Memory and Destiny

The Life of Glenn Janss

MEMORY
and
DESTINY

The Life of Glenn Janss

Glenn C. Janss
with
Tony Tekaroniake Evans

Memory and Destiny

The Life of Glenn Janss

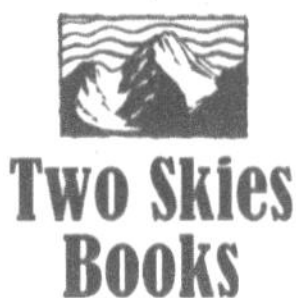

Published in the United States by Two Skies Books

P.O. Box 4372 • Ketchum, Idaho 83340

(208) 720-4821

twoskies@hotmail.com

ISBN 978-0-578-98545

Cover picture: Glenn Cooper with Christin Cooper

Cover design and book layout by Evelyn B. Phillips

To my children,
who will have learned the truth
about the good and bad decisions
in the life of their mother
and to whom I owe
Joy
Laughter
Love
Solace
and
Support

"It's not what we have in our life,
but who we have in our life that counts."

—J. M. Laurence

Contents

Foreword

The book you hold in your hands is a personal story of an extraordinary soul, a woman who was born into abundance and yet survived tragedy, someone who was strengthened, expanded, transformed, and served by every circumstance of her life. Glenn Janss's life story is filled with miracles because she is a miracle. She is the consummate mother, grandmother, teacher, student, activist, ecologist, artist, and lover of life.

We first met through close mutual friends in Sun Valley, Idaho, more than forty years ago. Glenn in many ways transformed Sun Valley and made it the cultural and wellness center that it is today. Our relationship deepened while serving together on the board of the Institute for Noetic Sciences (IONS), an organization founded by astronaut Edgar Mitchell to probe the frontiers of human consciousness. Even though I was younger by a decade or so, Glenn and I became close friends, drawn together by a shared destiny to be of service and make a difference with our lives. We shared a passion for fund-raising, for philanthropy in service to the natural world, for the community of life that has nourished our friendship and made us spiritual sisters forever. The transformational IONS board meetings sometimes lasted three or four days. I always sat with Glenn, shared meals and walks with her, and came to appreciate her deep wisdom and unconditional love for the world. She opened my own heart wider and wider each time we were together, and I continue to aspire to be the woman she sees I can be.

Glenn was born into a retail fortune in Los Angeles. She came to Sun Valley a widow with five remarkable children. Her love for my friend Bill Janss following the tragic loss of his wife Anne was an inspiration for me. They formed a life together that left a lasting legacy on the state of Idaho, the intermountain West, and their wide circle of friends. Bill's transformation of Sun Valley Resort paralleled Glenn's unyielding commitment to the arts, education, and culture of the rural Wood River Valley. This passion has always been an extension of her commitment to family and the natural world, to philosophy and the broadest understanding of the community of life. These principles have defined her life and the people and places that have been fortunate enough to know her: The Nature Conservancy, Sun Valley Center for the Arts and Humanities, the IONS, and the Idaho Heritage Trust are just some of the many initiatives and enterprises that were reshaped, nurtured, and uplifted by Glenn Cooper Janss. Her energy is boundless. Her effectiveness has been mindboggling. Her mission has been to serve, to move financial resources, both her own and others, toward the highest good. This book will be an inspiration to anyone determined to make a difference in the world while living life to its fullest.

To this day, Glenn chooses to learn and grow, following a spiritual path that engages her own transformation. Her commitment to her own integrity and the integrity of the world we live in is unflinching. Her contributions to the world of art, the environment, and the evolution of human consciousness are immeasurable. When I think of Glenn, I aspire to be a better human being myself. Her story is riveting, her experiences extraordinary. Read on and you will learn much about the world, but most of all, you will connect with her soul. This is clearly a story of a life worth living.

—Lynne Twist, author of *The Soul of Money*

Preface

I believe everyone's life has a worthwhile story, but why should I write about mine? I pondered when I began this project five years ago: Why is my story any more interesting than someone else's? I am not a seasoned writer, having majored in philosophy; and with no creative writing experience, I feared that I would not be able to tell my story in a compelling way. I wrestled with all of this before making the decision to move forward with this book.

I have always wanted, even from childhood, to be of help to others in a meaningful way. This theme is part of my story, and I hope to encourage others in this path. Giving is the primary means of achieving happiness. The reward is found in each deed done for someone else. I give you my story as proof that this is the foundation for a fulfilling life.

I asked my family about the prospect of writing a book, especially my children and longtime friends. My life has been varied by choice and altered by unexpected challenges, both of which have provided new perspectives that may have meaning for others. Primary in my decision to move forward was the understanding that I would be facing uncomfortable memories and actions I was not always proud of. But the intense self-examination of writing resulted in a golden reward of self-awareness that has made the struggle of writing worthwhile. It is my hope that this story will be a gift to others.

As I wrote, I recalled why I had moved many years ago from Sun Valley to Tetonia, Idaho. I wanted to live quietly for once, live in the moment, take time to assess my past, learn about myself, and consider whether I had lived my life well and fully. Had I accomplished my goal of giving back to humanity? I would have to be honest about the things I did wrong, honor what I learned from those experiences, and hope the wisdom I gained would be worth sharing.

For inspiration, I often reflected on the life of the Prince Siddhartha, for my story parallels his in some ways. As a youth, he climbed over the palace wall in hope of experiencing what the world outside was like, progressing through new worlds as they opened for him. He learned lessons, and only then would he move into a new realm of possibility. This is what I have tried to do in my life—not lingering to receive honors but passing on to others what has been created while moving to the next new experience of service that beckoned.

One of the great rewards of this project was in the assessment of my role as a parent. This required a deep and renewed connection with my children and the memories we shared. I explored common memories with each one individually, and I have written about those recollections from the perspective that age allows. We relished this experience. If I have any counsel for readers, it is to give yourself the honor of intensely reviewing memories within your family.

Equally rewarding was the reunion with old friends from around the world with whom I have shared my life. Deepest gratitude goes to my dear friends Bunny Fleming; Molly Chappellet; Harry Gesner, my childhood water-skiing companion and the designer of our "Wave House" in Malibu; and the adventurous Jimmy Pfleuger. Wally Huffman provided informative and entertaining stories about the history of the Sun Valley Resort and iconic stories about Bill Janss. These are joined by the memories of Harry Rinker, as well as Jim Belson and Michael Engl, who contributed their dependable memories of the early years of the Sun Valley Center for the Arts and Humanities. I am grateful for the ways Cecil Andrus, Julie Wrigley, Mariel Hemingway, Gaetha Pace, and many others contributed to the story. There are many people in this book who are no longer with us. I hope this story will provide a tribute to their memory. They include my parents and grandparents and the people they worked with who helped shape my destiny.

My years dedicated to environmental conservation opened a new world for me. I thank Lou Lunte for his memories about The Nature Conservancy (TNC) years. My love of nature has been a deep calling since childhood, but I had never considered it as a professional career. From my work on the first Blaine County Planning and Zoning Commission, I moved on to work with the Idaho Chapter of TNC and then evolved to work on TNC's Global Board of Governors. I was given the responsibility of traveling to all the western states, where I learned of their programs and encouraged participation in an early capital campaign. I was sent as an emissary to countries around the world to report on their programs and, while there, advise them as best I could. I had the unique opportunity to be part of the founding of China's first conservation program, which has since expanded throughout the country.

Writing this book has helped me recall many of these experiences as well as the extraordinary travels that helped shape my understanding of humanity and the natural world. My studies with fellow spiritual searchers in Sun Valley and at the Institute for Noetic Sciences (IONS) have also shaped my life immeasurably. It has been an adventure all its own to recall how my spiritual path has led to acceptance and faith in our purpose as human beings within a conscious universe.

Unending gratitude goes to those who had confidence in me and believed that I had a story to tell. Saul Turtletaub, an old friend in

Sun Valley and producer and director of many great television shows, was the first to agree to read and comment on the manuscript. He did so with directness and humor. Julie Weston, a noted author of several books both historical and fictional, provided the first thorough reading and sage advice in her responses to my storytelling.

All of this could never have happened unless my co-writer had agreed to accompany me in this challenging adventure. Tony Evans is a well-known journalist and author of books on Native American history in the West. We barely knew each other when we began. His friend, my oldest son Cameron, recommended him to me. I wonder now whether this story, which will be new to so many who idolized me, might weigh heavily on him—Tony knows more about my life than even my children do. Some might be shocked by what I have shared, but Tony has honored a life lived fully. I consider him a close friend, and I hope he feels the same about me. Such friendships can only develop from the sharing of closely held truths—truths that lead to an understanding of the totality of another's life. The work we have accomplished together has brought revelations, and I cherish each one for the peace it has brought me.

Although we are now sending this book out into the world, no story is ever complete. I am reminded of a Paul Gardner quote: "A painting is never finished. It simply stops in interesting places." I hope I have accomplished this.

Prologue
Avalanche

Some people believe we come into this world as blank canvases, gathering impressions from experience and from those around us until we are mature enough to take on the responsibilities of adulthood. Looking back on my own life, though, I can see that the invisible forces that make up our characters and our destinies are far more complex and compelling than that. Have I come into this life for a purpose? Have I fulfilled my destiny? It is this spiritual mystery that I now feel driven to reflect upon in the story of my life. I believe that the answers lie within the telling of this story.

My life was changed forever by tragedy one clear winter morning in January 1973 in Sun Valley, Idaho. I had lost my first husband several years earlier, after an accident left my five children without a father. And now we were all in a new place, facing new challenges. Our move to Sun Valley from Los Angeles in 1968 was a major decision for us. The rustic frontier town of Ketchum, Idaho, had a pioneer feel to it. It also happened to exist alongside the most famous ski resort in North America.

Sun Valley had a rustic glamour that dated from the Golden Age of Hollywood, when Ernest Hemingway, Gary Cooper, and Marilyn Monroe put the resort on the map. Although I had visited Sun Valley in my youth, I never dreamed I would live there. My children had grown up on the beach in Malibu, and now they were walking to school in the snow. We persevered, thanks to support from family connections that went back generations. Two of my closest friends in the Wood River Valley were Bill Janss and his lovely wife Anne. My parents had played poker at the home of Bill's mother Flossie in Beverly Hills during Prohibition. Our grandfathers had done business together back when Sunset Boulevard was still a dirt road. Although Bill and I had met in our youth, I never imagined that our paths would one day intertwine.

It was our love of art that brought the three of us together. While both of our families were still living in Los Angeles, Bill and Anne and I would meet frequently at art openings in the new Los Angeles County Museum of Art. We would walk together through a new exhibition and excitedly share thoughts about what we were seeing and how art could change lives. Bill and Anne knew of my work in the art world, especially my success in organizing and training docent guides for the opening of the museum in 1965.

Bill was now the owner and executive in charge of running Sun Valley Resort and implementing plans that would bring the resort into a new era. Immediately after I arrived there in 1968, he asked me to start an art center. I agreed to do so, even though I had my doubts about how well it would be received. Los Angeles was a world city on the cutting edge of modern art. Sun Valley in the late sixties still felt like a frontier mining town. I wondered if anyone would take interest in an arts center.

Anne and I met most mornings to practice our dance lessons at the Sun Valley Lodge ice rink. We commiserated as we struggled to perfect our moves, but we also found much joy in learning from our dedicated instructor, Herman Maricich. We still had so much to look forward to on that fateful day—January 22, 1973—when I received an early call from Anne, inviting me to join her and a few friends on a helicopter skiing excursion in the nearby mountains. The skies were deep blue and clear, so I could not beg off because of weather. Although I had been skiing for many years, I confessed that I had little experience skiing powder.

"Oh, it's really easy, and the snow is perfect," said Anne. "You will not have a worry. We will all be there to help you." How could I say no? Helicopter skiing was not a commercial enterprise at that time, and very few people were granted access to this kind of special adventure. It was an honor to be included.

Bill would not be joining us, I was told, because he had already departed for Salt Lake City to attend a First Security Bank board meeting. George S. Eccles was chairman of the board at the time. George's nephew, Spence Eccles, was on Bill's Sun Valley Company board. Spence and Bill had both been named to US Olympic Ski Teams and shared a love and passion for the sport, but on that day, they would have business to attend to.

Anne told me I would be replacing Bill on several helicopter flights to the top of nearby mountains. We were given some basic instructions before we boarded the helicopter, which then sped off and soon settled onto a level spot at the top of Balcom Ridge, a few miles northeast of Sun Valley. The deep snow was difficult for me, so I asked one of the guides if he would follow me and give me some tips. The rest of the group tracked single file across a gully ahead of us, settling one above the other on the opposite ridge. They were trying to reach a pristine and untracked ridgeline to ski but were grouping in an unsafe manner. Our guide went after them to bring them back when the entire mass under them rumbled loudly and broke loose; everyone on it was swept into the cascading snow and debris of a thundering avalanche.

After the snow settled and a search for survivors began, only my dear friend Anne was missing. We finally found her at the bottom of the slope, but it had taken twenty minutes. When we reached her, she was no longer breathing and could not be resuscitated. We fell silent, staggered by the tragedy that had overtaken us. An indescribable heaviness settled over us. We had just lost our leader and the queen of Sun Valley. I had lost a dear friend and was crushed to think how devastating this loss would be for Bill and his children.

When I did finally visit Bill to see how he was doing, we shared our grief together, an experience so profound and binding that we soon became inseparable. In the wake of this tragedy, Bill and I confided in one another and shared our deepest emotions. We found ourselves in a new life together, one that I had never dared imagine possible. I went to Bill to console him and never left his side for the rest of his life. I had finally found the deep love of a lifetime for an amazing individual who shared the same depth of love for me. This is the story of a life moving toward a dream of enduring happiness and the challenges and tragedies I encountered before realizing that dream.

PART I

ORIGINS

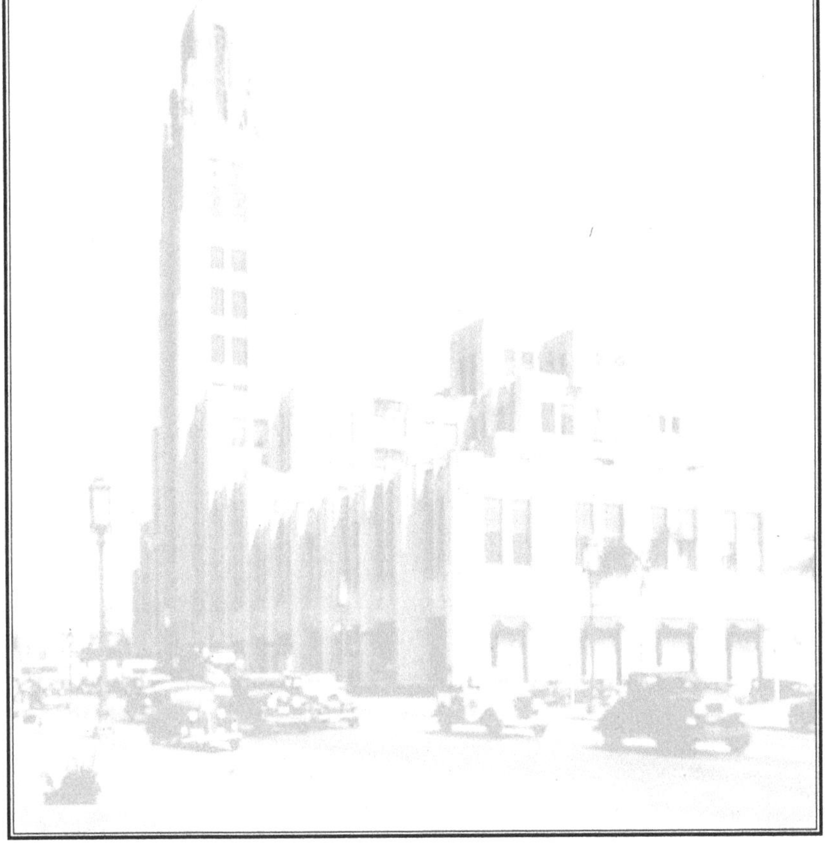

CHAPTER ONE

Little Princess

I was born on February 29, 1932, a leap-year Pisces daughter born between two brothers. My children and grandchildren recently called for a celebration of my twenty-first birthday. Since my birthday occurs only every four years, I received many invitations to go out and have a drink now that I was finally old enough. I am glad to see that a sense of humor runs in my family—humor is often the best way to get through hard times.

I have experienced a life of grace, unburdened by many of the financial concerns and fears that most people face. Yet, those born to wealth and privilege learn perhaps more readily that money cannot save us from the inevitable tragedies that are part of life.

In childhood, my life was simple. In some ways, my earliest memories are the clearest and most important. In one especially vivid recollection, I am standing beside my older brother Walter, looking upon a dazzling show of what appear to be giant, noisy, brightly colored birds moving past in the distance and then taking flight. I am three years old and Walter is four. My tiny fingers are entwined in a fence as I stare in wonder at what I later reasoned must have been some of the first private airplanes taking off from a runway in St. Louis, Missouri. This is a memory of wonder and transcendence. How could such things leave the ground and fly into the sky?

Another memory I carry is of Walter being reprimanded by someone for not eating his peas. He finally ate them, of course, a clear indication that we lived in an era when adult directions were strictly given and dutifully followed. I was shocked by this scolding voice and looked up to see what was amiss, paying close attention so as to avoid similar trouble myself.

These earliest memories carry a symbolic power, as though my life has taken place between the wonders of possibility and the hard boundaries imposed by those who keep order in this world. Perhaps we all live between these two poles: the hard facts of physical reality and the vast possibilities of our spiritual essence. By following the spark of our deepest desires, we can favor the spiritual in all we do. I have learned to take pleasure in every activity of my life, no matter how small and insignificant. This practice was intuitive for me as a child and grew in magnitude as my life evolved. Becoming fully present for any small joy, chore, or responsibility is the key; the more intensely I am involved in the details of life, the more rewarding and enlightening life becomes.

Despite being born to wealth and the wonders that it promised, it was many years before I found the courage to break through the limits that had been imposed upon me, or which I imposed upon myself, and then to act without doubt upon my soul's deepest truths. I was born into a palatial life—a true princess, you might say. Servants scurried to please me. As a little girl, I wore a dress of imported cotton embellished with delicate, intricate embroidery; white gloves; a matching patent leather purse and shoes; topped off by a hat with a ribbon band and streamers. Elegance was a way of life, and I thought nothing of it, looking down each day at my shiny Mary Jane shoes and lace-cuffed bobby socks.

We lived in a grand house at the end of a long gravel driveway on a large estate at 1111 San Vicente Boulevard in Santa Monica, only a fifteen-minute walk from my grandfather Percy Glen Winnett's much larger estate at 923 San Vicente. As a young child, I knew of nothing but play within the vast estate of gardens and manicured lawns that surrounded our home. These were the early, carefree years prior to World War II, the only years that I can really call carefree during my lifetime. These memories are so clear and easily conjured because they are remembered by the happiness in my heart before I ever experienced trauma or had a care in the world. I assumed that those places, those times, and those people I loved would always remain the same.

My father, Walter Weaver Candy Jr., announced his comings and goings with dance footwork he learned as a member of the Triangle Club at Princeton. He would occasionally let out an unforgettable bird whistle—long, shrill, and varied—which we all loved to hear. We would then join in his laughter and his pleasure in performing it for us. My mother, Kate Irene Winnett Candy, slept very late, and none of us were allowed to go to her until her breakfast had been served, for which she would have called to the kitchen. I quietly entered the forbidden area of her bedroom. There in her bed she sat before a shining tray of food with a basket on either side, one of which always held a newspaper. She sipped her coffee from elegant china as I bade her good morning. I wondered if I too would one day receive such a tray on my bed.

Once the queen had been honored, I was given permission to roam a landscape that was all my own. Our driveway, bordered by neatly trimmed box hedges, led through grounds with several buildings, elaborate gardens, an orchard, and an unused fenced-in children's play yard. Although I have clear memories of my mother and father, we children spent more time with the servants, who were all very loyal and attentive to us. My father taught me to ride a bike, an effort that sent me crashing into the hedges and taking out sections here and there, but most of his time was spent at work as president of the Bullock's department stores.

There were many other people around to look after us, including an English cook I only knew as Elsie, who rarely left the kitchen and lived above the garages. Our butler, Frank Bence, was married to Eleanor, our housemaid. Frank was a fixer of things. He also took care of the automobiles, chauffeured us around at times, and brought groceries and other deliveries to the house. The servants dressed in simple uniforms. The women wore ample white aprons over pastel-colored blouses.

And then there was our governess, Esther Perschnick, my second and most responsible mother, who had a great deal of influence during my upbringing. Esther was from the tiny town of St. Anthony, Idaho, not far from where I live today. She had an ample bosom that pressed close to us as she read or talked to us. A comforting presence in our lives, she gave us the freedom to play and explore, but she also taught us how to behave, which was no easy task.

Yet another servant came almost daily to do the laundry and hang it on the circular drying lines, the kind you could spin with your hand. I would often visit her, as she seemed to have such interesting work to do. She was a heavyset Black woman, as laundresses seemed to be in those days. One day we decided to tell the laundress that our pet alligator had gotten loose and could not be found. I suppose this seemed likely enough to her since the grounds were rather large and who knew what could be out there. She resigned at once and never came back, certain that said alligator would have her in mind when it was grown enough to stalk our property looking for a meal.

Our main house was a fortress. A heavy, carved-wood front door gave access directly into the Blue Room, which was covered with soft blue mirrors that induced different moods throughout the day, depending on the light. A much larger living room was used only during the holidays when our Christmas tree was placed there. Beyond the powder room were stairs to the second floor. To the left was a very formal Victorian dining room with a long, dark wooden table and heavy chairs. My father always sat in a smaller breakfast nook in the morning, reading his *LA Times*.

The iceman would come to the back door carrying tongs that clutched heavy ice blocks, which he placed through the many icebox doors that ran the entire wall of our kitchen. The milkman delivered at the back door, off the kitchen area, taking away our empty milk bottles and leaving in a wire basket whatever had been marked on the delivery list.

I had my own bedroom upstairs in the main house, as did Walter. My younger brother Peter shared a third room with Esther, our governess. Behind the main house and down a steep lawn was the Studio, a recreation house with a large, circular bar and no bedrooms. Guests were amazed to find a full-sized organ there, complete with shiny pipes. But didn't everyone have a pipe organ in their guest studio?

All the servants, including Esther, ate together at a pull-down wall table in a room off the kitchen. We were left alone to make trouble in our own private dining room—one of the garages adjoining the main house, which had been remodeled as the children's dining hall. Here, we would devise many creative ways to dispose of the less desirable portions of our meals.

I would open a window overlooking a spot on the lawn where two hungry dogs waited. They belonged to Uncle Bill, my father's fun-loving younger brother—William Ernst Candy—who was a mariner and president of the Santa Monica Beach Club. Uncle Bill was often away onboard his yacht, *Burra-peg*. It won first in its class at least once in the Transpacific Yacht Race. While Uncle Bill was away sailing, his dogs were fed a little extra by me and my brothers. Walter occasionally used his napkin to launch butter balls at the ceiling. This led to a competition to see who could get the most butter balls to stick there. If the servants ever looked up and discovered what we were up to, none ever mentioned it.

My mother had a repeating seven-day schedule of the same dinner menu each night of the week. We could have pot roast only on

Thursday nights, even though Daddy complained about this because he was fond of red meat. Being a bird hunter to the end of his days, his favorite dinner was wild duck. Friday was fish night, which none of us liked. On one occasion, I wrapped most of my fish dinner in my pocket and walked through the kitchen, declaring to the servants that I needed to go to the bathroom. I smiled with glee as I flushed the fish down the toilet. To my dismay, as I passed back through the kitchen, Elsie, our cook, said clearly to me, "Glenn, the next time you do not want your fish, just tell me." How did she know? Was there steam coming from my pocket? I never asked and will never know, but I was humbled by this experience. From then on, I knew Elsie had her eye on me.

If our mischief was sometimes tolerated, bad manners were not. One day when my brother and I were having an argument, he told me to "shut up." Servants in the kitchen overheard us; the bar of soap came out in Esther's hand, and both of us got heavy doses on the tongue, which sent us running outside gagging and laughing about what had happened.

In that era, proper speech and etiquette were a serious concern, and rude comments were simply not allowed. I was always being corrected for my improper diction at the evening dinner table. Correct English equalled good breeding, and it was instilled in me at a young age and reinforced later in school and college. Old habits die hard, even good ones, and so it still sounds like scratching on a blackboard when anyone misuses the "I and me" pronoun with the verb "to be" or if there are mistakes made regarding the object of a preposition. I still correct my children, but it is a lost cause. I thank my parents for their corrections when I was a child and sometimes wonder if even the British themselves still speak the old, proper English.

Two majestic pine trees stood like sentinels over the driveway circle in front of the main house. We knew somehow that they were off-limits as far as climbing or hiding or even touching. There were several other trees on our property that enchanted me in my early childhood. One was a jacaranda tree, often in full purple bloom. At the bottom of the sloping grass lawn, a giant magnolia tree also seemed to be in constant bloom, its giant white blossoms hanging determinedly onto their branches, not to wanting to give in to the inevitable fall. When I was old enough to see over the wall that marked the border of our property, I looked upon another vast property much like our own, with orchards and gardens and a tall castle of a house in the distance, another secret kingdom all to itself.

Down one side of our yard from the gravel circle was a fragrant rose garden, in which my mother took great pride. Her mother had one as well, even more spacious than ours. Beyond the rose garden was another groomed flower garden, and then the path took a wide circle around a fountain that spilled fresh water into the middle of a lily pond.

When I was a young girl, my mother spread a blanket on the lawn one afternoon and asked me to sit down and close my eyes. She went away, and I dared not open them until I was told. When I did, there was a tiny blond cocker spaniel puppy beside me on the blanket. My mother sat down, and we played with this amazing creature, all mine. It was as if my mother had given to me the jewels of the kingdom. I don't know why, but I decided to name this puppy Christopher. He gorged on the avocados that grew in the vast orchard on our property and was my constant companion until I left home for college in 1949.

One of my earliest memories is of my mother in Santa Monica was when I was just four years old. We were in the guest cottage on my maternal grandfather's estate. She must have been visiting her sister, Glenn Helen Winnett Boocock, nicknamed Dougie, who was staying there at that time. I went to sit on my mother's lap, and there was something so large in her tummy that I could not fit there. She told me that this was going to be a baby. My brother Peter was about to be born. It meant nothing to me at that time, but because this is such a clear memory, I wonder today if it was a premonition of what lay ahead—of having the responsibility of caring for Peter for many years to come.

Beyond the main house and outbuildings were a barn, stables, and tack room for the horses. When I grew older, Egon Merz trained me to ride my horse, Carnation Bonnie. The Carnation Farms were famous for their gaited horses, and Bonnie was one of them. She was a gift from my Aunt Peggy, half-sister to my father and Uncle Bill and the daughter of Walter W. Candy Sr., who then lived in Pasadena. When I was quite a bit older, I decided one day to ride Carnation Bonnie from where she was stabled at the Riviera Country Club in Santa Monica Canyon down San Vicente Boulevard to my house. I always chose to ride bareback, which most people found shocking. Having my horse at my house for the night was exciting and adventurous for me but, sadly, not for her. She was so nervous without her stable friends that she whinnied and paced through the night.

All around the barn were fields of grassland, sweeping down a gentle hill to the end of our property and a fence line, beyond which was the cliff that marked the edge of Santa Monica Canyon. Far below, we could hear the screeching of peacocks each morning at Leo Carillo's ranch.

My father's prized Ford convertible sat at one end of our separate six-car garage, a sporty automobile with whitewall tires and a chrome grill that seemed as tall as a locomotive's. The Ford had a rumble seat in the back, where we kids sat during Sunday drives down to the Third Street shops or along the beach front. My father drove a different car the many miles to work each day at the magnificent Bullocks Wilshire department store. The building could be seen from miles away, its beige ten-story spire, clad in green copper, towering above the glitzy homes on Wilshire Boulevard. At night, the building was lit up so magically that it looked like the Emerald City of Oz. This towering castle was the creation of my grandfather, Percy Glen Winnett, and his partner,

John G. Bullock.

Bullocks Wilshire was vast and unfathomable for a young child, but I have vivid memories of being there, memories that were brought back to me by Margaret Leslie Davis's extraordinary book *Bullocks Wilshire*, about the store and its history. I recall that it was a place where people hurried to attend us and where hundreds of well-dressed adults milled about, buying treasures from around the world. After shopping, they received their boxes of merchandise in the motor court for delivery to their cars by uniformed valets. The staff of attendants absolutely cherished my mother and did their best to please us, welcoming her as a queen into her palace. She was, after all, the heiress to her father's fortune. She always drove a black Cadillac convertible. Black must have been a prestigious color in the 1940s, when Hollywood film studios were transforming Los Angeles into the City of Dreams.

Artisans had labored for years to create Bullocks Wilshire, which was called a "cathedral to commerce" by one journalist. Completed in 1929 and ultramodern for its day, the building was designed in the latest art deco style. Movie stars Clark Gable, Greta Garbo, Mae West, and Marlene Dietrich came there to shop during my childhood. Angela Lansbury worked there as a salesgirl before taking a screen test and becoming a Hollywood actress.

This was a magical and overwhelming place for a child. If our home on San Vicente Boulevard was a private kingdom of lawns and gardens, Bullocks Wilshire was a labyrinth of elegance where each room was designed to cast a different spell. There were rooms and secret places in the Bullocks Wilshire building that I never entered and, just as surely, places that I have long forgotten. I was recognized there well into my adult years, enough so that it became embarrassing at times.

When I was a child, my mother arrived through a shining bronze gate and parked under an elaborate mural of naked gods and goddesses, airplanes, ships, and locomotives. Valets greeted us, and we were whisked away through polished marble arches under the sparkling chandeliers of an expansive perfume hall and into gold-mirrored elevators that transported us to the many rooms of this vast building. Opal glass lanterns hung from silver rings in the Fur Atelier. The Louis XVI Period Room was designed to mimic Marie Antoinette's own boudoir, with gold molding and crystal chandeliers that were reminiscent of the Palace of Versailles. The doorway to a room named for French designer Coco Chanel was guarded by a pair of her rather frightening life-size bronze monkeys. Store displays were created by famous artists and Hollywood set designers. One such display featured a life-size tree of feathers under which stood a Bullocks Wilshire mannequin wearing the latest designs from Paris or New York. The menswear department resembled a Mayan temple, a tribute to Frank Lloyd Wright. The Saddle Shop offered the latest riding gear.

My grandfather, an avid horseman, called for the creation of Bullocks Barney, a life-size plaster horse that equestrians could mount to test the fit of their jodhpurs. Nearby was the Doggery, where stylish collars and other accessories for canines could be found. The store also contained a banquet hall; beauty salon; barbershop; toy department; and millinery department, where women were fitted with elaborate custom hats in the latest styles. The rooftop Playdeck on the fifth floor was reserved for children, but my favorite destination was the Sportswear Department, where I could find the swimsuits and simple play dresses I liked to wear.

The second floor of Bullocks Wilshire housed creations by the most famous fashion designers in the world, each in separate departments designed by and for them—Bill Blass, Oscar de la Renta, Yves Saint Laurent, Halston, Hubert de Givenchy, and Christian Dior. The rooms were meant to evoke historical periods. The lights dimmed as clients relaxed in chairs and on sofas. Tall, elegant women modeled au courant fashions as though walking through a king's throne room. The famous Metro-Goldwyn-Mayer (MGM) fashion designer Irene Gibbons, who made designs for over fifty Hollywood films, had her own shop there, where she created exquisite gowns for the Los Angeles fashion elite. My mother proudly wore her designs.

My grandfather and John Bullock had envisioned this comingling of high fashion and movie star glamour when they built Bullocks Wilshire. The splendid entrance to the building on Wilshire Boulevard was capped by a design depicting perpetual success, carved in stone by George Stanley—the same artist who designed the Academy Award statuettes taken home by Oscar winners. The words inscribed over the entrance were as bold as the building itself: "To Build a Business That Will Never Know Completion."

Hollywood stars were welcomed and fawned over at Bullocks Wilshire. They, in turn, added legend to a business that had been conceived as a convergence of commerce, high fashion, and fine art—a store that would celebrate the new era of the automobile, speed, and abundance. Katharine Hepburn, Carole Lombard, Ingrid Bergman, and Gloria Swanson all shopped there. One store clerk recalled a surprise entrance by Greta Garbo in a trench coat, looking for swimsuits. When the attendant entered the fitting room with her, the trench coat came off and Garbo was wearing nothing underneath. Another salesclerk told the tale of being sent to bring actress Judy Garland a pile of clothes for fittings. She discovered the actress casually lying naked on the floor, sipping a martini.

Mae West, who lived in an apartment nearby, insisted on shopping from her car and so had packages of merchandise brought to the motor court. John Wayne, David Niven, Jack Palance, and Alfred Hitchcock all were regulars. Hitchcock later filmed scenes from his final 1976 film *Family Plot* at the store, continuing a tradition that had begun back in 1936 at Bullocks Wilshire with the filming of the comedy *Topper*, with Cary Grant and Constance Bennett.

I learned later in life that some of the wealthiest men in Los Angeles were invited to relax in a secret wood-paneled retreat in the Bullocks Wilshire tower, sipping cocktails and smoking cigars as they were shown the latest designs from the world of fashion. Presumably, they were there to shop for their wives.

What I recall most fondly from Bullocks Wilshire during my earliest years was the Tea Room, where the well-dressed and important ladies of Los Angeles gathered for lunch or tea while viewing the latest styles. I was especially happy to be invited to the Tea Room by my grandfather—he was so important and always made me feel special. There was a hush of anticipation before the fashion models walked out onstage wearing the very latest designs from Europe and New York City. After twirling on the raised walkway and while everyone was watching, they would come to my grandfather's table and plant a kiss on his cheek. He would laugh, call them by name, introduce me, and offer each of them a piece of hard candy he pulled from his pocket. The models would pop the candies right into their mouths before returning to the platform for one last twirl.

My grandfather always seemed to be happy. To me, he never displayed stress or concern. He was serious about business, and if I followed him around the store, he was absorbed in whatever he had on his mind. He seemed a contented man, happy with his life and with the legendary store that he and John Bullock had built. What I could not appreciate as a child was that Bullocks Wilshire was an enterprise of staggering complexity that had emerged out of the early days of Los Angeles against tremendous odds. This great emporium had survived the Great Depression to fuel the very heart of glamour during the Golden Age of Hollywood. Of course, at that young age I had no idea where my grandfather had come from nor what he had accomplished.

CHAPTER TWO

Merchant Prince

My grandfather, Percy Glen Winnett, disembarked with his family from the iron steamship *City of Puebla* at the port of San Francisco on May 15, 1896. He was fifteen years old, of slight build, and carried a wooden shoeshine box that he would use to earn money in the United States. A few years earlier, the Winnetts had traveled overland nearly fifteen hundred miles across the wheat fields and mountains of Canada from their hometown of Winnipeg, Manitoba, to Vancouver, British Columbia. The economic boom that was taking place in California at the turn of the century must have been irresistible, drawing the family south of the border and eventually to Los Angeles.

Percy's Irish immigrant parents had witnessed the transformation of Winnipeg from a dusty frontier town of fur trappers, Indian camps, and wagon trains into a modern city. By 1881, the year Percy was born, the Canadian Pacific Railway had arrived at Winnipeg, bringing mass immigration to the western Prairie Provinces. By the time Percy was a teenager, the city was a railway boomtown with department stores servicing a resident population of twenty-five thousand, many of whom had immigrated from Holland, France, the Ukraine, and elsewhere. The Winnett family was among the first wave of immigrants to arrive in Winnipeg. Percy's three older sisters—Ettie, Mamie, and Claire Ellen—no doubt doted on their two younger brothers and may have introduced Percy to the world of retail fashion.

Percy's father, John William Winnett, was born at Killaloe, Ireland, in 1853. He came to Canada in his youth, was educated in London, Ontario, and worked at the London Furniture Company before traveling in 1874 to Winnipeg, where he established a wholesale and retail furniture business. Two years later, he and Lydia Ann Roe were married and started a family that brought them five daughters and two sons. John Winnett built a furniture factory on Main Street that employed about forty men, including talented craftsmen able to build wooden rocking chairs, bureaus, and dining room sets for the settlers who were now arriving in droves. In 1884, the furniture company won a commission to manufacture the first wood blocks used in paving Winnipeg's streets in late 1884, earning him a mention in the Manitoba Historical Society's online resource, "Memorable Manitobans," a century later.

When Percy was eight years old, his father sold the furniture shop and moved to Victoria, British Columbia, where he took up the real estate business. But my grandfather would have learned as a child that his family's livelihood depended on the skill and artistry of craftsmen. This appreciation served him well in later years as a man who would bring together in one commercial enterprise both old-world artistry and the flash and promise of the modern era.

After coming ashore in California, the Winnetts headed south to Los Angeles, where the father sought real estate prospects while Percy took aim at making his mark on the retail industry. Los Angeles was suddenly thriving after languishing for decades. During the 1850s, it had a population of only two thousand, so few that city leaders eventually had to bribe the Southern Pacific Railroad in 1876 to link the city with the rest of the state. This worked like magic.

By 1885, the Santa Fe Railroad had also reached Southern

California, sparking a rate war that dropped the price of a trip from Midwestern cities like St. Louis and Kansas City to as low as a dollar. These screaming deals, along with promotional books and articles touting the healthy Mediterranean climate, brought Los Angeles an enormous surge in population, driving the incorporation of dozens of new towns. In 1887, 120,000 people arrived in the city by way of the Southern Pacific Railroad alone. By the turn of the twentieth century, thousands of new homes had sprung up in the arid valley that had hitherto been known only for its ranches and citrus farms.

Percy took a two-dollar-a-week cash boy job at a store owned by Arthur Letts, proprietor of the Broadway Department Store on the corner of Fourth and Broadway. Letts was destined to create a renowned retail empire in the growing metropolis, an empire that my grandfather would one day control in its entirety.

Arthur Letts came from England to Canada in 1882 and later to Seattle, working in the carpet department for Tolkas, Singerman and Company. On June 6 of that year, the entire fifty-block business district of Seattle was consumed by fire, leaving twenty-seven-year-old Letts, his wife, and their two-year-old daughter in desperate circumstances. According to the news of that time, Letts defiantly pitched a large tent amidst the ash and ruins of downtown Seattle; gathered what goods, supplies, and apparel he could find; and went into business. He slept with a gun inside the tent at night to protect his merchandise from thieves but was eventually shut down by the city.

With another child on the way, Letts left the city to clear land in Kitsap County and tried to homestead, but this venture ended in failure. By this time, with most of his savings gone, he moved his family back to Seattle, only to be caught in the financial Panic of 1893, once again losing everything he owned and going into debt. With nothing left to lose, Letts decided to move south to Los Angeles and begin again. By now, the city had sixty thousand inhabitants, many still reeling from the same economic recession that had devastated his own family's savings.

Letts walked the streets to get a feel for the city's movements before settling on a small one-room store far from the city center that he believed would one day be the center of commercial activity. One biographer described the store as having a collection of dry goods, cheap candy, a few pots and pans, and a number of old children's toys. But Letts was determined to stand out among competitors. He was the first merchant in the city to offer penny change to customers, and he later gifted each customer with a shiny new penny from a barrel he kept at the store. He also was the first to implement fixed pricing in the city, a strategy that reduced haggling and allowed younger kids to shop for items in a safe environment where they would not be cheated. Fixed pricing had begun in Paris at the storied Le Bon Marché and in Philadelphia, but it had yet to reach California.

Letts created enticing and provocative advertisements in the *Los Angeles Herald,* where he spent what some people considered an inordinate amount of money on year-long advertising contracts. He offered money-back guarantees on his merchandise in the form of store credits, not because it was a proven commercial strategy but because he considered it the right thing to do.

Only a few weeks after opening on February 24, 1896, the store at Fourth Avenue and Broadway was besieged by customers and littered with empty boxes while stacks of merchandise were piled in the aisles. By then Letts had hired a fellow Canadian by the name of John G. Bullock to run the menswear department. Letts was the general manager, while Bullock sold merchandise and chose new stock. Their partnership yielded tremendous success, and within three years, one hundred employees worked on the ground floor of the newly built Hallet and Pirtle Building. During the next few years, one wall after another was knocked down to make way for expansion of an enterprise that came to be known far and wide simply as the

Broadway.

Letts and Bullock came to Los Angeles during an era of epic transition. In 1892, Edward Doheny discovered oil in the city, bringing drilling gangs from far and wide. By 1894, eighty wells were producing oil in the Los Angeles area, a number that swelled to five hundred two years later, the same year Congress approved a massive $2.9 million deepwater harbor at San Pedro. The first automobile in Los Angeles appeared one year later, in 1897, built in a shop near the Broadway by S. D. Sturgis for J. Philip Erie. By 1904, sixteen hundred cars were cruising around Los Angeles at a maximum allowable speed of eight miles per hour in residential areas, six in business districts. By now, the city's population had soared to nearly two hundred thousand residents, many of whom were freed by the automobile to more easily visit areas outside the city center.

In 1899, my grandfather walked into the Broadway looking for a job. He was a soft-spoken man who stood five feet, four inches tall. John Bullock took a liking to him and hired him right away. In addition to guarding merchandise and running errands, he kept up the sizes of celluloid collars, which were flying off the shelves at three and a half cents each. PG, as he now preferred to be called, learned that despite the fuss over collars, they brought in nothing for the company. They were instead seen as a come-on item that drew customers into the store to buy more costly goods.

PG engaged customers and made quick sales whenever he could take a moment away from his errands or packaging duties. In later years, he would joke that the hard work of his early years stunted his size, but his slight stature was convenient for entering the packing cases. He would climb in, try something on for size and then throw the item out to Bullock and the others for inspection and sorting. They would stock the items immediately before knocking off for the night. On Saturdays, PG stayed on the job until ten at night.

He soon formed a strong bond with his boss. When Bullock

became superintendent of the Broadway, PG moved from a clerk position to running the menswear department. Perhaps they felt a kinship because they were both Canadian immigrants. They grew to rely upon one another and together learned from the older Letts how to succeed in business. One night, after the mopping up, Bullock took his young protégé to B. Hart and Bros. Importers on the Bryson Block and placed a Christmas order for silk handkerchiefs. This was PG's first experience in the buying of goods.

The older Letts was bold in pointing out the quality of the Broadway's merchandise and the weakness of the competition. In advertisements that resembled breaking news stories, he taunted his competitors with thinly veiled references to their shoddy workmanship and higher prices. "Men, Here's Certain Proof that We Have the Best $15.00 Suits in Los Angeles," read one advertisement. Of paramount concern to Letts and his protégés was an ethic that would come to be known in later years as the uncompromising "Bullock Ideal," which placed integrity, service, and fairness above all else.

Two months after starting work at the Broadway, PG was carrying the payroll to the store's twenty-six employees when he heard Mr. Letts call down from the mezzanine, "I am giving you a fifty-cent raise per week, PG!" When my grandfather reached the steps, Mrs. Arthur Letts was standing there. She looked down at him kindly and said, "You are a good boy."

PG learned the retail trade under Harry Phelp, Stanley McClung, and Ed Fox. Beginning with the women's and children's departments, the Broadway pioneered "unitization," which trained personnel to attend to specific clothing departments in an effort to reduce returns. The seller's detailed and specific knowledge resulted in tremendous success in the years to come. For example, the store carried very durable leather gloves for sale to Pacific Electric employees who operated the manual brakes on railways. The motormen came in asking for lighter gloves, but PG refused, even at the cost of losing a customer.

"A good many men walked out, but eventually they all came back," he later recalled. After a long day selling and strategizing, Bullock, PG, and other store managers would stroll Spring Street, then veer off at Third and Main, where they would have a tamale, sandwich, and coffee before going their separate ways into the bustling night.

PG was twenty-one years old in 1902 and doing rather well at the Broadway when he married Helen Hutton, the daughter of Judge and Mrs. A. W. Hutton of Los Angeles. The couple stood before the Reverend Baker P. Lee on the Hutton family's wide porch on Main Street in Los Angeles, under a canopy of ferns and Easter lilies hung with chimes of wedding bells. PG's bride was gowned in white embroidered chiffon over taffeta, and according to a society reporter, "a wealth of beautiful dark hair was partially-hidden beneath a long mull veil fastened with orange blossoms."

One of Helen's bridesmaids was Isabel Wolfskill, a descendent of the pioneer ranching and citrus farming Wolfskill family. The family's vast Wolfskill Ranch, which had been founded under an old Spanish land grant, encompassed what was soon to become downtown Los Angeles. Arthur Letts eventually acquired the ranch and, when the time came to develop it, looked to a land improvement company founded by a Danish immigrant doctor by the name of Peter Janss, grandfather of Bill Janss.

PG and his bride's wedding supper was served in the Hutton's dining room. The Nubila Brothers band played Schumann's "Träumerei." Pink sweet peas and lover's knots of tulle were festooned above the proceedings "with pink shaded candles casting a soft light over the whole," wrote a society reporter. The newlyweds then quickly departed for a short stay in Santa Barbara, with plans for an extended honeymoon later in New York City. This trip to New York may well have been a work trip for PG, who was by now head of the menswear department at the Broadway and no doubt in on plans to expand operations with his partner Bullock in a new venture financed by Arthur Letts.

Always on the lookout for an opportunity, Letts learned of a failed commercial venture at the corner of Broadway and Seventh Street where the steelwork frame for a seven-story building had been left standing. Letts struck a deal with Edwin T. Earl, publisher of the *Los Angeles Express,* to lease the building for fifty years, putting up $250,000 to complete construction and get the business up and running. He called on John G. Bullock to take over full responsibility for its operation, success, or failure.

PG was determined to follow Bullock in the new enterprise, but Letts answered "Pooh-pooh, you're too young and have no experience to speak of." But PG insisted until Letts relented. "Against my better judgment, I have been prevailed upon by Mr. Bullock and Mr. Phelp to give you a chance," said Letts.

As the new building neared completion, the two men shaped an ambition to create a department store that would rival that of Macy's in New York. They hired a sales staff of four hundred and set about finding merchandise that would lure the biggest spenders in the city. At eight o'clock on March 2, 1907, Bullock's opened to great fanfare with a lavish party for curious patrons and passersby that included bands on the brightly lit lower floor and a pony show on the rooftop terrace.

"That night all roads led to Bullock's," wrote Letts's biographer, Willam H. B. Kilner, years later. "Thousands crowded into Broadway and intersecting streets, and it was a perfect jam for blocks in every direction. Men, women, children, women with babies in their arms, street cars, automobiles, and carriages, were all packed together, and at times it was impossible for either one or the other to move."

Standing tall on top of the cream-colored building were the letters BULLOCK'S, brightly lit and visible from the outskirts of the city. Patrons arrived in droves during a grand opening that offered singing canaries and free violets to customers, a tradition that would be repeated annually on the fourth of March for many years. Yet, within weeks of opening, the Panic of 1907 caused Wall Street stocks to drop by 50 percent and sent merchants into a tizzy. Despite empty aisles and wary shoppers, Bullock and Winnett were aware that public perception was integral to their success and therefore ordered delivery wagons bearing the Bullock's coat of arms to ride through the streets even when empty of merchandise. The company also managed to create a list of a thousand customer credit accounts from dedicated clients. Within a year, Bullock and PG Winnett's strategy to accommodate high-end clientele at Bullock's had succeeded famously, enticing customers with exquisite merchandise from obscure sources. Other major retailers that had opened around the same time, including the Central Department Store and Bon Marché, could not weather the storm and closed operations, leaving Bullock's in a prominent position.

In 1909, PG signed in his fine hand a petition for naturalization as a US citizen, supported by his friend and mentor, John G. Bullock, who listed his protégé PG as "Assistant Manager of the Bullock's department store."

The following years were filled with hard work as Bullock and PG Winnett endeavored to transform Bullock's into a store that would justify the confidence Letts had shown in setting them up in business. Bullock and PG set about distinguishing the new Bullock's store as a place where clients could expect exceptional service and acquire almost anything they desired. An efficient system of wrapping, packaging, and shipping was established to keep up with the rush. Sold items were sent down a slide to lower floor levels where workers wrapped, boxed, and sent the equivalent of one package every ten seconds during the month of December 1915.

An article in *Women's Wear* that year told of a customer who purchased a steamer trunk at Bullock's. When she boarded her Europe-bound ship, she found that the trunk was improperly sized to fit under her berth. Upon reaching France, she wrote Bullock's a plaintive note describing her predicament. Within six days, the model trunk she specified was delivered to her by a representative of the company. The following year, in 1916, a front-page photograph in the Sunday *Los Angeles Times* showed a sweeping view of automobiles, horse-drawn wagons, and trolley cars in front of the Broadway. Beyond the store and for many blocks down Broadway Avenue, a tangle of thousands of pedestrians, carts, automobiles, and trolleys filled the streets as people poured into stores in the central business district.

Bullock and several other businessmen who benefited from the boom joined ranks to fight a "no parking" ordinance that they claimed was costing them hundreds of thousands of dollars in sales. The automobile age was exploding, and the two businessmen were determined to capitalize on it. The Broadway and Bullock's stores offered shiny bells, lights, rubber horns, and other automobile accessories alongside picnic baskets, driving gloves, toiletries, and spare tires. Their storefront displays were designed to enthrall passersby.

The displays featured mannequins wearing fur coats standing beside stuffed animals. Fine fabrics and furs lay draped over logs. These were the first stirrings of the theatrical window displays that became eagerly anticipated by the public in later years. Inside the Bullock's men's department, a cadre of impeccably dressed salesmen waited on customers who often shopped alone or took a break for a shave and haircut in the store's barber shop. A stationary department offered custom-designed products. Several lines of luggage, including steamer trunks, hatboxes, and valises were rated for durability and price according to the Bullock's "Indestructo Awards" index.

A spring window display in 1916 was filled with thousands of flowers and a backdrop mural of nymphs and goddesses cavorting beside a temple, all set about a display of ladies' dresses. Another displayed finely clad dolls in the latest buggies and strollers. As the years passed, these windows were filled with increasingly detailed and dramatic scenes that included pianos and harps, trees and ferns, and paintings on easels. The stories they presented were captivating to passersby and, of course, it was not bad for business to have crowds of window-shoppers gather on the sidewalk, enticed by what might await them inside.

In 1917, the United States entered World War I and the economy shifted to support the war effort. Bullock's was again in the news as a supporter of local craftsmen, designers, and traders. The business was lauded as a boon to the local economy, especially what was then called the "home product trade." Despite carrying stock from around the world and merchandise from obscure sources, the store also bought and resold $1 million in Los Angeles merchandise in one year and spent $3 million for merchandise, equipment, and supplies that had been made or distributed in the city. Bullock's was praised for what would today be called "buying local," but at the time it was a matter of necessity.

"If there ever was an opportunity for manufacturers to step into a territory ripe for profit, that opportunity exists now in southern California," John Bullock said at the time. "Railroad congestion, the difficulty in getting supplies and shipments of wares delivered, war conditions generally, offer a golden field for the manufacturer who seeks a new opening."

As the store expanded to take over the Pease Brothers Furniture Company's building nearby, newspapers paid close attention, eager for news on how Bullock's would impact the local economy. The store quickly became known for its bold and creative merchandising techniques. One year, a clan of Native Americans was hired to spend time in the store around a tipi and displays of Southwestern pottery, Pendleton blankets, and other wares. A short distance across the showroom floor, one could browse through an array of Scottish wool plaids, hats, and jumpers. Still farther on were offerings from "the Orient."

When the Great War ended, the entire ground floor of Bullock's was cleared for a grand party. More than a thousand employees, friends, and family gathered for a fine banquet and dancing. At the height of merriment, store superintendent H. M. Bigelow, wearing a fez, rode into the throng on a camel, the very image of a grand Pooh-Bah. When the roar of laughter and surprise abated, he read a telegram from company vice president PG Winnett that said, "Best wishes for a good and jolly party. Both Mrs. Winnett and myself regret we are not able to be with you." I knew that my grandmother as a retiring sort of woman, not always able to keep up appearances at company extravaganzas of this sort. In later years, I came to understand that her need for privacy was due to an unnamed family illness that has been passed down through generations in our family.

Meanwhile, the original Broadway store continued to flourish nearby, revealing plans in 1913 to demolish half of its structure and take over space in the adjacent Clark Hotel building, which fronted on Hill Street. A 1920 fall clearance sale drew a finely dressed mob that nearly filled the entire block, the men wearing straw hats and the women in scarves. That year, the Broadway expanded with a 11,000-square-foot Sports Shop, which became an enormous success for the company. Much of this had to do with impeccable timing. Los Angeles, with its warm climate, beaches, and sun, soon became a mecca for bathing and water sports. These leisure fashions were spreading around the world in popularity. A newly designed bathing suit could be nearly as extravagant as evening formal wear. The store's own designs were also making news.

"The supreme novelty of all . . . a bathing suit set consisting of breeches, top tunic and cape, hat cap and bag, in apple green silk with lining and trimmings of apricot"—designed and manufactured in Los Angeles, and later displayed on Fifth Avenue in New York City as a cutting-edge design—this Bullock's bathing suit turned heads around the world to the growing influence of West Coast fashion. "Los Angeles setting the fashion for Gotham!" screamed one headline.

The Broadway and Bullock's had established a policy of clearing out old merchandise in favor of the latest fashions, what PG later described as "last in, first out." In this way, the store was always known for being au courant and selling only the latest styles. Bullock's was quickly becoming an institution, with a busy kitchen producing fine cuisine and desserts for customers in the Tea Room. Servicemen and other notable speakers came to the store to lecture employees. *Bullock Way Magazine* was launched for customers and staff, providing news on travels, births and other notable events, civic notices, poetry, and philosophy.

The company provided not only a place to shop but a lifestyle formed from progressive ideals. Seals and flags from many countries around the world were displayed above glass counters that carried a cosmopolitan array of merchandise. A free "travel bureau" offered brochures describing exotic destinations, and a nearby American Express office sold railway and steamer tickets for foreign travel. A bookstore, a camera department, and handkerchief and dried fruit sections rounded out the offerings of supplies people needed for a life on the go.

Bullock's brought the wider world to California with room displays of rugs, furniture, and lamps from Europe and the Far East, enormous Persian carpets, Japanese kimonos, stuffed leopards, Italian lamps, and sculptures. Women sat patiently in the millinery department for hat fittings while gentlemen took turns at the indoor golf driving range, swatting balls at a target that hung from a curtain on a wall across the room. Children were dressed for pageants and photographed in the open on the upper deck, where skits were performed. On a lower floor, kids were treated to a life-sized puppet theater. There seemed to be no end to what Bullock's could do. During continual phases of expansion and new construction, a banner was hoisted above the sidewalk that read, "Bullock's is building continually to meet advancing conditions."

During the Roaring Twenties, the United States became the richest country in the world and consumers shopped accordingly, in a spirit of splendid excess. Bullock's and the Broadway delivered the goods that both the middle class and upper echelons of society required. Letts and his partners had masterminded an empire that was taking Los Angeles by storm. The store's imposing coat of arms read *Suprema Regnat Qualitas,* "Quality Reigns Supreme."

Yet, perhaps for political reasons, Letts drew the ire of at least one very powerful man—newspaper tycoon William Randolph Hearst. A very public row began when the Bullock's store purchased land on Hill Street and Seventh Avenue for expansion, with plans to connect several buildings by bridges to accommodate growth. An eight-story addition at St. Vincent's Court resulted in more than fifty thousand additional square feet. The company was now the largest retail store in the West.

Hearst had built the largest chain of newspapers in the country and wielded enormous power in Los Angeles and New York. He owned the *Los Angeles Examiner* and *Los Angeles Evening Herald,* newspapers in which the Broadway refused to advertise. When city leaders agreed to allow Bullock's to expand once more with a new bridge over St. Vincent's Court, Hearst declared war. He claimed that the city should charge Bullock's $80,000 per year in rent for the easement and ran front-page news articles calling for the revocation of its construction permits.

An offer by John Bullock to instead donate a much smaller sum each year to the city further enraged Hearst, who then formed the Taxpayer's Protective Association of Los Angeles, allegedly buying signatures at three cents each for a ballot initiative to revoke the permits. Hearst then mounted a public campaign to oust three city councilmen who had formerly supported Bullock and financed support for a gubernatorial candidate who would oppose the store. He launched scathing attacks in his newspapers against the company, describing its owners and managers as "purse-proud individuals [trying] to grab public assets from taxpayers already overburdened and underserved in police protection, street lighting, and highway maintenance."

Yet, Arthur Letts and John Bullock had powerful friends of their own. The Merchants and Manufacturing Association and Los Angeles Chamber of Commerce banded together to fight Hearst, rallying under the slogan, "Fair Play for Bullocks." The public also supported the store at the ballot box, voting six-to-one in favor of John Bullock and sending William Randolph Hearst and his backers a defeat. Hearst no doubt read a few years later, possibly while entertaining guests up the coast at his San Simeon mansion, that Bullock's had expanded once again to encompass an incredible 740,000 square feet of floor space. The companies founded by Letts were now in the national spotlight.

Bullock and PG worked as hard as ever, as Letts pulled back to focus on collecting rare plants and automobiles, breeding Ravenswood collies, and pursuing real estate ventures that would shape the city well into the twenty-first century.

Letts's developments included the Holmby Hills, which surrounded his Tudor-style Holmby mansion and splendid gardens. Then he turned his attention to the magnificent 3,296-acre Wolfskill Ranch he had purchased some years earlier. Stretching from a two-mile southern section along Pico Boulevard northward to the foothills three miles away, the ranch had been prized by land speculators since the 1800s. Letts's daughter Gladys had some years before married Harold Janss, one of physician and real estate developer Peter Janss's two sons. Peter, Harold, and Harold's brother Edwin "Doc" Janss Sr. formed the Janss Investment Company, which later developed numerous subdivisions in Los Angeles County, including Yorba Linda, Boyle Heights, and Monterey Park. They would continue developing planned communities across greater Los Angeles well into the 1960s, when Doc Janss's sons, Ed and Bill Janss, turned their expertise to expansions in the ski industry.

Letts enlisted the Janss Investment Company to subdivide the Wolfskill Ranch in 1923, directing the company to first donate 382 acres to the University of California for civic purposes. Other portions would become Westwood Village. The Janss Brothers' headquarters in Westwood Village, known as the Janss Dome, opened in 1929. Many streets in the neighborhood today have bronze Janss Investment Company "stamps" on their sidewalks.

Still other portions of the Wolfskill Ranch were set aside for movie studios in a city that had come to embrace this new industry. Century City, at one time owned by the Janss Corporation, was later sold following what I consider to be an ill-advised decision by then-CEO George Gregson.

When Letts died of pneumonia in 1923, he left behind a $7 million empire that had been incorporated as Bullock's, Inc. His managers and shareholders decided in 1927 to take the company public with the sale of $8.5 million in stocks and bonds—at that time, an unheard-of amount for a retail business. The shares were sold within hours, leaving the financial community astonished by the power and appeal of these thriving enterprises.

As the company continued to expand to more locations around the city, Bullock and his partner, PG Winnett, made plans for an even more extravagant enterprise on Wilshire Boulevard, just far enough from downtown to be risky, but well within reach in the flashy new automobiles then taking to American roads.

Within a year, the great tower of Bullocks Wilshire department store rose to dominate the skyline just outside the downtown commercial district. The art deco masterpiece they created became an emporium of glamour that had no equal during the Golden Age of Hollywood. Its allure proved inescapable for the rich and famous.

The movie industry exploded faster than anyone imagined possible. Whereas a generation earlier, movie actors had such bad reputations that they were often refused service at restaurants, by the 1920s and 1930s, stars like Charlie Chaplin, Lillian Gish, Rudolph Valentino, and Douglas Fairbanks were becoming folk heroes. Gradually, the city and its fashions came to be defined by the Hollywood film industry. My grandfather and his esteemed buyers and sellers at Bullocks Wilshire supplied much of the city's glamour.

CHAPTER THREE

Beyond the Palace Walls

When we are children, each new friend can bring a lifetime of adventures. The land around our house on San Vicente Boulevard was open countryside, rural enough to ride our horses to the corner drug store. To one side of our stables there was a large field bordered by a barbed wire fence that separated us from another field and the home of a young girl.

"Hey, what's your name?" my older brother yelled to her over the fence.

"Joan Morgan," replied the girl who would become my best friend and trusted ally.

Walter and Joan's brother Johnny Morgan sported BB guns and attacked almost anything that moved. Birds were likely prey, as were the frogs in the lower lily pond. The boys terrified us with tales of catching these poor creatures and inflating them with soda straws. Joan and I ran to get away from our hoodlum brothers by climbing over the fence, using a special four-part move that we had perfected for quick escape. But Walt and Johnny would lie in wait. With one leg up and almost over, our fannies would inevitably feel the sharp sting of a BB.

We were as wild in our own way as kids tend to be anywhere at that age but growing up free to roam our own domain instilled a sense of dignity and entitlement. I was a tomboy and therefore was expected to play and survive with the boys. Because there was no adult supervision, I learned to make my own decisions and take responsibility for them.

In our home and at school, things were quite different. There, we lived in a world of strict social rules and under the discipline of manners. One was supposed to respect and honor parents no matter the situation and not speak up or join in altercations of any kind. One was never to be disruptive or argumentative. Troubles at home were to be absorbed, digested, and endured. I was taught at school that I needed to work with others to gain their confidence and interact with them respectfully, always on an equal footing.

Other than the usual wild games outdoors, I was never belligerent because I never needed to be, nor did I ever have occasion to become aroused or come into conflict with others. During this time, I was provided social guidance by my dear Esther. From her, I learned to develop a confidence and resilience that served me well during my teenage years. It had not yet occurred to me to wonder why my mother was often nowhere to be found.

Despite having many rooms in our estate, we wanted a secret place of our own. Walter dug a hole in the yard and covered it with boards and dirt, just deep enough for the four of us to crawl into and light a candle. This was our own private subterranean clubhouse, spiders and all. To torture us, the boys would smear powder made from sycamore pods down our backs, causing us to itch terribly. They retrieved these pods by climbing the high branches of a sycamore tree that leaned out and over Santa Monica Canyon, a daring move that I greatly admired.

Joan and I became inseparable. I had been attending Brentwood Country Day School on San Vicente Boulevard before we met, usually dropped off there by our butler Frank. Next, Joan and I attended Marymount Catholic School on Sunset Boulevard in Westwood

Village until sixth grade. Then we both went to the Marlboro School. One of our classmates there was Darrylin Zanuck. My brother Peter would catch rides over to the Harvard Academy with her brother Richard Zanuck, who would one day run Twentieth Century Fox movie studios.

Marymount was a school for girls. There were uniforms, of course, and everyone took a penmanship class for an hour each day to learn to write in an elegant cursive script—without deviation—exactly alike. Although we are now well into our eighties, Joan and I still write in the same formal cursive we learned at Marymount. In addition to reading, writing, and mathematics, we learned social graces and such essential life skills as how to respond eloquently to invitations, address letters correctly, and place a stamp perfectly in the corner of an envelope.

Everyone was required to attend an hour of Catholic Mass each morning before the start of classes. Some girls got so tired on their knees that they fainted and had to be helped out. Since I was not Catholic, I did not have to take the hour of catechism each day; but at one point, I nevertheless became enthralled with Jesus Christ and the stories of Mary and Joseph; I spent my entire allowance on ceramic statues from the school church store, lining them up on a shelf in my room when I got home. My parents became so concerned about my sudden piety that I overheard them saying they thought it was time to send me to another school.

Joan's father, Colonel John Ainsworth Morgan, and her mother, actress Phyllis Cleveland, owned the Cock 'n Bull British Pub at the residential end of Sunset Strip, a place where movie stars, filmmakers, and writers hung out. Her father was a freelance Hollywood writer who served in US military intelligence under President Eisenhower. Tall and handsome, with a military bearing, Colonel Morgan was someone who commanded immediate respect.

Santa Monica in those days was a small town along the Pacific

Coast. Joan and I rode our bikes to the Third Street shopping area almost daily, usually to the Criterion or Aero Theatre on Montana Avenue around Twenty-sixth Street. These were the only theaters there at that time, and they mostly screened Westerns—so we dressed like cowgirls. The man punching tickets would look down at us with a grin and say, "Please check your guns at the box office, girls."

While biking home one afternoon, a dog on Tenth Street started barking, growling, and chasing us. It jumped up against our legs, gnashing its teeth. We sped up and, looking back to see if the dog was still there, I crashed into a parked car. The hook-shaped door handle sliced into my arm and pinioned me there. I pulled my arm out from the door handle and, though faint, went with Joan to ring the doorbell of a nearby house for help. We called my father and, it being Sunday, he came quickly in his black Ford convertible with the rumble seat, picked us up, and took me to the Santa Monica Hospital's emergency room, where the medical staff stitched me up. To this day, I carry a scar near my elbow from that gash. This was the beginning of a spell of memorable accidents for me and my brothers, but what I remember most was wondering at the time why this had happened to me on Tenth Street, since ten was my favorite number. For as long as I can remember, I have been prone to wonder why things happen when and where they do, as though there was an underlying pattern to the events in our lives.

Sometime later, Esther was driving through the neighborhood in our old Woody station wagon, with we three children in the back. Of course, there was no such thing as a seatbelt in those days. Peter, who was only three, leaned on a door handle; the unlocked door opened, and he flew out of the car. As he skidded across the pavement, everyone screamed. Esther hit the brakes, jumped out, and gathered up the battered and bloody little boy off the street. We drove straight to the hospital, where Peter stayed for several days, covered in bandages. It was Esther who suffered the most—Peter was "her baby." She may have been reprimanded, but she was not fired from her job as our governess.

Every now and then, it was over the hill and through the woods to Grandmother Helen Hutton Winnett's house we'd go. I would be dressed in a beautiful frock, wearing my Mary Jane patent leather shoes and all the rest. I took Esther's right hand and Peter took the left. Walter was older, so he was allowed to skip ahead. Those visits were big events for us, yet my grandmother, always very petite and fragile-looking, had little to say. I never learned about her early years, as no one, including Granddaddy PG, ever spoke of her after she died. She would greet us on the front porch of their white clapboard New England-style house with its tall, narrow, perfectly trimmed rosebushes lining the walkway to the porch. My grandparent's estate had extensive gardens, walking paths, and orchards, fully matured by the time of my youth. Much food was grown in those gardens, and there were many fruit trees. They had an avocado orchard like ours, but my favorites were the loquat trees, which I would climb to eat the fruits until I could eat no more. What ever happened to the loquat?

Down a slight hill behind the main house was the adobe house. It was entirely different from all the other structures, a rambling old one-story plastered building—a relic from the days of the Spanish missions—situated under ancient trees. This was where PG hosted his famous Sunday barbeques. He insisted on doing all the grilling, wearing a chef's hat and white apron in the wood smoke beside the barbecue. Bing Crosby would sing for our entertainment. Bob Hope was a regular family friend, as were Walt Disney and his wife Lilly.

What made these visits so memorable for my brothers and me was the Coca-Cola we were served over ice in elegant, sparkling crystal glasses on my grandmother's porch. Before we left, we were each given a new one-dollar bill. My grandmother had been raised in simpler circumstances. Her father was a judge; like most judges, he preferred to keep out of the public eye. The life into which she married demanded constant entertaining and frequent travel. While her husband PG was a well-known businessman with an engaging social life, she was incapable of being the center of her family in this way and always seemed to be left behind by the party.

When Grandmother Winnett passed away a few years later, I thought she must have died of loneliness. I know now that she had been slowly drifting deeper into alcoholism, a disease that was passed along to two of her three children. I never knew my grandmother well, but it was exciting to sit with her when I was a young girl and get a crisp, brand new one-dollar bill.

My mother grew up on the Winnett estate. Family lore held that she was delivered there by a doctor who arrived on horseback through one of the stout iron entrance gates. Nineteen years later, she was married to my father in the Long Garden, one of many gardens on the property. It must have been an amazing event in 1929, a few months before the stock market crashed. The wedding party was surrounded by five acres of mowed lawn that could only be reached by following a series of brick walled terraces to a fountain where a grotesque head continuously spouted water into the air.

Through another gap in a high wall was the guest cottage where my Aunt Dougie later lived with her two daughters while her husband, Kenyon Boocock, was away during World War II. Uncle Kenyon was thirty-three when he enlisted in 1940. He became a navy pilot and lieutenant commander who ferried airplanes across the Pacific.

When I was ten years old, my father decided it would be a good idea for me to know what it was like to fly in an airplane, so he planned a trip for us to visit Aunt Dougie, who then lived in New York City on Park Avenue. We boarded an airplane with two big propeller engines that pulled us loudly into the sky. The trip was terribly slow by today's standards, but we had first-class cabins with bunk beds and curtains for privacy. At some point in the long flight, we entered a lightning storm that sent the airplane falling quickly and then rising again. My father, who was in the bunk below mine, was obviously quite worried because he kept calling up to me and asking if I was okay. I giggled and laughed the whole time and thought it was great fun. My father was unimpressed with air travel, and he warned me never to invest in an airline.

Thanksgiving dinner at my grandparents' estate was a display of the kind of extravagance expected at that time. At a long table, twenty-five people sat behind dazzling china and glassware so beautiful and yet so unnecessary to a young girl who needed only a glass and a fork. The sparkle and shine from the table lit up the evening as waiters in uniform carried trays of sumptuous food to us.

It was our ritual each year to overeat so much that my siblings, cousins, and I would roll on the floor afterwards, groaning. My two cousins had a strict French governess who did not allow them to eat ice cream cones because they had to stick their tongues out to lick them, which she considered uncouth. We laughed about this at the time, but I soon came to feel sorry for all that they must have missed in their childhood. One afternoon, we brought them to the edge of the canyon, where there grew a giant eucalyptus tree that had a rope hanging from one of its limbs. This was where we tested our courage by running down the hill toward the canyon and swinging high into the air over the cliff.

My cousins were younger than us and, being from Manhattan, had never seen such a thing. These were not country girls. If their governess found out what was happening, there would be trouble. We swore them to secrecy before allowing each of them in turn to grab the rope and take a breathless and exhilarating swing out above the canyon, their lace dresses flapping, before returning safely to earth.

During World War II, gasoline was rationed, as were many other commodities and food products. Air raid sirens blew when a Japanese ship shelled an oil refinery near Santa Barbara. P-38 fighter planes roared along the shore. No lights could be on at night in homes or in cars. Not even a match could be lit. My mother worked as a volunteer for the USO at that time. She and other women met to sew upholstery for the war effort. She also hosted a circus fundraiser that featured stunts by none other than her two oldest children.

Walter and I were told this performance would be vitally important for the war effort, so we practiced for days prior to the main event. Walter seemed to have a black cloud over his head those days. He had pneumonia when he was six and was hospitalized for months with an open wound in his side to drain fluid from his lungs. When he healed from that, Esther allowed us to create an obstacle course in her bedroom, including stuffed chairs to jump over. I made the jump, but when Walter launched from it, he fell and broke his arm. On another occasion, while racing our bikes together around the circular front driveway, Walter's foot slipped off the pedal and into a wheel spoke, catching there and breaking his leg. He thought the world was against him, or at least that I was.

When the day came for the big circus, my mother invited all of her friends and their husbands to come to our sloping back lawn where Walter and I had built a large jump. The spectators sat at the top of the hill under the jacaranda tree. Now that there was a crowd, we were a bit nervous as Walter rode his scooter down the hill and over the jump. He landed badly and crashed spectacularly in front of the crowd. Terribly embarrassed, but relatively unhurt, he got up and rode the rest of the way down the hill as everyone applauded. Young Peter managed to avoid many of the dangers that Walter and I engaged in, but he had dramas of his own. In a fit of anger, he once threw a grapefruit at our father, who then chased him up the stairs and spanked him.

During World War II, Bullocks Wilshire was prohibited from selling silks and stockings, which were used for making parachutes. A banner above the women's department read, "In Skirts of Cotton

Bright and Free We're Working Hard for Victory." The mostly empty housewares department had a banner that recommended creative solutions during a time of scarce materials: "A Brush, Some Paint, a Frill or Two, and You Will Find That Very Soon We'll Have a Table as Good as New."

By then, the store had become known far and wide for its seasonal displays: sweetheart themes for Valentine's Day, extravagantly decorated Christmas displays, and a spring show that featured an actual dwarf, dressed as the Easter Bunny, who performed in the life-sized marionette puppet show. My father left this retail fantasy world to join the navy in 1943. That summer, my mother rented a beach house on the Island of Coronado in San Diego Bay, about two blocks from the Hotel Coronado. My father was stationed nearby until he shipped out to the Pacific theater, where the navy made use of his knowledge of inventory selection, distribution networks, and other logistical skills he had learned on the job at Bullocks Wilshire. Instead of selling and boxing elegant fashions, he was directed to prepare an airstrip on a Pacific island with storage and housing in Quonset huts for incoming planes and troops who would fight to secure the island.

Gas and food rationing were of little consequence to me personally. Of deeper concern was a subtle feeling that began to invade my quiet and secure life. After my father left for the war, men stayed for weekends in the guest room adjacent to the garage. They would be in uniform when I was introduced, and several I can even remember by name, as they were more frequent visitors. I felt strangely uncomfortable about them being in our house when my father was away. An odd, restless, and uncertain mood overtook me. I was anxious for my safety as a war of my own began to take shape in my mind.

My mother made certain that we had an ample vegetable garden, and the field by the stable was given over to turkeys and chickens.

But inside the house, noisy parties went on late into the night, with lots of drinking and laughing not far from my bedroom. I remember several occasions when my mother brought strangers into my room for a look at me while I pretend to be asleep. Quiet voices whispered above me. I was terrified by these strangers in my room, hovering over my bed in the dark of night.

My father came back when the war ended, having been wounded by shrapnel; he received the Bronze Star from the secretary of the navy. He also received a letter from the president of the United States that I still have today, addressed to Commander Walter Weaver Candy Jr.:

> For meritorious service as Administrative Officer of a Patrol Bombing Squadron and Assistant to the Commanding Officer of a Search Group during operations against enemy Japanese forces in the Central and Western Pacific Ocean Areas, from December 3, 1943, to April 19, 1945. Providing installation and services under combat conditions, Commander (then Lieutenant Commander) Candy enabled Naval search planes to operate at the earliest possible dates and, by his skill and efforts, contributed materially to the success of our forces. His professional ability and devotion to duty were in keeping with the highest traditions of the United States Naval Services.

After his return, my father immediately went back to work for Bullocks Wilshire. He never talked of his military service, and I never gave him credit for what he did during the war, but the war remained an important part of his life. At breakfast one morning before I went to school, he showed me a map of the Maginot Line, an expensive system of Allied fortifications and bunkers along the French-German border that was designed to deter a German invasion. In the end, it did not. The Germans simply invaded France by first invading neighboring Belgium.

Amazingly, my mother's parties for servicemen continued even after my father returned home. He worked hard at the store and looked forward to coming home at the end of the day, but my mother had by then found it impossible to give up alcohol in her life, and so the parties continued late into the night.

She had become addicted as well to the adulation she received from the men she was entertaining. My mother was beautiful and fun, so naturally any man who was invited to visit was honored to accept. These parties led to quarrels between my parents, which became more frequent and, ultimately, violent.

CHAPTER FOUR

The Gravy Train

About a year after the end of World War II, my grandfather wrote a letter to customers and staff in the *Bullock Way Magazine* to remind them of the grand opening of the original Bullock's store in 1907 that drew sixty thousand visitors to Seventh and Broadway. This history lesson was meant to inspire hundreds of company employees and excite thousands of loyal customers as Bullock's prepared for a new era. By then, my grandfather and John Bullock had acquired the I. Magnin & Company chain of upscale specialty stores and was preparing to expand to numerous other locations around Los Angeles. In addition to being a successful businessman, my grandfather was also an effective leader, with qualities I came to admire and emulate in later years.

Because of our retail connections, my family had one of the first television sets in our part of town. Joan and I stared at it in the corner of the room as though it was some kind of mysterious ghost. I don't even recall what we watched. It was just a novelty to see things move around on the screen, but there were so many more interesting things to do than watch television. My grandfather's 1,800-acre Rancho San Vicente was situated within the vast orange orchards of the San Fernando Valley. It was the first privately-owned ranch in the area, and it became a sanctuary for me. Prized horses were free to graze in broad pastures and stabled in immaculately clean and modern stalls. My grandfather arose early to ride these magnificent creatures, passing proudly by the ranch house in his English riding breeches and jacket.

After my grandmother died in 1949, I was permitted to sleep over at the ranch in her large bed, so luxurious for a young girl. At times, my cousins would also be there, but I always felt that I was PG's favorite, probably because I looked so much like my mother, who by then was losing her battle to the same disease that had afflicted his own wife. I did my best to fulfill the demanding social role of my mother. Whenever there was an evening gathering at the ranch for department store executives, I would serve as the hostess. My father would also be there, but never my mother. I was grateful for this responsibility and the opportunity it afforded me to become socially adept at a young age.

PG enjoyed indulging my genuine interest in the retail business. I asked questions, and we talked about the history of the stores and his goals for the future. Typical department stores had only one buyer for women's clothing and one for men's clothing. Bullock's stores had numerous buyers scouring the globe for purchases in their individual areas of expertise. Baby boom shoppers would soon be drawn to eclectic shopping centers in the emerging suburban areas around the city rather than to individual marquis store buildings. Each new store location would cater to specific neighborhoods, age groups, and tastes. The high-end Bullocks Wilshire store remained in a class all its own.

Because of the responsibility PG placed on me, I became an adult in my own mind well before my adult years. I was born with an innate curiosity to learn. My grandfather's attentions provided me with continual motivation to keep asking questions. This led to deeper understandings, which led to feelings of accomplishment. I refused to give in to the negative thoughts I had about my relationship with my mother. I would find a way to not only survive but also become successful on my own. I would never be dependent on anyone but myself. It was a bit egotistical to think that I could do all this, but I needed to believe in myself and display self-confidence at that time of my life in order move forward.

My grandfather's greatest travel extravagances were called the Gravy Trains, entourage tours attended by thirty or more close friends, business associates, and their families. These trips by cruise liner to Hawaii or by railway car to the Sierra Mountains became legendary throughout Los Angeles. Invitations were highly sought-after. My mother's packing for a Gravy Train trip was done by "Queenie," my nickname for Quinlock Sheen, her personal maid. Pieces of heavy Louis Vuitton luggage would come up from the basement and be opened around her bedroom. The finest new fashions from Bullocks Wilshire were purchased expressly for a trip to the Royal Hawaiian Hotel on Waikiki Beach and delivered to our house on hangers. Between each garment, Queenie laid several sheets of tissue paper, until the suitcase was filled with the neatly folded contents. It took days to prepare my mother's luggage for such an excursion.

My mother was considered the best-dressed woman in Los Angeles, and she had a retinue of fashion advisors and other personnel to make sure she upheld this reputation. Her "face lady," which is what I called her, taught her weekly exercises designed to activate the muscles in her face so that they would always be strong and not give way to sagging. While she was engaged in these exercises or some elaborate makeup detail, I sat looking up at the large mirror above and behind her ornately inlaid parquet dressing table. That mirror reflected a row of mirrored closet doors that ran the length of her dressing room. Brightly colored perfume bottles sat on the dressing table, each reflecting magically on all the mirrored surfaces. While I was in rapt attention, my mother dispensed what she deemed to be essential advice. She often reminded me that a woman's age can be judged by her elbows. She also advised me to put cold cream on my elbows after a bath, concerns that were trivial to me when I became a competitive athlete.

One of the most memorable Gravy Train excursions took us to Yosemite Valley to stay at the majestic Ahwahnee Hotel. Luxury railway cars pulled us away from the city through farm fields and desert until we reached the mountains. Yosemite Valley was a revelation of rugged wilderness. From our rooms we could see waterfalls. Half Dome towered nearby, as well as the enormous shard of Glacier Point. At night on the Fourth of July, a "firefall" of burning embers was pushed off the rocky top of Glacier Point, falling in a glowing stream of orange fire to the valley floor.

My first Gravy Train ski trip had been to Badger Pass near Yosemite when I was still quite young. We rode up in the *Queen Mary,* an old boat that had been converted into a lift of sorts, pulled uphill by a cable. I skied, tentatively at first, in a snowplow between the legs of an Austrian man named Siegfried "Sigi" Engl. My grandfather invited Sigi from Austria, where he had already made a name for himself as a ski racer. Sigi first came to Yosemite in 1936 when he was hired to teach and guide members of the Gravy Train. He stayed on for two more years at Badger Pass to run the ski school there and then moved on to teach skiing at the Sun Valley Resort in Idaho.

Sigi, who had learned to ski by imitating Austrian soldiers training on skis during World War I, joined the US Army's Tenth Mountain Division and fought the Germans in Italy. He then returned to Sun Valley to run what would become the biggest ski school in North America. He remained a close family friend for life. He and his wife Peggy Engl would become chaperones for me when I began to travel to Sun Valley in my teenage years.

During a special spring trip to Yosemite when I was still a young girl, my mother took me by the hand to join an Easter egg hunt outside the hotel. My memory of this trip is so vivid because a child never forgets such moments of tenderness. Under the giant sequoias behind the hotel, I followed her whispers as she led me to find the golden egg. The prize was an actual white rabbit, which we carried home with us.

My mother could express such warmth and loving attention to me in moments such as these. I must have looked up at her face with joy as I sat and cuddled my rabbit. Her love and attention were worth much more to me than the rabbit. I think back even now and grasp these precious moments, which would become rare as time went on and my mother's behavior grew increasingly erratic.

A few years after that Easter trip, I suffered a tremendous loss when my dear Esther suddenly left us. She had looked after us for so many years during my mother's incapacity. Her love and support were always present until one day she told us that she had been asked to leave. We cried for a long time on her more than ample lap and bosoms. It was hardest on Peter, as he was only four. She was our friend and confidant, our true mother. There was nothing we could not share with her, and then suddenly, mysteriously, she was gone, and life became terribly empty for what seemed like a very long time.

This first deep loss in my life brought about a lack of trust. I came to believe that whomever I loved would eventually disappoint or abandon me. After all, if my own mother could transform unexpectedly when she was drinking into someone I did not know, and if Esther could also abandon me for no apparent reason, who was there to depend on in a world such as this? My ensuing doubts about love and trust would negatively affect my relationship with my father and my first husband.

Although alcoholism ravaged many families during those years, it was not yet considered a disease. During Prohibition, people drank whatever they could find or make, including concoctions called "bathtub gin" that were made by Doc Janss and shared with my parents and their friends. Anyone with a predisposition to alcoholism would be quickly drawn to extremes under the influence of such high-octane cocktails. Those who became consumed by alcoholism would then disappear from sight, just like those with a mental illness.

When I was still quite young, my mother brought me to Good Samaritan Hospital in Los Angeles to visit my grandmother. She lay in bed, weak and feeble. I asked why, but my mother replied only that she was "sick." I felt that something was wrong with the situation, but at that age I could not comprehend what it was. I just felt sad for my grandmother. I learned later that she had been placed there because of her alcoholism. My grandfather had the money to pay for her care in such a facility and was no doubt a major financial donor to the hospital. Having my grandmother at home would have upset PG's organized routine and his reputation, so she was simply put away.

My mother was a kind and considerate person when she was not drinking. When I was a little older and after my grandmother died, we returned to the Good Samaritan Hospital for a lesson in volunteerism. My mother and other mothers in our social class were leading their daughters in a group called the Silver Spoons. We were taught at an early age that those who were born with "silver spoons in their mouths" had a duty to give back to those less fortunate. This idea of *noblesse oblige* was instilled in us in the hope that we would take on the responsibility of the well-to-do, that our entitlement in society would lead to positions of leadership where we could inspire people in our social class to make the world a better place. It was a matter of cultivating empathy for all people, regardless of their position in society.

I went with my mother to work at the hospital as a candy striper, delivering books and visiting with patients to provide comfort. I did not know at the time that this rewarding work would begin for me a lifetime of volunteerism and dedicated work in support of numerous nonprofit organizations across the country and around the world. At the time, I only felt a sense of purpose emerging from the confusing emotional landscape of my childhood. Personal tragedy can lead one to retreat from the world or engage more deeply with others for a positive purpose. The early support and encouragement I received from my father and grandfather, and the many teachers and mentors I met along my path, have propelled me to pursue the latter. In the years that followed, I found that I could communicate the values of empathy to others and lead by example. There were no requirements that people of my social class do these things, but for me it became a passion. A true leader must become a part of many people's lives, listen intently, and inspire them to come along on the journey.

Although Esther's departure left me feeling lost at sea, at least Joan Morgan and I had one another. Together, we continued to explore the world outside our classroom lessons. We snuck into the book stacks in the Blue Room at my house and found two remarkably interesting volumes, known as the Kinsey reports, on male and female sexuality. Although as yet we had no interest in boys, Joan and I were absolutely glued to these books. We were shocked by what we read about sexual behavior and said nothing to anyone about our furtive researches, always remembering to put the books back exactly where we found them.

PG was a cigar smoker. As curious girls would do, we slipped into the closet where he kept his cigars and took one, went outside with a match, tore the cigar in half and lit the two stogies. After one puff, we turned green, and that was it for us with smoking.

We found more enjoyment roller-skating around my grandfather's tennis courts, and later playing tennis on them. We became jocks, playing every varsity sport that was offered, including tennis, volleyball, and basketball. We met with a wider circle of friends and acquaintances at the Santa Monica Beach Club, an easy place to reach when we were kids and a regular destination for volleyball or bodysurfing. My first memory of the club is from when I was quite little and had to take a nap in the cabanas for little tots. It would be very hot, and I never slept. When I was allowed to escape, I would find my mother lounging with others under a bright blue umbrella.

A well-known yachtsman and president of the yacht club, Uncle Bill Candy was a favorite with everyone because he was fun, wild, and adventurous—and an eligible bachelor. My mother rarely ventured anywhere during my teenage years, so I spent time at the beach club with schoolmates or children whose parents who were acquainted with my family. To get there, Joan and I rode our bikes two and half miles along San Vicente, turned right at Seventh Street, and flew down the hill to the beach, passing rather dilapidated and simple one-story buildings, a grocer, a dry cleaner, and a bar. This was an area frequented by locals and, of course, anyone heading to the beach. Upon reaching the Pacific Coast Highway, we veered left at the stop sign and then pedaled another a few blocks to the club.

The Santa Monica Beach Club was for "members only" and their guests. The place was homey, safe, and fun. It provided a warm and welcoming place where many of my friends and relatives came to relax and socialize. The place to meet was under a large awning where we ordered lunches and dined in the shade. There were several other beach clubs along the coast that had volleyball teams. I was fast in the sand and able to get to the ball quicker than other, older players, so I was always in demand. As I grew taller and increasingly athletic, I accepted invitations from older men to be their setter in two-person games. There was also sunning, sunning, and sunning some more. In those days, the "blacker" you were, the more beautiful you were. I had olive skin, so I could gain a darker tan than almost anyone I knew.

It was very prestigious then to own a home on the Pacific Coast Highway in Santa Monica. Many Hollywood families we knew had homes there, including the Zanuck, Irving Thalberg, and Goetze families. Peter Lorre had a home there in later years. I was good friends with the Thalberg children—Irving Jr. and Katherine. Irving Sr., a legendary producer, was married to actress Norma Shearer at the time. I later become reacquainted with her in Sun Valley.

The Thalbergs' house had an extraordinary movie-viewing room that was very frequently in use. Plush couches provided seats for viewing. As children, we were more excited by the very large play loft that took up almost the entire top floor of the main house, complete with a rope swing that hung from the rafters, which we used to swoop from one end of the room to the other.

Next to the Santa Monica Beach Club was a beach house that belonged to actress Marion Davies, the mistress of William Randolph Hearst. This thirty-four-bedroom oceanfront mansion was off-limits and seemed empty most of the time. Who knew what went on in there? The compound was enormous. It stretched along more than a hundred yards of private beachfront behind a wall that separated the waves from its guesthouses, swimming pools, and tennis courts. Whatever differences the newspaper tycoon once had with my grandfather and John Bullock were long forgotten. Or perhaps the store was simply too irresistible to avoid. Davies had been known for walking the aisles of Bullocks Wilshire trailing a long fur coat as she shopped with Hearst for swimsuits and other sportswear for their guests at Hearst Castle above San Simeon up the coast.

When I turned fifteen, my life took on a bright new hue in the form of a yellow Ford convertible, a gift from my grandfather. We were allowed to drive at that age only to get to school or to work if we had no other means of travel. There was no school bus to Marlborough, and the ride with the Zanuck chauffeur had come to an end when these friends went off to other schools. My wondrous car elicited a great deal of envy from all my friends. I would pick them up on the forty-five-minute drive to Marlborough, cruising with the top down, weather permitting. But rarely did I dare invite anyone over to my house for an evening, much less a boy.

Proms were required annual social events. There was always the fear that you would be invited to dance by someone you barely knew or that you would not be invited to dance at all. Nevertheless, when I became student body president, I was expected to set an example at these social events.

I knew nothing about dancing or about boys. Joan set about changing this by arranging a private evening for us with two Harvard Academy boys we both knew. After they arrived at my house, we went down to the studio and put on a Frank Sinatra record. I had been to a Sinatra concert as a bobby-soxer and enjoyed his songs but was embarrassed at the screaming behavior of other girls in the audience. I do not recall who turned out the lights, but soon Joan and I and our two friends were dancing in the dark. My mother must have been watching from the main house above. We suddenly heard her screaming at us to turn the lights back on. I was mortified. The boys soon left, and we never dated them again.

So much for our experiment in dating and socializing. My date that night was Robert Wagner, whom we knew as R.J. He later became a famous actor in Hollywood, and even these days I see stories that relate to his wife Natalie Wood's untimely death and the ongoing suspicion that he had something to do with it. I saw R.J. a few years ago in Sun Valley at a fund-raising event, but I decided not to remind him of our dance in the dark that was cut short by my mother's screaming voice.

There was no real dating in those years, but I clearly recall the junior high school prom. My mother dropped me off in her black Cadillac convertible. Before I stepped out, she placed a finishing touch on my appearance by leaning over and, with a finger, wiping some lipstick off her lips and spreading it onto mine. It was a simple gesture of tenderness that I have treasured from those difficult years.

Its hard to say when I became fully conscious that my mother had a real problem with alcohol. The guilt and shame that comes along with this disease often leaves one in denial. My mother would disappear for days at a time, presumably to drink all she wanted. The police would eventually find her by locating her black Cadillac. She would be found alone and unconscious, locked in a nearby motel room.

One evening, I was studying, genuinely enjoying my time alone in peace, when my mother entered the room. She stood over me for a moment, swaying as though she were going to say something, but then suddenly fell to the floor. I had been advised and warned by her doctor that this could happen, that it would be a seizure from which she could die. I was to place a pencil in her mouth to prevent her from biting or swallowing her tongue. But my father took over and called an ambulance. She was taken to the Santa Monica Hospital and placed behind metal doors to detoxify. This was the only means of treatment then available.

Several times in later years, I took her to the same hospital, watching those metal doors slam behind her with a terrifying finality. Shock and fear for her eventually gave way to shame for me, and then shame gave way to grief. I also had a sense of wonder at why this was happening, at what was happening. I felt completely out of control, though I was more closely involved with these episodes than my brothers. Walter and Peter were away. Walter attended Lawrenceville School near Trenton, New Jersey—the high school our father and Uncle Bill had graduated from. By the time Peter was in eighth grade at Harvard Academy in Los Angeles, he was living at the home of Florence "Flossy" and Doc Janss on Sunset Boulevard in a house they had built back when Sunset was a dirt road. Flossy helped raise Peter as well as several other foster children she took in over the years. My father felt that Peter was better off there at the Jansses' than at our house until he was old enough to go back east to Lawrenceville.

One week my mother was gone for so many days that I experienced a terrible rash on my face and body. The emotional distress had brought on a physical condition, one that could not be ignored. I still attended school, but the teachers seemed to be more attentive to me than usual. I knew that they knew what was going on. My father must have called and informed them of the situation.

My mother could be so gentle and kind—until she started drinking; then she turned into another person entirely. There were many times when my mother acted perfectly normal. But even then, I was filled with anxiety about doing or saying the wrong thing, then losing her again and blaming myself for her condition. On one occasion, she took me to a luncheon at Chasen's in Beverly Hills, then the most famous restaurant in the area. Dave Chasen personally welcomed my mother, who looked fantastic in the latest fashions. All the waiters knew her by name. I was twelve years old and looked around wide-eyed at all the well-dressed people talking busily in their booths. Chasen's was famous for its original creation of the spinach salad, made of chopped spinach, boiled egg, bacon, and crumbled blue cheese. I followed my mother's suggestion and also ordered a spinach salad.

After we left the restaurant and were on the sidewalk heading for her car, a gentleman came toward us and gave my mother a big hug. I was introduced to Bill Hollingsworth. She smiled at him so unguardedly, I thought he must be a man of obvious significance to her. I learned much later that he had been her paramour during college and, supposedly, was a former fiancé.

As I understand it, many years earlier, when my mother was attending the prestigious Bennett School for Girls—a two-year finishing school in Millbrook, New York—along with her sister Dougie, a "mysterious occurrence" took place on campus one night. One of the younger girls on a lower floor of the stone-walled building was awakened by the sound of a rope knocking against her window. She was terrified to see that a man clung to it while descending from above.

"The house mother thought the children probably had some sort of nightmare or unfounded fright until she reached the room and saw the rope hanging outside the window. She got the night watchman immediately, and he not only saw the rope but tugged at it with both hands," the school principal wrote at the time. A Keystone Cops episode ensued in which various staff members with flashlights were enlisted to search the building. By the time they returned to the spot where the rope was hanging, it had disappeared.

"I was almost amused to have the several people who had been working on it tell me that the girls in the room upstairs (namely, Kate and Victoria) would be able to offer some light on the mystery," she wrote. But when questioned about the incident, my mother pleaded both innocence and ignorance, explaining that she and her roommate had slept soundly through the night, despite reports of loud "moving around" by the girls below. The principal discovered that Bill Hollingsworth had been on campus the night before and that there was good reason to believe he was there to pay a certain visit before sailing for Europe the next week.

"You can well imagine how much anxiety this matter has brought to us," wrote the principal in a letter to PG. "And I am surprised to see how little it appears to cause Kate . . . in the course of our investigations we came upon a fact entirely unconnected with the school, which makes us realize the young Hollingsworth would be capable of some adventurous escapade."

The girls must have known he was coming and contrived a means of secretly getting him upstairs from the ground level when he called up to them in the night. My mother's room was conveniently located over the entrance to the main building. Her roommate being an accomplished pianist, the girl's parents wanted her to have her piano with her at the school, so she was given the largest room available on the second floor.

When rub marks from the rope were discovered on my mother's

window ledge, she expressed only bewilderment over how anybody could enter her room, attach the rope, and then go out the window without waking her, especially since she was a rather light sleeper. The principal was unconvinced and requested that PG take the three-day trip east on the Union Pacific train to address her possible expulsion from Millbrook. He went to New York and no doubt paid the school generously to keep her enrolled.

Standing on the sidewalk outside of Chasen's, I had no idea yet who Bill Hollingsworth was, yet I could feel that my mother was excited and a bit flustered by this surprise meeting with him. As I listened and watched their spirited exchange, I noticed a piece of green spinach locked between my mother's two front teeth. Their animated conversation continued, during which time Bill Hollingsworth must also have noticed the green leaf in my mother's smile. Hollingsworth said nothing; and I knew I would get in trouble for interrupting their conversation, so I said nothing until later in the car. When I told her, she was furious; but with time and distance, some tragedies can become comedies.

Although my home life was chaotic and unpredictable, school held the promise of structure and purpose. I was a serious student and remained so through my college years, taking every opportunity to immerse myself in any and all learning environments. An honor roll student, I was elected student body president in both junior high and high school. My teachers loved me and openly shared their caring. They became the mothers that I needed at the time, as did the mothers of my many close friends. No matter how despairing I became, they were supportive and provided the encouragement that I craved.

I eventually learned to move beyond the shame and even gained confidence for having risen above my home situation. I was becoming a young woman, after all, and would soon need to make my own choices in life. Joan Morgan had plans to leave Los Angeles after ninth grade to attend school on the East Coast, but one night before she left, we stayed late at the Santa Monica Beach Club. After daring one another, we got up our courage, walked down the beach, and slipped over the wall of Marion Davies's mansion to take a moonlight swim in her pool. This small act of trespass marked a turning point in our lives. It made us feel brave and adventuresome.

Joan remained in close touch with our family, eventually marrying my brother Walter, the boy next door who used to torment her and chase her with a BB gun. She and Walter had shared all the adventures of growing up together, and Joan knew she had always been in love with him. They remained married for sixteen years and had three wonderful children.

CHAPTER FIVE

Money and Dignity

I always delved deeper into my studies than was necessary, especially in the subjects of languages and history. I wanted to travel, to know everything. I wanted to escape. Although I was venturing more and more outside the palace walls of my youth, I was beginning to build psychological walls of my own that I thought would protect me from the pain of being disappointed by others.

My father appreciated the fact that I loved Latin because it was the basis for the Romance languages that I was so keen to learn. A highly educated man, he would throw out a Latin phrase of note in the context of our conversations, such as *ex nihilo nihil fit,* which means "nothing comes from nothing," or *quisque comoedus est,* which means "everyone is a comedian." Once I figured out what he was saying, we would have a laugh over it.

At Marlborough, I learned that the ancient Greco-Roman period formed the basis for all Western culture and that European and American history were equally important in terms of the foundation of civic freedom and democracy. If only more people understood this today—that democracy is hardly an American invention.

Books and classes opened up entire worlds for me, ways of seeing life, art, and literature. Not only did I read assiduously, but I also listened to the mothers of my peers and to coaches and anyone else with wisdom to offer. My studies became the treasured reward for a dccp and lifelong desire to learn, to solve life's mysteries, and enjoy new enlightenments. I did not excel to be superior to my peers—I loved learning for learning's sake. I also needed to prove that I was academically competent; I needed to be as accomplished as possible to gain validation. My academic honors were a result of this need to achieve.

Academics also provided a positive diversion from the argumentative family dinners at home, from the alcoholism and quarreling. I found peace only when I could retire to my room to become completely absorbed in my studies. Oddly, the arguments always seemed to be about money, and yet we had an abundance of wealth, although our money was never put on display. These arguments over financial matters were only a pretense; on a deeper level, the fights were about my father's dignity as a human being and my mother's need to undermine it to defend her pride and avoid criticism for her drinking. My mother had been rich all her life. What she inherited from her father, she spent freely and unwisely. She thought nothing of renting a house in Del Mar right on the beach during horse racing season so that she could be close to the track and the festivities and watch her thoroughbred compete.

My father's childhood had been quite different. He grew up in a family that survived real challenges during the Great Depression. Before moving to Los Angeles, he earned his own living at the Busy Bee Candy Company, founded in St. Louis by his father, Walter J. Candy, in 1902. I have always thought it interesting that the family founded for itself a namesake business, just as families in old Europe once were named for their occupations: Coopers, Smiths, Carpenters, and the like. My father and uncle stretched taffy in the storefront window for passersby at their father's St. Louis store on Ninth and Broadway. My early memory of airplanes taking off was from those years before my parents moved west. They were persuaded to go to

California by PG, who missed his beautiful daughter and must have been in some control of her, even from far away. It was not so easy to travel back then. Visiting California would have taken two or three days by train.

When my father took a job with Bullock's, he worked hard to prove himself worthy, but he would not have been paid enough money for an estate such as ours, nor would he have had enough money to move us back west when I was four years old. I often wonder how different our lives might have been had we stayed in St. Louis. Having gone through the Depression years of the 1930s, my father would never have lived beyond his means, and he always warned his children not to take on debt.

So we moved to Los Angeles, and he went to work wrapping boxes at the Bullock's store at Seventh and Hill Streets. He worked tirelessly for decades, yet he had little authority as a husband or father over how his family's resources were spent. He also had no means of controlling my mother's increasingly volatile behavior. If he challenged her, she would say with defiance that she "paid all the bills" and who was he to complain. My father's very livelihood depended on my grandfather's approval, and our lifestyle could not have been supported without my mother's family's wealth. I grew so sick of the arguments at the dinner table, about who had the money and control, that I vowed never to discuss money if I got married.

My mother would never have given up the control she held over my father. She sometimes even spoiled for a fight, placing my father in a defensive mood. I am certain that he felt hurt by these attacks on his character, which were often made in front of his children. Afterward, he would try to defend himself to me, as though to regain his self-respect.

My father strove to support me with words that he hoped would help me find success in life. "If you do not blow your own horn, nobody else will," he would say. When he knew I was facing a difficult challenge, he reminded me to be like someone wearing a raincoat in the shower. "Just let it all run off you like rain, Glenn," he said. Above all, I remember him telling me, "Anything worth doing is worth doing well." Those words I took to heart, and they became a mantra for me throughout my life. Excellence was the only option. I can only hope that if he were alive today, he would be pleased with my track record.

When it became dangerous to my mother's survival for her to remain at home in a drunken state, it fell to me to take her to the hospital. When I dared to ask why this should be my responsibility, my father said, "Because she would be mad at me if I did." I interpreted this to mean that it was somehow all right if she was mad at me instead. A servant would help me get her into the car. At the hospital, an attendant would come and help her into the corridor that led through those metal doors that closed behind her with a loud clang. I was informed by her doctor on one occasion that she might not survive the next onset of seizures during a week of detoxification treatment. After detox, she would be shuffled off to an addiction recovery center where she was given Antabuse, which would cause stomach convulsions and upheavals if she took a drink. Eventually, this chemical deterrent wore off, and the cycle of addiction and abuse would begin all over again.

My mother never recalled what had taken place during her blackout binges, although she often had bruises to show for them. She acted as though nothing had occurred. Did she remember? Maybe she felt too ashamed to mention what she did remember. I was always hopeful that the next opportunity to spend time with her would be different. I joined her on a trip to Cabo San Lucas one year. She loved deep-sea fishing and would occasionally travel to a spectacular hotel at the end of the rocky promontory overlooking the sea.

On the second day of our stay, I went to her room in the morning to see if she was ready to go down for breakfast. I knocked but there was no response, so I entered the room and went to check the bathroom. It was locked and, again, there was no response. I hurried with trepidation and embarrassment to the front desk for help. We found her on the bathroom floor in a fetal position, unconscious. The owner of the hotel called my father, and later that day a doctor and nurse arrived from the states in a private airplane to transport my mother back to the Santa Monica Hospital for detox. It was many years before I felt comfortable being alone with my mother after that.

I later wanted my mother to attend Alcoholics Anonymous meetings and would gladly have gone with her. I attended some of these informal gatherings years later with an art teacher and was struck by the honest fellowship the people in this group created for themselves. Their confessions and sorrows led to mutual support and accountability that kept them sober. I knew my mother would have responded with compassion to these people, but she had the mistaken notion that such meetings were for lesser people—people "in the gutter."

If she had given it a chance, she might have understood that those who attended and learned to surrender to a higher power came from a broad range of socioeconomic backgrounds. She might have been able to give support and received it as well. But this was not to be. My mother had no support group to fall back on when she decided to get sober many years later. I learned later in life that, in many ways, I have been an enabler to some of my own family members regarding their addiction issues.

Each fall, my father departed for long weekends at the Bear River Gun Club in Utah to shoot ducks and spend time with his male friends. My mother would complain about his leaving on any trip such. She also complained about his departure for Sunday rounds of golf. Despite their regular fights and ambivalence toward one another, she needed to have him at home to share in her loneliness.

I wanted my father to be happy. I asked him why he did not

get a divorce. He said that would cost him his job. At the time, I thought this was a cowardly excuse, but I did not understand the impact a divorce would have had on our family. He was not selfish or ambitious. He had worked hard to get where he was. Many said he had succeeded only because he was PG's son-in-law. But his job was his life. He loved his work and saw more clearly than I that leaving my mother would have led to her destruction and the ruin of our family. It was only later in life, when I had a family of my own, that I gained some wisdom and was able to question my prior assumptions.

PG knew what was going on, of course, because he had been in a similar situation with his own wife. For all I know, he and my father may have bonded over this common tragedy. Yet, my grandfather never spoke to me about my mother's condition. Alcoholism was not addressed at that time. The thought was simply, "Oh well, she overdrank. Send her to a recovery center and she will be okay."

Although I found surrogate mothers, teachers, and mentors along the way, the insecurities I felt in my childhood and the resulting drive to succeed all contributed to the woman I have become. When the psyche is young, it can be easily damaged, but it is always in the process of evolution. We are who we are not only despite what we have been through but also because of what we have been through. It takes time and reflection to heal, to accept our past without judging it in relation to a new and wiser perspective.

I can say now that I am deeply grateful for the wisdom I gained from my parents, even through the traumas of my formative years. Because of the hard times, I am more compassionate and understanding toward those in similar situations and more capable of giving advice. I also learned to be independent and found that I was competent and capable of being alone, perhaps even to a fault. I too often strive to be perfect and prove once again that I am deserving of attention and accolades. I am aware of the danger this can bring, of building an invisible protective box around myself to avoid painful situations instead of immersing myself in them. Such an emotional barrier can be the result of attempting to control one's life in order to evade the pain that is an essential part of full involvement in life's journey.

CHAPTER SIX

Lake Arrowhead

Even as I ventured further beyond the walls of my youth, invisible social barriers continued to exist around me—not that this was overt or discussed. No one in our social set ever mentioned money or status, so the notion of class differences never occurred to us as kids. There was no television coverage about economic disparity and no one in our world to communicate the situation to us if it existed. We dated boys from Los Angeles High School, and some may have been on scholarship, but no one we knew of lived in poverty.

Monetary situations were never a topic among our friends, primarily because almost everyone we knew lived as we did. Yet, having money and having family comfort are two very different things. Unless I had to be around to pick up my brother Peter at Chadwick School, I spent weekends anywhere else but at home. I would stay with my friend Marnie Osthaus, whose family always welcomed me. They lived close to the Southwest Tennis Club, where I trained with the Marlborough tennis team on twenty courts in downtown Los Angeles. Sandy Moseley, another school classmate, also welcomed me into her Beverly Hills home, which was surrounded by expansive grass lawns with a swimming pool and guesthouse. Sandy's father, C. C. Moseley, was the founder of Western Airlines, one of the first commercial airlines.

These friends' families were cordial, but when we had dinner, it was similar to any other home at the time: kids didn't speak very much or ask questions. We mainly followed the policy of being "seen, but not heard." And the mothers typically acted less like individual human beings than women do today. Married women in the 1940s and 1950s were never allowed the independence to become important in their own right, instead serving more as an extension of their husband's life. Maybe that is why alcoholism was so prevalent among the mothers of girls I knew.

Sports became an obsession for me. In addition to tennis tournaments, I played on the varsity baseball and volleyball teams against other girls' schools. I felt that I had to be on the winning team even though the Marlborough Violets, always dressed in violet and white, were teased for having such a weak and willowy team name. We would have preferred tiger orange or anything other than the timid lilac color that said nothing about us. Our league competitions were tough, we fought to win, and we gained respect because we often triumphed over the ten other girls' schools in the area.

My parents were not athletic people, and my grandfather's only sport was horseback riding at his ranch on weekends. But I do remember finding him late one afternoon working out on a rowing machine that he kept on a raised brick walkway under a canopy of trellised vines beside his tennis court. He was concentrating hard, pushing back and forth with his legs and pulling with his arms. He seemed to take his health and exercise seriously, and one did not dare disturb him at moments like this.

My first tennis lessons were on PG's tennis court with the Doeg sisters and later at the Santa Monica home of Bob Harmon, a respected coach in the area. Santa Monica was known for having great players, but I was not intimidated and won in my division at the Santa Monica Open when I was eleven. That was the first tournament I competed in; and during the years that followed, I amassed a rather large collection of tennis trophies. Sports were a positive focus in my life and a source of confidence, but the greatest escape during my high school years was to Lake Arrowhead, an alpine resort high in the San Bernardino Mountains.

Lake Arrowhead attracted the upper echelon of Los Angeles society. Baron Hilton of the Hilton hotel dynasty had a house there, as did the Chandler family, which owned the *Los Angeles Times*. Hotels and restaurants, a pavilion, and beaches made up the lake's waterfront village. My grandfather had one of the largest homes on the lake, built of stacked stone like a medieval castle. When I was a young girl, I stayed in a tiny bedroom in a tower-like corner on the top floor of the main house, which had men's and women's dormitories for our guests. The women's dorm filled the entire top story of the main building and had a beautician's salon with several stylist's chairs for all the ladies to do their coiffeurs at the same time. My own small room was intended for a maid, but within my little aerie, I could feel peaceful and alone. As I matured, I became better known, well-liked, and included everywhere with my peers.

My grandfather's membership in the Lake Arrowhead Yacht Club allowed him to park his motorboat at the docks adjacent to the village, where everyone went to shop. Dozens of boats gathered there for awards banquets and evening dances. On Sundays, the lake filled with white sails. Until I was fifteen, I raced my Falcon sailing dinghy on the lake. That all changed when I discovered the exciting new sport of water-skiing, and the Lake Arrowhead Water Ski Club became my territory. The club was a center of summer activity and a source of fun and frolic that led to lifelong friendships.

Evenings could be quite cold in the mountains, so there was a fireplace in the large living room of PG's house. Our devoted Black servant Willie Davis carted big logs in for the fire. Willie was born at the PG Winnett Estate in Santa Monica and grew up there. During his many years of service to our family, he remained a trusted friend.

He eventually held the prestigious position of head elevator operator at Bullocks Wilshire and traveled with my mother and her guests to the Del Mar beach house she rented to attend the horse races.

For dinners, everyone sat on long wooden benches at the dining table while Willie served meals from large platters to each individual guest. A housekeeper made up our beds and cleaned daily. The servants lived in quarters above the garage, which was a separate structure at the very top of the hill along the road. I can only imagine now how hard they worked, taking our meals and other supplies up and down those steep paths.

PG lived in what he called the "guesthouse," which was built from the same heavy stone as the main house. It was, in fact, very spacious, with a master bedroom upstairs and living area and bar downstairs that opened out to a balcony with a commanding view of the lake. The boat dock below the house was attached by a gangplank to an awning area where lunches were served and we could relax and look out over the lake and down the long beach to other docks farther on. We knew everyone in our cove. Two docks over from ours was the boat belonging to Charles and Harriet Cooper, owners of the W. E. Cooper Lumber Company. Next to them was the dock of Hollywood actress June Lockhart, who was frequently visited there by actor Dan Dailey and his wife Liz. Matinee idol Van Johnson joined them from time to time.

Although we all socialized together, our gang was a younger bunch of daredevils who were drawn to the speed of motorboats and the thrill of water-skiing. When the sport was invented in Santa Monica, it was called aquaplaning and involved just standing up on a board that was tied with a rope to the back of a motorboat. Aeronautical engineer Jack Northrup had a home at Lake Arrowhead during the 1930s. One of his nephews was Harry Gesner, a man seven years my senior who brought his high school big band to the lake to play for parties at the pavilion. Harry said his uncle had been experimenting with aquaplaning by nailing his two nephews' sneakers to two separate seven-foot skis and throwing a fifty-foot rope out to them with a broom handle attached. Northrup towed the boys behind his Chris-Craft speedboat, and soon they were doing all sorts of tricks. At some point, the sport was renamed water-skiing and quickly became popular from California and Florida to the French Riviera.

Before Harry went overseas to fight in World War II, he taught some of us how to water-ski at Lake Arrowhead. One of Harry's friends was Bill "Gerry" Cooper, a handsome, charismatic boy three years older than me who had a reputation for derring-do. Gerry and his older half-brother Jim were born into the family lumber business. Their father, Charlie Cooper, liked to be called Buck. He was a quiet, serious man and a skilled horseman. He rode a tall horse of his own and took time to teach younger members of his family how to ride English style. The Cooper family bought a house at Lake Arrowhead near another family whose last name was also Cooper. The first Cooper family had named their house "Windswept." Harriett Cooper's family, always ready to delight, moved in next door and dubbed their home "Unswept."

I was attracted to Gerry during those first years at the lake, but he was so much older than me that I would never have admitted it. He was interested in a senior at the Marlborough School when I was only a freshman, so we were worlds apart. I nevertheless water-skied with Gerry and Harry and others at a time when the sport was growing in popularity and expanding into slalom racing, jumping, and tricks. Our dock was taller than most and became a favorite for skiers wanting to take off from it while standing on one ski. It had a large slip for our Chris-Craft speedboat, the *Pee Gee.* The boat had two rows of seats up front and one in the back for whoever was working with the ski rope and picking up fallen skiers. The *Pee Gee* was the envy of the lake because it produced the biggest wake and therefore had the most challenging wake to jump.

After breakfast each morning, we skiers got out onto the water as early as possible, while the surface was still glassy smooth. Willie was always there to deliver lunches to us at the stone-walled alcove above the dock, adjacent to the beach. My cousins Susie and Leslie Boocock were often there with their mother, along with many other guests. My favorite playmates were Eddie and Patsy Janss Gregson, who were my age. Their grandmother, Flossie Janss, had taken in my younger brother Peter during his grade school years, so we all felt like family. At that time, I could never have imagined how closely my life would someday intersect with the Janss family.

I remember when I first saw the photograph of the beautiful Patsy Janss on the wall of the Marlborough School, along with all the other student body presidents. My photo soon joined hers. Patsy, Bill Janss's sister, married George Gregson, a good friend of my parents. A few years after their marriage, in 1938, George was driving with his wife back to Yosemite Village from Badger Pass Ski Area in Yosemite National Park when he came out of the tunnel, hit the ice, and lost control of his car. He survived the crash, but Patsy suffered a severe head injury and never recovered from a coma. George had been drinking after skiing that day and apparently miscalculated his speed as he exited the tunnel. Flossie, who everyone so loved, never really recovered from the tragedy of losing her only daughter. Perhaps because of this loss, she became known over the years for taking other children into her Beverly Hills home. George must have been crushed by guilt over the accident, but his and Patsy's children—Eddie and Patsy—were regulars at the lake each summer.

When I was quite young, my parents went to the Janss's to play poker once a week, as they had during Prohibition, no doubt drinking Doc's bathtub gin. I played in their pool on those hot summer days. While floating on a tube in the water one afternoon, a handsome young man with blue eyes walked by. We glanced at one another for just an instant. This was Doc and Flossie's son Bill. His glance was extraordinary, and it left me with such a clear memory. Why would I have remembered this? Was there some premonition?

Bill must have been attending Stanford University at the time. The Janss family and the family of Arthur Letts had been brought together through marriage many years before, so perhaps it was inevitable that we would one day become friends through our social circle, but in hindsight it appears that our destinies were already more deeply connected. I have come to realize that we are surrounded by these connections and synchronicities, and they can become more apparent to our intuition.

One summer, an older woman named Marian Pike came to stay at my grandfather's house on the lake. An artist, Marian painted all day, every day, wearing painter's garb—pants and an apron or smock. I often sat for a portrait while she painted and talked. She never tried to do much with her hair, leaving it short, straight, and simple. When she was painting, loud and dramatic classical music blasted out to all corners of the lake from our living room. I had never heard that kind of music before, and I had never met a woman quite like Marian—nor have I since. She had a sense of joie de vivre that was unusual in our social group. Her personality went somewhat against the grain of our culture.

My mother's age, Marian lived adjacent to the Marlborough School, so I often visited her after school in Los Angeles. I wanted to be with her instead of spending afternoons at the home of one of my teenage friends. Marian inspired me to take an interest in art history. From her, I learned how important art and mythology were to the history of the world, and thus began one of the great passions of my life. I could talk to her about anything. She was different and refreshing. Her portraits of me still exist in the homes of my children. It turned out that Marian had been married to an ambitious businessman who bored her. She eventually divorced him and moved to Paris to live and paint. I visited her there shortly before she became romantically involved with Coco Chanel, the designer who had her own style emporium at Bullocks Wilshire.

Harry Gesner was badly injured in combat during the war, but he recuperated and eventually returned to Lake Arrowhead. Little had changed. June Lockhart was a Broadway star. Dan and Liz Daley were having a baby and then breaking up. Harry went to work in construction, building expensive homes in Lake Arrowhead's North Shore area. He set his sights on becoming an architect and decided to learn how to design homes by first becoming a builder. We were all once again part of the inner circle at the lake, skiing by moonlight and doing other outrageous things.

Word got around after the war that a new trick had been introduced at skiing competitions; it involved spinning in the air after launching from a jump. The best male skier at the lake said he was not yet ready to try it, but I was eager to give it a go. I had him show me how to wind the rope and handles around my body before taking off over the jump. All I had to do was let go of one hand and the pull of the boat would propel me in a 360-degree spin while I was in the air.

I wanted to show everyone that I was brave and confident enough to be the first one on the lake to achieve this feat. I wrapped the rope around myself and was pulled quickly toward the jump. I released it too soon and struck the jump sideways, bumping my head and momentarily knocking myself out. Hitting the water quickly revived me, but I rested for a full day afterward in case I had a concussion. This incident failed to teach me a lesson in risk-taking, a lesson that I only learned much later in life.

Gerry Cooper asked me one moonless night if I wanted to take a night tour. My Uncle Jack and Aunt Martha Winnett trusted me enough to let me go. Once we were out on the water and out of sight, Gerry tied the boat to a buoy and we necked. It wasn't the first time this happened, and I was thrilled to be winning him over from an older girl. It was exciting for me to have been chosen by handsome Gerry Cooper.

When we returned to the dock and shined the spotlight at the beach, a large black bear was walking on the sand. Scared that we would have to interact with the beast, Gerry turned the boat around and we went back out into the lake for another hour. The bear was gone when we returned, but I could not be sure it wasn't still lurking in the shadows. I ran scared and breathless up the path.

Everyone chose to question our bear story the next morning. They chuckled and shared knowing looks whenever it was mentioned, as though there was another, more scandalous reason we for us coming back so late. Gerry and I would laugh about the bear episode during the first years of our marriage.

Even then, there were reasons to be cautious about Gerry. He had a habit of winning over others by putting them down. He would frequently come over to me on the dock when I was dry and warm and push me off into the water. I tried to be nice and laugh about it, but inside I was furious. He seemed not to care how angry we became with his antics.

As president of the student body my senior year, I stood at the podium each morning before the assembly to address the high school classes. Previous presidents had simply announced schedule changes for the day, but I did my best to be creative and add something philosophical and instructive. I wanted to serve as a role model and provide a message of wisdom, so I would stress our need to work harder to meet a teacher's standards when we received a bad grade or talk about the importance of presenting a sportsmanlike attitude if we lost a game against another school.

The tennis tournament I loved most each year took place at the Hotel del Coronado in San Diego. Built back in the 1800s, the towering red and white hotel was a landmark resort visited by royalty, celebrities, and heads of state. I was chaperoned at tournaments there by the parents of one or more of my tennis-playing schoolmates. Our chaperones never really had to watch over us because, in those days, there was no evil lurking nearby, nor would we ever have participated in questionable behavior. Nowadays, children are so "protected" by their hovering parents that they cannot experience the freedom they need to grow into independent and mature individuals.

During my senior year, our tennis team ended up in the Southern California high school finals at the Ojai Valley Tennis Tournament. My partner, Molly Shea, and I competed in the girls' doubles finals. It was the first time that my father came to watch, so I was more nervous than usual. We played a long three sets, with points that seemed to go on forever. Our opponents were lobbers, just what one did not want to face in a long match; Molly and I preferred a well-placed hard hit. With consistency and focus, we persevered and won the tournament.

As our high school years came to an end, we began to consider where we would attend college. Most Marlborough girls knew they would be accepted at the college of their choice because of the rigorous academic schedule we had faced over the past six years. I found that all of my friends wanted to attend a co-ed university, Stanford being the first choice for almost everyone. But my parents had attended prestigious East Coast colleges; they wanted me to have the same "broadening experience" and be exposed to the older values and cultural offerings of a way of life far removed from the sunny beaches of California. Because I was determined to concentrate on my studies and not be distracted by boys, I chose Wellesley College near Boston, one of seven well-known women's colleges in the area.

As the day of our high school graduation approached, we all ate lunch and sunned ourselves in our bathing suits in the school's inner garden so as to be as darkly tanned as possible against our long white dresses. My father attended my graduation, but not my mother. I would not have expected her to attend. By that time, she had been out of the public eye for some time and had not participated in any of my high school events. Before the graduation ceremony was even over, I was already looking forward to another way of life and any freedom it might offer.

All these years later, I most enjoy drifting back to the memories of Lake Arrowhead, when everything was still possible and our lives had only just begun. One night under a full moon, before any of us had quite become adults, Gerry Cooper pulled Harry Gesner and me behind the *Pee Gee* on separate ropes. Gerry preferred to drive the boat rather than ski, so Harry and I danced back and forth behind the boat like Ginger Rogers and Fred Astaire. It felt like those halcyon days and moonlit nights would last forever.

I was seventeen the summer after my high school graduation. Harry spent day after day pulling me behind the *Pee Gee* to ready me for the Pacific Coast water ski championship competition in August. We set up a slalom course with spaced buoys and a single floating, wooden ramp. Our jumps would be judged on form and distance. I spent hours practicing my tricks, and Harry never tired of helping me. Thanks to his patience and attentiveness, I won the championship in all three events: slalom, jumping, and tricks. I barely had a chance to celebrate this victory before it was time for me to leave for Massachusetts.

PART II

Adventures in Academia

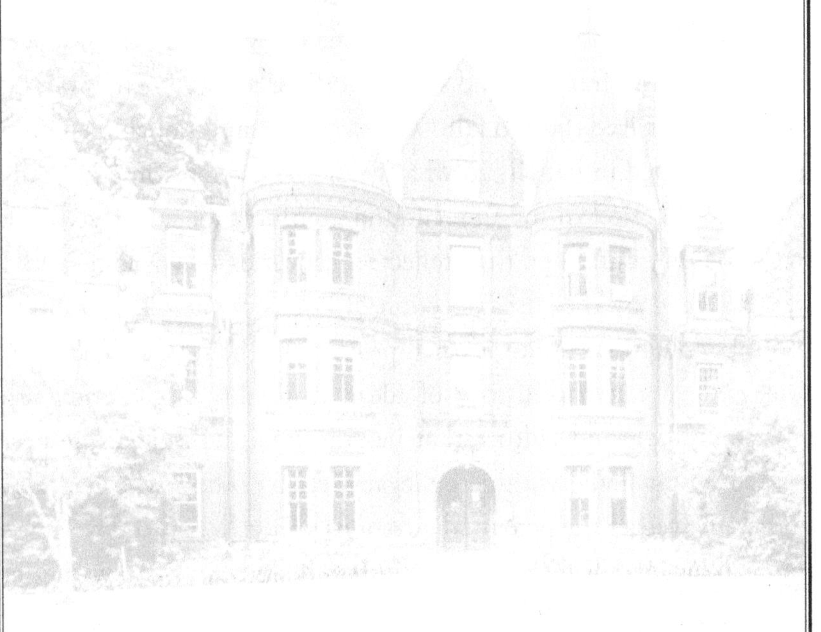

CHAPTER SEVEN

The Platonic Way: A Path of Inquiry

Universities are often called "ivory towers" because they are considered places of privilege removed from the practicalities of the real world. Wellesley College was truly an ivory tower for me. There, I discovered a refuge of peace, equanimity, and learning that I had sought but never found in my childhood. The campus itself was a sanctuary of forested hills and manicured greens surrounded by nineteenth-century buildings that resonated with deep knowledge. This was the inspirational and secure world I had been searching for.

When I arrived there in fall 1949, I was as impressionable as could be, but I settled in happily to what would be the most intellectually stimulating period in my life. I found comfort and security within the old stone buildings that reflected centuries of wisdom, and I was intrigued by the vast collection of books at the Clapp Library and the reputations of our learned professors. The time I spent there conversing about the history of ideas sparked a fascination with philosophy, art, and culture that has inspired and guided me ever since. I felt at home within the legacy left by others who had also sought answers to the perennial questions of life: Where did we come from? What does it mean to be a human being? How can we better the lives of others?

Because I had never lived away from home, the first semester was intimidating. The college had nurtured the intellects of many famous female scholars and scientists long before I arrived, including Marjory Stoneman Douglas, the author and suffragette known for her defense of the Florida Everglades. Everybody I met there was bright and motivated. It was clear that each of us was expected to make our mark on the world. In years to come, Wellesley would graduate Madeleine Albright, Hillary Clinton, and Diane Sawyer.

I took up residence as a freshman in an old house in town that served as a dorm. It was a twenty-minute walk or a short bike ride to campus on my clunky old balloon-tired bike that had been passed down from a graduate student happy to leave it behind at a bargain price. I had no idea yet for a major and wanted to delve into what was then called a liberal arts education. My first-year requirements were English 100 and a year of Bible history, to which I added art history, Spanish, and philosophy, trusting that this mix of ideas would provide me with challenging new perspectives.

Despite my high academic standing at Marlborough, Wellesley proved far more challenging than I expected. We were given lengthy reading assignments and essays to complete on our own. The large classrooms and lecture halls provided less personal contact with professors than I had been accustomed to at Marlborough. I was excited by the atmosphere at Wellesley but overwhelmed by the college's daunting expectations. I tried out for crew that first year, a new sport for me. The workouts every afternoon after class proved to be exhausting and debilitating, cutting into much-needed time for studies, so I chose not to continue that sport.

My first grades came back as a shock. The papers I submitted were returned with a frightening amount of red-inked corrections. I had left California a straight-A student, but at Wellesley I received only a C in English. I was devastated. I had attended what was considered to be one of the best private schools in one of the best educational systems in the United States, yet my East Coast schoolmates were clearly better prepared for university than those of us from "out west." I worked hard on those corrections, digested the lessons, and was rewarded with higher grades as well as an expanded understanding of the English language. While home for the holidays, I found myself correcting the verbal faux pas of my family members.

I was surprised to be so stimulated by study of the Bible and impressed by the depth of consequences this book has had upon the world. We read it as a collection of tales both historical and mythological that shaped Western culture and tradition following the fall of the Greek and Roman empires. It would become foundational in my continuing studies of the humanities, but I never took it literally as an infallible text or the "word of God."

Art history provided a perspective on the past that was at least as provocative as Bible history. Learning about the great artists who had shaped our sensibilities through the ages awakened new realms of understanding that would influence my future in ways I could not yet foresee. I was introduced to the incremental expansion of mankind's creative interpretation of experience, from archaic rock art in caves to paintings in Gothic cathedrals and on into our modern era of personal artistic expression. I came to believe that the role of creativity was grounded in mankind's ultimate spirituality. In the years to come, I would dedicate my time to the study of artistic treasures and eventually work to bring the firsthand experience of great art to others.

My first year of study in Greek philosophy had the greatest influence on my path forward. Perhaps this was because so little of my reading before then had much meaning or comfort for me, or perhaps I was just overly curious about the deeper mysteries of life. Some people go through life as pragmatic realists, never wondering about anything beyond their creature comforts. Many have no interest in conscious evolution or are simply so caught up in the immediate challenges of survival that little time or mental energy is left for philosophical pursuits.

I learned while studying the Greeks how these ancient thinkers studied the world around them and analyzed thinking itself, establishing the basis for scientific inquiry, aesthetics, and the quest to find mankind's place in the cosmos. My philosophy professor was an older gentleman, soft-spoken, yet possessed of an intricate belief system based upon a lifetime of systematic philosophical thinking. He taught that mythology had once supplied meaning for cultures that both philosophy and science would later add to in more rational ways. The philosophical rationale of the Greeks was based upon a mathematical logic, but the Greek worldview combined a rational approach with parallel thinking that connected man with the world of the gods. The Romans later became more dependent on the gods for their well-being and survival, even casting themselves as incarnations of these gods. The original Greek philosophers Plato and Socrates appealed to me most because they applied reason to the original questions that have perplexed man from the beginning: Why is there life? What are we here for?

I decided to major in philosophy after a year devoted to the study of the *Dialogues of Plato*. The syllabus required reading Plato's *Dialogues* in order to give us knowledge of Socratic and Platonic questioning and the resulting theories of reality. Plato was inquisitive, rational, and probing. Plato's *Phaedo,* a collection of dialectical discussions upon the death of Socrates, was and still remains my favorite. In this dialogue, Plato uses the occasion of the death by suicide of his beloved teacher, Socrates, to assure readers of the immortality of the soul. He uses several of Socrates's philosophical arguments to reveal that body and soul, reason and emotion, and mortality and immortality are merely different perspectives on life. Life must come from somewhere, and that somewhere is the immortal soul.

Plato's teachings informed the later Christian theological tradition, and parallels to his thinking can also be found in the

Eastern idea of reincarnation. Even the Renaissance, during which the more secular arts flourished after the Dark Ages, was based upon Neoplatonism. The process of inquiry in the dialogues between Plato and Socrates became the basis in history for dialogue and debate as a means of finding deeper truths. Much later in my life, when I was exposed to investigations of the physical mysteries of energy in the universe, I came to realize that Plato and his theory of ideas provided a philosophical basis for the notion of quantum energy and likewise for the field theory of Rupert Sheldrake.

One of the primary reasons I decided to major in philosophy was the inspirational experience I had with my philosophy professor. He was a living, breathing Platonist. He exposed me to philosophical theories that expanded my thinking far beyond the limited and restrictive belief systems and dogma espoused by the Episcopal Church of my youth; there was Descartes, and there were the logical assumptions of Hegel and Nietzsche and Existentialism. I came to see these studies as "intensive" reading rather than "extensive," because they required completely adopting one individual philosopher's belief system—in effect, to accept it as one's own—before moving on to a new paradigm. The impact was transformative and created in me an open-minded flexibility of thought.

Philosophy at Wellesley was a difficult major, and it was avoided by most students in those years. There was only one other philosophy major in my graduating class of 1954. She was known for having a photographic memory, so I redoubled my efforts to keep up with her. The race was on.

My concentration on studies was disrupted at one point by a call from Gerry Cooper, who professed his love for me and informed me that he would soon be arriving for a visit. He said he was on his way east to try to join the US Navy Air Corps in Pensacola, Florida. Within hours, Gerry arrived with his mischievous friend Bill Anderson. The two of them together always meant trouble. They found inexpensive housing in town and opened a car wash business, brandishing a sign on the street. They were successful enough to survive for three weeks, during which time Gerry and I talked in the sitting room at the dorm in the evenings—in those years, men were not allowed in women's dormitory rooms. From our conversation, I learned that his college years at the University of Santa Barbara were quite different from mine, with less emphasis on studies and more dedication to partying. He had no idea of the stress I was under to simply survive with adequate grades.

When my father learned of Gerry's visit, he was incensed and called me to say, "You get that boy out of there. It will affect your studies! And I am paying for you to get an education!" I was grateful that my father was paying for my education, and I also wanted Gerry to leave. I had no time for romance or any other interferences. Thankfully, Wellesley Hills was a quiet town with no nighttime activities, and I had an early curfew as a freshman. I told Gerry how displeased my father was that he had come for a visit; he soon left, although I suspect he departed out of boredom as much as anything.

I studied so late into the night my freshman year that it became impossible to quiet my mind, and I slept very little. Another privation came in the form of bland potatoes-and-gravy-style dormitory food. As a result, I returned home for Christmas vacation twenty pounds lighter than when I had entered Wellesley. That holiday season, when my parents asked what I wanted for Christmas, I chose my usual gift, a trip to Sun Valley, Idaho. After being home in California for the Christmas holidays, my father dropped me off at Union Station in downtown Los Angeles, greeting and thanking my chaperones for a week in Idaho. My assigned caretakers were to be Daryl and Virginia Zanuck, who were traveling with their children—my friends Darrylin and Dicky. Sun Valley ski instructor Otto Lang also joined us and promised to watch over me in Idaho.

CHAPTER EIGHT

The Three Musketeers

My first trip to Sun Valley had been in 1947 when the resort reopened after serving as a rehabilitation center for World War II veterans. Now, two years later, it still held a certain mystique. Sun Valley was exclusive, hard to get to, and surrounded by Idaho wilderness, much as it is today. I had an adventure ahead of me into a relatively unknown and isolated world of new friends and experiences. On the train, I had my own room and berth but shared meals with my friends in the dining car. It was exciting to have a sense of freedom from school, and it was a relief to leave behind the usual family worries that came along with spending the Christmas holidays at home.

We arrived a day and a half later, after the midnight clanging and bumping in Salt Lake City, where train engines were exchanged and some railway cars left behind. After crossing an open expanse for many miles, the train came to its final stop on a frigid and beautiful blue-sky morning at the Ketchum, Idaho, Railway Station. We were greeted by horse-drawn sleighs and the Sun Valley buses that would take us on the short ride from Ketchum to the Sun Valley Lodge, which was a world unto itself. The only reason anyone would frequent the nearby frontier mining town of Ketchum at that time was to gamble.

In the lodge, everyone wore baggy woolen ski clothes with leather boots as they rested and socialized after a day of skiing. We all met upstairs in the lodge dining room for breakfast, lunch, and dinner. The fire burned brightly during teatime in the lobby, which shined with Christmas decorations. I was reunited that winter with Michael and Nina Engl, the children of Sigi and Peggy Engl. Together, we explored every hidden corner of the lodge, searching through darkened rooms and opening storage trunks in the loft that were filled with discarded china, old costumes, and theatrical artifacts that had been cast aside after years of use.

One afternoon, Sigi decided it was time for me to grow up a bit and have my first drink. He felt that he was the proper man to introduce me to this experience, having known me since I was four years old. He drove me to Ketchum, to the Christiana, which was a gambling casino at the time. "I will order you a Coca-Cola," he said, but when I scrunched up my face over its horrible taste, Sigi admitted that rum had been added to it. To please him, I drank it. It was my first experience with alcohol; embarrassingly, I was not able to keep it down.

That week, I joined a ski school class taught by a Canadian instructor named Yves Latreille. I had no idea at that time how close a relationship I would build with this man and his two friends, Yvan Tache and Ernie McCullough. All three were from Mont-Tremblant in Quebec. They were dashing, athletic, and popular—called the Three Musketeers by all who knew and treasured them. After a week in ski school, Yves asked me if I would like to ski with him just for fun on Sunday. I was honored and a bit surprised that he would have taken such a liking to me, but I had already agreed to ski with one of my ski school classmates, a Catholic priest from Seattle.

My friend and I skied all the Bald Mountain (Baldy) runs that were open that day and then decided to end the afternoon with a challenging run down the mogul-ridden Exhibition slope. There was a low cloud over Baldy late in the day, creating a dense fog and flat light. We could not see at all. I was slowly traversing when I dropped down into a deep gulley. My uphill ski went into the opposite snowbank, throwing my weight onto the downhill ski and twisting all my weight against my lower hip. I heard a loud crack, unforgettable to this day. Alone on the mountain in the wet and cold fog, I waited in agony until my friend was able to chase down the ski patrol.

The bumpy rescue ride down to the bottom of River Run brought excruciating pain. I was taken to what passed for a hospital back in 1949. A few rooms on the lodge's closed-off third floor corridor had been dedicated to the sick and injured, with one operating room, one receiving room, and two recovery rooms. John Moritz was the attending local physician. I meekly asked him for pain medication. After a brief examination, I watched him take down from a high shelf a large, heavy book titled *Orthopedic Surgery.*

By now, I just wanted to pass out, imagining that this doctor had no knowledge of how to treat a broken hip. Happily, at that moment, the pain medication took me into oblivion. I woke up later that evening in a recovery room following the operation. I was told that a doctor named Sawny Renard Gaston from the Harkness Pavilion Hospital in New York had stayed over in Sun Valley that night to perform the surgery, with which he was familiar. It involved pounding a steel rod the size of a thumb into my femur. This was the only medical solution at that time for a broken hip. As I grew more conscious each day, I was better able to greet visitors to my room after their day of skiing. The Three Musketeers came every afternoon and took turns pushing me in a wheelchair down to the lobby for teatime. Our lives would intersect for years to come.

The early Austrian connection to Sun Valley is well-known, but what many people do not know is that there was a Canadian connection as well during the early days of the resort. One afternoon at the lodge during tea, I met Norma Shearer, who had grown up in Montreal before going to Hollywood to become a movie star. Her husband, Irving Thalberg, whose home we played in as kids, was considered to be a genius in Hollywood. He started out at Universal Studios as a secretary and then helped Louis B. Mayer create MGM. He oversaw the production of hundreds of films—winning two academy awards—before he died of consumption at the tragically young age of thirty-six. Two years after Irving died, Norma met and married Marti Arrouge, a ski instructor whose family once owned nearly all of Squaw Valley, near Lake Tahoe, California, before it was developed into a ski area.

Norma and Marti traveled to Mont-Tremblant to ski one winter during World War II, when the Sun Valley Lodge was being used to treat injured military veterans. It was at Mont-Tremblant that Norma met Yvan Tache, one of the Three Musketeers. Norma mentioned to Otto Lang, the director of the Sun Valley Ski School, that she knew some talented instructors from Quebec. Soon, the other two Musketeers were off to Idaho, where Yvan gave lessons to Norma and her daughter, Katherine Thalberg, whenever they came to Sun Valley. He also gave skiing lessons to the Zanucks.

The second Musketeer, Yves, taught Darryl's wife Virginia. Darryl was so impressed with Yvan and Yves that he invited them down to Los Angeles for a visit after the ski season one year. They stayed in the Zanuck houses in Santa Monica and Palm Springs where, waited on by servants and treated like royalty, they spent their days golfing. Yvan said Darryl, the movie mogul and screenwriter, would stay up all night writing and then join them at the pool later in the day. Although Yvan has long since passed away, his widow, Marie Tache, still has the letter Otto sent to Yvan and Yves, inviting them to Idaho. I know this because my daughter Christin married Yvan's son, Mark Tache, many years later.

During my college years, the Sporthaus in Westwood Village

came into being. This was the first up-to-date source for ski gear in the city of Los Angeles. There were few, if any, other ski stores, probably because local Baldy Mountain oftentimes had no snow. The store's success was due to its sponsors, Otto Lang and Darryl Zanuck, and their befriending of Yves Latreille and Yvan Tache. I was familiar with Westwood because Bullock's Westwood, where I shopped for the latest pedal-pushers and saddle shoes of the day, was near the Sporthaus. Westwood Village was developed by the Janss Corporation. The artistic iron manhole covers on the streets read "Janss Corporation." Many years later, during my marriage to Bill Janss, I pestered him on one of our trips to "lift" one for old time's sake, just to have a piece of Janss history. They were perfectly functional and very heavy, so there was no way we could have actually taken one.

At the Sporthaus, I met Betty Jane and Sylvester "Vetz" Morning. They had a home in Mammoth, California, and three of their children became noted ski racers. Their daughter Katie lived with us in Sun Valley many years later in order to train there with Michel Rudigoz and our Sun Valley Ski Education Foundation team as a World Cup racer. Betty Jane become godmother to my daughter Kelley. All these children grew up together and have been close friends ever since. Betty Jane would come to my family's rescue some years later when we needed a place to stay.

Names and faces run together as I tell my story, and I have surely forgotten many. I eventually lost touch with young Irving Thalberg Jr., who lost his father when he was only six years old. But I did look up his sister Katie in Aspen a few years ago; she was owner and manager of the Explore Book Store for many years, a literary hub of the town.

The last time I saw Otto Lang must have been twenty years ago, when he was signing copies of his autobiography by the fire in Sun Valley Lodge. So much has changed since those early years.

First invited to Sun Valley by Nelson Rockefeller, Otto became the preeminent ski instructor for the Hollywood stars, eventually parlaying his friendship with Darryl Zanuck into a second career as a film producer and director. He lived to be ninety-eight.

Even though I was still on crutches, I began to feel like a princess again with all the attention from the Three Musketeers. A week later, my mother arrived by train to be with me for a few days and accompany me back home. By then, the Christmas holidays were over and most of the celebrities and members of Los Angeles society she knew had returned home. The doctors decided that I would have to spend six months on crutches, with no weight on the hip, so returning to the snowy, icy paths between the dorm and classes on the Wellesley campus was out of the question. This was terrible news. I had only just been set free to venture forth beyond the palace walls to a new life of independence. Now, instead, I had to return home to recuperate, missing the remainder of my freshman year.

CHAPTER NINE

Gap Year

I hadn't expected to be back home while all of my friends from high school were away at college. I found out that my dog Christopher had been put down the minute I left for college. My mother said he he had become ill. I wanted to believe that he grew disoriented after I left because no one cared for him and, at fourteen years of age, he simply wanted to depart this world.

Elsie, our cook, agreed to help keep me busy by teaching me to cook. I spent many hours with her in the kitchen, hobbling around on my crutches, learning the basics of baking, and preparing meals. Elsie was sweet and caring, as were all the servants. I found her to be talkative—I hope because she enjoyed my company. It must have been boring for her to cook the same meals week in and week out for so many years in accordance with the strict, unvarying schedule set for her.

Aware of my situation at home, my Aunt Dougie invited me to her Park Avenue penthouse apartment in New York City during vacations and cared for me a year later when I went to the Harkness Pavilion Hospital during the Thanksgiving holiday so that Dr. Gaston could remove the metal rod from my hip.

Dougie was a force for the arts. She dedicated much of her life to the success and expansion of the New York City Opera. She also loved to travel; she took my two cousins and me on the final transatlantic crossing of the ocean liner America during the summer of 1951. The ship was one enormous playground for us, but my cousins and I dreaded being invited to sit at the captain's table, where we were expected to be elegantly dressed, mind our manners, and carry on adult conversation. Dougie insisted on bringing her own car on the ship to Europe, a new Chevrolet convertible. When we disembarked in England, we left the dock in this enormous vehicle, which was not well-suited for the narrow roadways of Britain—even less so the roads in Ireland. We motored through the countryside on lanes so narrow that another car could not pass by without us having to drive over the hedgerows. Men in the fields behind rock walls craned their necks to see what had just come down the road and shook their heads in amazement and dismay. If the "ugly American" stereotype had been invented by then, it would have been us. My cousins and I scrunched as low as possible in our seats to hide from view.

During those first few months at home from college I became a whiz on crutches, stretching the weight distribution restrictions in creative ways. By the time I went back to Lake Arrowhead that summer, I could sit on the edge of the dock and take off on one ski on my right leg—the good, weight-bearing leg. I was ecstatic to feel once again the freedom of carving sharp turns and then jumping the wake. The Gravy Train trips continued, as they had since I was a small child. My mother, her close friends, and some of their family members joined us, but never my father. He stayed behind to work at Bullock's. Perhaps PG never invited him. The guest list was selected for younger, fun-loving, and entertaining companions; PG enjoyed being idolized by them. I cannot recall my grandfather ever inviting anyone close to his own age to come along.

As a young girl, I had been embarrassed by the special attention I received prior to these trips, beginning with the visit to Bullocks Wilshire, where the Candy children were treated like young royalty, escorted from department to department by buyers for the store. The children's sporting clothes section had always been my favorite, with its bathing suits, shorts, tank tops, and light summer dresses. We would then be whisked away to the dressier children's clothing section and paraded around to see if the dress would billow out perfectly when twirling. This was done for the purpose of our high-style presentation during the early days of the Royal Hawaiian Hotel. The hotel boasted a grand outdoor ballroom by the ocean, with a dance floor surrounded by dinner tables. As young girls, we dreaded the moment on the veranda during dinner when each of us would be invited in turn to dance with our grandfather PG, who twirled us in the latest Bullock's fashions for all the guests who happened to be dining out that evening on the terrace. These were awkward moments of display for us.

On the other hand, I loved the attention we received from the Kahanamoku family. Duke Kahanamoku was a famous swimmer, a five-time Olympic medalist who popularized the ancient art of Hawaiian surfing in America. He was famous for having saved thirteen fishermen off the coast of California in 1925. In later years, his brother Sargent, or "Sarge," took over Duke's responsibilities as host and continued the tradition of entertaining guests as an ambassador of sorts on the island. The Kahanamokus joined us regularly at the Royal Hawaiian as PG's guests for dinner. They, in turn, introduced PG to their own circle of indigenous Hawaiians.

Sarge would meet us on the beach at Waikiki, gathering us together and helping us into the largest of the hotel's outrigger canoes. He guided us out over the smaller waves and then through the heavier surf. After passing the breakers, he had us quickly turn the boat around and paddle hard so we could catch the perfect size wave he had picked out for us.

Sarge invited our group to dinner at the exclusive Hawaiian Citizenry Outrigger Canoe Club, known by Hawaiians simply as the

Outrigger Canoe Club. I grew to love Sarge and his wife Anna. They were passionate and loving people, always there for us—although I assume that they were paid royally for their services.

CHAPTER TEN

The Guinea Pig

Back at Wellesley in the fall of 1950 for my second freshman year, I chose a large dormitory in the middle of the campus called Tower Court. The building was a fortress of stone covered with climbing ivy vines. There I met Gracie Vogel, a wonderful girl whose Milwaukee family had made a fortune in the beer industry. She too was a year behind, but that was a result of studying for a year in Switzerland, a common practice for families who could afford this luxury. Gracie was from the Midwest, open-minded and, after her year in Europe, fluent in French—a fact that would influence our mutual choice of dormitory for the next year. Gracie had been invited to join the advanced French students on the French Corridor, where only *français* could be spoken. The madame in charge wanted Gracie to live on the corridor because to her fluency in the language. Gracie told the madame that she would not leave Tower Court without me.

I had only studied French for one year, but because Gracie would be such a valuable addition to the French Corridor, I was allowed to live there too. I was called the *cochon d' inde,* the guinea pig, because no "one-year" French student had ever been permitted to live there before. It was both a challenge and a frustration as I stumbled to communicate, even with Gracie. In addition to the language regulations on the French Corridor, we were required to sit at designated dinner tables together. I decided to only listen, and not talk, during dinner table conversations for the first few months, reasoning that this would be better for my digestion, but *français* came to me eventually. I became somewhat fluent by the end of the year, thanks to total immersion in the French Corridor.

I continued to keep in touch with Marian Pike, much as I had after school during the Marlborough years. She remained a tremendous influence in my life, insisting that I continue my art history studies and take studio art classes as well. I was also encouraged to pursue art studies by Gracie, who decided to major in art history, no doubt with her family's encouragement. The Vogels were well-known for their collection of French Impressionists.

I was dismayed to return to California for Christmas vacation that year to find that "home" was now a high-rise apartment building, in which I had been assigned a tiny bedroom. Unbeknownst to me, my parents had sold our San Vicente estate and moved to the upscale Cordingly Apartments on Wilshire Boulevard. These apartments were conveniently close to the Los Angeles Country Club where my father played golf on Sundays and a shorter drive to the Bullock's offices. I knew it was a disastrous move for my mother and that she would have rebelled if she had any influence over the decision, but her circumstances had changed. Although she had once been proclaimed the best-dressed woman in Los Angeles, those days had ended during her long illness and increasingly solitary life. She had also lost much of the control she once exercised over her own affairs. She was accustomed from childhood to having vast gardens, whether she walked them or not. Now, there was nothing for her to do each day other than to order the evening meal.

It was strange for me to drive home into an underground parking lot, find my designated parking space, and use an elevator to get to our front door. How odd and confining it was to be suddenly living high over the city, with no yard, and just one small room to call my own. I had no opportunity to say farewell to San Vicente, which was soon split into a developer's dream of smaller parcels and less luxurious but very expensive homes.

After my sophomore year, I wanted to spend my junior year abroad—as Gracie had—but that is not at all what happened. Instead, I returned home for a year of classes at the University of California, Los Angeles (UCLA). I told friends and family that I wanted to compare the experience of an East Coast women's college to a university with thousands of male and female students and little, if any, contact with our professors. But there was a deeper and more personal reason for my decision. The situation at home had worsened in my absence, and I naïvely believed that my presence there could be helpful. I had seen during my previous Christmas vacation just how much my mother's disease had progressed. My father reacted to her behavior with rage and, at times, violence. I went home under the unrealistic assumption that I could provide the company my mother longed for after her other children had left. By then, Walter had joined the Navy Air Corps and was living in Florida, married to Joan Morgan, with a baby girl on the way. Peter was a senior at Lawrenceville. My mother and I could do things together and she would no longer be lonely, or so I wishfully believed.

In reality, life at our new high-rise home was a scene of domestic mayhem. My mother had taken to staying home all day and all night. She was drowning in alcoholic binges between trips to the hospital and trips to the recovery center. She displayed increasingly bizarre and frightening behavior. There were fights at night between my mother and father. The next morning, my mother would come to breakfast with a black eye or bruised face. My father would say this was due to a fall, hitting a doorknob, or some other excuse. My mother would say nothing at all. To sit through dinner was an ordeal.

By this time in my life, I had developed complete philosophical trust in the universe and its outcomes, but despite my trust in destiny,

I also believed that I could make a difference in the lives of others. I was completely ignorant of the realities of alcoholism—that no one can prevent an alcoholic from drinking but the alcoholic. Little was known then about alcoholism. Doctors considered the condition to reflect one's unhappiness with life or a simple lack of self-discipline. It was not yet considered a disease.

I harbored a deep mistrust of the single employee my parents hired, a supposedly loyal Filipino servant by the name of Lucky. I was convinced that he was using my family for his own financial advancement. I frequently found blank checks lying around the apartment, signed but not yet made out to anyone. They may have been intended for the grocer, the cleaners, or the gas station, but I was certain that they were being cashed by Lucky with at least a portion going into his pocket. My mother never bothered to balance her checkbook, so she would never have known of these transactions. There had always been money available for her, and she presumed that this would never change. But one day it did.

My father was pleased with Lucky's service and had no desire to make any disruptive changes. Despite my pleas, he would not consider letting him go—no wonder, as Lucky was always solicitous toward my father, preparing all his favorite meals, which by now were no longer scheduled by my mother.

If there is any assumption that I did not love my mother at this time, it would be untrue. My love for her remained below the surface. It was difficult at times, but a child's love for her mother runs deep, even if it becomes darkened or even obliterated at times. The good memories are the ones we struggle to hold onto amid all the trauma and tragedy. During this period, I finally came to accept that there was little I could do to help her avoid what appeared to be her inevitable self-destruction.

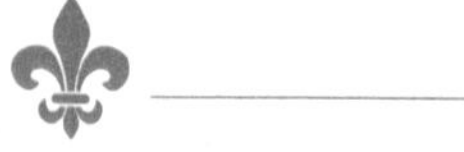

CHAPTER ELEVEN

The Turning Point

My experience at UCLA was surprisingly challenging. I thought studies there would be easier and less demanding than Wellesley, but I was wrong. Ambitious Korean War military veterans had returned to civilian life and were determined to enter into the professional world with a resumé of high achievement. The competition was intense, but I managed to keep my grades high. I continued to take philosophy classes toward my major but added a number of elective courses, such as astronomy. The most influential and provocative class that year was a review of world mythology, which proved essential to my later studies in art history. I studied in the library late into the night to maintain high grades to return for my senior year and graduation from Wellesley.

Sports continued to be my tonic. I skied whenever there was snow on Mount Baldy in the San Bernardino Mountains. Yves and Yvan were by then running the small resort and ski school there at Snow Valley Mountain Resort. It wasn't a challenging hill, but it brought me time away from home and my studies. My father was welcoming to both Yves and Yvan, inviting them to play golf at the Los Angeles Country Club as his guests. He was comfortable talking with them and enjoyed golf with them on weekends.

I confided in Yves over those painful months. As we became

close friends, he gave me his limitless emotional support. He was a father figure for me, supportive and consoling. I grew to trust him more than any other individual in my life at that time. But what I failed to consider was that, in my parents' eyes, he was merely a ski instructor and therefore not at all suitable for me as a mate. They went into catatonic upheaval when I asked if I could accompany Yves that summer to ski in Chile. "No, you cannot go to South America alone with that man," my father stated firmly.

Gerry, on the other hand, was deemed acceptable. We had kept in touch and were seeing each other occasionally when our vacations coincided. By 1953, he was stationed on a US Marine base in Hawaii, where he met Jimmy Pfleuger, the scion of a Hawaiian family that owned a great deal of property on the islands. Jimmy had an automobile dealership. The two men, who met on Waikiki Beach while surfing and canoeing, soon found that they shared a passion for daredevil motorsports.

Gerry was presumably in the Marine Corps, but somehow, he also had all the time he needed to race jalopies in the evening and hang out at the beach during the day. No one ever knew exactly what Gerry did as a Marine, but the job had to be a soft one that did not demand much of his time. His brother Jim was running the Cooper Lumber Company at that time in Los Angeles. I must admit, there have been times when I doubted whether Gerry ever served in the military at all.

After the end of my junior year at UCLA, I accepted Gerry's invitation to visit him in Hawaii. For my parents, this was a more acceptable alternative than going to South America with Yves. On our first night together in Hawaii, Gerry drove us to Diamond Head's famous Lover's Point and proposed to me. I was surprised, flattered, and a bit taken off guard, but I immediately said yes, although I did so with the deep realization that I had no idea why. Now, looking back so many years later, I still have to wonder why I said yes.

I had been enamored with William Gerritt Cooper since I was a girl. He was the attractive older boy at the Santa Monica Beach Club. Three years older than me, he was at that time out of reach. Nevertheless, I decided to try to attract his attention. During my senior year in high school, when my friends asked me what I was going to do that summer, I responded decisively and with characteristic boldness that I was going to "win" Bill Cooper as my boyfriend. And now this man who had always been considered such a catch was proposing to me. Gerry was socially acceptable in all ways. He had attended Harvard Academy, that prestigious, private boys' military school, which corresponded to Marlborough as a private girls' school. He was handsome, charismatic, and privileged. He would also one day be an heir to the Cooper Lumber Company.

Perhaps most significantly, he was the first boy I had ever been physically attracted to, and I was delighted to have finally become attractive to him. I also knew marriage would provide an escape route for me. I could see no other avenue along which to move with my life besides beginning a family within my social circle. I had already asked my father if I could travel in Europe for a year or even attend secretarial school. He replied that a girl of my birth and education did not do such things. Only marriage would gain the approval of both my parents. At least then, I thought, I would finally be able to jump over the palace walls once and for all. Several of my friends had already taken this path. Some had even married before finishing college.

Gerry and I called our parents together to give them the news. They were elated. My father was especially delighted because he had been worried about my continued exposure to my mother. But he made it clear that he wanted me to finish my final year of college, a goal I also shared, so we all settled on a June marriage the next summer, right after graduation.

Arriving home from Hawaii, I faced the challenge of telling Yves of my engagement. He had driven me to the airport for my trip, and Gerry had picked me up in Honolulu—a fact that must have been distressing enough for Yves. Even though over the years I had grown dependent on him for his loving care and support, I was not in love with Yves. He was like a father to me—always tender, loving, and loyal. Yet, I broke Yves's heart by telling him the news of my engagement. I had never wanted to hurt anyone like that.

Yves married several months later, divorced, and then married again several times more. He eventually returned to Mont-Tremblant, where he died at a relatively young age. Only in retrospect did I understand the importance of his friendship and generosity during that difficult period in my life. Perhaps Yves would have continued to be there for me in ways that Gerry could not, but I had made a choice and there was no looking back.

My father could not contain his pride when I received the Phi Beta Kappa key, a prestigious scholastic award, as well as Wellesley's highest academic award, that of Durant Scholar. It was a wish come true for both of us. After my years of hard work, graduation was a triumph, and I was leaving Wellesley with great personal confidence in my future. My father was there for the celebration, but my mother did not attend, having long since become incapable of leaving our apartment.

I looked forward to returning to California and the journey of starting a family. Although I was uncertain as to exactly how it would all work out, at least I knew that there would no longer be anything keeping me from moving toward the future I desired. I saw marriage as a new adventure that would bring me a family of my own and protect me psychologically and emotionally from what I considered to be my greatest failure—my inability to defeat my mother's disease. I had persisted until then in the idealism of youth, wanting something I could not have, and then blaming myself for the failure. Now there would be an entirely new beginning. Unsurprisingly, my old belief that I could effect change in others accompanied me well into my married years.

During the Christmas and spring vacations of my senior year, I went home to California to plan my wedding. I was a princess again, but my mother was not physically able to accompany me and share in the excitement and joy of this moment at Bullocks Wilshire. In truth, that made it easier for me—I could avoid disappointment by avoiding expectations. Now, at twenty-one, I felt capable of handling almost anything that confronted me. I realized, though, that my mother would one day feel tremendous guilt for missing her daughter's wedding, and that would weigh heavily upon her for the rest of her life. She had become a recluse, avoiding the store where she used to be venerated. She could no longer bear to be seen by those who had known her as she had once been.

Now I was taking my mother's place, and Bullocks Wilshire opened its gilded doors to me. My father and grandfather made it immediately clear that my every wish was to be fulfilled. The department heads and other employees I had known for many years expressed their excitement and welcomed me with open arms. I signed up with the Bullocks Wilshire wedding registry for all my gifts. My grandfather said I was to select whatever silver pattern I desired and all the silver serving dishes that accompanied it. I welcomed motherly advice from the store managers and buyers at that time, as though they could fill the gap in my soul. So many childhood conversations with my mother had centered around our looks or how to prevent the inevitable aging processes, rather than any emotional guidance about relationships or how to make sound life decisions while venturing into marriage and family life.

I was given my own dressing room at Bullocks Wilshire, and the lead store dress designer was appointed to create my wedding dress. It would be simple in design but decorated exquisitely with antique Irish lace. My father and grandfather looked in on me during the design process with glowing pride. I felt as though I were Cinderella in a fairy tale, soon to be swept along in a carriage drawn by two white stallions. Perhaps I might even lose my slipper at the grand party as I ran from the reception in the getaway car.

As bridesmaids, I chose my closest high school girlfriend Joan Morgan, my cousin Susie Boocock, and Gracie Vogel, along with three other high school friends. I designed their dresses as well. Kimberly Cooper, the oldest daughter of Carole and Jim Cooper, was my flower girl. I was free to select all the flowers I most loved to decorate the church, the bridesmaids' bouquets, and my own.

The wedding ceremony took place at St. Augustine by-the-Sea in Santa Monica—the most beautiful church—made of dark wood and built for the community by my grandfather, PG Winnett. I was thrilled to see my mother appear like an apparition in a long gown of deep blue. She had mustered the courage to make an appearance despite her swollen features and obvious fragility. This was the first social engagement of any kind that she had attended for years, and I so loved and appreciated her for being there.

The reception followed at the Los Angeles Country Club. Gerry and I changed clothes at the club before our classic crazy honeymoon departure. Rice rained down on us as I ran to get into Gerry's black Austin Healey before we peeled away from the crowd for a night at the Ambassador Hotel on Wilshire Boulevard. Several ushers told us later that the trunk of the car was so small, they had to sit on it to get it closed over my suitcases. My mother had selected the splendid clothes she imagined I would want on a honeymoon. Neither she nor I had any idea I was going on a West Coast driving honeymoon and would have no need for fancy clothes.

The following day, we took off with great haste, heading for the Northwest. Above all things, Gerry loved to drive, even more than to eat or sleep, so off we raced for ten days, up the coast from Los Angeles to San Francisco and farther north on twisting Highway 1. It was a beautiful and dramatic drive, with cliffs dropping to the ocean below, but there was little to do along the way. We stayed in hotels and motels, making a stop to visit a lumber mill in Bend, Oregon, for Gerry's family business. Our entire honeymoon was spent driving, with only one short side trip to view Mount St. Helens. Although it was romantic to be newlyweds, there was nothing inspiring about the trip—nothing historical, artistic, or educational. I had just graduated from a prestigious institution with studies that had sparked in me a passion for art and philosophy. With Gerry now at the wheel, even in the afterglow of a romantic departure toward our new lives together, I began to wonder what dreams I might have left behind.

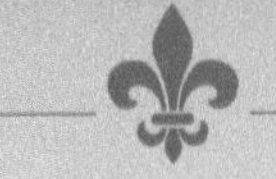

PART III

A New Family

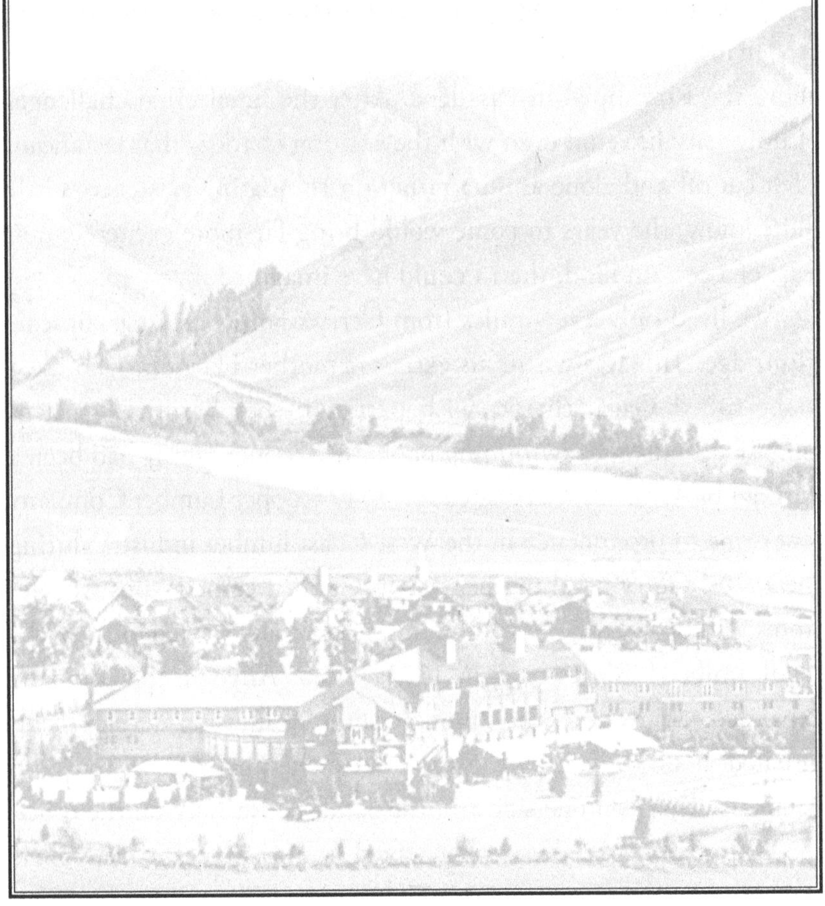

CHAPTER TWELVE

At the Cliff's Edge

By 1954, we were awaiting the birth of our first child and living in a modest new home that Gerry had built on stilts, high above the Rose Bowl in Pasadena. After the intellectual challenges of university life, and even with the exciting changes that lay ahead, I felt cut off and alone amid a rather unstimulating existence. Little did I know, the years to come would bring far more excitement, at least of a certain kind, than I could have imagined.

We lived only a few miles from Gerry's family estate in upscale Flintridge. This was where his extravert mother Harriett, who liked to be called Gaga, threw lavish parties in her beautiful gardens alongside a saltwater swimming pool. The Cooper family had been a part of Los Angeles society since the W. E. Cooper Lumber Company first came to prominence in the West Coast lumber industry during the 1920s. Gerry's grandfather, W. E. Cooper, came to Los Angeles from Wisconsin, where he and his father had started out in the retail lumber business back in 1893. In Los Angeles, the company expanded rapidly with the dramatic surge in housing development. Situated at 2035 East 15th Street, between spurs of the Southern Pacific Railroad on one side and the Santa Fe Railway on the other, the W. E. Cooper lumberyard benefited from easy access to suppliers of hardwoods, pine, white cedar, and spruce.

In 1921, *California Lumber Merchant* and *Western Building Review-Journal* heralded the success of W. E. Cooper's enterprise. But at that time, the lumber industry was wreaking havoc on the old-growth coastal redwood forest. A year later, the same journal ran a story about Joseph D. Grant's Save the Redwoods League. The league had produced a play called *Ersa of the Red Trees,* which was performed in state parks to impress upon the public the need to preserve the ancient giants that grew to more than three hundred feet in height. Grant and his supporters managed to pool half a million dollars to preserve two thousand acres of old-growth forest along the same California state highway that Gerry and I traveled during our honeymoon.

Charlie Cooper's two sons each took different paths in the family business. Jim, the eldest, went into the wholesale side of the company, traveling to lumber towns and learning to grade and value timber, while Gerry, seven years younger, chose to take on the retail end of the business. Gerry's engaging personality was better suited for work in the city with customers who would soon be seeking more than just stacks of lumber. Gerry eventually bought out his brother in the company, turning it into a successful hardware retail operation.

When he wasn't at work at the store or building homes to sell, such as the one in which we were living, Gerry stayed busy boat racing and motorcycle hill climbing on weekends. A mischievous rebel, Gerry lived in the glow of overwhelming adoration from his doting parents. In a rare moment of emotional intimacy during the first years of our marriage, he confided to me that he was "smother loved" by his mother. Yet, I could see that as an adult he continued to yearn for even more attention and recognition from others.

Before we married, Gerry boasted about stealing the family car when he was fifteen and running into someone on the street with it, surely a wild exaggeration. Another story he told of took place at Harvard Military Academy with his prankster friend Bill Anderson.

They laid down on the road around a curve in front of the school bus, pretending to be killed or injured. When the bus screeched to a halt and the bus driver ran out to help, they jumped up laughing. On yet another occasion, Gerry stole his parents' boat *Sweet Chariot* to attempt racing upstream through the formidable rapids on the Colorado River.

These stories were no doubt embellished, but the common theme was that Gerry was always getting away with something bordering on criminal activity. His parents always forgave him and seemed to disregard his transgressive behavior, thus encouraging his attention-getting pranks even more.

I imagined that marriage and family life would end his childlike behavior, that Gerry's needs would at last be satisfied and he would find contentment in life with just me and our children. My expectations grew from an idealistic and innately positive outlook on life; being negative and suspicious has never been a part of my psyche. I believed that what I put out there in the world would attract what came back to me, like a magnet. On the other hand, I felt that people who see themselves as victims dominated by negative experiences can become a magnet for disastrous circumstances and situations. I continued to believe that my positive outlook would prevail and that Gerry would change.

We lived in the stilt house until Lea Candy Cooper, our first daughter, was born in 1955. Gerry's mother Gaga convinced us of the real danger of a crawling child falling off the balcony and down the hillside toward the Rose Bowl. She invited us to live for as long as we wished in the two-room bathhouse of the pool in her garden. It was sufficient for our needs at that time. We lived there for a year as I became accustomed to caring for a baby, a creature such as I had never held and hardly even seen up to that point in my life. Of course, I had to do it as perfectly as possible, which created stress and brought little sleep.

By the time our second child, Cameron Scott Cooper, was born a year later, we had moved into one of those wonderful old houses that still line the streets of Manhattan Beach. We lived on a steep and wide pedestrian walkway with no cars. My clearest memory of Manhattan Beach is of struggling to push a heavy baby boy in a stroller up from the beach. My life was solid and secure in the sense that I knew what I had to do and when I had to do it. There is no question of avoiding or postponing daily tasks when you are raising small children.

Yet, I was frustrated with my situation and decided to visit Marian Pike for her sage counsel. I was missing the study of art history, with its visual impact and the creative inspiration of its compositions, colors, and representations. Los Angeles was attracting a new generation of artists who were working in new mediums and with eye-opening contemporary themes. Marian had not yet moved to Paris. After a brief conversation, her solution was quick and persuasive. She convinced me that I needed to find a new outlet in my life—not another academic pursuit, but a creative and personally expressive one.

"You have been gathering all these ideas and theories in college," said Marian. "How can you expect to be content now that your rational mind and creative instincts have no expressive outlet?" She told me about her friend and fellow artist Dorothy Royer's Creative Art Workshop, which focused on learning to explore—hands-on—every aspect of visual expression. I attended as soon as I could and dove into drawing figures and abstract patterns; working with models; and creating works in watercolors, pencil, oils, and even clay and glass.

I was encouraged to explore the subjective emotional and spiritual experience of art making, as opposed to only reading the objective, rational analyses that I had formerly studied in historical works. I learned to feel and understand art from the inside out and came to appreciate the challenges an artist faces within a particular composition. During Dorothy's workshop, I learned firsthand about the constraints of personal expression and how an artist's choices can truthfully express a particular vision.

About this time, Gerry was building another house as an investment. It was on a beautiful lot overlooking the ocean in a new development called Palos Verdes Estates, situated on a cliff high above the waves that crashed onto boulders far below. A snorkeling area below our house was accessed by a steep trail. On at least one occasion I can recall, a helicopter hovered above the rocks below our house on a search and rescue mission for survivors.

Gerry and I agreed that, when the home was finished, we would live there for a year or so until it sold. The building turned out to be more open, welcoming, and spacious than our first home, with a master bedroom and two children's rooms in one wing, a living and dining area in the center, and a kitchen adjacent to a playroom in another wing. With a third child on the way, my life continued to revolve around childcare, grocery shopping, and pediatrician appointments. Thanks to Marian and Dorothy, I now also had an essential creative outlet that both tied me to earlier intellectual interests and brought daily visual inspiration to everything I was observing around me.

Gerry and I often took our two children down to the beach at San Onofre. We pulled a trailer behind the car so they could get out of the sun or nap. To join the San Onofre Beach Club, one had to be recommended by an existing member. The club had recently been divided into two separate groups that tended not to mix. The early members established their domain on the south beach, while newcomers were relegated to the north beach. One could note the boundary between these two groups by their cars. The south end had older cars and trucks while the north end sported flashy new surfboards on expensive new cars. These two domains were divided by a volleyball court.

The south beach had a more relaxed atmosphere for the old-timers, and they had first rights to the volleyball court. At one time, I had been a member of this older group, but now we belonged to the northern, more recent and supposedly wealthier members who could afford the new, higher membership prices. The south group referred jokingly to the north group as the "martini and diaphragm club."

I first got to know Sam Grossman at San Onofre. He was known for taking girls "tandem surfing" to get to know them. For Sam, lying together on a surfboard was an effective way to get acquainted. Although the term "nouveau riche" could have been applied to us "north beachers," money was never a spoken issue. There was no class consciousness—the separation had to do with seniority. If one had money, whether it was inherited or earned, it was simply enjoyed. There was little gossip among members at the time, and if there was, it was never about money.

Our Palos Verdes home had an extraordinary view, perched as it was on a cliff. But as with many of our homes, the location brought risk. Gerry built a secure chain-link fence along the boundary of the property. Grass lawn stretched to the cliff's edge, and the fence provided safety for our curious children—or so we thought. I was eight months pregnant when, after a week of heavy rains, I faced the most horrifying day of my young married life.

One afternoon, I returned from the market with my two children and walked them to the sandy, fenced-in play yard adjacent to the house, where they were eager to play on the slide and swing set. I closed the gate securely before going into the house. I put away the groceries and, within a short while, went out to call the children in for their lunch. I looked out and noticed that only Candy was in the play yard. I asked her where her brother Cam had gone, and she sheepishly refused to answer me. It was a game they played with me, like hide-and-seek, so I was not panicked, thinking he would be somewhere around the perimeter of the house.

After I walked circled the house and did not find him, I went out to the street to call for him. No response. Next, my heart racing, I went to the neighbor's house to check out their pool area. Thankfully, he had not fallen into the pool. I finally went to the last place I wanted to look, over the cliff edge and down two hundred feet to the rocks and ocean below.

As I approached the fence, I saw to my horror that after days of rainfall the mud had slid out from under the fence, leaving a large, gaping hole. I was traumatized and shaking as I looked over the fence. There, far below and barely visible, was the hunched figure of my son Cameron lying on a boulder. I had to get him to safety.

I thought of the time when the helicopter had come very near this spot, seemingly searching for someone, and the hordes of people, their cars parked on the cliff, wanting to share in the excitement. Now I was facing a similar drama, and all I could think of was how to get to my son and bring him back up the cliff. If I did not do something immediately, he would surely tumble farther, possibly to his death. I had no doubt in my mind what I needed to do. I needed to be with my baby boy, to hold and comfort him. I ran over to the snorkeler's path by my neighbor's house, shouting angrily at Candy to frighten her away from following me. Anyone who has been in a situation where a child's life depends on you will acknowledge how adrenaline takes over and beyond-human strength prevails.

The heavy rains had washed out the path of descent, so I slid more than climbed down the washed-out steps, grabbing boulders as I passed them to slow me down, and clambering over others. My huge belly threw off my balance, but finally I reached Cam, who was sitting hunched over on the boulder. When I reached for him, he groaned with pain and passed out. The slippery path upward was an enormous struggle with a heavy two-year-old. I lifted him bit by bit as far as I could, laying him down on a large rock or flat spot so I could then maneuver myself a little higher. On sections of the muddy path, I set him down as far ahead of me as I could reach and then pulled myself up to him, often slipping backward. He seemed to go in and out of consciousness and groaned as I moved him.

I found Candy at the top of the cliff, exactly where I had ordered her to remain. We rushed to the car, and I placed Cam on the front seat beside me. He still was groaning from time to time. I began to sob uncontrollably. Then my three-year-old daughter had the presence of mind to quietly say, "Mommy, it is going to be fine." Gerry met me at the Palos Verdes Hospital, where we found that Cameron had no broken bones. His bulky clothing during the winter months had protected him from more serious injury. The doctor told us to keep him in his crib for a day to watch for any sign of a concussion. He was badly bruised but recovered in a few days and soon returned to his "curious toddler" explorations. It is said that babies and drunks know how to fall, loosely and relaxed. That had to have been a factor in Cam's life-threatening fall.

I cannot say whether this incident traumatized Cam in his early years, but when his father threw him into the air in fun, he would just freeze. Yet, as Cam grew up, he showed no fear of heights or of falling. Quite the contrary—he became a pilot, a fearless skier unafraid of skiing the bumps, and a kayaker eager to go over the falls in a rapid. Perhaps because of surviving that fall at Palos Verdes, Cameron exhibited bravado and confidence in his later years. He would fly high, know no fear, and roll with life and whatever it would bring.

Candy surely knew where Cam had gone but was afraid to tell me. She later said that they had gone to the fence to watch a large freighter passing close to the shoreline. Cam wanted to get a better look, and the rain-soaked mud under his feet had given way. I never regretted the risk I took that day. Only in my later years have I begun to concede that risk-taking should no longer be an option. But by trusting in my intuition to save my child that day, I found a path to deep, inner wisdom that has served me ever since.

My second daughter, Kelley Winnett Cooper, was born in 1958. Happily, she loved to sleep. Perhaps this was a natural reflex and protective mechanism to escape the noise and folly of three and four-year-old siblings who spent their waking hours trying to outwit one another in their attempts to elude the oversight of a potentially overprotective parent.

After two years, we moved on from Palos Verdes. This was a regular occurrence as Gerry continued to build and sell our homes. He set his eyes next on a move to the isolated coast of Malibu, where my children would experience a period of wildness, unbridled freedom, and exploration. The years ahead would dispel any notion I once held that marriage was a safe refuge. Gratefully, they also brought me to a new level of personal independence and self-confidence that I would eventually need to make big changes in my life.

CHAPTER THIRTEEN

Point Zero

SOME PEOPLE BELIEVE THAT CHAOS MEANS LACK OF CONTROL. Physicists now know that mysteriously organized patterns lie behind even the most chaotic and unpredictable natural processes. Our early years in Malibu were both real and surreal, an experiment in chaos theory. Some deeper principle of organization must have magically saved us, because somehow we all survived. I intuitively felt in those years that this underlying organizational principle was there for us. It all began in 1958 at a rented home about a mile south of the Ventura County line, or Point Zero, as it was known by surfers. That was where I became accustomed to a way of life full of risk and constant activity. Even by the freewheeling standards of that time in Southern California, no one else played as wildly as we did.

Gerry became the pied piper of an endless beach party that drew friends from far and wide. It was like Disneyland, except that it was free to anyone willing to play and take the ride. The home we lived in for the first two years was perched above the sea beside a short dirt road that descended steeply to the beach. The Coopers and our entourage transformed the placid beach at Point Zero into a lively commotion of go-carts, motorcycles, boats, surfboards, bikes, and an army surplus amphibious vehicle named The Duck.

Gerry's loyal subjects followed him with unquestioning trust and devotion. The children gathered around him each morning in worshipful attendance. He made sure each of them had a toy—pedal cars and wagons for the wee ones; and bicycles, tricycles and pull-behind wagons for those a bit older. All the men had Triumph motorcycles, bought at a discount thanks to Clarence Fleming, a close friend from Lake Arrowhead whose uncle, Bill Johnson, was the first man to import Triumph motorcycles from England to California. The men would take to the harder sands of the beach or go up into the Malibu hills to ride on rough trails or strike out on their own across the hills. There was stiff competition to be the one to lead the way and return first, hopefully unscathed. Accidents were frequent. Jimmy Pfleuger broke a rib on at least one occasion when Gerry accidentally rode over him. Actor Steve McQueen rode with them from time to time, but Gerry's indispensable companion was Jimmy. The two men were eager to break any and all barriers for the sake of an adventure and their enduring friendship.

"These older men were like gods to us," my son Cameron recalled. "We never knew what was going to happen next, but we always knew it was going to be fun. I hated leaving the beach to go to school."

I expected these Malibu years to be my first experience of true freedom from societal expectations, and I welcomed this new life of reckless abandon, eagerly participating in whatever came next. But this new kingdom had a ruler—Gerry's word was the word, and no one dared to question the risk-taking he demanded.

On weekends, I took on the responsibility of hosting and looking after thirty or more people on the beach, racing about on all sorts of machines. After my daughter Christin was born in 1959, I was so busy with four children under the age of six that I asked visiting families to bring their own picnics as part of our open-door policy. Most would stay late on Sundays to miss the Pacific Coast Highway traffic heading back to LA. I was always exhausted at the end of a weekend, despite having all the energy of a woman in her twenties.

Every now and then, I grabbed a moment of relaxation by lying on a towel and resting in the sun. But as soon as I managed to drift off, the jeep would roar by just above the ocean shallows. A water-skier swinging wildly from a rope behind it pulled across the shallows atop the remnants of a wave that left a shallow skim of foaming water. To prevent a dangerous landing on the sand, the skier would carve out to sea and jump a wave before cutting back in toward the beach. The jeep was always packed with younger kids waiting their turn with the water skiis or to be dragged behind on rubber mats—the precursors of boogie boards.

The only non-mechanical toy we had was a trampoline, which was situated, of course, on the back porch between a glass window and a steep ice plant-covered hill down to the beach. Gerry was convinced that the vegetation would provide a soft landing for any kids unlucky enough to launch off in that direction. The trampoline was popular with my children, who competed for height in their jumps, but few other parents would allow their kids near it.

Kids aged four and up, like Cameron, were given go-carts to race up and down the road and around the driveway of the Tainter family, the first residence on Point Zero Road. Just opposite our house was an incline up to the home of Don and Jeannette Lanctot. They were quiet residents until we came along, but they quickly joined as eager participants in our playtime adventures. Down the road from the Tainters lived the Taskers with their four children. They also joined in our circus of exploits and adventures, as did the Porter family—Cal and Cathy and their son and daughter, Lon and Cathy-Ann. At that time, Cal was a Los Angeles County lifeguard at Zuma Beach. He taught all of the local small beach rats how to swim, including the Cooper children. This was the only safeguard that anyone took seriously during those years. Life jackets were simply not a part of our lives.

Our close family of friends gathered from as far away as Pasadena,

Palos Verdes, and Beverly Hills. Clarence Fleming's wife Anne, or Bunny, became godmother to my youngest daughter Christin. The entire Morning family became regulars. Mike Hynes, then assistant manager of the Cooper Lumber Company and beloved by all the children, became my younger son Brant's godfather after Brant was born in 1961. Years later, after Mike lost a leg in a motorcycle accident, he visited us in Sun Valley, where he was well-known as "the one-legged skier," using an arm support with a ski attachment under his missing leg. Mike was with us every weekend in Malibu, and he introduced us to Michelle Doerner, known as Michou, and her sons Darrick and Marc Doerner. Darrick became a lifeguard on the North Shore of Oahu and a renowned big wave surfer. His brother Marc still dives for lobsters off the rocks of the cove at Point Zero.

Gerry and his brother Jim threw a huge feast at Point Zero every Fourth of July, shot skeet off the deck, and held a volleyball tournament. At dusk, they set off an impressive array of fireworks that drew people from miles around. The two men crawled on their bellies across the sand with lit sticks in their mouths to light the fuses and then quickly scrambled away before the explosions began. Our fireworks were the kind you might see at the Rose Bowl.

One afternoon, the waves were rather large; and when the tide came in, surrounding the rocks about one hundred yards from shore, I heard the scream of children—you know, that special kind of scream that indicates something serious. I had already done up my hair in curlers for an event Gerry and I had planned to attend in the city when I looked out and saw my niece, Kim Cooper, clinging to a rock far from the shore. As soon as I saw what was happening, I grabbed a surfboard and trotted down to the beach.

Kim was a water baby, just like all the Cooper kids. In the pre-boogie board era, they all rode waves on yellow surf mats and learned early on to respect the ocean. But on that particular day, Kim got flustered by the breakers and, instead of coming ashore, paddled out farther to get beyond them. Then she was hit by a wave and lost her mat. She swam to a large rock and climbed up, awaiting rescue. Stranded by the breakers, she had yelled to the other kids on the beach to call the coast guard. I didn't think that was necessary, so I paddled out through the waves, trying to avoid the foam to keep my hair dry. After I made it beyond the break, I drew up alongside the rock and had Kim dive off and climb aboard. I gave her a hard time as we paddled back to shore, catching some waves along the way to get home more quickly. She really should have known better, I told her. Then I went inside to finish my hair and get dressed for the evening—just another day at Point Zero.

Within a few years, Kim would be working for a summer at the W. E. Cooper Lumber Company and driving a forklift. Gerry hung the company sign upside down that summer on Pico Boulevard. He said it would "get talk" and that meant free advertising. Gerry and his brother Jim were known to drive very fast on the Pacific Coast Highway and, as a result, were well-known by every policeman from the Santa Monica tunnel to Malibu. They were two rich brothers who didn't spend much time in the office. It was all about fun at the cove. Kim and Candy, the two kids old enough to know best what was going on, called it "bikinis and martinis" time at the beach.

Vetz and Betty Jane Morning and their four children were then living, of all places, in the rebuilt six-car garage of my childhood home on San Vicente. They had converted the building into a lovely home. It was strange to visit the Mornings by first driving on a new road through what had once been Joan Morgan's family estate next door. From the second story of the Mornings' new home, I could see that our avocado orchard and gardens were now filled with new homes that surrounded our old house.

The Chappellet and Wetzel families also came to Point Zero. They had moved to the Napa Valley area in the late sixties and founded successful wineries. Donn and Molly Chappellet owned a beach house five miles south in what is now the private celebrity beach area of Malibu called Trancas Beach, or Broad Beach. Molly's sister, Luanne Wells, and her husband Frank visited them on Broad Beach in a family house next door to the Chappellets. In the years to come, Frank would serve as president of the Walt Disney Company when the company expressed an interest in acquiring Sun Valley Resort. Within a few years, my mother would also own a home on Broad Beach.

Meanwhile, the Coopers assembled their forces to the north, where things were a bit less tranquil. The Duck was one toy at Point Zero that stood out from all the rest, an amphibious military vehicle that was designed to transport troops and supplies onto beaches. Ours was painted bright blue rather than military green. A toilet was hoisted permanently over the transom, with flags flying around it to bring it to everyone's attention. The machine could move at a decent speed along the Pacific Coast Highway and, whenever the occasion called for it, veer off into the surf and crash through the waves as it headed out to sea. Gerry had no license to operate The Duck, on sea or land. But he did have a plan. If pulled over on the highway, he would tell the police it was a boat and that he didn't need a license for a boat on the highway. If the coast guard came alongside at sea, he would claim it was a truck and therefore exempt from a boating license.

The Duck served to bolster Gerry's hard-won reputation as a motor sports hero. Gerry enjoyed racing the family station wagon against fast cars in the neighborhood because it had been souped-up and could "burn rubber." He once posed for an advertising photograph for his home-building company beside a red "bird-cage" Maserati, helmet in hand. The ad in the *Los Angeles Times* was meant to show Los Angelinos that owning a home in Malibu was convenient. Under the photograph were the words, "Los Angeles to Malibu in 15 minutes." Jimmy Pfleuger once told me that Gerry drove in reverse all the way from Malibu to Los Angeles on a dare, leaving at three in the morning to avoid traffic. But really, I never knew what to believe.

One weekend, the Cooper family loaded into the Duck to visit the Chappellets, who had a home at Broad Beach. We crashed into the surf and turned south out past the breakers. An hour later, we arrived outside the break and turned toward land, revving up the wheels at the last minute for a beach landing. The Duck performed admirably, taking us ashore for an afternoon picnic and a game of volleyball with Molly and Donn and their kids, before turning back into the surf for the cruise home. Just another day with the Coopers.

Point Zero was quite a bit more exotic than Trancas. We had a collection of animals that came and went. There were snakes, rabbits, dogs, and cats. Doc Tainter had a flock of peacocks that wandered freely and a coop of chickens that were of great interest to our hunting dog Tazio Nuvolari, named after a famed Italian race car driver of the day. Tazio was completely untrained and therefore chased anything that moved. He eventually found a way into Doc Tainter's chicken coop and soon had to be on his way far from our beach. On the other hand, our two baby alligators gave us no trouble at all. "We named them Tigger and Eeyore, after the characters in Winnie the Pooh," said Cameron. "We played with them for hours. It was always fun to see the look on people's faces if they were walking by and looked in on us to see alligators there in the sand with us."

Nothing would have surprised us. One day, a burro appeared. I have no idea where it came from nor where it ended up a few weeks later. We named it "Clarence." It stayed next door at the Lanctots for a few weeks and then disappeared just as mysteriously as it had arrived. I never knew what type of slithering, terrorizing beast Gerry might bring home for the amusement of the children—certainly not for mine. At various times, we had living with us everything from horned toads to boa constrictors. To feed some of these predators, we raised white mice, which escaped to run freely around the house.

They ran up our pants legs and turned up in our beds. I managed to catch a few and release them outside.

Alligators and snakes brought me the most distress. The small alligators were placed in a large fish tank with rocks to climb up on. Who knew how big they would become? They had little else to do each day but eat. To keep them fed, I sent the children out to catch baby frogs in the pond and creek that trickled down the hill beside our house. I did my best to be out of the room when feeding time came because the little frogs' squeals as they were chomped with sharp teeth and devoured brought agony to my heart.

I had no idea where the reptiles retired to when the children tired of feeding them. This uncertainty brought to mind our childhood prank of telling the laundress that we had a pet alligator on the loose—she had left without a backward glance. Now I lived in a home where we, and our neighbors, never knew where an alligator might appear. In the laundry? Under a couch?

The worst scene came when live animals were fed to the boa constrictor. The snake was a gift to Candy from her father. It lived in a cage in the lower service bathroom, but Candy would take him out and carry him to her bedroom. One day, I walked in and found this large snake wrapped around Candy's neck. She apparently had no idea that constrictors evolved to strangle their prey. Trying not to curse, I screamed out "Godfrey," and because that seemed so funny to the children, Godfrey became the boa's name.

Another time, Candy took Godfrey out onto the beach. She then wandered away to explore and returned to find that Godfrey had done the same. The loose boa must have wandered the neighborhood until it was swept away by a high tide from under the house deck. Or it might have survived for years in the brush. Candy was distraught over this loss, so home came an even a larger boa, Godfrey II. The first boa preferred mice for its meal. Godfrey II preferred little birds, canaries to be exact, since they were the only ones available for purchase at the pet store. I had to leave the room as that lovely bird slowly went down the snake's writhing body. I was aghast at my daughter's ability to feed a live bird to a snake and watch it be killed after a few pitiful peeps. I asked her how she could do this, and she gave the very simple answer, "I like my snake better."

Weezy Tasker, one of the neighborhood kids, came by to babysit from time to time. That all ended one day after the door to Godfrey's cage in the utility room was found open. We searched the house, the gardens, and the beach area. He was lost for days, and even I was nervous, watching where I stepped and peeking carefully inside cupboards and closets as the doors were slowly opened. Weezy was in the swivel chair in the TV room about a week later when Godfrey slowly came out from under the back of the chair, then slowly crawled over her shoulder and down into her lap. She leapt up, screamed, and ran from the house, never to return. I suspected Candy of leaving the cage door open just for the delight of surprise. She later claimed, "We never left the door to the cage open to scare anyone. We just didn't think animals in general should be caged."

There came the day that Candy decided to take Godfrey to school for show-and-tell. He would be in his cage, so we thought all would be well. But when Candy went to carry him down to the house after returning from school, she found the cage door open. There was no Godfrey II to be found. We looked everywhere, the entire family, but there was no sign of Candy's six-foot-long, three-inch-thick pet. I decided to take the car to the local gas station and have the service men take out the car seats and look through the car and engine, "anywhere a snake could curl up and hide," I said. They reported that they had found nothing. I later realized that they probably feared encountering such a monster and only claimed to have searched the car.

Two weeks later, the children and I went to Needles, California, with a close friend, Randolph "Ran" Galt, to water-ski for the weekend. Needles is situated on the Colorado River, just across the bridge from Arizona and on the tip of Nevada in the Mohave Desert. We checked into a motel close to the river.

The first day of our vacation, we were off across the lake in the boat we had towed along with us. The temperature was over one hundred degrees. When we returned to the car at the end of the day, there on the driver's floorboard side was Godfrey II, horribly shriveled and completely dead due to the heat and lack of water. We knew that snakes could go a long time without food, but not without water at those temperatures. Ran, who had invited us on the trip and driven us there in my station wagon, was visibly shaken when he realized that this snake had no doubt been in the car and most likely coiled up under his seat during the entire drive.

Candy ran into the motel, placing him in a bathtub of cold water to revive him. She did not think it at all odd to ask the desk attendant for some ice "to revive her overheated boa constrictor." But Godfrey could not be revived. The children rallied to create a prank to honor him, placing his body on a floating boat pillow and sending him off for one final ride. They thought that some unsuspecting water-skier passing by might see this large snake lying in the sun on the Colorado River and think they were going crazy.

It never entered my mind to take my young children to nursery school. That would have meant more bouncing around in the car on the highway—before the days of safety seats or seat belts—so I decided that our eclectic life in the wilds of Malibu would be its own nursery school. With all the frenetic activity around us, it is a miracle there were so few accidents. The worst mishap I can recall was when my third daughter, Christin, brought down a scalding hot cup of tea upon herself. I had placed it on the bedside table and laid down for a moment's rest. I opened my eyes just as she pulled it onto her terry cloth pajamas. She screamed and writhed as I tried to get the absorbent garment off her, and she continued to howl during the entire five-mile drive to the pediatrician in Malibu. He did what he could for her, but she suffered terribly and had scars on her shoulder and arm for years.

My mother-in-law, Gaga, must have known I was feeling overwhelmed. She offered to "loan" me her Black servant, Maddy, for as long as I wished. Maddy was a gem, a mothering, loving woman. But she was also quite heavy and not very maneuverable. Only with great effort did she manage to get down the steep dirt road to go fishing. There she taught young Cam and Candy how to bait a line. Maddy could stand there on the sand for hours in the hope of catching a fish, although I do not recall her ever catching one.

The only quiet escape I could find with my children was when I joined them for art sessions a short drive down the Pacific Coast Highway at the home of Lenore Wright. The first thing we did was explore the rocks and tidal pools at the end of Point Zero Beach, searching for smoothed out rock surfaces to create Rock People. This began with searching for that one rock that would be the best face, body, leg, or arm. My kids imagined their own creatures, with painted eyes, nose and mouth; a sad face, happy face, or silly face, with painted buttons and shoes; well-dressed, naked, or even with a hat. These prized collections of humorous rock people came home to inhabit each child's room.

Bob Brandt, a successful stockbroker in Beverly Hills and a motorcycling buddy of Gerry's, was often at our house. One day, through a window, I could see Bob walking toward our front door with a large, blond puppy in his arms. I did not answer the door. He knocked harder. Surely, this creature would be the last straw that broke my back. "No, I cannot handle a puppy right now," I yelled to him through the door, and then I broke down into tears.

Gerry and the children ultimately won out with their pleas. As a result, we ended up owning the greatest family dog one could ever hope for. Archie became a loving and faithful member of the family.

The children were devoted to him and he to them. Instead of becoming another burden, Archie helped raise my kids, always watching over them and keeping them company. He was ever available to wrestle with, trip over, or serve as someone's pillow.

• • •

Harry Gesner entered our lives again during our last year at Point Zero with an idea for a grand adventure—an expedition to the island of San Miguel, part of the Channel Islands, to search for the lost gold of sixteenth-century conquistador Juan Rodríguez Cabrillo. Cabrillo had joined forces as a young man with conquistador Hernán Cortés in Central America, thereby becoming one of the richest men of his day. During the 1540s, he was the first European explorer to navigate the California coast, apparently burying his treasures before dying of gangrene after an attack by local Tongva warriors. Legend had it that Carbrillo's treasure was buried along with him at a secret location.

Harry told us of an old map that his father had kept, found within the adobe walls of the Gesner house in Santa Barbara before it was demolished. Harry was convinced that it revealed the location of the conquistador's treasure, buried at "the horse's neck" on deserted San Miguel Island, a rocky and desolate spot about 140 miles west of Malibu. Harry surmised from the description that their target had to be a narrow place near shore that resembled a horse's neck. Finding the treasure became an obsession for Harry. He had already made one attempt, years earlier, with filmmaker Bill Baird aboard the schooner *Resolute*, to locate Juan Cabrillo's treasure once and for all. With a USGS map and a World War II Raytheon mine locator for assistance, they launched a longboat for the shore. Certain that the mine locating device would show where Cabrillo had been buried in his armor, they marked out a grid and went to work. It was not long before the work crew received a signal that showed they were above metal, so they went to work digging. They had been warned that the island was used during the war as a listening station and that any leftover ordnance scattered about could explode. They dug down ten feet but found nothing until the ground gave way and they found themselves in a fox den. They wondered how far they might have to dig to unearth three hundred years of sediment, but the weather suddenly changed for the worse and the ship had to move, so the crew gave up and went home.

By the time Harry managed to convince Gerry and Clarence Fleming to search once more for the treasure, the island was off-limits, except for temporary beach landings. This little detail wasn't going to stop them. Soon they had planned an expedition that involved airplanes, jeeps, motorcycles, and at least twenty people—and, of course, surfboards. Gerry leased a Douglas DC-3 cargo plane to carry the jeep, digging machinery, food, and cooking supplies. He had to improvise at Oxnard Airport to get the jeep ten feet off the ground and into the airplane. He used wooden ramps that slipped loose, sending him crashing to the ground. The jeep bounced a few feet in the air, but no one was seriously hurt.

Some friends braved this wild idea of a treasure hunt with us. Cap Watkins; Clarence Fleming; Sterling and Tookie Dietz (Clarence's sister); the entire Tasker family; Cal and Cathy Porter; Lenore Wright; Bob Brandt; Mike Hynes; Dr. Dan Hillman, a pilot; and last but not least, our dog Archie. Candy, Cameron, and Kelley were with me. They needed constant monitoring because of the moving machinery and airplanes that were necessary to transport supplies and fuel. Harry and Mike Hynes flew on the first supply trip to the island. Dan Hillman had arrived earlier in a smaller plane to place a flare at the top of the runway that would guide the cargo plane to a safe landing. Gerry and I and the three children came by boat, landing on a beautiful sandy beach and then trekking to the last remaining old bungalow on the island. My assignment was to help Vera Tasker organize the supplies and to cook and serve all the meals.

Feral sheep that had not been shorn in many years wandered the island, each of them just huge bundles of wool waddling around. The men went to work with a conveyor belt at the "treasure" site, removing a twenty-foot-wide, fifteen-foot-deep section of ground, but again found nothing—no bombs and no Juan Cabrillo. The mine locator was still showing a metal signal when they called it quits, Harry told me later. Everyone then explored the island on motorcycles, filming as we went. We returned to the mainland with no treasure, but plenty of home movies and memories.

As exciting and daring as our lives were at Point Zero, the location was merely a proving ground for greater adventures elsewhere. Looking back now, some things seem predetermined. My husband's destiny began to unfold years before we were married when he first met Jimmy Pfleuger on Waikiki Beach. Jimmy's company sponsored jalopy racers on a quarter-mile racetrack in Honolulu. Gerry raced a 1932 Ford three-window coupe there and had the best mechanic in town, a guy by the name of Benny Lovell. Their biggest competitor was Jerry Unser Jr., of the famed New Mexico car racing family. Thousands of people showed up to watch.

Jimmy told me that Gerry won more races than most, including almost all of the "trophy dashes" that started each race. This would handicap him and put him near the back of the pack for the forty-lap main event. Despite all the money spent by company sponsors, there was little at stake for the drivers other than their lives. Winners only took home a tin cup trophy. It was entirely for "fun and frolic," as Jimmy would say.

In 1957, Jerry Unser won the United States Auto Club stock car championship. Tragically, he died in 1959 in a fiery crash during a practice run for the Indianapolis 500. His younger brother, Bobby Unser, went on to Indianapolis 500 glory and in later years patented a radar detector to help drivers avoid speeding tickets. For this reason alone, he would have seemed like a hero to my speed-demon husband.

The Unsers first came to fame as the family that dominated

the 14,110-foot, twelve-mile Pikes Peak Hill Climb car race on the southern Front Range of the Rocky Mountains in Colorado. Jimmy and Gerry followed their example by taking on the 13,800-foot Mauna Kea volcano on the Big Island of Hawaii before there was even a road to the top. Gerry was along for the first of Jimmy's several attempts, using a jeep equipped with tires from a DC-3 airplane. A "snorkel" was attached to the intake to keep lava dust from the carburetor. It took five years and several tries for Jimmy to finally reach the summit.

Gerry and Jimmy's first hill climb challenge together came when a man named Bart Erdman, who owned a ranch on Maui, had the nerve to tell Jimmy that he couldn't ride a motorcycle up the eight-mile Kaupō Gap, a steep and narrow cow trail that crossed harsh terrain on Haleakalā, the massive shield volcano that forms most of the island of Maui. Whenever Jimmy faced a challenge, he called Gerry, who in this case quickly flew his latest Triumph motorcycle to Hawaii for the big day. Determined to prove Bart wrong, they roared off from the village of Kaupō and were done with the climb in about two hours.

Jimmy and Gerry courted danger as though it were some kind of addiction. They raced speedboats from Los Angeles to Catalina Island, and hatched a plan to race more seaworthy boats from California to Hawaii, but their plan fell apart when they discovered that the resupply fuel tanks they planned to drop from airplanes along the route would disintegrate upon hitting the surface of the sea. Gerry, however, remained obsessed with setting records, winning races, and becoming famous. In those days, Jimmy beached his Chris-Craft speedboat at Sand Island in Kāne'ohe Bay on Oahu. The water was a vivid blue and clear near the shore's edge. Gerry and I joined him there for water-skiing and to show him some tricks he had never seen before.

My favorite trick at that time was taking off backward on two skis. I told him to take me out of the water slowly. He thought it was funny that my fanny came up out of the water first. I then dropped one ski and flipped around to go forward. Time and again, Jimmy told me that I was the best athlete in the bunch. But his friendship with my husband would take them on adventures to places I rarely followed. One big exception was when Gerry asked me to join them on an expedition up the Colorado River into the Grand Canyon. To me, this seemed the most thrilling and dangerous adventure of all.

On one particular Sunday, the swells at Point Zero were large but the ocean was quiet and windless. Gerry yelled to everyone on the beach, "Who wants to go for a ride?" Of course, everyone did, and they began to scramble onboard. Small children were hoisted up to the arms of waiting adults. The Duck set to sea with close to thirty people aboard. I could hear their laughter from shore and their cheers as The Duck crashed through breaking waves, amidst showers of spray, into the deep sea ahead.

Gerry maneuvered out beyond the kelp beds, killed the engine, and they all had a picnic. There was a quiet time, and I watched from shore as several adults went overboard to snorkel. I didn't go along because I had toddlers to care for. It was peaceful as The Duck later cruised up and down a half mile out to sea. Eventually, Gerry knew it was time to bring the restless children ashore, back to their sandcastles. The Duck turned and tugged steadily toward the beach. I noticed that the waves had become a bit larger. Gerry gunned the engine as usual so The Duck would storm the shoreline with as much speed as possible until the wheels caught on sand. The Duck routinely made landfall in this way, chugging to a stop at its parking space by the beach towels. But about twenty yards offshore The Duck's motor quit. There was no power left for that last surge onto the sand and beyond the crashing waves, no chance for it to transition from a watercraft to a land vehicle. After slogging around for a minute or two, the mighty and invincible vehicle went broadside in the surf.

Adults scrambled into the waves, reaching up for their children to be lowered into their arms, then struggling ashore in the shallow surf in hope of not being hit by a wave—or by The Duck. They also risked being swept back out to the sea by a retreating wave. Everything had suddenly gone terribly wrong.

The Duck eventually careened over in the surf and lay beaten, with waves splashing around it as everyone's belongings washed about in the surf. By some miracle, no one was injured. Gerry planned to have an excavation tractor come to the rescue the next morning to dig The Duck out of the sand and repair the motor for future adventures. He felt confident that he could fix this, just as he always fixed everything. But heavy surf continued into the night, and The Duck slowly became mired in the sand, impossible to move. In the next days and weeks, it slowly sank deeper with each new tide.

Months turned into years as The Duck was slowly taken by the sea, all but an axle and wheel sticking up occasionally from the surf. For me, the demise of The Duck meant the end of an era free from regulations and filled with adventure. It signaled the end of a unique and carefree time of sheer playfulness—and yes, recklessness—that brought together parents and children for the ride of a lifetime. Rules were few and boundaries were tested, but are we so much better now for all the limits we have created to protect ourselves? I treasure that time when my family lived and loved with abandon, assuming life would never change.

There were those of us who loyally held out hope for years and would go back to Point Zero Beach for a possible last look and tearful goodbye. At low tide, we would occasionally be rewarded with a glimpse before The Duck disappeared finally beneath the waves.

CHAPTER FOURTEEN

UP THE RAGING COLORADO RIVER

GERRY WORSHIPED ADVENTUROUS EXPLORERS, especially one-armed boatman John Wesley Powell, who in 1869 led the first expedition into the Grand Canyon. Powell had faced Indian attacks, mutiny, and dangerous rapids through unknown terrain. But now the Colorado River was charted and the canyon fully explored. Its tamed waters flowed into Lake Mead where Gerry and I water-skied in the summer. Yet, Gerry often looked upstream to the lake's far end with ambition. His dream was to take on the canyon in a motorboat, from the bottom up. It would be a new conquest over the forces of nature by man and machine.

Back when Gerry was in his early twenties, without his family's knowledge, he drove his father's Chris-Craft speedboat up the lower section of the Colorado River until he was turned back by the rapids. After bouncing off some rocks, he turned around and quickly headed home to repair and repaint the hull before his parents noticed the boat was missing. Now it was 1959, and Gerry was determined to succeed where once he had failed. The plan was to motor up through the Grand Canyon during spring flood, when the water was at its highest. At that time of year, the waves in the rapids would be enormous, especially at the treacherous Lava Falls, about halfway up the 365-mile reach of the Colorado. The boats were outfitted with outboard motors so they could maneuver over and around the rocks.

Gerry and I were familiar with the boat ramps and beaches at Lake Mead. A few years earlier, we had entered the one-hundred-mile water ski race at Lake Mead. Gerry was my driver as I skied behind *Sweet Chariot* on the lake's glassy waters. But for this new adventure up the river, he invited along Jack Davis, a wealthy investor in New Jersey hotels and casinos, a mechanic friend, and several other boat-worthy men. Our cars pulled three boats to Las Vegas and then on to Lake Mead. Two of them were outfitted with specially powered outboard engines. The third boat would carry supplies. It would be necessary to portage supplies from this third boat to get above the more dangerous rapids. The final major challenge on the route from Lake Mead to Lees Ferry would be Lava Falls. Its fearful drop of nearly forty feet led to carnage for some who took the falls from above. From below, it could be even more perilous. The most powerful motors at that time were seventy-five-horsepower Mercuries, mounted on lightweight boats for maximum power. The boats were built at the Cooper Lumber Company of the strongest hardwood plywood available. We also brought along carefully selected spare motor parts and extra propellers to replace the ones that would be destroyed by unseen rocks.

The memory of that adventure comes flowing back to me today as clear as the Colorado River was then muddy and cold. Our boats crossed placid Lake Mead and left its calm waters to head upstream, easily navigating the smaller rapids and even some of the larger, rough sections for the first three days. Our bodies suffered from hours of constant bouncing and banging; and now, as the canyon grew narrower, the boat was rising and falling even more over each large wave. This was not a trip for the weak of heart, I realized. But I had not yet begun to question such risks and still had complete trust in Gerry's judgment and proven boating skills.

Sleep did not come easily on the sandy riverbanks. We had to remain vigilant for possible flash floods from heavy rains upstream, so the boats were pulled high onto the shore and camp was made well above the river's edge. Our supplies had to be portaged around raging rapids that the heavily laden supply boat could not surmount unless it was empty. Losing our supplies would have meant a retreat and failure. Some of the men probably wished that I had not come along since my presence meant their language and etiquette were somewhat restricted. They would surely have to walk farther away than usual to pee.

Frequent stops were made to replace damaged propellers. On the fourth day, the expedition reached the series of rapids known as Lava Falls. There was no way up the sides, where foaming, roiling waters ran over shallow rock protrusions. The lowest of the rapids were mild, but farther upriver the channel narrowed, and the river became a tumultuous waterfall of rapids. It would take excellent boatmanship to read the water and guide a boat at full throttle through waves that came at us from all angles. Gerry was a champion boatman.

Looking up at Lava Falls from a safe distance, I could see a lava rock cliff over which poured an enormous amount of water that gathered in the center of the river. Some boaters coming downstream over this rapid hadn't lived to tell their stories. We pulled ashore well below the rapids and Gerry ventured upstream alone in his boat to read the water and find the best possible route through the convulsive waves. I took one look from shore and was convinced it would be impossible. The center cascade of the falls was at least twelve feet high, with the heaviest fall converging in the center. To the sides were rocky and impossibly shallow entries that would have been sheer madness to attempt with an outboard.

Gerry returned to announce that he had found the best possible route. With fearful anticipation, I joined him and Jack in the lead boat, and we headed into the maelstrom. The falls grew so loud that it was impossible to hear anything else. As we approached, they appeared to grow larger and roar even louder. There would be no retreat once inside the largest of the waves.

I felt a deep awe for the crashing power of this place, and it occurred to me that we should turn back out of respect. There was only a moment to consider such a thing before Gerry gave full throttle toward the centermost and biggest wave, easily ten feet high; but no amount of thrust would allow our boat to climb over the top of the wave.

I was prepared for action, even if that meant abandoning ship and swimming for it, when something unexpected and terrifying happened. The boat held steady for a long moment in the raging torrent, with the bow in the air and the propellers shaking wildly in cavitation. I must have glanced around, wondering what to do next, when the props finally caught water and pitched the boat violently forward, high over the top of the wave and down into its backwaters, burying the bow beneath the next enormous wave. By some miracle, none of us were thrown from the boat. We sat immovable as the river poured in over the bow.

My instinct was to jump out immediately, but Gerry shouted, "Don't leave the boat!" As the cold water surrounded us, I looked to Jack, who was equally aghast, and then to Gerry at the helm, who I hoped had a plan for our survival. As the boat continued to sink and drift downriver half submerged, Jack and I held on to the sides as we were rocked by wave after enormous wave. An eternity passed before the boat was three-quarters filled with water and Gerry finally gave the command to jump from the boat and swim like hell.

Once away from the boat, I found myself giggling with joy, bouncing in my life jacket as I was swept up and over one tall wave, and down into the next trough, and then up again for another ride. When I reached an eddy, I swam to the rocks at the side of the river and climbed onto a large boulder, absolutely ecstatic despite having been turned back by Lava Falls. I spotted Jack a few yards below on another rock and went to join him. Scared and totally shaken by trauma, he was not a happy man. I felt sorry for this dedicated and successful New York investment manager who had little or no outdoor experience. Having had absolutely no idea what he was signing up for, he had just risked his life willingly for a friend. I tried to bring some levity to the occasion, bragging about our feat of survival and how it would be such a great story for his grandchildren, but it was some time before he could be cheered up.

Gerry did have a plan for our survival, and it worked: let the boat sink first so it would not hit us after we went overboard. He floated farther down the river, staying close to our submerged craft, and was finally picked up by the second boat, which towed the waterlogged vessel to the closest sandy shore. Jack and I remained on the rocks for several hours, happily warming ourselves in the sun until we were rescued. We spent that night planning our retreat and preparing the sunken boat for towing. It could still be used to carry supplies.

The return to the Lake Mead boat ramp was slow and tedious, and everyone was in a depressed mood. Gerry was solemn after the defeat, but neither he nor I had ever doubted that we would survive the attempt. For me, this was just business as usual after deciding to spend my life with an adventurous soul. I came to believe in the old adage: "In the end, we only regret the chances we didn't take."

Gerry brought a great deal of excitement and danger into our lives, and I was determined to find the courage to live through just such challenging adventures as running the Colorado River backwards in a speedboat. Gerry had a way with people and could talk them into things they considered impossible. Undaunted by what had happened on his second try, he enlisted pioneer ski filmmaker Warren Miller to document his third attempt. Gerry would pay for the boats and gear, and Warren and he would share the royalties from the movie.

Jimmy Pflueger immediately agreed to come along. He and Gerry were both strong, mechanically minded, and seasoned boatmen.

There was also a journalist, a Malibu dentist named Jim Beardmore, and another friend of Gerry's, Chuck Fester, who begged to be included. Jimmy brought along a surfer friend from Hawaii. The preparations and specific timing of the trip were kept secret, since failure was likely, in which case negative public scrutiny was assured. On the day of departure, Jimmy sat on the sand at Lake Mead with the two boats, which were designed to ramp up on a plane but turned out to be doggedly slow. After Jimmy took apart the engine covers and adjusted the timing, Gerry got behind the wheel and hit the gas. It took off like a rocket, planed up, and hit the high speeds for which it was designed. He took a wide turn and then passed back by Jimmy and said, "See you later," and sped away, leaving Jimmy to get the other boat going.

"Nobody catches Gerry Cooper," Jimmy always said. "Unless Gerry is asleep."

On the fourth day, the expedition reached Lava Falls. Chuck Fester joined Gerry in his boat as they tried to climb up and over the largest central wave, could not reach sufficient speed, and were quickly swallowed by the next one. The boat's bow was again plunged underwater and sank rapidly. The two men jumped from the boat to swim down through the rapids and were rescued by Jimmy in the second boat. The engines of both boats were damaged by the infiltration of cold water and silt. The sunken vessel was pulled ashore into an eddy below the rapids. The trip downriver was yet another sad retreat as well as a financial disaster. *Life* magazine published an article about Gerry and the expedition, which surely was more important to him than any financial reward.

Despite being turned back at Lava Falls, Warren's film captured the high drama and spectacular scenery of the Grand Canyon, including footage of strapping men carrying supplies and manning the helms of their high-performance powerboats. The film was sold as Up the Raging Colorado to a successful television series called

Man and the Challenge. Warren and Gerry shared royalty checks from their adventure for years to come. The film celebrated the indomitable spirit of men who raced their boats into danger. Few people knew that a woman had been along on an identical attempt a year earlier.

Only a year after Gerry's third failed attempt, there were advances in nautical engineering that transformed travel on the Colorado River. Jetboats allowed boaters to go over the rocks in ways that no propeller boat ever could. It is ironic that what Gerry admired most, the cutting edge of motorsports technology and innovation, ultimately outpaced him. I never asked him if he felt defeated by this. In any case, his courage and determination have become a part of family legend.

Many years later, a group of Cooper family members ran the Colorado River in rafts. On the appropriate day of the journey, my youngest son Brant mentioned to his raft guide that he was likely going to swim Lava Falls himself in honor of his father. The river guide said he thought it was a bad idea—falling into forty-nine-degree water that was roiled into house-sized waves. But Brant is nothing if not his father's son, so you can probably guess how that turned out.

CHAPTER FIFTEEN

Cap's Cove

One morning, Gerry called Harry Gesner to show him a piece of property for sale north of Malibu. They met at the Trancas Restaurant, drove north four miles to Nicholas Beach, walked to the cliff's edge, and looked down to see a perfect wave breaking toward shore. Somewhere down there was a beachfront lot for sale. Harry took one look at that wave and said, "Buy it," and only then asked, "So, where exactly is the lot?"

Our land turned out to be at the south end of a half-mile-long stretch of pristine beach with a few old beach homes above the sand on a steep, grassy hill. Gerry loaned Harry $10,000 of the $35,000 he needed to buy the lot next to ours. Harry then walked into a bank in Santa Monica to arrange financing for construction and found that banks wouldn't make a loan for a house that far out of the city on a nearly deserted beach. "Then I noticed a face in the bank, a guy sitting in the back who I had designed a house for," Harry recalled. "I waved at him and he waved back. I looked down at the sign on his desk, and it said 'President.' So, that's how I got the loan."

Harry had recently gone from building homes to designing them. Even without an architect's license, he completed "Eagle's Watch" in 1958 in the Malibu Hills, accessible only by a three-hundred-foot tramway. He also designed the famous Fred Cole house above the

Sunset Strip in Hollywood. When it came time to build our dream house, we called our old friend Harry.

Only later did we find out that Nicholas Beach was called Cap's Cove, named after Cap Watkins. The former captain of all Santa Monica lifeguards, Watkins still lived on the rocks above the point, in a wheelhouse he salvaged off a tugboat. He was a grand old man and still very active, as we later found to our amazement. Cap's office had once been on the Santa Monica Pier in the La Monica Ballroom, a favorite destination for roller-skating before it was demolished after being damaged by fire in 1962. Anyone who grew up in Santa Monica at that time knew the pier intimately. As a youngster, I rode the old carousel on the pier and sometimes succeeded in grabbing the gold ring. The reward was one free ride.

Cap's Cove was a secret surf spot on the wild northern edge of Malibu. Cap's wheelhouse was surrounded by heaps of driftwood and seashells cemented into mosaics, all "very Gaudí," as my daughter Candy remembers it. My daughter Kelley called it an "elf boathouse" and as a kid wanted nothing more than to live there. Cap always slept outside unless it was raining. Inside, there were two bunks and a galley. The first time my children ever heard a man snoring was when they sneaked over to Cap's one day to find him sleeping in his hammock.

Cap was always happy to see the children, but he also loved to party in his retired years, and many celebrities came to party with him, including Marilyn Monroe. Johnny Weissmuller and his costar, Maureen O'Sullivan, well-known for acting in the Tarzan films, also came to the cove. Although famous surfers like Joe Quigg, Tom Zahn, and Duke Kahanamoku all surfed there, the locals always said with a straight face that there was never any good surf at Cap's Cove. Harry made several trips to the cove to get the feel of the place. After sketching designs from shore, he found that the best place to view the site would be from the ocean, so he took his old Velzy Jacobs twelve-foot balsa wood surfboard out through the waves and made sketches with a grease pencil while rolling up and down on the swells outside the break.

We rented an old beach shack in Cap's Cove while Harry and Gerry formed plans for an ambitious residence that came to be known as Wave House. While our home was being built, we survived many months of dampness, bugs, and difficult sleeping conditions in this dilapidated old structure that was barely sealed against the weather. We had four small children at the time, but the house had only two small bedrooms upstairs and one downstairs. Gerry and I were in one bedroom, with Kelley and Christin in the other. Alberta Harris came to live with us, replacing Maddie, and she took the downstairs room, which was a makeshift living space in the garage. Candy and Cam lived in the adjacent "dollhouse," furnished with two bunk beds. It was truly the size of a dollhouse, and barely habitable.

The only noticeable comfort we had as a family was safety. No one we didn't know ever entered the remote cove, so there were no dangers from the outside world. Cam and Candy were nevertheless frightened at times and occasionally came to our room after waking from bad dreams. I encouraged them to last out the months until our home was finished and read them happy fairytales at night to put them to sleep. Our dog Archie was always nearby to serve as their trusted protector.

Nature brought unexpected wonders. Grunion hunting was said to take place after midnight, an activity preceded by drinking and laughter. For a few years, when I heard this talk, I thought it was all a big joke. But one full-moon night, we went to the beach and found millions of tiny fish squirming and flopping around and over our feet, a living silvery vision stretching off into the distance under the moonlight. I grabbed as many as I could, as fast as I could, but they were slippery; that's when I knew this was a game—one that was always accompanied by much laughter. We bucketed a few, but they were so small that no one had any idea what to do with them. We dove into the shallow waters after them, squealing and laughing and diving again into the silvery mass.

Harry knew we would give him free rein to create our house. He could avail himself of any type of specialty woods available at the lumber company. Gerry took him to an old warehouse and walked him down an aisle to an unused area where he found what he was looking for—wide, eight-inch-thick planks of wood obtained by the W. E. Cooper Lumber Company from an ancient coastal redwood tree many years earlier. The two men brushed a thick layer of dust from the redwood lumber as Harry's mind began to race with the possibilities.

The Duck was no more, but the jeep remained an essential part of our lives. Gerry installed a mechanical lift on it to move rocks and boulders from the surf where Harry made plans to drive seventy wooden pilings that would support the home's foundation. An enormous 176-foot deck was to be built on the pilings, extending out over the surf at high tide. The house Harry had in mind for us would ride out to meet the sea. I hoped it would also provide a warm sanctuary for our growing family. The traffic on the Pacific Coast Highway had increased on the weekends since we first arrived in Malibu, so the number of friends visiting us dropped off somewhat, except for locals in the area. Many of the parents we knew began to involve their kids in after-school activities, but those who continued to join us at the beach faced continuing contests of courage.

Bob Brandt brought his then-girlfriend Janet Leigh and her kids Kelly and Jamie Lee Curtis to Cap's Cove. Our lifestyle must have been a far cry from the urban delights and Hollywood parties Janet had grown accustomed to during the time she was married to Tony Curtis. Kelly slept overnight in the dollhouse bunks with Cameron and Candy.

"The image I have from those days is of five Adonis-like men on surfboards, riding in together on the same wave," Kelly Curtis recalled. "People were still so healthy and there were bonfires and kids always running around. Those days were the beginning of the 1960s counterculture, and the last of the Los Angeles glamour days."

Bob and Gerry both enjoyed riding the latest Triumph motorcycles. Bob also had a Mercedes-Benz Gullwing coupe, but he preferred to ride his racing bicycle on the steep hill from his home to work at 9200 Sunset Boulevard. He crashed and went into the office bloody all over on at least one occasion. Bob was a helicopter skier and a general wild man about sports, so he fit right in with our crowd.

Kelly tells of the day when Bob took her on the back of his Triumph to Armstrong Schroder's Restaurant in Beverly Hills for breakfast; and then they stopped by to visit Gerry at the Cooper Lumber Company on Pico Boulevard. In the sidecar was Janet with little Jamie Lee between her legs. A successful stockbroker, Bob married Janet six months after she divorced Tony Curtis and took her children into his active lifestyle. Bob's mother had remarried into the Hatfield store chain in the Midwest. His stepfather, Walter Brandt, had a huge estate in Burlingame, on the San Francisco Peninsula. "Bob was a great man and fine husband for my mother," said Kelly. "His idea of a home life suited her."

Our home life was a bit different, I suppose, and more dangerous. Gerry was roaring along in the jeep at high speed over the sand dunes one morning when our Kelley and Cam were thrown from the back. Gerry did not even realize they were gone until he reached the far end of the beach. As soon as Cameron was old enough to sit on a motorcycle, Gerry took him for a ride. When they returned, I saw that Cam had suffered a deep burn on his leg from the hot exhaust pipe. Gerry showed no concern and expected no tears. Even at five years old, Cam was supposed to be a tough boy. Despite Gerry's obvious disappointment in the lack of courage displayed by his son,

I took my boy in my arms and let him cry.

As the house took shape, I began to realize just how magnificent it would be. Harry designed with circles and curves rather than straight lines. The roof of the house was made of three vaulted "waves" reaching seaward, up and out, just to the point where they begin to curl into what surfers call the shoulder of the wave. Spherical and bold, resting on single beams of thick wood at the peak of each wave, the home's front faced the sea. Massive glass windows formed the front view of the fifty-six-foot by forty-four-foot sunken living area facing the ocean. It was as if we lived within rather than apart from the forces of nature, and our family's energies surged with their changing moods.

The spaces that surround us when we are young influence us forever. Our constant confrontation with the sea encouraged risk-taking. The architecture of the Wave House would surely help prepare our children to face future challenges in their lives. There were no railings on the outer deck, just a ten-foot drop to the sand below. Raised with a natural fear of the ocean's power, the children were instinctively aware of the danger, so no one ever fell off the deck. And yet, there were many close calls.

Kelley and Cameron wandered down the beach to the base of Cap's Rock one day to watch huge waves crash up against the cliffs. They determined where the high-water mark on the cliffs was and decided to climb to about six feet above it and let the waves crash just below them. "Of course, a rogue wave came barreling in, and we clutched the cliff face, only to have me swept off and pulled out to sea," Kelley recalled. "Cam dragged me back onto the beach against the suction of the water and walked me home, limping and with blood running down the back of my upper thigh." This was just another day at Cap's Cove with yet another trip to the Malibu clinic, this time for stitches.

Gerry so believed in sunbathing oils that he slathered Cam all over his body, neglecting to realize that our son would become as slippery as a grunion in the ocean. Gerry's plan was to push him on a rubber raft onto a wave close to shore to give him the thrill of riding a wave. But Cam slipped off and disappeared into the seafoam. We searched the breaking waves close to shore and for a horrified moment or two believed that our son was drowned and lost forever. At last a hand appeared, and then a foot, above the foam. We frantically grabbed him and pulled him ashore.

The changing tides reminded me continually of the rhythms of life. A sense of wonder and amazement accompanied me those years, but there was also a growing unease about the life we were living. The continuing quest for risk and danger worried me, yet there seemed to be no escape. I grew fearful for the safety of my children, and for myself. I recall also feeling distressed that I was in danger of losing my identity. I had little control over my life, but the loss of my true being was what frightened me most. Retaining my basic sense of self would, in the years to come, allow me to break through certain barriers and expand my understanding of life. But those new frontiers would have to wait until their time. Life doesn't happen all at once.

The inside of the Wave House provided safety and comfort. A massive stone fireplace, its back to the sea, broke up the sweeping view of the ocean. Harry knew it would provide solace for the eyes and give a feeling of security against the forces of nature beyond the glass. As a mother, I experienced the inner space of our home as being under an enormous bird with its body and two wings covering and protecting me and my brood, even as the storms brought surging waves under our deck.

Kelley was eight when her father came out onto the beach to drag his little outboard skiff into the water. Knowing that he would grab whichever kid was in the vicinity to join him, she hid under the deck. The waves were giant that day, and she had no desire to be in them, especially in a boat with her dad. "He peered under the deck and said something like, 'C'mon Kelley, let's go,'" she recalled. "One didn't say no to him, so out we went over the waves of the breaking surf to the still rolling water beyond. He turned off the engine and we sat there together, listening to the radio, *Time* magazine opened on his lap, lying back on the gunwale, a Pall Mall between his lips, Bain de Soleil slathered on his body."

Kelley was fingering the kelp, idly swirling the water beside the boat, when she glanced up at the horizon to see a monster swell approaching and realized that it would break over them. Kelley dared not show fear as she watched the wave steadily approach, gaining speed and mass. She finally uttered, "Dad." No response. Louder, "DAD!" He looked up, calmly extinguished his cigarette, turned off the radio, laid down his magazine, and reached for the engine pull. It started up on the first pull, thank god, and Gerry drove the boat straight up to the top of the wave as it broke, crashing down heavily on the other side, all just in time. "I remember feeling as a child that I had just escaped death," said Kelley, "and that my safety was not my father's priority. After that day, I found deeper, darker places to hide underneath the deck."

I understood Kelley's fear because I had lived through it myself; yet, since becoming a mother, I had pushed my fears into the back of my mind. I suppose this denial was necessary for me to accept the paradoxical predicament of my marriage to Gerry; the solace and independence of having my own family came with this constant risk of mortal peril. This was the half-conscious bargain I had struck years before. Gerry had been true to form since I was a girl, and so his compulsively daring nature should not have come as a surprise.

In Hawaii years before, during the summer that we became engaged, the waves grew to epic size. We were told they only got that big once every ten years. The swells were so large that the surf was breaking way out beyond the cliff and beach area of Waikiki, at "Steamer Lane"—so named because the steamers delivering tourists were not allowed closer in, where it became too shallow. Gerry arrived at the beach in front of the Royal Hawaiian Hotel where I was quietly sunning, beaching his outboard motorboat onto the sand. He called to me and Dr. Cameron Hall, a particular friend of ours who was also on the beach, to come with him for a ride. Thinking nothing of it, we climbed into the boat and roared out to sea, and by that I truly mean "out to sea." I had no idea that Gerry planned to ride those thirty-foot waves. He took us out to the break and we waited as the waves rolled in and towered over us. Just as they peaked and began to break, he gunned the motor and gained enough speed to charge over them, launching us into the air each time to come down with a hard crash on the far side in a flurry of foam. No one else was anywhere near us. No surfers at that time dared to brave this kind of surf. I am not sure we would have survived if the boat capsized. We finally took a circuitous route between the breaking waves to return to the beach. Even now, I can feel the depth of that true terror. Gerry seemed to enjoy bringing our fears into focus and testing everyone's courage.

Our new home turned out to be as audacious as the lifestyle Gerry had created for us. *Life* magazine published a five-page feature story about Wave House, cementing Harry's career and shining a spotlight on the Cooper family. The story, titled "A Bold Splash of a Beach Home," featured our family living and playing within the rambling six-bedroom structure that included a children's wing, courtyard, art studio, and dining room. A stained-glass wall was designed in a water, seaweed, and turbulent sky pattern to reflect the ocean elements.

The ancient redwood slabs were fashioned into long tables that extended from each side of the living area, with one full-length redwood table at the center. The children used them as springboards during their competitive play and antics. The master bedroom and bath had a large sunken bath that could fit all the children for bathing together in the evenings. Alberta Harris, our live-in help, took the bedroom and bath closest to the kitchen. Although we lived on a rugged shoreline at the base of a cliff, every modern convenience filled our home, including a state-of-the-art entertainment center and one of the first microwave ovens among our circle of friends. Alberta and the kids were trained to keep a glass of water inside it at all times because we heard that the thing would explode if it were turned on when empty.

Following the *Life* magazine story was an article in the *Los Angeles Times* with a full front-page photograph of Gerry and yet more coverage about our home and our lives, with full-color photographs. In the story, Gerry described himself as a "motorsports millionaire." This article would prove to be a source of friction between Gerry and me, as it was a graphic mirror of the lies and deceptions that were becoming disruptive to our relationship. He was not a millionaire but wanted to come off as one. Everything he said to the journalist was an exaggeration of who he was. I grew up in Los Angeles, and the people reading this were my friends. Gerry just shrugged it off and laughed about it. Everything was a joke to him. I can see now that he had low self-esteem and was trying to build himself up. Perhaps this also explained his many ensuing affairs.

In 1960, we lived on the Malibu frontier. There were only four or five old beach homes in Cap's Cove at that time. To our north was the empty lot where Harry built his home, Sandcastle, in 1970. Somewhere down the beach lived Hank Searls, the author of Overboard. His films were already being made into movies. After the heyday of our years at Cap's Cove, Hank wrote a poem honoring our dog Archie and his master:

THE SURVIVOR
Archie limped past on the beach today
Where the wet sand meets the dry.
(His God used to heave him, you see,

All the brutal mastiff pounds,
To the Triumph's battered gas-tank,
Paws scratching for a hold, and
Steady him between arms and handlebars.)
"Never wash a motorcycle," God would say,
"the dirt holds it all together."
And they would race their reflection
down the shimmering low-tide sand,
Archie for once outdistancing shepherds
And labs and lesser breeds.
(Archie also taxied lightplanes until they were caught.)
Anyway, he limped past today, tongue lolling,
He must have been twelve, right foot sore
(or faking it: "Biggest ham in the world.")
God knows what he was looking for.
—Hank Searls, Malibu, 1971

Today, all but the old beach house we first rented, Harry's Sandcastle, and our Wave House have been demolished and renovated. Many have been renovated by Harry, who has stayed on at Cap's Cove. There are eight homes in the cove today. The original house my family huddled into when we were building our own home has been added onto numerous times and now boasts a swimming pool. It recently sold for $26 million.

One day shortly after we moved into the Wave House, Harry received a surprise telephone call from Danish architect Jørn Utzon, who had won the design competition for the Sydney Opera House in 1957. Utzon's original design had the appearance of a fleet of high masts with billowy white sails. The sails were planned to be in the shape of a parabola or ellipse. But according to Harry, in 1961 the engineers decided that it would be more structurally sound to have the sails in the shape of a prescribed segment of a sphere. Our house had been highly publicized by then, with recognition from as far away as Russia. After seeing the Wave House in a European magazine, Utzon called Harry to express his appreciation of the design. He introduced himself simply as "an architect" and said he was very taken with the design and how fitting it was for the site.

Harry said he was honored and impressed by the call, as it was from overseas and an expensive call in those days. He has never claimed any influence on Utzon's Opera House, but it does share many of the same motifs as our Wave House. He humbly explained the coincidence in this way: "An inspirational concept comes from a collection of parts and pieces of all we experience in the act of everyday living and that wonderful sauce called imagination."

In 2012, a book titled *Houses of the Sundown Sea: The Architectural Vision of Harry Gesner* was published. The Cooper Wave House is pictured full-page on the front cover and has its own chapter, accompanied by photos of the home and our family living there. As Harry's designs became well-known around the world, he received letters requesting that he take the California architect certification tests. He never responded to those letters, nor did he take the required classes or tests, officially remaining a "designer." At some point later in his career, he received a letter informing him that he was now certified as an architect in the state of California. Harry said he was grateful for the honor but had already done quite well without a license. At ninety-five, he still climbs the spiraling driftwood stairs high up into an aerie of a studio, completing his architectural drawings by hand.

CHAPTER SIXTEEN

The Human Taxicab

My primary role in life during the Malibu years became that of family chauffeur. I transported my growing brood to an ever-shifting landscape of schools, dance halls, sports fields, and horse-riding arenas. The venues changed regularly based on the children's ages. It was a game of musical chairs that leaves my head spinning as I reflect on it.

Candy and Cameron started kindergarten and then first grade at the nearby Juan Cabrillo Elementary School, named after the man whose treasure we failed to unearth. They later attended St. Augustine by the Sea School, farther away in Santa Monica. Cam then attended Carlthorp School until sixth grade and went on to Lincoln Junior High School for seventh. Candy went to St. Augustine through the sixth grade and then attended Marlborough for two years. By then, Kelley had attended a new Montessori School in Malibu, then Carlthorp from grades one through six. Christin and Brant, my two youngest, attended St. Aidan's School in Malibu. Christin then switched to St. Augustine for one year before she and Brant went together to Carlthorp. It's like we were a band of gypsies, covering thousands of miles of highway travel even before they were old enough to require transportation to a myriad of after-school activities at various locations around Malibu and Santa Monica. Gerry would deliver kids on his way to work in the morning. I picked them up in the afternoon. The uniforms came off the minute they arrived home, and out onto the beach they ran.

Christin's attendance at St. Augustine came to an end when her older sister Candy came running down from her sixth-grade classroom to grab her from the basement. The building was on fire, and the children were evacuated in time to watch both the school and church burn to the ground. Up in smoke went the church where Gerry and I were married. Although my grandfather, PG Winnett, never said a word about it, it must have been devastating for him to lose the church he had commissioned so many years before and which held so many family memories.

By the time all five kids were in schools, our morning departures bordered on chaotic. They each needed to be dressed in the clothes laid out for them the night before, their rooms picked up, beds made. After breakfast, there would be a call to arms in my best trumpet voice: "Do you have your homework, your books, your lunch boxes, and whatever for show and tell?" Then they all ran for the car. Our black Chrysler Woody station wagon had a large, protective box designed at the Cooper Lumber Company to harness the two youngest wildlings in the rearmost seat. It was a clever prototype of the child's safety seat, made of the strongest wood, four feet by four feet in size and lined on all sides with deep green padded leather. With no seat belts in use at that time, this was their father's way to keep them from being tossed around and hurt from a sudden stop or change of direction. The Cooper Lumber Company would have done well to market this clever child carrier.

Cam and Candy traded off sitting in the front seat with me—a special treat reserved for anyone disciplined enough to keep from wiggling around. Behind us sat whoever had not called shotgun or been previously assigned a seat alongside Kelley. The farthest back seat held Christin and Brant, who eagerly awaited graduation from the wooden safety box to a spot with more visibility. Nothing could prevent Cam from creating bedlam when he was in the middle seat. He wrestled and poked anyone close to him. His jibes were returned until it turned into a fighting match. Shouting over my shoulder while cruising down the Pacific Coast Highway had no effect. On several occasions, I became so exasperated that I pulled over and ordered the miscreants out, slammed the door, and drove away. I could see in the rearview mirror their shocked faces as I drove out of sight. Of course, I did a U-turn and came back for them. It would be blissfully quiet for the rest of that drive. A parent caught doing this today would surely end up with a jail sentence for child abandonment.

I made an attempt to interest my kids in Sunday school and even taught a Sunday school class to get them to go with me, but their father was no help. He teased them as they left, telling them with his sly smile of temptation about the exciting activities they would be missing at the beach. They sulked and complained so much on the way to church that I abandoned my intention to introduce them to religion. If they were going to find spirituality in their lives, it would be through their own personal discoveries and chosen paths. However, I may have earned points in heaven for looking out for my kids' nutrition.

I was an early devotee of Adele Davis, a nutritionist who first started writing cookbooks in the 1940s. I found a copy of her book *Let's have Healthy Children* and at once took to her nutritional advice, avoiding unprocessed foods and giving them vitamin supplements. By the 1960s, Davis was getting media attention for pointing out the dangers of pesticide residue, vitamin deficiencies, extensive intake of fats and sugar, and the benefits of healthy eating and exercise. Her ideas came at a perfect time for me as a mother, and they continue to influence my lifestyle to this day.

Yet, Adele Davis's ideas weren't always met with enthusiasm by my ravenous youngsters. On the way home from school, we always made a stop at the nutritional food store on the highway in Malibu because everyone wanted a treat. I allowed them each a carob brownie, the same healthy treat I added to their school lunches. But the grumbling grew louder each day as I heard that all the other children had Twinkies in their lunch boxes. As a mother, you have to pick your battles to win the war, so Twinkies became their lunch box dessert—just so that they would not be ostracized by their friends. At that time, I also added spinach to their eggs in the morning. They said it only became edible when added with tiny slices of hot dog, sausage, or bacon. For desserts, I presented "strawberries and cream," which was in fact plain yogurt and frozen berries. They never knew the difference, and I am happy now that my early obsession with health foods had a positive influence on their lives.

My career as a human taxicab quickened when a diverse schedule of extracurricular activities and sports were added to the mix. Candy owned her own horse, Calazar's High Voltage, which was stabled in Pacific Palisades, where she took riding lessons. Gerry took such an interest in her sport that he spent a weekend building jumps out of driftwood on the hard sand above the high tide line. The whole family sat entranced while we watched her practice at Cap's Cove.

A few years later, Candy was appointed to the prestigious Trainer's Team of four horse-and-rider pairs selected to represent their stables at a three-event show in Fresno. She won third place in cross-country and second place in stadium jumping. This earned Candy the title of "reserve champion," with three trophies overall. When Candy received her awards, the woman presenting them said she hoped that now her mother would buy her some riding clothes that did not look like hand-me-downs. That got my attention. I whisked Candy off to a local saddle shop and purchased some beautiful new riding outfits and boots.

Cam, the next in line, joined the baseball and swim teams. The third oldest, Kelley, became a dedicated ice-skater, studying with some of the finest instructors available at the Santa Monica Ice Rink, including John Nicks, the coach of famous pair skaters Tai Babilonia and Randy Gardner. I drove Kelley to practice almost daily since she was committed to entering competitions.

Another popular activity was ballroom dancing with the Unander Cotillion at the Wilshire Ebell Theatre. This was a popular destination, also on Wilshire Boulevard. Cam especially loved the opportunity to dress in a suit and tie and dance with the girls. Candy was less thrilled. She complained about having to dance with "yucky boys and wear pointy shoes," calling the dancehall a "torture chamber." Kelley loved dressing up in her lace socks, patent leather shoes, and a fancy dress, just as I did when I was a girl. She had two decidedly un-yucky boys from Carlthorp School with whom she very much liked to dance. The evening dance school was offered by Commander Richard Unander and his wife Jayne, the sister of Luanne Wells and Molly Chappellet. Commander was there when he was not off flying as a commercial pilot. These classes were fully attended every night they were scheduled, a sign of the times.

My shopping trips to Bullock's became fewer because the store seemed so far away now, and I was reluctant to endure yet another chaotic drive through downtown with my kids. I never admitted this to my parents, but I found a shop in Westwood that outdid even the Bullocks Wilshire children's department. It was called Dena Carl. My babysitter, Peggy O'Neill, worked there. She convinced me of the quality of the clothing, hand-sewn and widely embroidered, with a child's monogram upon request. In some mother's fantasy of perfection, I dressed Candy and Cam in matching Dena Carl outfits until they were old enough to rebel. Standing there like little junior aristocrats, they thought I must be joking. They made it clear that the JCPenney department store in Santa Monica was their preferred shopping destination. We did, however, always go to Bullocks Wilshire for Christmas because they had a very convincing

Santa Claus—surely the real one. The salespersons knew me and loved to see the children, PG's great-grandchildren. We went to the children's barbershop, noted for its excellence. Some parents would take their children nowhere else. Bullocks Wilshire still had a certain old Los Angeles mystique, even though the world outside its doors was changing. I would look up at the once towering and impressive spire on the building to see other tall buildings now crowded around it. The neighborhood was not as desirable for a shopping destination as it had once been.

During the holidays, there was a Christmas dance and table ornament decoration contest at the Ebell Theatre. Cam created a volcano with dry ice one year, but the smoke came out at the bottom instead of the top, to the dismay of all the adults and the amusement of the children. Alberta saved a turkey bone one year, and my kids painted it gold so that it looked like a sled and placed a Santa and reindeer in front of it, with presents on top. The next year, they made an igloo out of sugar cubes.

I felt that my own creativity had been stifled since leaving college, or just subsumed in the affairs of starting a family, which was, of course, a creative and rewarding journey of a different sort. But something else was brewing for me in the background. Thanks to Alberta's help at home, I was able to steal away for art history studies in early 1961 to become a guide for the art department at the Los Angeles Museum of Natural History, Science, and Art in Exposition Park. These studies revived in me interests that had lain dormant for a number of years. Following this path altered my life in ways I could not yet imagine.

Meanwhile, Gerry's motorsports activities proceeded as before. He was gone most weekends. I still trusted him, and it never occurred to me that he would be up to anything but racing with his friends.

CHAPTER SEVENTEEN

A European Perspective

Gerry and I managed to take a vacation during those first hectic years in the Wave House—a ski trip to Europe with Warren Miller and his wife. The Millers invited us to join them at several resorts while Warren shot one of his increasingly popular ski movies. Although Gerry didn't care for the sport, the opportunity to ski in the Alps with Warren as our guide was too much for me to resist. I, for one, longed to return to Europe for any reason at all. Gerry seemed less thrilled as it would put him out of his element and away from his boats and other motor-racing machines. But we came together on a plan once we acknowledged that this was to be a once-in-a-lifetime adventure with our good friends.

I insisted that our oldest children, Candy and Cameron, join us for the experience. Kelley and Christin happily stayed behind with a wonderful older lady who loved small children and had proven herself to be caring and competent. Gerry planned to return to California earlier than the rest of us; I assumed he would then spend time on the weekends with our kids. Desiring to speak as much French as possible, after we arrived in Paris, I hired a young French girl named Caterine de Barbarin to travel with us. She turned out to be delightfully naïve and gullible when it came to Cam and Candy's jokes.

We went first to Milan to visit some friends—Will Hanley and his family, whom we knew from Malibu. This gave the children a chance to see kids their age. The Milan Cathedral, piazzas, and the Sforza Castle were a revelation to me. There was so much history and such a short amount of time to soak it up. Gerry was not at all interested. He had never been to a country where English was not the dominant language, so he felt bereft and incompetent as a tourist in a foreign land. While I expressed wonder, trying to engage my children in the sights around them, he spoke only of his distaste for the "big, noisy city."

The skiing was extraordinary and unbounded, so different from the tightly confined resorts of America. Lifts took us up from charming towns to wide open, treeless runs that led over one mountain to an entirely different town on the other side, and to yet another tempting resort. We stopped first at Kitzbühel, Austria, in the Tyrolean Alps, a wonderful medieval town of heavily buttressed walls and painted frescoes, perhaps the most beautiful town in Austria. The terrain was staggering in its richness, with the Alps rising above the valley on all sides. I stood at the top of a run and took in a deep breath of disbelief at what lay before me.

The hotels Warren brought us to were mystifying in their simple homeliness; we felt comfortable and relaxed in their welcoming ambience. I noticed the exquisite old furnishings of masterfully carved wood that must have been inherited from generations of earlier hoteliers. We almost always chose the Post Hotel, reputed to have come down through decades of ownership and always located in the center of a town. More than once I found an Austrian ski instructor who had worked in Sun Valley, Idaho, before returning home with improved English to take over a family's Post Hotel.

Warren filmed as we went. We met his contacts, made new friends, and of course skied every day. He took us next to the Lech Zürs am Arlberg ski resort. I arranged ski lessons for Candy, Cam, and for Caterine. The children by now had decided that they wanted to teach Caterine the California slang English she really wanted to learn but played tricks on her as well. They convinced her that "water" in English was pronounced "vasser," which they had only just picked up in Austria. I had to spend some time straightening all this out. Meanwhile, Gerry struck out to find other adventures on his own.

I was sitting with the Millers and my kids on the train a day or two later, en route to another resort in Austria, when we looked out the window to see on the highway next to the train tracks a sports car driving at top speed to keep up with us. Gerry had finally found a way to make himself feel a part of European culture. He had traveled to Stuttgart, Germany, for a visit to the Mercedes factory. There, he managed to commandeer a Mercedes-Benz 300 SL Gullwing. We all knew it was Gerry racing along beside us, no doubt wearing that grin of his. I suspect he was quite disappointed when the train finally outpaced him. In any case, Gerry was finally happy, driving the European highways at full speed in a roadster. He ended up buying the car, the last one to come off the factory line, according to him, and had it shipped home. This purchase made the entire European trip worthwhile for him.

At our final ski resort in the Chamonix Valley, I was given what remains my iconic memory of all European skiing. From Chamonix rises the massive Mont Blanc, the highest peak in Europe, situated on the border of France and Italy and reaching into Switzerland. Its summit is in France. From the valley floor rise all the *aiguilles* (rock pinnacles) *de Chamonix*. The view of the glaciers from there left an unforgettable sense of the Alps' magnitude. We rode the Aiguille de Midi cable car from the center of Chamonix to reach the highest peak above the town. At the top, the cable car entered into a cliff where it deposited us at a stairway to terraces on the surface of a glacier. From there, we had a 360-degree view of the Swiss, Italian, and French Alps and a clear view of Mont Blanc. After one more lift, we could have skied down into Italy.

Warren's plan was, instead, to guide us across the Col du Midi glacier. Also called the Vallée Blanche, it is a twenty-kilometer ski route with the challenge and thrill that can only come from continual navigation around crevasses. With total trust in Warren and his skiing and guiding capabilities, I set off behind him, my heart beating wildly. During moments of rest, I could look up and see awesome views of the Alps. Warren would regularly shout at me not to stray from the "piste," or track. He had earlier lectured us about what lay to the side of the trail—deep crevasses from which one could not be rescued. It seemed an endless descent before we skied over the most critical terrain of ice blocks to a road where a bus met skiers to return them to their hotels.

Our final family days were spent in Paris, where I looked up an old friend, Marian Pike. Gerry had by this time departed for California. Marian invited us to stay at L'hôtel Madison, where she lived and painted. It was an older hotel on the left bank of the Seine in Saint-Germain-des-Prés in the Sixth Arrondissement. The elevator was housed in old cage-like doors cast in iron with ornate designs. They clanged musically when they closed; this fascinated the children, who wanted to drive the elevator themselves using its single lever. The hotel's dining room was small, as were all the famous local restaurants, such as the Les Deux Magots and Brasserie Lipp, which were frequented by artists. The Saint-Germain area was an artists' enclave and a bustle of feverish excitement. In the 1940s and 1950s, the quarter had been the center of the existentialist movement. Marian always wanted to be in the center of anything even slightly revolutionary, so Saint-Germain's reputation would have drawn her naturally to this part of Paris.

We enjoyed many hours together, visiting Marian's favorite hideouts and restaurants. As she painted in her hotel room, we talked late into the night about the issues that were beginning to surface in my marriage to Gerry and the possibility that I might one day pursue a career in the arts. I confessed that Gerry did not share my interests. She told me that this had been the reason for her own divorce years earlier.

That night, she painted a portrait of me to join the others from my high school years, all the while talking, occasionally studying my face before going back to work on the canvas. She told me of her affair with Coco Channel and the possibility that they would soon be living together in Coco's luxurious apartment.

Marian, as always, inspired me to follow my deepest dreams and desires, no matter how radical they seemed to others. It is a gift to know someone like that—a person who helps you understand who you are and what you can achieve in your life. I left Paris with a renewed confidence in my own interests and a growing faith that I would one day move toward the fulfillment of my own destiny.

CHAPTER EIGHTEEN

Hollywood and Politics

Although I never pursued friendships with Hollywood celebrities, associations with them came as an inevitable result of the glamourous ambience of Bullocks Wilshire and the natural development of childhood friendships. The movie industry always seemed cliquish and ephemeral in its tastes and preoccupations. But of course, we all loved going to the movies, and occasionally some actors and filmmakers even became close friends.

Bob Brandt, Janet Leigh's husband, had many Beverly Hills investment contacts. He was an attractive bachelor and a popular guest at Hollywood gatherings. Bob had met Janet through a Hollywood agent named Mort Viner. The wedding took place in Las Vegas, and Gerry served as an usher. We sat with Janet and Bob at their table during the reception, when their friend Dean Martin sang one of his best crooning songs for the bride and groom, "Fly Me to the Moon."

Janet and Bob remained family friends, even more so when we all came together again during the Sun Valley years. Our kids all meshed in ages, so there were trips together to the Colorado River, where everyone raced about in motorboats or floated around together on tubes, by then even wearing lifejackets. I guess family life had tamed us somewhat.

Bob and Janet invited us to attend a Democratic fundraiser for

John F. Kennedy at the home of actor Peter Lorre, who owned one of those oceanfront Santa Monica beach houses on the Pacific Coast Highway still so treasured by celebrities. As Republicans, neither Gerry nor I knew anyone at the party, nor did anyone care to talk to us. It was not my favorite Hollywood event. Later, I heard the rumor that Jack Kennedy met Marilyn Monroe in one of those beachfront houses.

I was not influenced to change political parties after attending any of Janet's events, hearing the speeches and calls to arms. I was turned off by the fact that the celebrities felt they all had to belong to the same political party and entertain only their favorite Democratic candidates. I remained at that time the product of my upbringing. My grandfather and father embodied the traditional Eisenhower Republican agenda: lower taxes and reduced government spending and regulations were all incentives for investment that resulted in the stimulation of a strong economy. In any case, I was not involved in politics, as were some of our friends.

Although I like to think I am immune to the popular fascination with celebrities, I got a little wobbly in the knees when Bob and Janet introduced me to Gene Kelly at a tennis tournament fundraiser. He and I were to play together as a mixed doubles team. I had played on those courts many times before as Bob's partner, but on that day I was so nervous and starstruck that I could hardly get a ball over the net. I kept apologizing, and Gene—fine man that he was—kept telling me it didn't matter. But it did matter to me that I lost my wits and became discombobulated while playing tennis with this actor who was larger than life in my imagination.

Janet was a proud member of the Academy Awards Committee, which nominated the final films and creators for the coveted golden Oscar statuettes. She explained to us each year why these films—around thirty of them—were critically acclaimed. She had to watch them all before her vote could be counted. On one occasion, she invited us to a large, elegant party at the home of Kirk Douglas. The rooms in his extravagant home were filled with beautifully dressed celebrities and their friends. The champagne flowed continually. Many of the guests were leaders in the film industry and contenders for Academy Awards. But this really wasn't our crowd, and Gerry and I felt out of place.

When it came time to leave, I went to pick up my coat, but it was no longer there. This was the finest, most beloved coat I have ever owned—a full-length wraparound white cashmere given to me by my mother, something from Bullocks Wilshire that I never would have bought for myself. I was distraught. When I found Janet and told her what had happened, she did not seem at all interested in getting involved or hearing anything further about it. These were, after all, her associates and friends. I returned to the coatroom and searched for it myself, the attendants carefully following my every move. I mentioned it to the host, but no one seemed to think this was anything to be bothered about. Gerry was no help. He just wanted to get out of there before I embarrassed both of us. I mistakenly thought that this would be one party venue in which I could place my highest trust. My distress surely had to do with the fact that by then my mother had succumbed almost entirely to her illness. I treasured that coat as emblematic of the fine taste she was once known for and the fading memory of her once-iconic status.

Through Janet and her kids, we were also invited to attend Hollywood-style birthday parties, which turned out to be competitions for extravagance. The goal was to be so over-the-top that the parties would be talked about—meaning, they were really for the adults. But the kids had a lot of fun too. There was a circus party that included elephant rides, clowns, music men with dancing monkeys, and animals everywhere. Jamie Lee Curtis had a memorable party at The Luau, a famous 1950s tropical restaurant on Rodeo Drive in Beverly Hills. A simulated tropical rainstorm in the background at times grew so loud that nothing else could be heard.

Steve McQueen, a huge star at the time, was also a well-known motorcycle rider. For this reason, he and Gerry became good friends and rode together in the Malibu Hills. Christin went to school with the McQueens' daughter Terry, and Brant became friends for life with their son Chad through their schooling years together at Carlthorp. The McQueen and Cooper homes provided play yards for the children, and their friendships continued after our move to Sun Valley. Christin was especially fond of Steve's wife, Neale, who warmly welcomed our kids into her home. They were let in through a locked gate with an intercom, then driven up a long winding driveway and dropped by a ten-bay stone garage filled with a collection of fancy cars and motorcycles. Steve was often in the garage, working on one of his machines. The secluded grounds were expansive and included a large pool. In the house's dark and soothing den were bookshelves with large leather-bound manuscripts of the films in which he had starred. Christin recalls leafing through scripts for *The Sand Pebbles* and *The Great Escape*.

The Cooper-McQueen family friendship was one of many relationships that circle back mysteriously, as though the enduring connection was meant to be. A few years after I arrived in Sun Valley, Steve turned up with his motorcycles to find us once again. He ultimately bought a house in North Fork along the Big Wood River and married a Wood River Valley woman. Bob and Janet also came to Sun Valley, bought a condominium, and skied there every winter. Janet worked less in the movie business after marrying Bob, doing mostly variety shows and TV series. She preferred to stay home with him and support him in his business affairs.

Hollywood stardom can cast a limelight on actors and have a beguiling effect on our culture, but at the end of the day, life is just life, no matter who you are. At least, that is what I like to tell myself. But for me, Gene Kelly was in a class all his own.

CHAPTER NINETEEN

The Proxy Fight

During our years in Wave House my family was hit by an unexpected storm that impacted us for years to come. It didn't arrive in the form of wind and rain, nor did it have anything to do with the situation between Gerry and me. The metaphorical storm I describe was a prolonged battle over control of the Bullock's empire. By the time it ended, we were all forced to face new life circumstances.

My grandfather, PG Winnett, was legendary for his shrewdness, but his prowess as an old guard mercantile businessman could not prepare him for what lay ahead. The merchandizing industry was undergoing widespread growth and change across the country. In Southern California, this meant sprawling new communities that included new commercial developments and increased retail competition. The grand spire of Bullocks Wilshire, once rising on the outskirts of the City of Dreams, now sat in an urban area that was less desirable than it had been a generation earlier.

Yet, Bullock's, Inc. had also been growing and consolidating its holdings. In 1943, the company had bought the venerable I. Magnin & Co. store chain, which was founded in 1876 and based in San Francisco. With stores throughout the entire West Coast, I. Magnin was deemed the nation's second largest retailer of fine women's wear after Saks Fifth Avenue in New York. In 1950, PG was named chairman of Bullock's-I.

Magnin. He oversaw the expansion of store locations to Santa Ana and the San Fernando Valley. In 1963, Bullock's purchased the Ralph's supermarket chain and, as with the Bullock's-I. Magnin stores, now owned the land beneath their buildings. Whoever owned the company would control an increasing revenue stream from the property leases alone. PG, now eighty-three, retained personal ownership.

My father, Walter Candy, who started out wrapping boxes in the Bullock's store at Seventh and Hill Streets after he married my mother, slowly worked his way up over the years. He bragged about never missing a day's work, yet he was also there for us as a father. My brother Peter attended my father's alma mater, the Lawrenceville School near Trenton, New Jersey, before going to Stanford.

By the mid 1960s, Peter was working at Security First National Bank in Los Angeles in various capacities, having adopted a work ethic instilled in him by his father. As a young man, he took various jobs in the family business, loading trucks at Bullock's during the summer when he wasn't in school. Peter told me of those days: "I would get two weeks off from work at the beginning and end of each summer. I wasn't allowed to hang out at the beach."

Work was my father's number one priority. He was so punctual that Peter could step out of the bank building at exactly half past five and, without looking, point behind him at the line of cars on the road and know our father would be passing by at that exact time every day. He was absolutely methodical about work.

This work ethic paid off. By 1964, my father was president of Bullock's, Inc., with my grandfather serving as chairman of the board. Yet, there arose a public rift between the two men that involved the entire family. It all began when PG commissioned research by Dean Witter & Co. on a merger proposal from Federated Department Stores, Inc. If such a report is completed, federal regulations require that it be presented to the stockholders for a vote, Peter informed me.

"PG was a trailblazer in the merchandizing industry, a man

with a great eye for fashion and talent for organization," said Peter. "Bullock's had separate buyers for each department who would be sent to merchandise sources to purchase items. In Orange County, he later established the modern model for shopping centers and malls when he invited his primary competitors to join Bullock's in the shopping center. He knew that this would create a bigger geographic draw for them all, from San Bernardino, San Diego, and elsewhere. And it worked."

Yet, PG was quite authoritative and insisted on making most if not all executive decisions. This was not due to insecurity on his part but rather to his perception that he could do it better than anyone else, and he wanted things done right. But the management at Bullock's could see that, despite PG's best efforts, the marketshare they had secured was being lost to competing department stores that opened new territories in the rapidly spreading Southern California suburbs. The managers also realized that the "unitization plan" unique to Bullock's was outdated. It empowered each department of each store to have its own buyer, and each store its own executive buyers. This meant that opening a new store was far more complex, expensive, and time-consuming.

Peter was working at Security First National Bank when he received a call from the chief financial officer at Bullock's. "He was a tough guy, Mahlon Arnett," Peter said. "He said to come down by nine the next morning. When I got there, I was told that PG had given him the authority to bring me into the business, that I would train under him and possibly run the entire business one day."

Peter accepted the proposal, only to find that PG later changed his mind. He was told by other staff that our grandfather had suddenly decided not to have any more relatives working for him, and even wrote this into the company bylaws. Perhaps it went back to when PG's only son Jack had been fired twice for running things badly at the Bullock's Westwood location. Jack was an alcoholic. Perhaps it was due instead to his recognition that there was destined to be an ensuing family battle for control of the company.

"PG didn't look back much," Peter told me. "Unfortunately, he also didn't look forward. He had no management prospects rising through ranks. It was true that the doorman at the back of Bullocks Wilshire knew the name of every person who came through the portico, but Bullock's had no young, talented people in senior management capacity."

After the report from Dean Witter came back showing that a merger would be a positive development for the company's shareholders, PG simply refused to accept the offer. My grandfather was seen by the managers as unwilling to expand the business and keep pace with a rapidly expanding city. PG dug in, placing him alone in a struggle against the proposed merger with Federated Department Stores, Inc.

PG's entrenchment also pitted my immediate family against PG. If we were to vote our shares in unison with the vote of the board and our father, we would be voting against the man who created the empire and was the principal stockholder, the man to whom we owed our heritage and inheritance and the assurance of current and future comforts. For me to side with my father would mean having to vote against a grandfather I deeply loved and respected and from whom I had learned so much. My inclination was to back my grandfather, without whom there would never have been a retail empire to begin with.

It was a bitter and very public fight. PG argued in the press that the book value of Bullock's had a better earnings record than that of Federated. His opponents on the board argued that Federated would be able to present to the stockholders the safety of geographical diversification, thereby increasing marketability and the market price of shares—and, in turn, dividends. Federated would have gained an enormous income stream by having all the prime real estate under the Bullock's-I. Magnin stores to lease out.

During this period of heartbreak and confusion, a miracle occurred. My mother suddenly stopped drinking, instantaneously chose to support my father through the challenges he faced, and never drank again in her lifetime. Their love for one another resurfaced, and a wonderful and enduring relationship was reawakened. It was a marvel to experience.

I received a telephone call from PG, inviting me to join him for lunch in the Tea Room at Bullocks Wilshire, where he continued to hold court as a purveyor of LA fashion. "If you do not vote with me, I will cut you out of my will," he said. I was stunned and gave no answer. I had five children and wanted to protect their financial futures. My own father had said to me that I should vote my conscience and do whatever was best for my family, aware of the loss I could face if I sided with him.

During the proxy fight, my siblings decided at once to vote with my father; and, amazingly, so had my mother. Their newfound love and commitment to one another inspired me to stand together with my family. It brought tears to my eyes to see my mother back up my father against her own father, to whom she owed everything—every trip, every gown, every house she had ever owned. The proxy war went on for four months. PG was eventually deposed by the Bullock's board, and my father was elected chairman. Mahlon Arnett, then treasurer and loyal to the company since 1929, was elected president. Those who favored PG felt that he had been unfairly ousted from the chairmanship, and my father was blamed for that. "Walter Candy sold him out," said a friend of my grandfather's. "Walter Candy was a nice man, a good-looking handsome man, but he was not a merchant. He just married the boss's daughter."

People I knew who were employed at Bullock's spoke in favor of my father, saying it was a "very logical decision" to merge with Federated. "Candy had seen the writing on the wall," they said, "and had been kicked around long enough by Mr. Winnett. The son-in-law never had a free lunch being president of Bullock's."

The vote by the board was nearly unanimous in favor of the merger, due to its benefits to the corporation and its stockholders. In the end, PG cast the only dissenting vote. One of PG's historic quotes was used ironically in the press at the time: "Never fight change. It is our most valuable ally."

Another great irony is that the automobile, which had helped bring Bullocks Wilshire its fame during the Jazz Age, now contributed to its doom. Expansive development in Southern California created many new suburbs, and the car made them all accessible, drawing customers away from the mid-Wilshire shopping district. In an attempt to deter this migration of interest, a group of concerned Bullocks Wilshire supporters held elegant, lavish black-tie parties to which were invited foreign dignitaries, celebrities, the city's wealthiest patrons, and government officials. But the progression of inevitable urban decay and the rapid development of new suburban neighborhoods with extensive malls proved to be an indomitable force. The automobile that Bullocks Wilshire celebrated during its heyday eventually led to its demise.

With no clear road to a decision during the proxy fight and because of the emotional confusion I felt over family loyalties at that time, I decided to vote with my father and mother. As a result, not only were we children cut out of PG's will, but so was our mother. PG's estate was willed entirely to PG's other daughter, Helen Winnett Boocock—my Aunt Dougie—and her two daughters—our cousins Susie and Leslie—all of whom lived in New York, far removed from the conflict. I suppose their decision was an easy one. I have many times wondered if I made the right choice. Perhaps not. My family would not have been as impacted financially as we were. My grandfather would have loved me until his death four years later in 1968 at age eighty-seven. Perhaps he forgave me in his own way.

Despite the betrayal that PG must have felt from us, my mother continued to visit him and to lunch with him in the Tea Room. I wonder even now whether he forgave her and what they talked about after she became sober. These are questions we did not dare ask at the time, and so the answers are lost forever.

I wish I could have comprehended then what a difficult and sad time this was for my father. Public sympathy had favored my grandfather. As if wanting to put the battle behind him, my father soon retired. He was eager to enjoy the last years together with his beloved, recovered, and rediscovered wife. He never spoke about the proxy fight because it was typical in those days to keep disappointments and losses to oneself. Since there was no apparent need, I offered little support or compassion as he retired into relative solitude. He even gave up his weekend golf games with his best friends. He became sedentary and increasingly immobile and unmotivated.

In later years, I learned from my brother Peter that my father no longer attended the Los Angeles Country Club because he could not face being questioned about the family proxy fight. I am left with yet another wish that I had broken the expected silence of the times and instead reached out to him with more love and compassion.

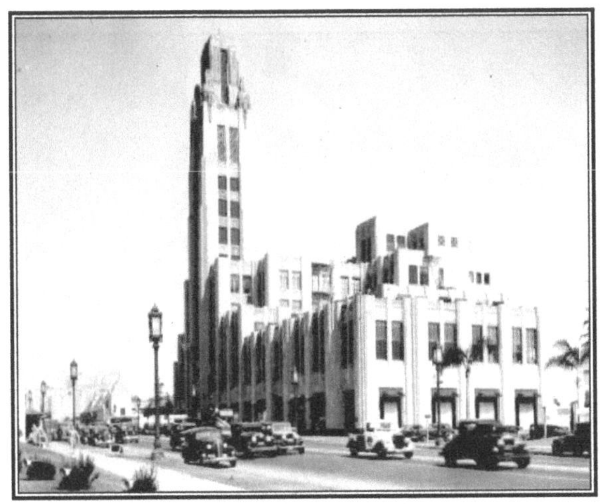

Bullocks Wilshire in the 1930s, the glamorous store built by my grandfather Percy Glenn Winnett and John G. Bullock. I was awed by the place. Attendants took me by the hand like a princess. Today the store is a historic landmark and considered an Art Deco masterpiece. Photo courtesy of the USC Digital Library, California Historical Society Collection.

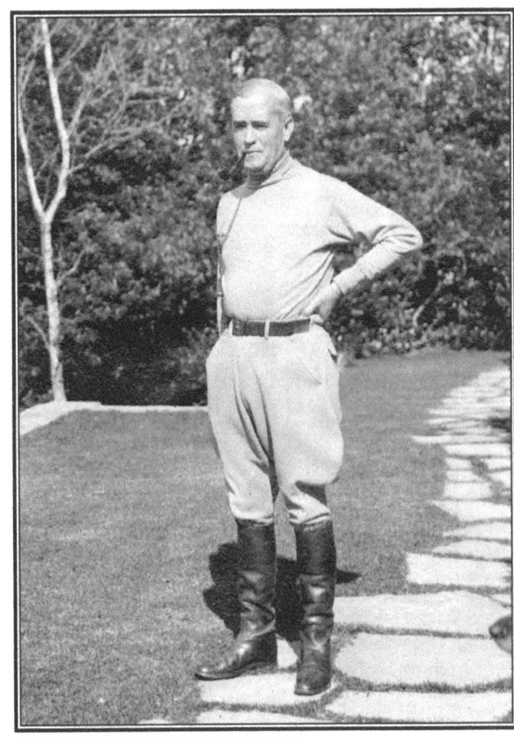

My grandfather stands in his riding attire at his ranch in Orange County, California during the 1940s. I spent weekends there with him. We had a great love for one another. He was a mentor for me.

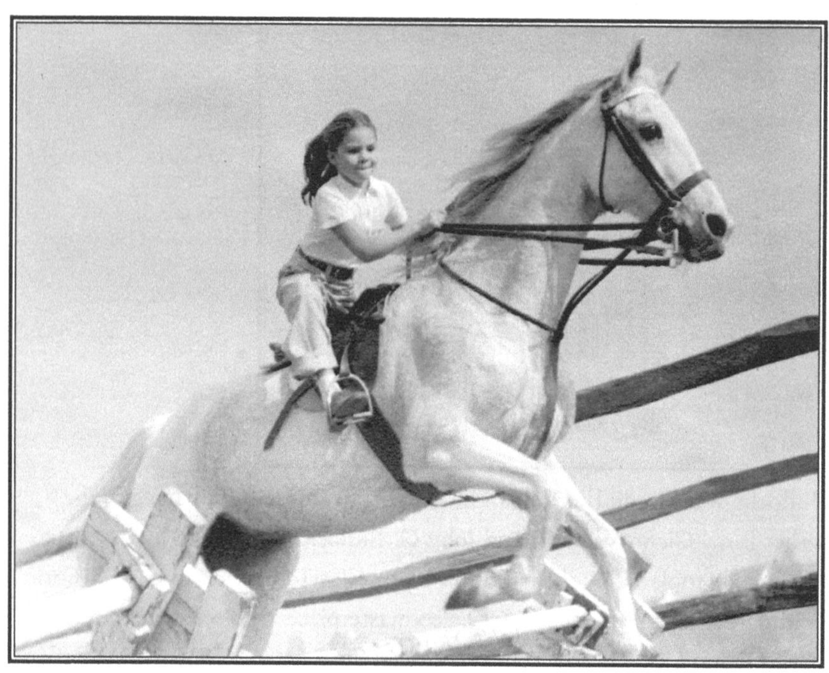

My beloved horse Lady Grey took me over jumps at Egon Mertz's Stables in Brentwood during the early 1940s.

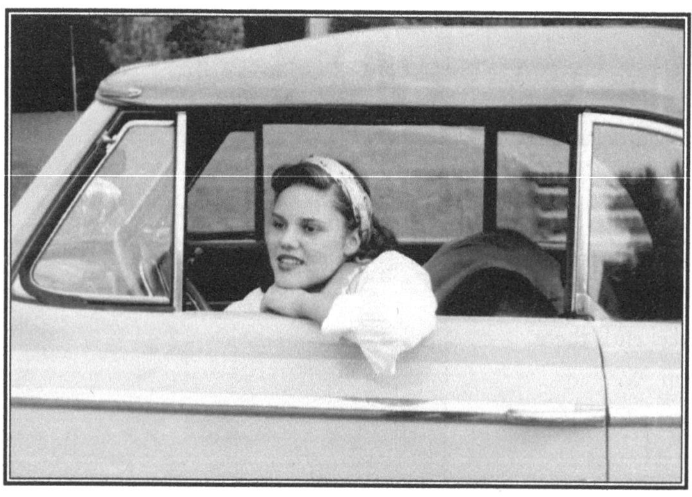

This yellow Ford convertible was a gift from my grandfather when I was 15 years old. All my friends wanted me to pick them up on the way to the Marlborough School.

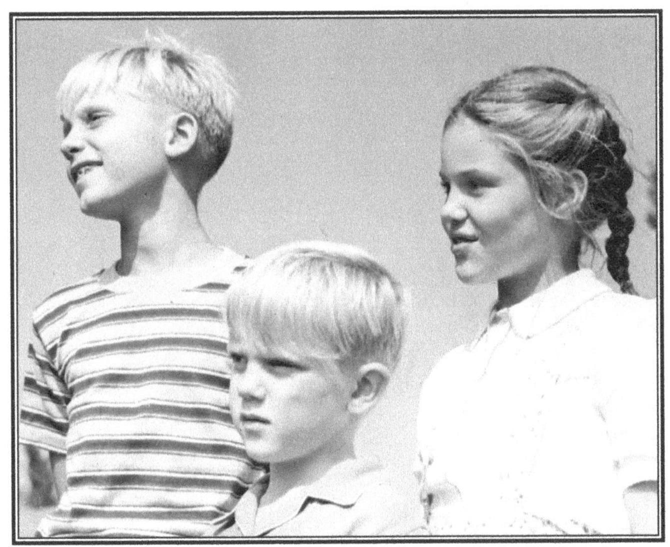

This picture of my brothers and I was taken in 1943 at our home in Santa Monica. Walter, the oldest, is on the left. Peter is in the center.

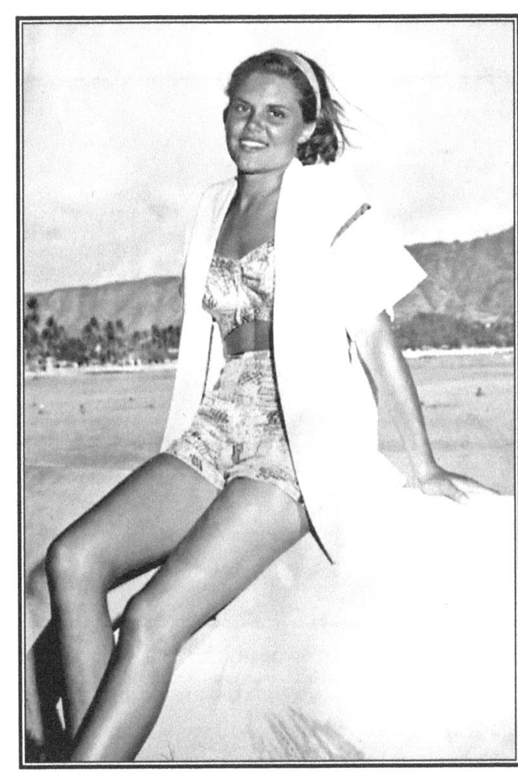

I was 17 when this picture was taken in Hawaii. We went there on my grandfather's Gravy Train excursions with family and business associates.

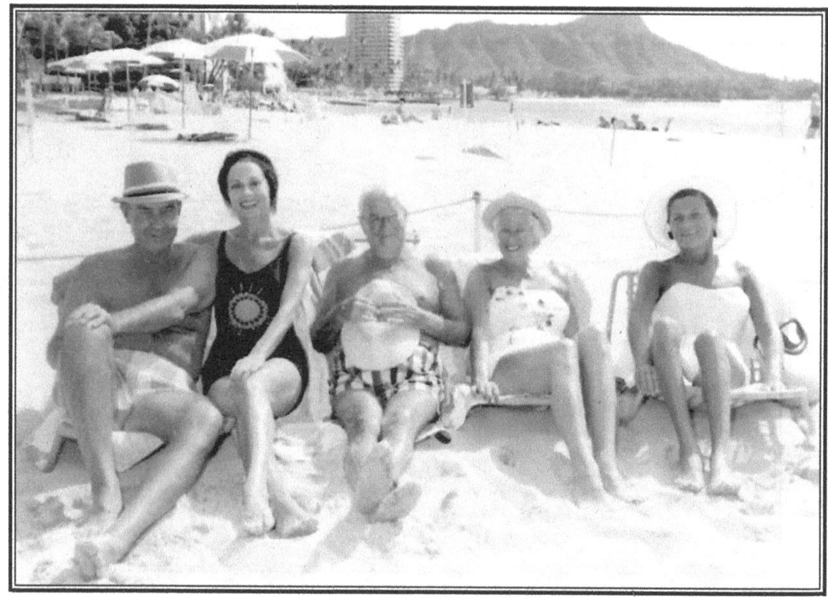

This picture was taken on Waikiki Beach in about 1950 in front of the Royal Hawaiian Hotel during one of my grandfather's Gravy Train excursions. My grandfather, center, and mother on the far right, were joined by other guests from Los Angeles.

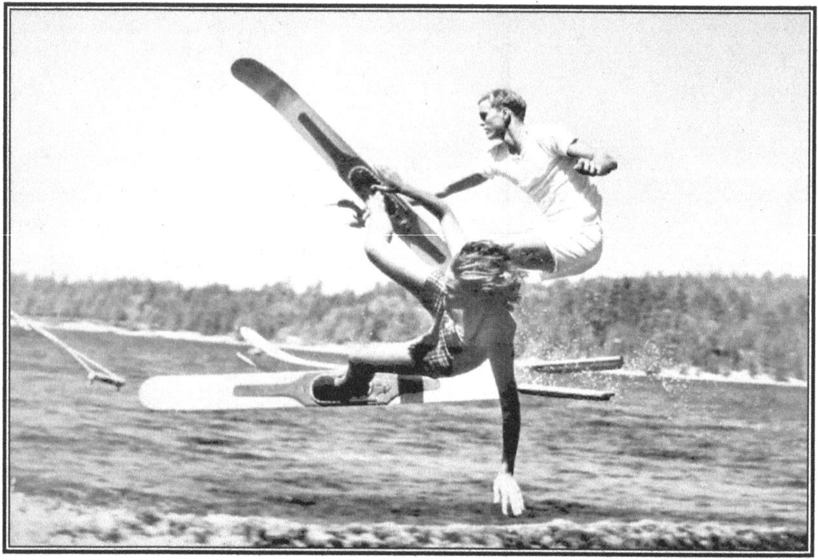

In 1949 at Lake Arrowhead, the year I graduated from high school, Gerry Cooper and I flew through the air for a magazine photographer. The jump was made for only one person, so I went sideways but no one was hurt.

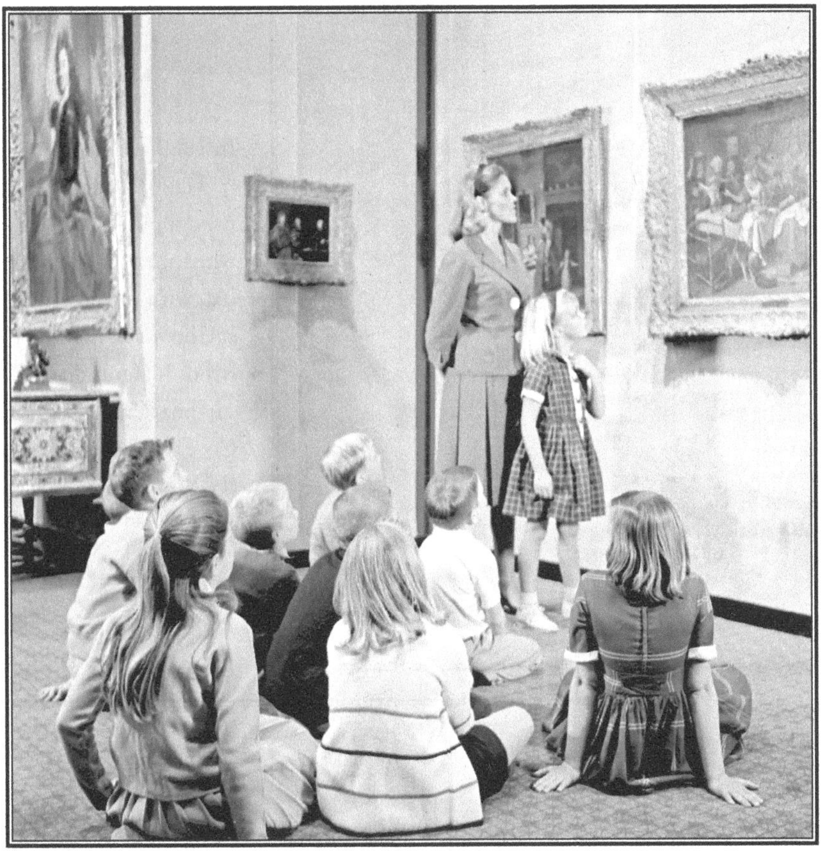

I gave talks to schoolchildren at the Los Angeles County Museum of Art during the late 1960s after founding the Docent Council at the museum.

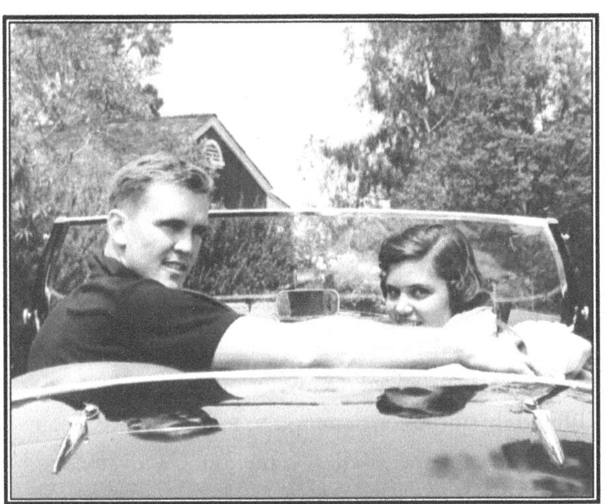

My first husband Gerry Cooper loved sports cars. This one took us up the California coast on our honeymoon in 1954.

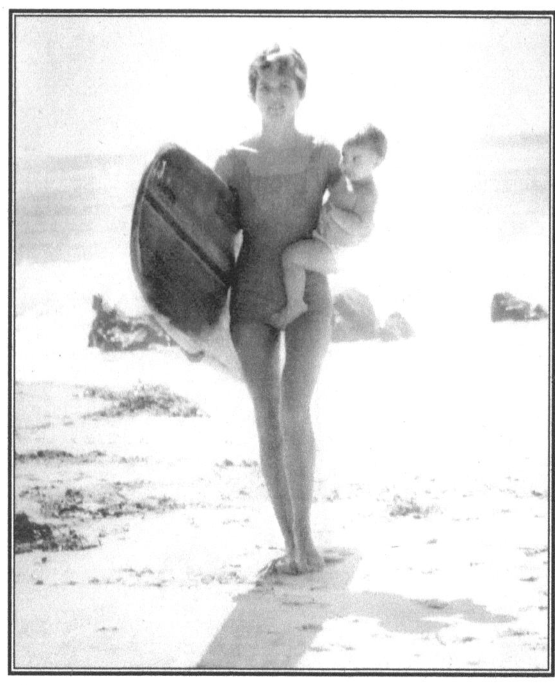

In 1960 at Point Zero in Malibu I carried my daughter Christin when she was one year old, with my favorite surfboard in the other hand. I later rode that surfboard at Cap's Cove, where we built the Wave House.

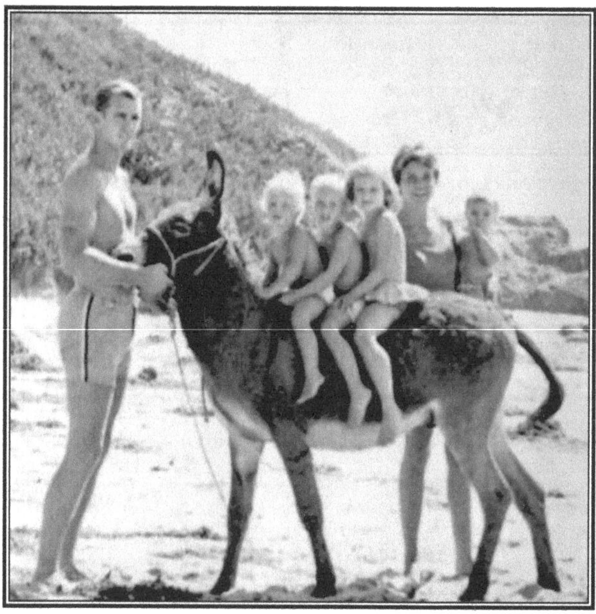

The donkey that showed up mysteriously at Point Zero in 1960 only stayed long enough to take a picture. From left are Gerry Cooper, Kelley, Cameron, Candy, me, and Christin. Brant was born a few years later.

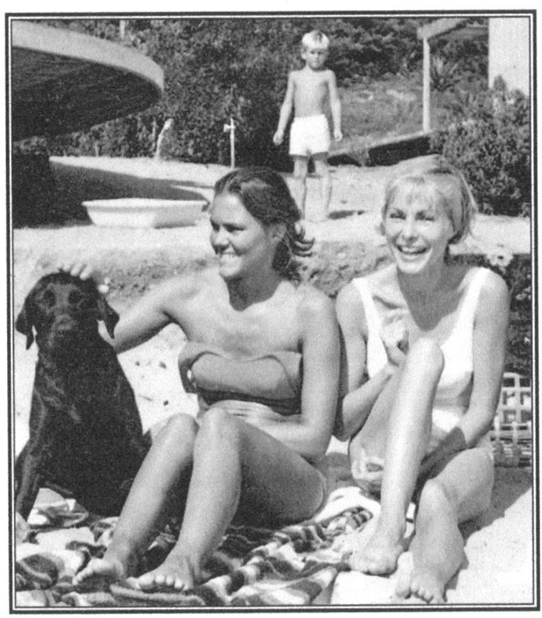

Janet Leigh Brandt and I spent time together at the Malibu Wave House during the late 1960s. Janet and I remained close friends during tumultuous years in California, and later in Sun Valley. My oldest son Cameron is in the background.

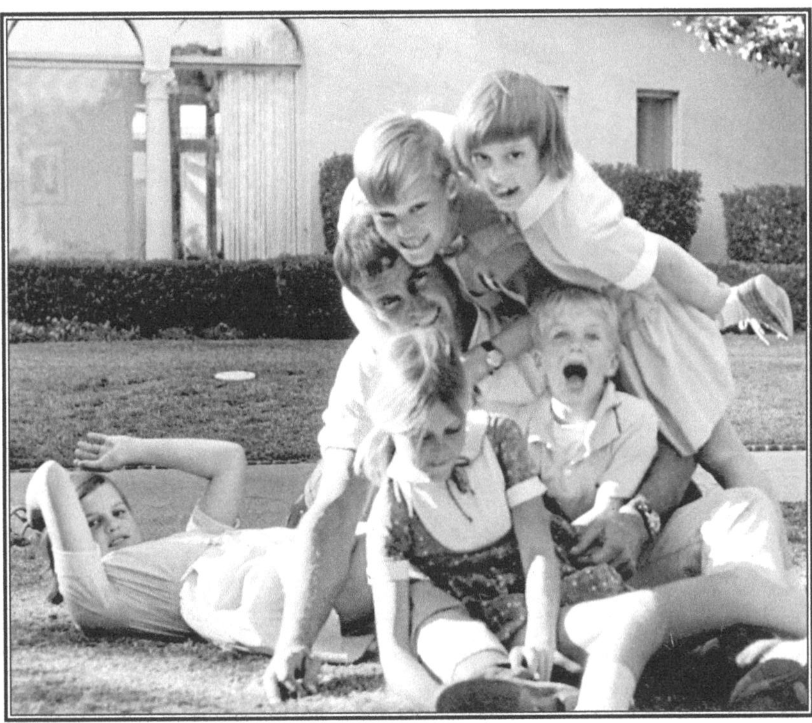

The Cooper children smothering their dad Gerry Cooper at play at the La Mesa house in Santa Monica in 1968.

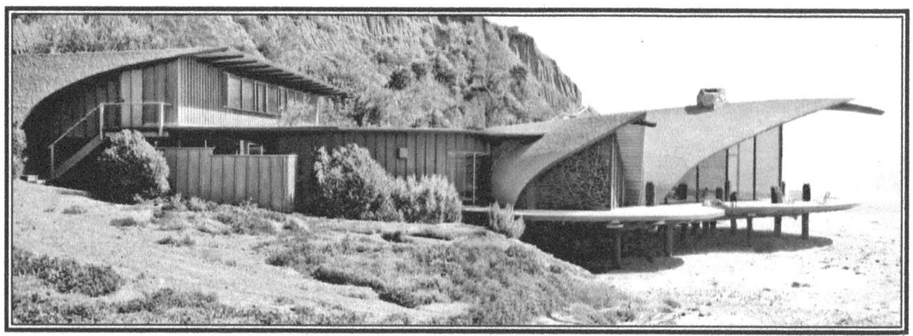

Our iconic Wave House in Cap's Cove in Malibu was photographed by *Life* Magazine in 1965. It was designed by our old friend Harry Gesner and is now considered an architectural masterpiece. This photo is by Fred Lyon.

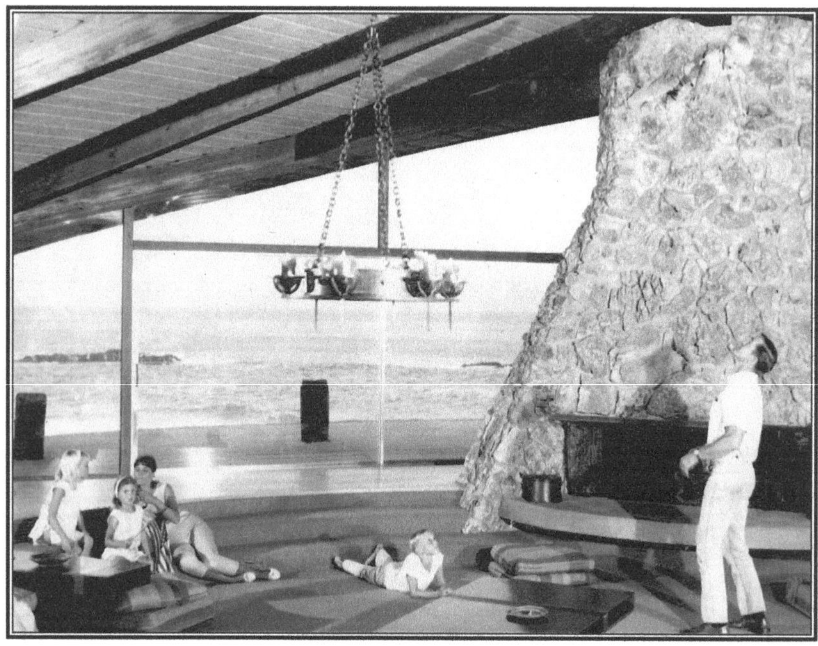

This picture was taken at high tide in 1963 inside the Wave House, designed by our friend Harry Gesner. From left are Kelley, Candy, me (Glenn Cooper) and Cameron. My youngest son Brant has been tossed high in the air by my husband Gerry.

PART IV

Turning to Art

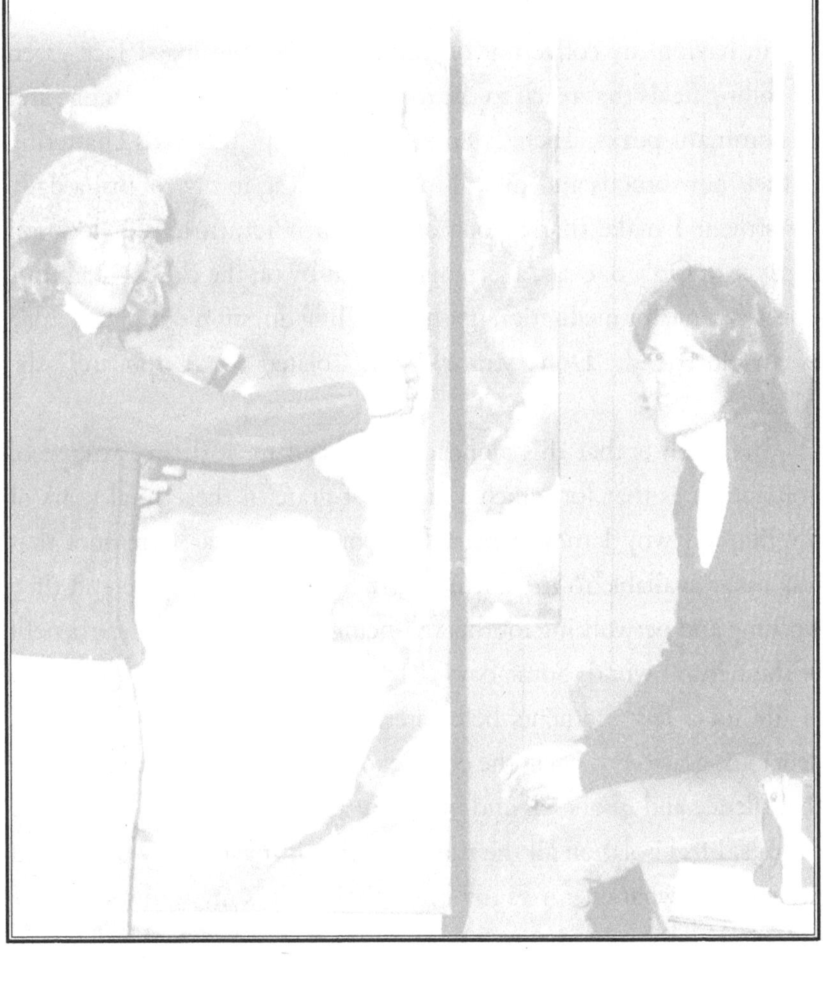

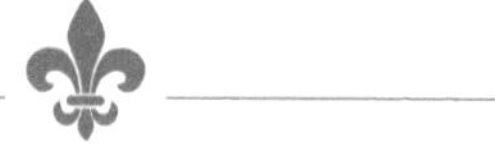

CHAPTER TWENTY

Following Bliss

I am having my coffee out on the deck this morning. I face green rolling fields that reach to the forests rising to the Teton Range and its dominant peaks. There is not a sound except the birds chattering to their new broods and me calling and talking to my robins, a daily investment I make that I hope ensures their return to this location every year. Only one car, a jeep, has passed by on the closest road. It is a perfect time for meditation upon a puzzling question raised yesterday by an old friend. "Don't you ever feel isolated where you are?" she asked.

The truth is that this aloneness is what I most desire, a sense of isolation. It is that for which I am most grateful these final years of my life and why I moved here. It is something that I treasure that was never available to me during all the years of family life and then working and networking for the well-being of others and for the benefit of the natural world. Some days, I want to just enjoy the simple gifts of life for a few moments before returning to my story—beautiful, delicious, gracious silence; the chance to listen, the chance to just be in that silence and in oneself and in nature all at once.

Yes, I feel isolation all the time, and that is my love, my peace, and my joy. It is what energizes my heart chakra. It is my soul source and my meditation. I thank you for asking, dear friend. Now I will return to my deck and its silence and talk to my birds once more and be the better soul for it.

Back now to writing. I recall a timely quote from Georgia O'Keeffe: "Take time to look." I add to that, "Take time to be." And maybe that will be my best and last experience. The consolations of art and philosophy have come back to save me at many times during my life. Wise voices from the past can be a lifeline during times of despair. The great mythologist Joseph Campbell left us many sage and quotable statements. But the one that has come to mind while recalling those last years of living in the Wave House goes like this:

> If you follow your bliss, you put yourself on a track that has been there all the while, waiting for you, and the life that you ought to be living is the one you are living. When you can see that, you begin to meet people who are in your field of bliss, and they open doors to you. I say follow your bliss and don't be afraid, and doors will open where you didn't know they were going to be.

Long before the proxy fight over Bullock's, things were not as they appeared to be for the Cooper family in Malibu. My own feelings never matched the outward appearance of our lives. Despite the envy of friends for what appeared to be a blessed life within our giant wave of a house, I had for years been discontent. The turmoil between my father and grandfather was not the problem. My lovely children were not the problem. Nor was the issue related to the increasingly divergent interests of my husband and myself. The real problem was the churning and inescapable feeling that something important was missing from my life: balance. I had felt an intuitive need for balance since childhood. And now I desperately needed to feed the intellectual curiosity I once enjoyed. Perhaps this would balance the physical and athletic expressions that were called for each day as a part of our active lifestyle.

This lack of intellectual and spiritual fulfillment had become a thorn in my side, causing ever-increasing discomfort in my deepest being. My husband could not understand the insatiable need I felt to follow academic pursuits. Gerry had proclaimed to others that I was "curious to a fault." Fortunately, I had taken small steps over the years in the direction of my soul's calling, and just as Joseph Campbell had said, the proper helpers and guides appeared when I needed them.

I had quietly renewed my academic interest during the days of my first pregnancy, studying to become a docent for the art division of the Los Angeles Museum of Natural History, Science, and Art in downtown LA. I was following an early desire to learn about the arts and pass that knowledge on to others. Little did I know what a passion this would become in the years that followed.

When the feeling of discontent arose during those later years in Malibu, I recalled the words of Ralph Waldo Emerson: "What lies behind us and what lies before us are tiny matters compared to what lies within us." Yet, I had to admit to myself that what lay within me had drifted unnoticeably onto a barren, arid desert. Most of my waking hours were involved with the daily routines of family and children: grocery shopping, doctor appointments, school deliveries and pick-ups, and a growing list of extracurricular activities filled my days. Picking up the threads of my true calling would take courage and initiative.

Marian Pike had encouraged me to attend an art workshop during my first year of marriage. We touched on some of these memories while I was in Paris. The journey she encouraged me to take brought me into contact with two men who would influence my life beyond measure. The first of these was Henry T. Hopkins, who by the mid 1960s was serving as director of the education department for the art division of the Los Angeles Museum. I first met Henry back in 1955 when he invited me to attend his night course on Modern Art at the University of California, Los Angeles. The awakening I had at that time to the art of the late nineteenth and early twentieth centuries proved crucial to the focus of much of my life in later years.

Only lately have I come to recognize the impact Henry Hopkins had at that time upon the art world of the 1950s and 1960s in Los Angeles and elsewhere in the United States. Henry was an Idaho boy. In his youth, he decided he was interested in the fine arts and wanted to pursue a career in that field. This had to come as a shock to his parents, who lived far from the mainstream urban art world. After attending the College of Idaho, Henry entered the prestigious Chicago Art Institute and graduated with both bachelor's and master's degrees. He then studied for a doctorate at UCLA and later received two honorary doctoral degrees for running some of the most prestigious art institutions in America.

When I first met Henry, he had been selected to head the education department of a new museum planned for Wilshire Boulevard that would one day house the Los Angeles Museum's art collection. I must have stood out as an avid student and quick learner, for Henry took a particular liking to me and scheduled courses outside of the museum that would provide the necessary preparation for guiding in the new facility. I did not realize then that I was being groomed to organize the guides for the future opening of this new museum, the Los Angeles County Museum of Art.

Los Angeles was at that time second only to New York City as the center of the contemporary art world. At the time I was taking his night course at UCLA, Henry owned and managed an art gallery on La Cienega Boulevard that specialized in contemporary art. I attended the Friday openings at La Cienega galleries during this seminal period. They were festive and memorable occasions. I met many of the artists who were part of the Abstract Expressionism movement that was sweeping the country, a movement that would become as important to the future of contemporary art as French Impressionism had been to the art of the mid to late nineteenth century.

I bought my first painting at that time, a watercolor by Paul Wonner, one of a number of San Francisco Bay Area artists who were recognized for their figurative painting styles. This was a group known for abandoning the then-prevalent style of Abstract Expressionism. By the 1950s and into the 1960s, they became known as the Bay Area Figurative School. David Park and James Weeks were original members of the group, but the ones most recognized were Richard Diebenkorn and Wayne Thiebaud. The group met together weekly to draw from live nude models, limiting themselves to black ink drawings. The medium was unforgiving, demanding spontaneity and control. Elmer Bischoff, Nathan Olivera, and Theophilus Brown later joined this notorious school.

I bought paintings by these artists because they appealed to my aesthetic sensibility—some for less than $1,000. Having come to know these artists personally through gallery openings, it became my responsibility to introduce docents-in-training to as many artists in their studios as possible. Meeting and talking to the artists about their intentions and painting styles was essential to understanding their creative intentions as expressed in their work.

My friendship and respect for Henry grew as our collaborative effort to train the women who volunteered as guides became more intense. Each piece of art tells a story, just as each work in turn becomes part of the larger story of art history. The artists' temperaments, their influences, and their aesthetic challenges are all part of this history. This new direction in my life opened a door into a new way of seeing the art world; it was possible to relate my own perceptions to the inner experience of artists who were reflecting their souls through their artistic visions. It was also a heavy responsibility for someone like myself, who had only recently begun to study the genre. My background in art education had been dedicated only to the old masters. These contemporary artists were on the cutting edge of a new frontier.

The second person who influenced me strongly in those years was Richard Fargo Brown, a graduate of Harvard University who had lectured at the Frick gallery in New York after receiving his PhD in

1952 with a dissertation on Camille Pissarro. Ric, as he wished to be called, and his wife Polly visited us in Malibu on more than one occasion. Polly was completely paralyzed from polio. She always had a supplementary oxygen supply with her and was confined to a bed. Nevertheless, every now and then, Ric would bring her on a wheeled bed, with a nurse and all the necessary emergency equipment, to the Wave House so that she could enjoy the ocean from out on the deck for a few hours. I watched as Ric paid such devoted attention to his dear wife and was touched by his tenderness. Their son Michael often came with them. Through Michael, I met his girlfriend, Peggy O'Neill. Peggy became our most treasured babysitter, even into our Sun Valley years.

Ric had been selected in 1954 to serve as director of the newly planned Los Angeles County Museum of Art, or LACMA, as it soon became known. The three of us—Ric, Henry, and I—decided that the organization for the new museum's guides would be called the Docent Council. The word docent derives from the Latin *docere,* which means "to teach."

When I learned that we were to be the first all-volunteer docent organization in the country, I decided it was essential to visit the guides at the Metropolitan Museum of Art in New York and the Art Institute of Chicago. Each of these institutions was recognized for its highly trained professional staff of guides. Our docents would only be passionate amateurs. I wondered if we could maintain a comparable degree of professionalism.

After personal conversations with museum managers in New York and Chicago, I realized that speaking skills would be just as essential as an in-depth art history education for our docents. It would take both academic learning and charisma to leave our museum visitors with a deeper understanding of the artwork in our collection, which we hoped would ensure future visits and enduring support of the arts in Los Angeles.

Because it had been my desire for academic discipline that brought me into the job, I wondered if there might be other women seeking a similar experience. As it turned out, many women with master's degrees and even PhDs in a variety of disciplines were going unutilized as they stayed home to raise children. They oftentimes mirrored my own situation—they had children at home or in school, yet they had spare hours to contribute to the love of learning and the love of giving. It helped that the Junior League of Los Angeles promoted this docent experience as a fulfillment of that organization's volunteer work requirement. Soon enough, word spread. Guiding in the galleries of a new art museum began to look like a unique social opportunity and a way to enrich one's own life as well as that of thousands of others throughout Los Angeles County. My own close friends Anne Fleming, Molly Chappellet, and Maggie Wetzel joined the training, to name just a few.

It was now left for Henry and me to create a curriculum for this group of eager women. With all of his contacts in the contemporary art world, Henry was invaluable. He scheduled lectures by artists in the community, including many rising stars—young artists just beginning in their careers who would become famous worldwide and overtake the embedded artistic culture of New York: Ed Ruscha, Larry Bell, Ed Kienholz, Kenneth Price, David Hockney, and Philip Guston, among others. Henry scheduled visits to their studios, where we were given a deeper introduction to their methods and immediate access to each artist's personal vision.

The story of art in Los Angeles is one of an emerging world city with a cultural inferiority complex. LA was perceived as a cultural backwater, even as the city was giving birth to a generation of artists whose local styles would soon have global appeal. The Los Angeles artists of that era were so innovative that the city would eventually dominate New York as the world center of art. We had three years in which to prepare for the opening in 1965. With Henry's guidance, I scheduled professors for a docents-in-training program; they lectured on the periods of art history that were to be represented in the new museum. As I prepared the academic curriculum for our docent recruits, I realized that due to the amount of organizational time this required, I would not be able to participate in any of the academic education I so desired. I was instead appointed chair of the Docent Council. While this leadership position had not been my original goal—I had only sought to find in my studies a personal refuge from the emotionally painful aspects of my marriage—the appointment was an honor, and I did not take it lightly.

I founded the organization in 1962 and applied for its nonprofit status, which was granted later that year, creating a unique nonprofit entity. To achieve this, I formed a board of trustees and created a budget that would establish the nonprofit as a stable and self-enduring organization with a guaranteed funding source. This experience would prove invaluable for future arts education undertakings that I had not yet imagined.

After the new museum opened, I resigned from the Docent Council and returned to UCLA to begin a diverse curriculum of art history classes, using any spare time I could find to pursue my newfound passion. Gerry and I had been drifting inexorably apart. He was following his dreams, and I was following mine. Our foundations for individual happiness were as disparate as two souls living active lives together could have been. Gerry loved his motorsports and followed his quest for speed. I loved my studies and followed my pursuit of art history. His involvement with life was physical. Mine was intellectual and artistic. And yet, I acknowledge that this is inadequate to explain the pain we were inflicting upon each other.

For example, Gerry decided one day that it was time I learned to ride a motorcycle, that this was undoubtedly something I would love and we could enjoy doing together. He bought me a small Triumph. Rather than starting out on the pavement, an easy flat surface on which to learn to shift gears, apply gas, and brake, he said we should instead go into the Malibu Hills. Still trusting his judgment in those days, I followed him very slowly across the highway and onto a dirt trail.

On the way back down, I had to brake hard and, with no experience, lost both my balance and my courage, crashing mentally and physically. I leaned the wrong way on a curve and went over the embankment, plunging down several yards. I suffered only minor bruises to my body, but the insult and injury to my pride were massive. Before coming to my aid, Gerry stood on the trail above, laughing, not even inquiring whether I was all right. I began to realize that Gerry enjoyed seeing me fail at anything at which he excelled. This added to my emotional turmoil and latent suspicions about him.

By the mid 1960s, Gerry was a renowned boat racer, having funded the construction of one of the fastest racing boats on ocean or lake. His adventures took him far and wide. The ocean race across the channel from Los Angeles to Catalina Island encountered swells so high that the force of encountering them was enough to collapse muscles, bones, or bodily organs. Gerry had another boat built for calmer waters on inland lakes throughout the West. Life in Wave House was not enough to satisfy his craving for personal fame. Motors and speed supplied him with an increasing source of attention and recognition. An article about him in the *Los Angeles Sunday Times* surprised me. I was aghast at the outright exaggerations in the coverage, which made him out to be very rich. Gerry just laughed when I questioned him, retorting with the simple comment, "Oh, I was just having fun."

I too was having my own kind of fun at the time, but it took me in an entirely different direction. By 1965, we were ready when the Los Angeles County Museum of Art opened to much fanfare along the same boulevard on which my grandfather had opened Bullocks Wilshire in 1929.

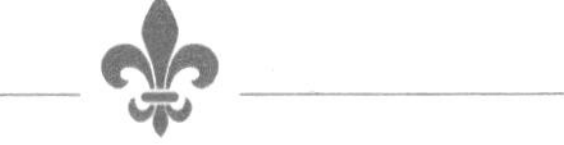

CHAPTER TWENTY-ONE

Blood in the Water

Los Angeles in the 1940s and 1950s was undergoing an art renaissance, and civic leaders knew it was time for an institution that would reflect this. Richard "Ric" Fargo Brown, a great-grandson of the founder of Wells Fargo Bank, was the man for the job. Initially lured by LACMA board member William Sesnon Jr. from New York City, Ric had been a research assistant and lecturer at the Frick Collection and published a thesis titled "The Color Theories of Camille Pissarro." Sesnon invited him to LA; and Ric, fascinated by what was going on in California, decided to take up the challenge. Soon hired as director of the planned Los Angeles County Museum of Art, Ric was developing museum shows, lecturing, buying art, and running a gauntlet of powerful California personalities, all while shaping a new art museum that would match its trustees' ambition to turn LA into the world's latest cultural center.

A *Life* magazine article at the time described Ric as a force of nature:

His boyish face, his eloquent tongue, his zeal for the beautiful swept over the city like a great wind. His lectures charmed young society ladies to sign up by the dozen for art courses and become "docents," shepherding visitors around the galleries of the museum. He chatted about Cézanne and chiaroscuro over innumerable martinis.

He became an indispensable guest at dinner parties. He traveled to Europe to help novice patrons find Picassos.

Among those novice patrons was Norton Simon, a wealthy industrialist whom Ric convinced to provide $1 million in 1957 to fund the new museum. By then, Simon had several Cézanne paintings in his bedroom. Clearly, his growing collection of old masters needed a public home. In addition to Simon, many of the city's other wealthy donors also got behind the effort to move the Los Angeles Museum of History, Science, and Art's $20 million collection into a new art museum. Among them was merchant-magnate Ed Carter, who served as chair of the nascent museum board. He drew more than two hundred additional donors whose names would be emblazoned on a benefactors' wall in a script borrowed from Trajan's column in Rome, a clear indication of the imperial ambitions of the museum's trustees. Hollywood royalty stepped forward to take part, as did the city's old and new money. Among them was billionaire insurance tycoon Howard Ahmanson, who was quickly acquiring an art collection of his own.

Ahmanson's ambition extended to the design of the museum building itself. Why not hire the same architect who had built his Los Angeles business headquarters? Ahmanson agreed to donate $2 million, which he considered enough to have the entire museum named after him. Simon learned of this, became disgruntled, and dropped the amount of his contribution considerably. Other major donors and art collectors pulled out completely, while other well-heeled donors stepped in. The feud was only settled when Ric proposed building two separate museum buildings. Only one of them would have Ahmanson's name on it. This quadrupled the cost to more than $12 million, but no one seemed to mind.

The LACMA board very much wanted Norton Simon's collection, largely because Ric had for years been Simon's curatorial advisor. He knew the collection as well as anyone. It included many paintings by

Italian and Dutch masters. But when Norton pushed for his paintings to be exhibited, Ric brought a level of professional scrutiny to the process that Simon did not always welcome. For example, if Simon had a painting that he claimed was a Bellini—which it was not—Ric would inform him that it was instead an example from the "school of Bellini," painted by a protégé or imitator of the same period. For Ric, it was a matter of integrity. For others, it was more a matter of pride and display.

Ahmanson's collection also grew in significance, as did his clout. He put forward Edward Stone as the museum architect, the same man who had designed Ahmanson's Wilshire Boulevard headquarters, a move that would tie his business legacy together with his legacy as an art donor. Ric had yet more ambitious ideas and favored world-renowned architect Ludwig Mies van de Rohe. He wanted the museum structure to be its own lasting work of art. Eventually, the dispute was settled when the board handed the commission to William Pereira, a Los Angeles architect whom I knew well. It took two years and $12.2 million to complete the buildings in 1965, nearly three times the original estimate.

At the grand opening, donors who had given at least $25,000 gathered for a black-tie dinner in the museum's lobby. They were entertained by classical music from the stairways while they socialized with one another, as various museum representatives told the story of how their contributions would benefit Los Angeles society for generations to come. Thankfully, all these boisterous egos had been tempered enough by their shared humanitarian urges to preserve and display their great art for posterity in magnificent buildings. Situated next to and above the La Brea Tar Pits, the museum seemed to rise from primordial circumstances.

Prior to the grand opening party, a strange mishap took place that seemed to reveal the true story of the museum's roilsome birth. Chemicals put into the pond beside the museum were intended to turn its murky water black for the occasion but instead left it blood red. The symbolism was not lost on me, and I wondered if someone familiar with the inner workings of the museum board had intended it as an inaugural prank. Ric still found himself caught between the towering egos of Simon, Carter, and Ahmanson, and adrift among an ever-increasing number of the twenty or so museum trustees vying for control of the exhibitions. In any case, the museum exploded in popularity, with memberships selling in numbers far greater than anyone imagined.

Matters came to a head over a major acquisition that would become a hallmark of the museum's permanent display: a large Syrian palace relief dating from the late eighth century BC hung in limbo while the museum board dithered over whether to spend $350,000 to purchase it. Ric grew impatient and brokered its sale to a new art museum being planned in Fort Worth, Texas.

Only under panic did the board finally coalesce and spend enough money to acquire the relief for Los Angeles. But by then, the board had mobilized to have Ric removed from his position as museum director. Because he was not afraid to speak his mind when it came to his academic expertise, the board decided to replace him with an individual whose skill set was purely administrative. The push to get Ric out was reported on by the *LA Times* for weeks, and he received a lot of local praise and support from the outside community.

Amid all the turmoil, Ric eventually accepted an offer to leave Los Angeles for Fort Worth, where he set about establishing yet another world-class institution, the Kimbell Art Museum. The trustees there realized the importance of having an actual art historian in charge of a leading art institution. Over time, this opportunity allowed Ric to finally create a major art museum designed by a world-class architect. The Kimbell, designed by Louis Kahn, was hailed as one of the greatest architectural achievements of the era.

In 1965, LACMA opened to much fanfare along the same boulevard on which my grandfather opened Bullocks Wilshire in 1929. Ric Brown, Henry, and I brought together two extraordinary exhibitions for the opening: a Renoir show in 1965 and a Van Gogh show to follow in 1966. The new museum garnered rave reviews worldwide. Our docents skillfully guided the public through the exhibitions. The Docent Council fulfilled its grand mission of idealism and hope. On the museum's opening day, my personal dream came true when the first lines of school buses brimming with children from Los Angeles city and county schools pulled up in front of the impressive façade. For most of these children, this field trip would be their first experience of the rich history of world art treasures.

In 1964, I received recognition for my efforts in the form of the Los Angeles Times Women of the Year Award. The *LA Times* was then a prominent and universally recognized American newspaper, and it was a great honor to receive this award before a crowd of well-known and key community leaders. The Chandler family owned the newspaper then, and Dorothy Buffum Chandler (or Buffy, as she was familiarly known) presented me with the award. On a silver cup in my house in Tetonia are inscribed these words:

Los Angeles Times
Women of the Year
Award
1964
Mrs. William Cooper
For Outstanding Achievement

But my true reward came from the smiles of the children sitting before a painting, asking docents questions about what they were seeing, and hearing a response that would awaken them to the creations of individuals who see and interpret the world in fascinating new ways. The most memorable experience for me was hearing the children express their own personal responses to a work of art.

Having studied the artwork on display and the eras from which it emerged, our docents proved themselves uniquely successful as the first volunteer guiding group for a major art museum in the United States. Upon the occasion of museum's fiftieth anniversary in 2012, the Los Angeles County website boasted that 521 men and women docents belonged to the council. Docent guides have led more than two million visitors through the museum since 1962, and they have guided an additional one million Southern California schoolchildren during field trips. LACMA is recognized worldwide for its contemporary and historical art collections. It is the largest museum in the West, with 150,000 pieces of art ranging from antiquity to the modern art of today.

I learned from these experiences that what I most enjoy is answering a need, creating a new organization to fill that need, giving it the stability it requires to continue, and then passing on the gavel to the next leader. The establishment of the Docent Council harkened back to a time when my mother encouraged me to work as a candy striper at a convalescent hospital. As a "silver spoon" of society, I was taught to expect less from others and more from myself. I learned that giving freely and without restrictions is the true gift of life. By 1965, I had combined the art of giving with the giving of art.

My mentor Henry Hopkins gave to me in ways that I can never repay. He continued a career of special significance to California, gaining national recognition as director of the San Francisco Museum of Modern Art from 1974 to 1986. He later returned to Los Angeles, serving as director of the Frederic R. Weisman Foundation, where he took on the responsibility of collecting works for that highly acclaimed contemporary art collection. He then renewed his long relationship with UCLA, chairing the art department from 1991 to 1994, while simultaneously serving as director of the Wight Art Gallery, UCLA's collection specializing in works on paper. During his tenure as chair of the UCLA Department of Art, Henry recruited an outstanding roster of artists to its faculty. He received the honored title of professor emeritus and is still credited with making UCLA one of the most noted and respected art schools in the country.

When UCLA was negotiating the university's ultimate management of the Armand Hammer art collection, Henry's diplomacy and wisdom were credited with the dissolution of tensions over the museum's location. Ultimately, he was chosen as director of the Hammer Museum. Our paths continued to cross for many years, primarily during my efforts to expand arts education in Sun Valley and elsewhere in Idaho. In his later years, I enjoyed seeing Henry return to creating his own paintings—light-filled and softly rendered. They reflected his personality; quiet yet commanding. After a long and honored career, Henry finally retired to his cabin on Henrys Lake in eastern Idaho to enjoy his passion for fishing.

Ric went on to serve as director of the Kimbell Art Foundation, which inherited the art collection of prominent Fort Worth, Texas, businessman Kay Kimbell. The Kimbell Art Museum building is considered one of Louis Kahn's greatest achievements and an important monument to museum architecture. Ric expanded the collection by acquiring works of worldwide acclaim, growing the inherited English portraiture collection into a wide range of the finest works in Western art; paintings by Duccio, El Greco, Rubens, and Rembrandt, including such eclectic pieces as Picasso's *Man with a Pipe*, a Duccio altarpiece, a twelfth-century Avignon wall painting, and an enthroned Khmer Buddha.

History has a way of repeating itself. I was shocked just recently to learn of the planned demolition of the Los Angeles County Museum of Art. The situation is so similar to the time of Ric Brown's directorship, of which I am now writing, that I feel compelled to comment on it. While our goal for the Docent Council at LACMA was to educate the public on the historical significance of the collection as it was to be displayed, the goal of the museum director today appears to be quite the opposite.

In the 1960s, $12 million was considered astronomical. In the 2020s, Michael Govan plans to create a memorable edifice at a cost of $650 million, but his plan doesn't include enough spaces to display the collection, which has vastly increased over the last fifty years. Once again, Los Angeles is divided over the future of LACMA, and some of the same families are involved in the controversy. Howard Ahmanson's great nephew, William H. Ahmanson, expressed dismay over the plan. The Ahmanson family has contributed over $150 million worth of art since one of the original buildings was named for his uncle. The Ahmanson Foundation has now declared it will no longer support LACMA.

I am reminded of the public fight over architecture that once took place between Ahmanson and Norton Simon, in which Ric Brown was caught up. Govan and his architect, Peter Zumthor, believe that what is now termed an "encyclopedic museum"—one that contains art from many cultures throughout history—fails the viewer and is somehow obsolete. They are even considering removing the educational labels that accompany the artwork, in what I consider the mistaken belief that an emotional response should be first and foremost.

In his day, Ric Brown wisely settled the power struggle with a Solomonic decision to split the campus into more than one building. Ric was pulling for a renowned architect, but he would never have sacrificed the treasured significance of the collection for an architectural wonder. I believe, as Ric did, in the relevance of an artwork's place in history. I certainly would not have studied the history of art as I did and relished the travels with Ric and others that brought the history of a work of art into perspective had it not added to an appreciation and understanding of a piece. Great art provides more than an aesthetic experience. Beyond its intrinsic value lies the recognition of its place in the culture of the time and its significance as a beacon to the future.

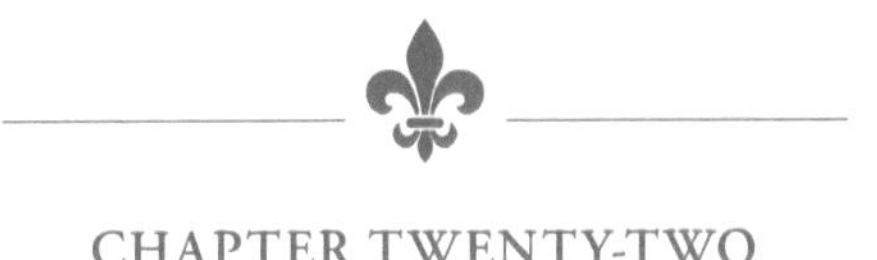

CHAPTER TWENTY-TWO

My Retail Misadventure

In late 1965, my friend Bunny Fleming and I decided to open an arts and furniture store of our own across from the new Los Angeles County Museum of Art on Wilshire Boulevard, next door to The Egg and the Eye Restaurant. Anticipating business from the steady stream of visitors to the museum, we named our enterprise "Art Imports."

Investing in the art and antique furniture market would never have occurred to me without Ric Brown and Bunny's encouragement, and yet my family was recognized for having expertise in retail and merchandising. Bunny was a highly respected interior decorator and an expert in the historical relevance of antiques. Together, we hoped to create a place where customers could find an unexpected combination of fine art, furniture, and treasures from around the world that could not be found elsewhere in Los Angeles.

Bunny guided Gerry in a renovation of our location that transformed a dull retail space into a place with old-world atmosphere. Bunny could walk into a room full of furniture and, as if she smelled it, point immediately to any restoration that had been made to a piece. Her particular expertise was in continental furniture, specifically Italian, Spanish, and German. My goal was to focus on fine art, sculpture, and accessories.

London was the center of galleries that specialized in the kind of furniture and antiques we both liked, so Bunny and I traveled there most often. The best antiquities were obtained through auctions or at the shops of Portobello Market. We learned quickly as we made purchases, and both of us enjoyed the education as much as we enjoyed the travel.

We determined that our initial inventory—enough for the grand opening of our store—would fill one entire shipping container. Since crate prices were charged according to volume, we filled every drawer, cabinet, and empty niche with small accessories and other items. These were the objets d'art for which I was responsible, anything other than furniture that would entice shoppers. Our goal for our initial selection was to offer our customers as diverse an inventory as possible, including whatever we found to be unique, historic, and beautiful. Our first container had all types of furniture, rugs, and lamps, as well as old-master drawings, Asian scrolls and ceramics, decorative historic lanterns and candlesticks, pewter items, Isnik ware, early Roman stone sculptures, and collections of intaglio stamps.

Art Imports was more like a London antique shop than anything Los Angeles had ever experienced. I like to think it was ahead of its time, but we learned that it takes more than good taste to run a successful business. Just finding our way around Europe posed challenges. On one trip, we got lost in the confusion of roads within the five countries that border Switzerland. The names for routes and destinations in several different languages did not always correspond to the same ones on our trusty but outdated fold-out map. We crossed one border so many times one afternoon that the customs agents just started laughing and waving us through as we approached.

One night, after finding that most of the better hotels in London were booked, we ventured into a lesser-known area. We checked into one of the last available places; and as we relaxed after a long travel day, drinking and smoking in the bar, we looked around to see many scantily clad women also drinking and smoking in the bar. Bunny dared to approach the man at the reception desk to inquire if these women were prostitutes. His answer was to simply roll his eyes and not implicate himself further in the running of a brothel. That night, we double-locked our door.

We came to be seen as "*dégagé* but fly" by one art dealer, which meant we were easygoing and a bit naïve, but stylish and capable. Our inexperience must have been obvious to some of the people we dealt with. Bunny and I fought back giggles at one London auction when we realized how ridiculously uninformed we were about the lots for sale. But after all the trouble we went through to get into the auction room, we were determined to buy something, anything, so I bid on a Roman marble sculptured bust of a child. We persisted, and I won the bid. Although I lived with it for many years, loving its presence by the side of my bathtub, we never knew whether it was truly an ancient Roman piece.

Our excitement at receiving a shipment of crates in Los Angeles was unbounded as we reviewed our lists with the customs agents and arranged for the items to be delivered to our waiting space. But as time passed, disappointment heaped upon disappointment. Buyers did not flock to visit. Our only serious buyers were those in the antique retail business from the San Francisco area, which was at that time the West Coast center of old-world antiques. They remained over time our primary buyers, but as retailers themselves, they required us to greatly discount their purchases.

One of Bunny's more spectacular purchases was made at a London gallery in Portobello, where she found an intaglio seal collection of very old rings and official seals dating to the Roman period. They had been used on documents two millennia earlier to create wax impressions unique to their owners. Bunny was so taken with the collection that she told the owner, "I'll buy the lot," trying to sound very British. Mostly, it was a "lot" of trouble.

We also made purchases at a London store called Spink & Son, founded in 1666. There, I bought an Egyptian ibis sculpture made of bronze and gilded wood that dated from the first century BC. I assessed its value based on its aesthetic qualities and historical purpose rather than on the more traditional foundation of academic research. What mattered most to Bunny and me was its place in ancient Egyptian culture. The ibis bird was associated with Thoth, the god of wisdom and writing, held sacred to the scribes who recorded Egyptian history for the ancient dynasties. Ric recommended that we send the ibis to his associates at Harvard, where it could be treated for a bronze disease. It was returned months later after treatment and restoration. My dream for the piece was that it end up on display at a museum.

Ric was at that time still director of LACMA. He provided generous support and guidance by sending me salesmen who had already visited the museum in the hope of selling an artwork for its collection. If what they had was not of museum quality or if LACMA already had a similar but better piece in its collection, Ric sent them to us. These salesmen became my sources for old-master drawings and Asian ceramics. I felt confident that Ric would only recommend to us sellers offering objects of the highest quality and authenticity.

Ric called me one morning from LACMA to tell me that he was sending over the daughter of Amon Carter, founder of the Amon Carter Museum in Fort Worth. I looked forward to meeting Ruth Carter Johnson and wondered what me might have in our store to interest her. The Amon Carter Museum focused entirely on American Art. It turned out that she had her own excellent and varied personal art collection. Ric encouraged her to look at our Egyptian ibis and advised her of its importance as a piece deserving of her attention. I was thrilled when she decided to buy the piece, and Bunny and I arranged to ship it to Texas. Ruth loaned it for display at the Kimbell Art Museum and, doubtless with Ric's encouragement, eventually donated it to the Kimbell, where it remains to this day.

It was a joyous surprise when one day my grandfather walked into the store, unannounced and unexpected. Despite the awful family division that had taken place during the proxy fight over Bullock's, PG wanted to know what his granddaughter was up to and asked to be shown all the inventory. He asked many questions that only a seasoned retailer would think to ask. He was proud of what I had done, no doubt remembering his tentative beginnings in the retail world before being proclaimed the "merchant prince" of Los Angeles. PG had been a forerunner in the retail business and held out hope that I also could succeed. His visit and words of support meant everything to me.

One day not long afterward, two well-dressed men of large stature dressed in suits and ties entered the store. Bunny was in the back of the store, and I was in the front. One of the men occupied my attention by asking questions about some of the items on display. The other man wandered elsewhere. I turned my back to the first man in order to follow the other man with my eyes to see what he was interested in. In that moment, the man closest to me opened the glass top vitrine, which displayed the entire intaglio collection from ancient Rome, and swiftly scooped up a major portion of them and then briskly and quietly walked to the exit door. He was quickly joined by the second man before we discovered what had happened.

We were at a loss as to what to do. Run outside and shout for help? Yell, "Robbers!" and run after them? Or just accept the loss and sit down together and weep? We quickly discarded the thought of calling the police, as the theft would only be of minor concern to them; we felt we should be grateful that at least we had not been threatened. However, this theft marked a turning point for us that propelled us toward the decision to close the business and take our losses.

At Art Imports, I gained a deep appreciation for the business profession—budgeting, accounting, buying, and selling. I became aware of the daily demands of the service industry, including the need to dress appropriately and be cordial and helpful to customers.

I encountered a wide range of people in the course of our retail adventures, people beyond my usual frame of social reference. Along the way, I learned something unexpected: how important it is to carry on casually and graciously with everyday people. As a result, I became less formal with people I did not know. When I later became a leader in the nonprofit and public domains, this proved a most useful lesson. I have come to believe that the service industry should serve as the foundation for any and all community service.

Bunny and I did indeed find treasures, but our business expertise left much to be desired. The joy and fun we had together sustained us until we finally closed our doors after two years. There were specific reasons for our failure. The first was our location, and PG might have suspected this—we should have located ourselves amid all the other antique stores. A large, bulky, and unattractive building in Beverly Hills, nicknamed The Blue Whale, was the central site for most of the designer shops and many of the art and antique galleries. The Blue Whale anchored a district where busy shoppers came for home décor and furnishings, knowing they could find what they wanted. My grandfather had shown through his example that competition between stores in the same area would draw more business for all.

There was also the issue of timing. The Southern California design market was in its "bamboo period." Decor was light and tropical. We should have recognized this preference; instead, we indulged our love of the dark walnut furniture favored during the Renaissance. We should not have expected an appreciation for our tastes in such a light-hearted, contemporary time and place. We could have considered our business venture as a grand failure, but instead I have come to see the experience as deeply rewarding. Our import store misadventure allowed us to see the world through many cultures. Furniture and art objects we sold still reside in many upscale homes in California.

Despite our ill-advised decisions and misadventures, the store was not a long-term economic loss. Many of the treasures from our store still dwell with me to this day or were kept by friends or family as gifts. Most of the collection of sixteenth-, seventeenth- and eighteenth-century furniture was later sold at considerable profit or given to my children. Because I had funded the venture, I was the eventual grand winner of many of the finest pieces. They lived with me for another fifty years, combining later in life with the very same style of furniture collected and treasured by Bill Janss. I found the old retail advice learned through my family's involvement in Bullock's to be true: "Always buy the best." I think that, when he visited our store, my grandfather saw that we were at least on the right track in that respect.

With the demise of Art Imports, I could not help pondering whether the failure was reflective of other poor choices I had made in my life. My marriage was supposed to protect me behind the sturdiest and most enduring of walls, yet it was now facing collapse. For a while, I feared one personal failure might bring more. Over time, I came to realize that all experiences have their rewards. I chose to follow the advice of my father, who said that to achieve success, one must find a way to "just dance in the rain."

CHAPTER TWENTY-THREE

Rogue Wave

A rogue is defined as an unprincipled person, a scoundrel, and a rascal. A rogue wave comes unexpectedly, sweeping away all that lies in its path. The rogue wave that swept through my early life was my husband, Gerry Cooper. For many years, I refused to recognize the unfolding drama that would destroy our family and sweep me and the children away from Malibu forever. I did what people too often do when faced with an oncoming disaster: I refused to accept it.

It is difficult after all these years to untangle the series of events that led to the end of our marriage. Perhaps it was doomed from the start. Yet, there were specific events that caused the entire edifice to crack wide open, impossible to repair.

As my own interests veered toward my museum work and academic studies, Gerry involved himself even more aggressively in his boat racing. He retrofitted a bus that could trailer his boat and provide a traveling home for him within the constant commotion of the races—trucks pulling boats on trailers in every direction, race crews, mechanics, adoring young women standing in attendance around the drivers. He welcomed the attention of his many friends and hangers-on at these events and told me that he also wanted his children to be there with him. At first, I allowed them to go along, but after attending a race myself and witnessing the dangers involved,

I refused to let them go again. It was clear to me that Gerry was not there to be with his family. He paid us little attention. He was there for the adoring crowds, and this was not a place for unwatched children. His primary reason for having them at the races, I realized, was to assuage his guilt over leaving the family nearly every weekend for his own pleasure and acclaim.

During the week, Gerry also spent more evenings away from us, supposedly working at the lumber company. When he did come home, it was often in the company of questionable friends: mechanics, fellow racers, and distraught-looking women who appeared to be lost, seeking fulfillment in their admired leader. I might have been jealous under different circumstances; instead, I had to face the truth that I simply no longer loved him. He was not the man I thought I had married. Instead of the comfort and support I dreamed a family would bring, he brought only insecurity and danger.

There was a joke Gerry loved to make in front of our friends: "Keep your wife barefoot in the winter and pregnant in the summer." And this was exactly what I had been doing, willingly and lovingly serving as mother to five children in six years.

"We need to talk," I said to him one night over dinner. "We are no longer living our lives together." There was an awkward silence, and then he rose and left the table and walked away. This was the usual stalemate. He avoided all such conversations. Admittedly, he too could not yet accept the truth of a failed marriage. I wanted any failures in my life to be a part of my past. I assumed that following my own interests would conceal them forever.

Life became more challenging when Alberta left. She lived in Pasadena and had been working for us ten days straight, taking every other weekend off. She took on the cleaning, laundry, meal preparation, and all the other daily needs of five children. She loved them, and they loved her; but to get home, she had to follow a circuitous and time-consuming route.

In Alberta's absence, I began to employ local sitters, some of whom were more than just admiring of my husband. The existence of other women in Gerry's life became obvious, but I continued to turn away from this truth. Had I desired to look more deeply, I would have recognized a pattern in Gerry's behavior: the closer he could bring his lies and subterfuge to discovery by those he loved, the prouder he was of the feat.

In the years before our marriage, I had thought he was only playing the role of a scamp and scoundrel. Surely, he would outgrow these shortcomings of character. Instead, it was in his character to expand upon these deceitful habits in new and creative ways.

Of course, there were also many bright spots in our lives during those years. In 1961, we took a trip to Hawaii with Clarence and Bunny Fleming and Harry Gesner. We visited with Jimmy Pfleuger, played in the ocean, and had a wonderful time. In fact, Gerry and I were close on the trip and, as a result, conceived our fifth child, Brant Cooper. When we returned to Malibu, our family spent time with our neighbors, the Porters. Our children were the same ages, so we always enjoyed spending time together. I was blind at the time to what else was transpiring.

On what turned out to be our final Thanksgiving vacation together, Gerry decided that we should all take a drive up the coast in his bus. It had been revamped and decorated as a traveling home, complete with bunk beds, kitchen, and bathroom. The expense was written off to the lumber company. A road trip with five young children was not what I had in mind for the holiday, but he convinced the children of all the amazing natural wonders and fun surprises he had in store for them. And of course, we could not leave the family dogs Lizzie and Archie home. Lizzy was nursing her six puppies at the time, so they earned one bunk bed all to themselves.

I accepted my fate and took along a large turkey, with all the trimmings, to cook in the bus's oven for a grand Thanksgiving dinner.

When I heard that Gerry had plans to drive on the twisting Highway 101 up the coast, I wondered if this was some kind of punishment. Only a sports car driver could enjoy such a drive. This was the same road we had taken on our honeymoon, but now there were seven of us and our pets. The sharp turns in the road were nauseating.

We did see the redwood trees, but only in passing, never stopping for any playtime. On Thanksgiving Day, the turkey was roasting in the oven when Gerry took an especially sharp curve too fast. The oven door flew open, and the turkey and all its trimmings shot out and onto the floor. I yelled and wanted to break down and cry, but that would have been a victory for him. Instead, I rescued what I could, and we had a dinner of sorts. It was not a fun trip, and I was close to tears all the way home. The children had little to do in the bus other than fight and wrestle. I don't even think the dogs had a good time. We just drove and drove, and then drove some more. It was a stark reminder of my honeymoon drive on this same highway, when I first reflected upon what might be missing in the relationship that was just beginning. Now I could see that, despite the gift of our five children, we had drifted ever further apart.

My husband's deceits came in many forms. When Gerry and my brother Walter decided to quit smoking, they bet $1,000 on who could keep from smoking the longest. One day, I went out to the garage to call Gerry to the telephone. Smoke filled the garage, and I found a familiar sight—Gerry with a cigarette hanging from his mouth as he worked on a motor. He sheepishly said, "You are not going to tell your brother, are you? You better not!" I was astounded by this and told him that I expected him to tell Walter himself that he had lost the bet, which he did. It was agonizing to realize that Gerry could be deceitful to someone so close to me. "Glenn, you're honest to a fault," he often said to me.

And yet, we continued to have intimate relations. One night after making love, I was lying in bed and suddenly realized that he had not flushed any protection down the toilet. I asked him about this when he returned to bed, and he said, "Of course I did." I accepted what he said, but with deep reservation. I soon found that I was indeed pregnant and knew exactly how and when it had happened. But why?

We had agreed that our family was large enough, and my doctor had become concerned about my health should I attempt another pregnancy. He had told me months earlier during a physical check-up that I should not have any more children, that five births had already taken a toll on my body and it would be dangerous for me to carry another child. Gerry knew this. I had suffered during my later pregnancies with varicose veins so painful that I was barely able to remain standing at times. And now, with five young children to look after, my situation would be even more difficult and dangerous. I asked the doctor what I could do about the pregnancy.

Abortions were illegal at the time, but he said he would perform this for me as a special friend. He told me to come back to his office at night. The procedure was unknown to me, so I had no idea what to expect. I was awake the entire time. Afterward, he stuffed my uterus with large handfuls of gauze, instructing me to take it all out five days later, at night, and throw it into the ocean.

As the days progressed, I became increasingly sick with infection. Before five days had passed, I could barely struggle down to the beach. I called in a sitter to come care for the children and then I called the doctor. He advised me to come directly to the emergency room. I managed to drive to the hospital, where I was given anesthesia before the doctor performed a dilation and curettage operation to clear out my uterus. When I awoke the next day, he told me that he had performed an emergency surgery to clear the area of infection and that I was lucky to be alive. At one point, my breathing had slowed and I was close to death.

Gerry had been away for one of his racing weekends. When he returned, I called and told him I would need a ride home from the hospital. When I told him why I had been there and what had taken place, I could not tell if he was shocked and saddened by what I had been through or only dismayed by his failure to get me pregnant again.

Life resumed, and I imagined that all was normal. I returned from a London buying trip with Bunny. The children were happy to have had playtime with their favorite sitter, Peggy O'Neill; but as she left, Peggy seemed restless and anxious to tell me something. Her sister had also come to stay and was close to Gerry's side the entire weekend. Peggy's story made it obvious that there was everything going on between the two of them. She left with tears in her eyes. I stood there stunned, but I said nothing of that incident to anyone. I knew that I could no longer hide from what was going on.

I decided to confront Gerry. He readily admitted to having an affair with Cathy Porter, which surprised me. Cathy and Cal, our longtime Malibu friends, appeared to have been happily married with two children. Perhaps Gerry decided to tell me of this one affair because everyone else in the community already knew about it and he was afraid I might hear of it from someone else.

Grateful for his admission, I thought this might possibly mean he was becoming contrite, but deep inside I knew that I could not trust him, admissions or not. I also could not let myself feel the rage that was brewing inside me. I had grown up with so much verbal and physical hostility in my childhood that I was determined to solve tense situations with either negotiation or truce—harmony but never anger. Anger for me was a personal defeat, a loss of control, a defect in my character. But it was only a matter of time before I lost my composure and the pent-up anger exploded.

Gerry arrived home late one evening without calling to explain why. Dinner had been ready for an hour. The children were already in bed. When he walked in with no excuse whatsoever, I just lost it. The stress had been building for months if not years. I took the heavy roasting pot and threw it to the floor with all the force I could muster. The cast-iron pot landed so hard that its handle flew off and hit one of the three large windows that formed the wall of the breakfast nook, leaving a large crack in it. Pot roast spewed across the floor as though some poor beast had been disemboweled in my kitchen. Gerry simply smiled with contentment at being able to crack my fortitude after years of resolving to remain calm and collected in the face of his blatant infidelities. I was mortified by my behavior and retreated to the bedroom.

Some days later, Gerry told me that he had to go to San Francisco for a business conference. He left me with the telephone number for his hotel. It was a Sunday, and my brain switched to that of an enemy spy. In ten years, he had never been to a lumber conference. When I called the hotel number and asked for Mr. Cooper, the receptionist politely responded, "Oh, I am so sorry, you missed Mr. and Mrs. Cooper. They just checked out." I confronted him when he got home that evening. He said nothing and left the house. We both remained silent during this period of increasing emotional conflict and desperation, neither of us wanting to accept the finality of our doomed relationship.

The final bomb detonated at Christmastime, when Gerry begged me to include Cathy Porter and her now three children to stay with us for Christmas. He said that Cal had recently asked for a divorce, so Cathy and her kids were going to be all alone for the holidays. Our family Christmases were a treasured time for me. Happiness flowed from the children and enveloped us all, while everything troubling in our lives was forgotten. I went upstairs to my studio, away from everyone, and began to sob. It was an impossible request to add another family to ours at such a time, especially Cathy, whom I realized had remained close to Gerry over the years. I called Bunny and told her what Gerry had asked. She blurted out, "You do know who her new child's father is, don't you?"

And in that instant, I did! My son Brant had been conceived during our vacation in Hawaii while visiting Jimmy Pfleuger. He was born in the month of December, nine months after our trip. After we returned home from Hawaii, Gerry had also returned to Cathy Porter. Her child and mine were born in the same month of December. Gerry was the father of both children. I went immediately to Gerry and told him that I now knew everything and calmly ordered him to get out of the house. He looked bewildered. It had never occurred to him that I would throw him out. He rummaged around and grabbed a few things. He seemed to think I was joking, that this would all blow over. His departure was for good, but only because I vowed that I would never allow him to return.

Our life together was finished—the years of raising a family in the Wave House, enjoying the simple elegance I treasured, my studies, the children happy in their lives and schools, their friends and activities. It had seemed an incredibly blessed life. People who knew us from afar thought we were the happiest of couples. Now it was all over. And the truth is, I was as guilty as he was. Dear reader, lest you think I am only a victim in this mess, let me tell you that by the time my marriage came to an end, I also had endeavored to find love elsewhere. What Gerry did not know as he walked out of my life that day is that I was already several months into an affair of my own.

CHAPTER TWENTY-FOUR

Dark Ages

True romance can begin anywhere. To explain the secret love that gave my life purpose and clarity during those last years in Malibu, I must first take you back to one of the darkest periods in human history, one that I had become familiar with while traveling with Ric Brown. In 1348, the Black Death swept out of Central Asia with a lethal power unmatched even by the Golden Horde of the Mongol Empire. People first noticed the plague when rashes appeared. Boils then grew in their groin and armpits. Within a few days, victims were overtaken by a high fever, vomiting blood before they died. Those who survived long enough watched as patches of their skin turned black and peeled.

Artists, always in the vanguard of spiritual expression, struggled to make sense of the apocalyptic scene unfolding around them. For centuries, they had brought solace to the people in their representations of Jesus, the Virgin Mary, and the apostles, but now they wondered if they had strayed from God's path. Patrons who saw a connection between art and religion, creativity and divine justice, now questioned the naturalistic tendencies in art that they had supported in recent years and considered a return to the rigid and conservative iconography of earlier centuries.

By the time the walls around my marriage disintegrated, I had been on several adventures through the wonders and terrors of European art history with Ric. The passion we felt for one another blended with the passion we both felt for the vivid tableau of history and creativity that lay across the Atlantic Ocean. He was an expert guide who became a partner in my quest to understand life in terms of art. With his help, I was able to find an academic focus centered on the interplay between art and religion and understand how a catastrophe like the bubonic plague could alter the history of both. Over several years, during which we traveled together in Europe, I became intrigued by the plague's influence upon art and introduced it into to my graduate studies at UCLA.

When I first started working as the docent program leader for LACMA, Ric invited me to New York to help him at the Knoedler Gallery when it was closing. It had been the finest old master gallery in New York, and we were to assess the collection and determine which paintings should go to auction, which should be held for future sales, and which might best be placed in other galleries or sold to museum collections. Ric convinced me that my researching skills would be of use in the decision-making process.

We studied the gallery's records, which included each piece's provenance, sometimes gathered over centuries. I often wondered in those years if my calling was to serve as Ric's amanuensis, as had been suggested to me by a friend. I was gaining "an eye" for quality and had even come to recognize the evolution of style over time in an artist's oeuvre. But after traveling with Ric, I learned just how rudimentary my skills were. Ric could spot a copy or a forgery from a distance.

The closer we grew, the more enthralled I became with his historical knowledge of the world. During one of our trips to New York, Ric and I enjoyed a long conversation in the hotel at the end of a workday. It seemed so natural when our relationship turned from an intellectual one to a more intimate affair. He was not only brilliant intellectually but also emotional about his work. He was warm and affectionate toward others, reminding me of my grandfather, who was also a man of short stature with an engaging personality.

I later joined Ric in pursuit of works for Norton Simon, a collection so broad that it gave me the opportunity to study some of the best-known works available by old masters of the Trecento, Renaissance, Baroque, Rococo, Neoclassic, Romantic, and Impressionistic periods. While helping Ric curate for the Norton Simon collection, I was also exposed to nineteenth- and twentieth-century modernism and contemporary art, a period that in later years came to form the foundation of my own art collection.

Ric had every expectation that Simon's collection was destined for LACMA. Simon was, after all, on the LACMA board of directors and implied that LACMA was to inherit his collection. As it turned out, Simon decided to create his own monument, the grand architectural triumph of the Norton Simon Museum in Pasadena, California.

Our greatest adventures involved following the path of artists and their works "in situ"—in churches, monasteries, or historic but forgotten piazzas. No goal was too far afield for Ric to search out for study—an altar piece or painting, for example, in the location for which it had been commissioned and where it would remain for posterity. My eagerness for adventure and discovery was kindled under his tutelage. During this time, I was discovering my own path for research in the world of art history.

The Black Death killed millions across Asia before entering Europe by overland trade routes and by sea. Physicians at first had no idea that fleas and rats carried the illness to the Mediterranean. With no understanding that bacteria carried the plague, many attributed the sudden scourge to a curse from God. The bodies of innocents fell by the thousands in cities, floated in rivers, and were carried away on wagons through the streets to be burned or buried. Within four years, half of the inhabitants in some regions of Europe were dead. Historians believe that the devastation was so vast and unprecedented that it may have brought an end to the Western Roman Empire. Nearly a thousand years after the fall of Rome, after generations of gradual artistic development, economic expansion, and trade, the Black Death cast the world into darkness once again. It was not until the Renaissance in the fifteenth century that art returned from stereotypical iconic worship scenes to the more realistic renderings of everyday secular life. It was this perspective that provided the backdrop for my research and studies.

One summer, we followed the Piero della Francesca Trail through the hill towns of Tuscany to find the panels painted by this Renaissance painter and mathematician. We found them hidden in small chapels or neglected in monasteries or cemeteries where they had been commissioned by donors five hundred years earlier to decorate their tombs. During the evenings, we usually discussed our discoveries over dinner at a piazza café. Ric guided me in exploring my deepening interest in the Trecento, which refers to Italian art in the 1300s. In this period, I found examples of paintings from before and after the Black Death. These works supported my theory that a plague had set back the evolution of naturalistic painting for generations.

Ric also knew where to find the monasteries that held closely guarded treasures, protected from the upheaval of the Medieval period and rarely revealed to anyone but art scholars. He led us to Piero's fresco series in Arezzo, *The Legend of the True Cross,* which depicts the chronology of Jacopo da Varagine's *The Golden Legend*—the story of the cross upon which Christ was said to have been crucified; and to the *Madonna del Parto* in Monterchi, which depicted a pregnant Virgin Mary painted with exotic colors brought from Central Asia by the Venetian doges; and to the *Polyptych of the Misericordia* in Borgo San Sepulchro (now Sansepolcro), one of Piero's earliest works, depicting the "Virgin of Mercy"—also painted in uniquely precious Asian pigments.

In pursuit of the Sienese School, in which Simone Martini was so noted, there was *Maesta* by Guido da Siena in the Palazzo Pubblico in Siena as well as the *Maesta of Duccio* in the museum of the Siena Cathedral. Ric introduced me to the lower story of the Basilica of St. Francis of Assisi, where the walls are covered with frescoes by Martini. We found our way to other examples by Martini, including the *Saint Catherine of Alexandria Polyptych* in the National Museum in Pisa and the painting of *Saint Louis of Toulouse Crowning His Brother Robert of Anjou* in the National Museum of Naples. These paintings retold stories and legends of Christendom in styles and perspectives that are the hallmark of the Renaissance. Everywhere we went, I looked for examples of how and when such art had changed in the face of the Black Death.

Ric's professional standing granted him access to treasures that were not open to the public. We visited the protected vaults of European libraries and museums for clues. We traversed the continent, seeking out the well-known and the least known art treasures wherever they were displayed. He led me to the Mausoleum of Galla Placidia in Ravenna, remarkable for its fifth-century mosaics in all their brilliance. There, I first learned the story of a remarkable woman whose tumultuous life spanned the fall of Rome and the rise of the Visigoths.

Galla Placidia was born in AD 388 and came of age as the classically educated daughter of the Roman Emperor Theodosius I. Her father became the last emperor to rule over both the eastern and western halves of the Roman Empire. During the ensuing battles for Rome, Galla Placidia was captured by Alaric I, first king of the Visigoths, and taken from the Italian Peninsula to Gaul. In AD 410, Rome fell to the Visigoths under Alaric, and Galla was then given as queen consort to Alaric's successor, King Ataulf, to broker peace between the two halves of the Roman Empire. She bore him a child that died in infancy. Following Ataulf's death, Galla Placidia was returned to her brother, Flavius Honorius, as part of yet another peace treaty when Rome once again gained power. Then forced to marry the general Constantius

III, she was named empress consort in AD 417. When Constantius was proclaimed emporer, his wife Galla was given the title Augusta, proclaiming her to be the only empress in the West. The two had three children, including Augustus Valentinian, the son for whom she served as regent.

Galla Placidia was a strong-willed and determined woman who remained a devout Chalcedonian Christian all her life, a faith that perhaps influenced the Visigoths to eventually support Rome. Her continuing influence upon Roman politics enabled her to build and restore a number of churches throughout her lifetime. Even as a young girl, she was known as *nobilissima puella*, or "most noble girl," and that is how history remembers her. Yet, despite her noble title, or perhaps because of it, her life was fraught with terror and dislocation.

Ric and I walked through the modest Mausoleum of Galla Placidia while discussing her extraordinary legacy. She had commissioned it herself and designed it in the shape of a Greek cross. The walls were intended from the beginning to be covered with mosaics expanding into the lunettes and cupola. They are the oldest and most brilliantly colored mosaics in Ravenna, creating an illusionistic light source within alabaster window panels. These mosaics represent perhaps the finest example from the Byzantine Empire, a period that represents a departure from the art of the Western Roman Empire and its legacy of Greco-Roman art. A salient feature of this Byzantine aesthetic was the presence of a more naturalistic representation, so prevalent in the figures of the apostles, the four evangelists, and Christ as the "Good Shepherd." It became for me a significant example of an early stylistic attempt at realism, though still tempered by conservative religious constraints. The iconic themes developed in these decorations represent the victory of eternal life over death.

Some years later, I called Ric when he was working in Fort Worth, Texas, at the Kimbell Art Museum and left a message for his secretary to tell him that Galla Placidia was calling. He rushed to the phone with merriment in his voice, and I could imagine his sparkling, laughing eyes. Yet, I was not the only woman in Ric's life, and I knew I never would be. His dear wife Polly had suffered from polio since the earliest years of their marriage, and she was the only true love of his life. Ric told me that polio had been the one illness that she had feared more than any other, and yet it had taken her.

Polly was intelligent, bright, thoughtful, and perceptive. I have learned that when a person's physical abilities decrease, other senses can become keener, including the sense of intuition. As a woman, I was convinced that she knew what was happening between Ric and me. I could see it when she looked my way. She seemed able to accept that our love for one another was pure and necessary, and we both accepted that I could never take her place.

During our research trips, Ric and I documented that a sea change had taken place in art during the Black Death and the social collapse that followed. Back in Los Angeles, I decided to work toward a master's degree in art history, encouraged by my professor, Karl Birkmeyer, at UCLA. My thesis was based upon past research as well as upon what I was learning and interpreting from the frescoes, mosaics, and paintings we had visited in Europe. Following the Black Death, artists turned back from styles of tentative realism for fear of divine retribution. The plague had set Renaissance culture back by at least one hundred years in some places.

I decided to introduce a new theory based on my familiarity with and attraction to the painters of the Trecento, calling it "Realism in Trecento Painting." Three specific venues were key to my studies. I visited them more than once, taking notes and then researching them further upon returning home.

The art of the 1300s had opened with mostly flat depictions of religious icons: saints, apostles, the Madonna and child, gilded depictions ordered by donors—and in which the donors were featured. The first of my three examples of an innovative, realistic style change were in the painted frescoes of Giotto in the Scrovegni Chapel in Padua, near Venice. There, the faces of Christ, Mary, and other biblical characters look back at us with a familiarity unknown during the Byzantine era. The Cappella degli Scrovegni, as it is known locally, was completed in 1305. In Giotto's frescoes, one can see a new presentation of realistic figures going about their daily activities, their faces calling out with human emotion. They move within innovative architectural and space perspectives amid natural surroundings. The depiction of shepherds in their pastoral landscapes is a quintessential example of the artist representing the everyday person in his day's work, a clear departure from the typical iconography of the preceding period.

My second source lay hundreds of miles south of Padua: the Basilica of St. Francis in Assisi. Its walls were also covered in frescoes by many artists of the period, including several chapels decorated by Giotto. The final and most significant depiction of a realistic figure was the famous fresco of Simone Martini in the Palazzo Pubblico of Siena, depicting the city's war captain, Guidoriccio da Fogliano, riding across the hills as the victorious leader of an important battle. This fresco provides the best example of an early thirteenth-century fusion of realism and imagination in the pictorial elements. In 1348, the Black Death had come to Sienna and killed half its inhabitants, rendering the exquisite walled city an economic and artistic backwater for decades. The Catholic Franciscans had risen to prominence, and this fresco was covered over with more conservative iconic religious figures.

Thanks to Ric, I had found an academic path that balanced my life in Malibu with the needs of my soul. Ric affectionately called me Galla, harkening back to our adventures in Italy. I was flattered and yet aware of Galla's troubled life. She was used as a pawn in the war of empires that surged around her and yet remained a woman of great influence. I was entranced by the idea that I too was might be called *nobilissima puella*; after all, I too was born into a palatial life and studied the arts in hope of becoming a valued patron. Perhaps one day

I would find a way to prove my worthiness.

Ric Brown was more than a teacher and a lover. He provided me with a confirmation of my deepest being, who I truly was in my soul. I learned from him that I could be loved for who I am. This confirmation had to come from someone I honored. Ric's love enabled me to persevere on a path that I hoped would one day allow me to help preserve and allow others to experience the creative gifts of our shared humanity. For the first time, I had found a romance that fulfilled both mind and body.

As the walls around my family came tumbling down, I held onto this inspiration. All I had ever wanted was to live simply but elegantly. And now my family life seemed like a hiding place where I had become unwilling to give up a dream of grace and bounty. In the wake of my imminent divorce from Gerry, I could not yet foresee that many miracles lay ahead and that my true life's work had only just begun.

CHAPTER TWENTY-FIVE

Tidal Pools

What remains after a rogue wave are the tidal pools. They settle quietly among the rocks, desiring only the peace that follows a storm. Zen masters say it's impossible to see our reflection in running water. That is only possible when looking into a still pool. It takes an act of will to go further than the surface and look into a deeper reflection of the self.

As my marriage fell apart and I was drawn deeper into my psyche to find reasons for its failures, I entered psychotherapy. Janet Leigh Brandt had the connections for this new road to self-discovery because therapy was becoming common among Hollywood celebrities. She recommended a Beverly Hills psychiatrist, an older man who listened carefully and made notes as I talked. I suppose he had the basic Freudian background of the time. We met once a week for about one hour over a two-year period, during which time Gerry and I continued divorce proceedings.

I welcomed this analytical process with my usual curiosity, loyally attending the weekly sessions in the hope of finding out just who I was and how I came to be this way. The process entailed an intense and honest examination of my past and the influences that brought me to the current moment. If there was any benefit from psychotherapy, it lay in seeing and honoring a clear and honest picture of myself. I was eager to learn and to move on with my life. I chose as a starting point of inquiry a conversation my mother related to me. Gerry had gone to see her after he was no longer living with us and divorce proceedings had begun. He professed with his usual self-assuredness to my mother that I had been "a good wife and a good mother, but never a good woman." I puzzled over that statement until it became an obsession. What did it mean to be a good woman? More sex? More tenderness? More expressions of love? Had five pregnancies in six years destroyed the chance for deeper expressions of love and enjoyment of the sexual act? Had our different interests driven us apart? Where does the blame reside when the pursuit of happiness divides into two vastly different paths?

The comment Gerry made to my mother triggered me in such a powerful way that it led to an obsession with uncovering the truth. The idea that I was somehow incomplete compared to the other women in Gerry's life was only a small part of the story. Gerry was not an emotionally expressive person; and in relation to him, I did not become more open and loving myself. Growing up with an alcoholic mother I could never fully trust or get close to and a father who was always away at work left me with no examples of how to be open and vulnerable with a partner. I focused on academics and athletics to feel worthwhile, and no doubt some of the competitive spirit I had developed in my youth followed me into marriage. Gerry saw me as strong in all ways because this was the persona I inhabited. He made it a contest to see how he could undermine my strength. Being open and vulnerable with Gerry seemed impossible because I had the feeling that he was out to destroy me.

I had unconsciously chosen just such a relationship because I had learned to surround myself in a protective box. There were walls in my psyche that would need to be broken down for me to have a lasting and loving relationship. I had co-created the situation with Gerry because I never revealed to him my basic human frailties. That is the only reason

I could think of for his hostility. It must have been maddening for him.

In psychoanalysis, one finds one's own answers. In the process, a new person emerges, with renewed confidence and honesty. I wanted to honor the new person I had become. Now, many years later, I have come to believe that this new perspective presents itself as a possibility for each new moment of each new day. It is a gift, as is each hour or minute of every day. But I still had so many questions at that time, some of which would only be answered in the actual living of life in the years that followed.

Psychotherapy showed me that I had acquired coping skills while growing up that stressed excellence even as they separated me from others. I learned that I had every reason to believe in myself as a woman and that I would only learn to trust men when I came to truly know and trust myself. The hardest thing to accept was that it had had been impossible in my youth to please my parents, yet this was the one thing I most wanted to do. The lack of self-worth that resulted from this dilemma could only be filled at the time with accolades from teachers and friends.

Then Gerry came along with the right background and a winning personality. He charmed my mother and flattered her, calling her "sporty" and making her laugh. He won her over; and because I needed her approval, to please her I leaned more and more toward accepting Gerry as a husband. The Canadian ski instructor Yves Latreille had already won my heart, but my parents would have none of it. He was not on par with Gerry because he was, in their eyes, a lowly ski instructor and not part of our social set. I felt powerless to protest at the time. Gerry had used his charisma to win over my parents and me, and our marriage would have been a total disaster if not for my wonderful children.

I too had been unfaithful, and now here I was on a therapist's couch, still an attractive woman, wondering what was next. Ric Brown was the first man I felt free with because he accepted me for who I was.

He appreciated my gifts and opened the door to a new self-appreciation. After being with Ric, I would no longer need to be put down by men. I learned from Ric that there is no danger in a truly loving relationship.

My friends and relatives pleaded with me not to divorce Gerry but, instead, to separate from him until I gathered more insight about the relationship. But even before entering therapy, I knew that no one could convince me to trust Gerry and take him back. Psychotherapy only confirmed this. The final judgment of our divorce came in August 1969. I continued to drive all five children to their respective schools for that year, but I was increasingly distressed by the hours and distances required. I decided to place Wave House up for sale and rent a house in Santa Monica. If Wave House were for sale today, it would likely fetch about $70 million. I sometimes wonder what kind of positive impact that money might have had on my family and on the network of philanthropic interests that became so much a part of my life in later years. But at the time, I needed to move on. There was no point in looking back.

After Ric moved to Texas, two other men entered my life. Randolph Galt or "Ran" as he was called, was an heir to the Signal Oil and Gas Company fortune. His father had been instrumental in founding the company, and Galt family members were still major stockholders. Ran had two children by his former wife, actress Anne Baxter. Anne was friends with Molly Chappellet, who introduced me to Ran. Their daughters Melissa and Maginel Galt became close friends with my children.

Ran was raised in Hawaii, where his family had a grand estate. He invited us all to join him there before Ran and I journeyed farther on to Australia. It was an offer I did not want to refuse. Jimmy Pfleuger and his wife Nancy kept all the Cooper children busy in Hawaii. Jimmy provided the "fun and frolic" they had become accustomed to in Malibu, including all the toys. Ran and I flew from Honolulu to eastern Australia for a visit to Sydney and the Great Barrier Reef. We then flew across the continent to Perth. After a short time in that city, we took a lengthy drive across rugged country to Ran's expansive sheep ranch. We rode horses across wide, rolling grasslands and enjoyed picnics under trees while looking out at the distant horizon. We stayed in a shack of a cabin where I did not sleep a wink because, while we lay in bed, scores of large rats ran across the ceiling above me. Ran assured me that I was perfectly safe, that they would not come close or hurt me. This did little to assuage my discomfort. I asked how his wife Anne had reacted to such a place. He smiled and admitted that she had only visited the ranch once, never to return. I doubt that I would have returned either, without some major remodeling to the cabin.

Corporations were purchasing resorts at that time. Just as Johns Manville bought Elkhorn in Sun Valley, Signal Oil decided it must have a resort on the island of Hawaii. Since it appeared that Ran was drifting in the corporate world, they placed him in charge of its development. Construction was beginning on a beach property near Kona called Kona Village, where thatched houses perched on stilts over the water.

Ran treated my children and me to yet another trip to Hawaii. As they slept above the changing tides at Kona Village, I was grateful that the kids had all learned to swim. During the first year of operation, the resort was practically empty of other guests, so we felt especially welcome. We became part of the employee staff, joining in volleyball games and water sports. We drove around the island, discovering hidden coves and beaches and hiking to the uppermost section of the Kīlauea volcano. It was a special family trip, and our constant activities doubtless helped the children adjust to the absence of their father.

The second man in my life during these years was Page Jenkins. I met him at the Anderson Company accounting firm after he was assigned to my account. He was younger than me by a few years and very much a bachelor in the new Los Angeles discotheque culture of the sixties. I loved to dance, so we frequented bars and discos on the Sunset

Strip, including P.J.'s, Troubadour, and Whiskey à Go Go. With these two adoring men in my life, I began to feel that I was still a desirable woman after all. In fact, my feminine confidence grew exponentially. I was also beginning to see the changing world beyond the insular level of society in which I had been raised and into which I had married. It came as a shock to me at one of the discos one night when I caught sight of a Black man dancing with a white woman. I had grown up in a time and place where Black people were our servants and we typically only knew their first names. I now lived in a world of new freedoms. I felt as though I had finally gone over the palace walls and was now experiencing the real world.

This new life was also fraught with new challenges: for the first time in my experience, I found it difficult to pay all the bills. For years, Gerry had taken care of spending on the house while I had cared for the children and their expenses. Now it was all up to me. What saved me was the prudence of my father. He had bought US Treasury war bonds for all his children, and I still had a stack of them in a Santa Monica bank. With excitement, I would go to the bank, open my safety deposit box, and cash several at a time. I was grateful for my father's thoughtfulness and generosity and thanked him for his foresight numerous times.

Over the years, I had also received some stock in Bullock's from both my grandfather and my father, and it had increased in value. My plan had been to save that for a rainy day, but this plan became tenuous when the divorce was finalized. I received no cash award. My lawyer assured me that he had conducted a thorough investigation into Cooper Lumber Company accounting. There was no trace of a salary having been paid to Gerry for many years, at least since his brother Jim Cooper had left the wholesale division of the company and Gerry had taken over the retail business. His salary had been surreptitiously hidden in company expenses.

I did at least receive the Malibu house and was now grateful that

I had decided to sell it. I also would receive an inheritance from the Cooper Lumber Company, but at that time I thought Gerry might outlive me or just happily spend those funds if the company was ever sold. Even with no salary and no record of such, Gerry had somehow managed to charge considerable expenses to the company, including boats, trailers, motorcycles, the remodeled bus, and now, the redesigned ferryboat he lived in. This new home, called *Nickel Grabber*, was an extravagant relic and a reminder of his expensive toys and lifestyle during our Malibu years. In its previous incarnation, the ferry had been used to cross Long Beach Bay before the bridge was built. During the boat's remodel, no expense was spared. Gerry hired Harry Gesner to redesign the exterior and interior to Gerry's liking and comfort. The boat was a home and, of course, faster than it needed to be.

During the divorce proceedings, Gerry informed my lawyer that if I wanted the children to go to private schools, I would have to pay for this "extravagance." It was clear that he wanted to punish me and see us suffer. It was up to me to adapt. There is an old saying, "Spend money wishfully but wisely." Wisely became the dominant theme in our lives, with anything "wishful" getting sidelined. Suddenly on my own with five growing children, finances became a serious concern. I embarked on an accounting addiction. I needed some kind of addiction at the time and this was a relatively purposeful one. I kept a ledger of every penny spent—and I mean every penny. We loved our trips to Brentwood's Twenty-sixth Street market, the toy store, the pharmacy with its ice cream counter, the cleaners, and other old stomping grounds from my childhood. But now, every ice cream cone, every stick of gum, every one-cent lollypop was entered into the ledger. I have that ledger today to share with the children and remind them of these years in our lives. Looking at the numbers brings a shocking reminder of the inflation in the cost of living that has taken place since the 1960s.

By now, I had grown close to my mother and father. After becoming sober, my mother was in a good place emotionally and spiritually, so I took my children frequently to visit their grandparents at their Trancas beach house. I had a renewed feeling of love for her, and I know she loved me. She was a delight when she was not drinking. There is no telling what she could have accomplished in Los Angeles if she had been sober all those years. My father might also have been a different person had he not had to prove himself to the world by working his life away at Bullock's. I also have pondered how my own life might have been different if I had not been driven to excel in order to cope with my insecurities. Looking back now, I can see that many of the philanthropic duties to which I was committed took me away from being there for my children when they needed me. I can only hope that I also set an example for them of how to proceed in life as an effective and caring individual.

During our last year in Los Angeles, I introduced our friend and babysitter Peggy O'Neil to my brother Walter. The three of us had visited Mike Hynes together in St. John's Hospital after he lost a leg as a result of a motorcycle accident. Later, I asked Peggy if she wanted to visit my brother before I dropped her home—I had promised him that I would come by and sit in his Formula Ford open-wheel race car while he adjusted the shocks and suspension before a race. He asked Peggy to do this instead; when I was ready to leave, he was not finished, and he asked Peggy if she would stay. She was there again the following night and the next night, and so began a romance that many years later led to their engagement, marriage, and home together in the Wood River Valley.

Great changes in life sometimes begin with the smallest of ideas. Because Kelley was determined to continue her ice-skating career, I undertook frequent drives to the Santa Monica Ice Rink—frequent because the hours differed depending on whether she was attending "patch" sessions, free skating, or lessons. While driving through traffic one day, I dreamed of having an ice rink available by bicycle or even in walking distance and suddenly flashed back upon my Sun Valley holiday in the 1940s. I called my old friend and ski instructor Bill Butterfield to ask him about the ice rink behind the lodge. Was it open during the summer months? He said that it was, this fact being the best-kept secret in Sun Valley. The few people who used the rink in the off-season had it practically to themselves.

I asked Bill if he could find me a rental; he called me several days later to say that he had found a place called the Miller House in the old mining town of Ketchum. The wood on the house was so old that it looked as if it had been recycled, he said, but it had ample bedrooms for all of us and a fenced-in yard for dogs. I immediately rented it for the following summer. We all went through our summer possessions to cut down on extraneous items and, when the time came, packed everything that fit into a trailer we pulled behind our black Chrysler Woody for the drive away from the sea, over the mountains, and across the vast desert to Idaho.

That joyous summer of 1968 changed our lives forever. I had been warned that the Wood River Valley was rustic, with few civilized offerings, but we were enchanted. We found ourselves doing everything together as a family. We rented bikes to use as our transportation, went fishing, rode horses, and hiked together to mountain lakes. The most amazing thing to me was that we all learned to ice-skate. I quickly became enamored with the idea of living in Sun Valley, as far away from Los Angeles as I could get. This was the way families were supposed to live, fully and happily together. It was normal and expected in Los Angeles to live with highway traffic and for kids to get dropped off at an activity and then retrieved hours later. Life in Idaho was so much less complicated and more natural. I arranged to rent the Miller House again the following summer and launched plans for a permanent move to Sun Valley during the next school year.

I wanted our last year in Santa Monica to be a reminder of the playful environment in which my children had been raised. I wanted them to have happy memories instead of the fraught memories that I carried, so I rented a large property and home on La Mesa Street near San Vicente. The property had a tennis court plus a pool and pool house with extensive gardens manicured by a gardener. Looking back on it now, I should not have been aghast at the monthly rental price of $1,000, but at that time it was a stretch for our budget.

The children excelled in school and in their social lives that last year. Their father came to visit and, in his usual fashion, threw them one at a time ten or twelve feet into the air before catching them. It was extraordinary that anyone could throw a child so high. Of all the children, only Cam would freeze in shock as he flew up in the air, which I attributed to his fall off the Palos Verdes cliff years earlier.

With a move to Idaho scheduled for the following summer, I concentrated on my academics. I planned to complete all aspects of my master's degree other than the actual writing of my thesis, which I would undertake to finish in Sun Valley. I reviewed the notes from all the courses I had taken over the previous five years in preparation for taking the multiday art history comprehensive exams. These took all day and covered the many cultures of world art. I passed the comprehensive exam as well as the required language exam. Thankfully, I was still competent in French.

That last year of decisions included "refining" our belongings, which is the nicest way to describe going through everything a family of six possesses and treasures with the intention of discarding much of it. Every parent knows the heart-rending decisions that must be made by a child who has created a diversity of collections with pride. They ranged from Cam's extensive comic book collection to Candy's plastic horses. She owned every horse that had ever been created in a popular series, now numbering over two dozen. Kelley treasured her collection of Hummel figurines. My own collections included a trove of at least two dozen sports trophies, large and small, that had been packed away during our many moves. After some thought, I swallowed my pride and placed them all in the trash can at the end of the driveway. I was confronted several days later by the gardener who sheepishly confessed to me that he had taken them out of the can and given them to his children. I gave him a big hug for that, and we smiled at each other, agreeing to keep it a secret.

I had lived in California for thirty-eight years. My friends and family thought I was crazy for moving to Idaho. My mother knew the reputation of Sun Valley for attracting celebrities and was certain that I was moving there to find a husband. This is what Sun Valley was known for in its early years. Divorces could be quickly decreed in Idaho, and there were always interesting and wealthy guests around who might be looking for a new relationship. I chuckled at the thought. I had a life so full of challenges that a new marriage was the last thing on my mind.

Gerry continued to follow the boat racing circuit. Mike Hynes was made manager of the Cooper Lumber Company. He was an excellent choice, astute in managing people and the details of a retail operation. This gave Gerry total freedom to roam and play. He would come by to visit us at the La Mesa house, which was always painful for me. It seemed as though he came to show off some blonde and buxom babe rather than to spend any length of time with his children. It was also an opportunity for him to show off his beautiful children to his girlfriend of the moment.

Besides our dogs, we acquired one new pet—exotic as usual. For some reason, Ric Brown thought we should have a skunk. One was available from the Fort Worth Zoo, so he brought it by plane as a gift to the children. I was aghast at such a pet, even if it had been de-skunked. It turned out to be the worst choice of pet. A nocturnal animal, it came into view only at night when we were all asleep, and by day it simply hid under some piece of furniture—usually my bed, since that was the quietest spot in the house.

My last time with Ric was sad and distressing. As his new life unfolded back in Texas, he continued to visit Los Angeles to finalize details of his permanent move. His wife Polly had died. He grieved as one does for the love of one's life. He had been dedicated to making her life as livable as possible; and now that she was gone, he was distraught. Ric arrived at our house one day a few weeks before we were scheduled to leave for Sun Valley. He seemed very disturbed and anxious, and he said that I must come to live with him in Texas immediately.

Perhaps Polly's death had made him slightly irrational. I told him I could not move to Texas, that we had a plan already and needed time to adjust to our new lives. I also told him of my progress in psychoanalysis and what I had been learning about myself. Rather than take interest or provide understanding, Ric was distressed by what I shared with him. He declared that what he had to offer me was far more important—a dedicated husband, a life in the art world and all that would bring me—far better than what he assumed some doctor was telling me about what was best for me. He slammed his fist upon the table. "You don't need therapy," he shouted. "You need me!"

He then left abruptly, saying he was going to marry Jane, his longtime secretary, even though she was still married and had a son. Jane and her family were friends who had come to the Malibu house occasionally. Indeed, Ric soon married Jane and they had two more children.

I remained in contact with Ric, but he had decided to move on, even though he was not willing to let me move on. What he could not understand was that I needed time to evolve into someone who was more confident of her own decisions. I needed time for the sake of my children too. I could not make a decision of such magnitude.

Just as I was ready to move on to a new experience in Idaho, everything suddenly changed. Ric stormed off, and only ten days before our scheduled departure for Sun Valley, I received a frantic telephone call from the Wallaces, friends of ours in Houston. There had been a terrible accident, and they begged me to come at once to the hospital where Gerry was in intensive care, unresponsive.

CHAPTER TWENTY-SIX

The Crash

I arrived at the hospital in Houston to find Gerry still unconscious. His head and body were swathed in bandages. Stitches covered parts of his head, neck, chest, and abdomen. I found out later that surgeons had sewn up a major artery in his neck after he was pulled from the water and rushed to the emergency room. I walked into the intensive care unit and quietly spoke his name. He opened his eyes and took my hand. It occurred to me that I might be the only person left in his life he would want by his side. His parents had already died, and he was no longer close to his brother.

The medical staff told me that Gerry had been in a terrible crash while boat racing and that surgeries had been undertaken to close the many gashes on his body. The situation was still tenuous; but once he had awakened to the sound of my voice in intensive care, he was moved to a regular room. Gerry was grateful to know that I had traveled such a long way just for him. For three days, I stayed by his side, doing what I could to keep him quiet and calm and keep others out of his room.

Mike Wallace was a close friend of Gerry's, even though they competed constantly in boat races. He told me what had happened that day in Houston as high-speed motorboats prepared for the start of a 250-mile race. I pieced together other details from a sensationalized account in the *LA Times's West* magazine, which came out months later. The press, determined to make Gerry larger than life, was gullible in accepting his tales of heroic determination.

"If you are a woman, beautiful and charming, living near the water in California, Florida—anywhere, really, where speedboat racing is in vogue—then there is a sporting chance that a lanky millionaire with a broken nose and a boyish grin will show you his scar. . . ." Thus began starstruck Patrick McNulty's February 23, 1969, article in *West.* He went on to describe the scar as fitting Gerry's "outdoorsy, handsome face like the Heidelberg dueling marks of a Prussian aristocrat or a Maasai warrior's facial tattoos."

The story included a lengthy interview with Gerry. Apparently, he arrived in Houston in time to help install a supercharger in his light single-seat racing boat, which he compared to driving a Grand Prix car. "So, we had 700 horsepower—about 200 more than the boat was designed for," Gerry said. But after a few test runs, the boat checked out and he joined the field of thirty-six boats jockeying for starting positions. "To Cooper's annoyance, the start was by a helicopter dropping a bag of flour when the boats were properly lined up," McNulty continued. "As was his habit as a daring competitor, he gave it full throttle at the lineup start, so he would be first to the first buoy turn."

Gerry told McNulty, "I don't like helicopter starts, because you have to look up and watch for this cornmeal when you may be running at 90 miles an hour with full fuel tanks, a hot engine, and thirty-five boats around you. You have to look at both sides, too, and watch your instruments and the water and all at the same time. I'm short of eyes for this."

Gerry planned to position himself right under the helicopter until he saw the flour bags drop; but when it cut across the lake and he tried to follow, he was faced with a shallow section of water that he knew might be treacherous. Rather than turning back, he lost his temper and floored the engine. "She was running around 112 an hour," Gerry said. "I had no reason to be going that fast. I was over my head and I misjudged the wind and it caught up with me."

One moment the three-thousand-pound boat was skipping across the choppy lake, and the next moment it was cartwheeling in the air. It landed on Gerry in shallow water as the crowd screamed and gasped. He was rescued unconscious from the water and rushed to the hospital. The surgeon who had to sew the two thousand stitches to close up his wounds said it looked like the boat's propeller had landed on his head and body, causing deep lacerations. The magazine story noted that Gerry went into the intensive care unit and for several days the team of doctors attending him said it was touch and go. "But speedboat racers and especially Cooper are made of sterner stuff, and soon Cooper was sitting up, joking, and even hosting informal daytime parties in his hospital room with local racers and friends who had flown in from California," McNulty wrote.

The parties in his hospital room never took place, although I was dismayed and concerned by the commotion caused by a number of women in the hallway waiting to get in to see him. Each of them had a different plea . . . a wife, a sister, a cousin, an old friend. I quickly set boundaries for no visitors at all. The doctors expected Gerry to recover in the hospital for at least two weeks. He pleaded with me to stay and keep everyone else away. For that reason alone, I remained until he was in stable condition. Despite Gerry's apparent popularity, I went to Houston because the Wallaces had implored me to come before he died alone with no family present.

"However, the man of action quickly became restless," McNulty continued. He wrote that Gerry soon got up and walked out—well before doctors would have authorized his release—borrowed some clothes from an orderly, flagged a cab, and flew home to LA. Harry Gesner recalled seeing him at the LA airport when he arrived from Houston—emaciated, bandaged, and in terrible shape. Apparently, about a month later, Gerry was again behind the wheel of a speedboat, bounding over the Pacific swells in California's rugged Hennessy Cup around Catalina Island. "He finished first in his class," wrote McNulty. "In four other post-Houston races, Cooper placed second and earned enough points to become last year's Pacific Coast Offshore Racing Champion."

I will not argue with the race results, but I find this hard to believe since it took Gerry some time to recover enough strength to even leave his hospital bed. Gerry's stories were different for different people. McNulty asked his readers, "Why would a man so cruelly mutilated, almost killed, return to such a violent pastime?" I could never answer for Gerry. It seemed that his life path, as many friends verified, was a suicide-mission ego trip, something based on a death wish.

But Gerry did answer that question for McNulty. "I never considered quitting because of the accident," Gerry told him. "The suggestion was put to me by many people, but I treated it in the manner you would treat a proposition to give up driving after smashing a front fender. An accident like the one at Houston is frightening when you don't know why it happened. Everyone tends to fear what they don't understand, and I knew I had an overpowering machine at Houston. I knew I was racing a boat capable of exceeding its design speed. It had to be driven with care. It wasn't. It will be next time."

I can't pretend to understand all of Gerry's motivations or his apparent addiction to danger, but I returned home after he was two days out of the ICU to tell the children of their father's courage, confirming that he was going to be just fine. It was a shock when Gerry, weak and bandaged, stumbled into the La Mesa house just a few days later. He was in no condition to travel, let alone be out of the hospital. I put him to bed in one of the children's rooms. He stayed with us until the day before we departed for Idaho.

I told Gerry that he would have to make plans for a place to stay. I heard later that he had gone to the home of Carole Cooper and her two girls, Kim and K.C. Carole was now divorced from Gerry's brother

Jim. At least Gerry had a place to stay and someone to look after him. I pondered at the time whether his early departure from the hospital could come back to haunt him. In any case, it was time for me and my children to get back on track.

Our journey to the Wood River Valley might have been a script for Comedy Central amusement. Page Jenkins and I took turns driving the large, rented van filled with all of our remaining treasured possessions and our dogs, Archie and Lizzy. We towed our family car behind us. "No exotic pets allowed!" I insisted. Two days later, as we passed Twin Falls en route to the Wood River Valley, Page asked me why I would willingly choose to live in such god-forsaken, dry sagebrush country? "Are you out of your mind?" he wanted to know.

I began to wonder myself until we dropped down into the valley from Timmerman Hill and the landscape before us turned lush green. I had never before driven to the valley, always arriving by train or plane. It was the Fourth of July weekend, and the Wood River Valley spread out before us like Shangri-La, with rugged mountain peaks in the distance.

After settling in for a day, Page left to return the van to California. The children, accompanied by Peggy O'Neill, were due to arrive the next day by train in the nearby town of Shoshone. Mike Hynes had dropped them off at Union Station in downtown Los Angeles. Gerry managed to be there and said his farewells. The children ranged in age from eight to fourteen at that time, so the train ride was a novel experience for them. The rail route had changed since I traveled to Sun Valley in the mid to late 1940s. The new, overnight route was to Green River, Wyoming, where they transferred to the City of Portland passenger train.

Physician George Saviers, a new Sun Valley friend, offered to drive me to Shoshone to meet them. I welcomed the offer since I as yet had no idea of about routes and travel times in the area, especially at night. We arrived to find Indians sitting on the train platform with their artwork and trinkets for sale. Sadly, those too inebriated to stand were seated cross-legged against the train station wall. The scene was so rural and unusual that my children had to be wondering what else this new land had in store for them.

When Page Jenkins turned back for California and George Saviers entered my life as a devoted friend, I could finally accept that my newly found career as a woman was flourishing. Yet, somewhere in the back of my mind was a little voice that said, "Be careful what you wish for."

CHAPTER TWENTY-SEVEN

The Rogue Wave Recedes

When a wave retreats, it once again becomes part of the vast ocean waters and its tides. It is never destroyed or eliminated—except in form—from the universe. Water evaporates and falls again as rain, becoming part of the planet's giant recycling plan. I believe that our souls are also part of this enduring cycle of birth, death, and regeneration.

After our second summer in Sun Valley, I received a telephone call from Gerry. He said that, not feeling well, he had checked in with a doctor, who discovered tumors in both of his lymph nodes. The doctor had prescribed surgery to remove the tumors and then radiation. Gerry assured me that it was nothing and that all would be fine. I suspected that this was the rogue in him talking. Scoundrels often think they are exempt from the laws of nature and society.

I accepted the medical diagnosis that all would go well after the procedures, but deep in my heart I feared the worst, remembering Gerry's early departure from the Houston hospital without a doctor's approval and the way he had failed to care for himself during recovery, even boat racing again one month later. The fact that the tumors were located exactly where the propeller had cut across his neck hardly seemed coincidental.

The children had just started their new schools in Blaine County that fall. I focused on their needs as we settled into a new rental home on Bitterroot Road, owned by Rosemary Bradford, recently married to William R. Hewlett, cofounder of Hewlett-Packard. The Bradford house was one of the first homes built on quiet Bitterroot Road, a place removed from the bustle of condominium life in the resort.

During our recent months in Sun Valley, I had reunited with some old friends from Los Angeles, including Bill and Anne Janss. Bill Hewlett was a close friend of Bill's. They had attended Stanford together, and their families enjoyed summers together in the Sierras. Anne and I started ice-skating together behind the Sun Valley Lodge, and we were all looking forward to a winter of skiing.

Lots were not selling well in the late 1960s because Sun Valley was just beginning to be renovated as a ski resort. Wanting to help his friend Bill Janss through a period of slow sales, Bill Hewlett bought four Lodge I condominiums; but Rosemary preferred her small, cozy house, with all its upstairs bunk beds for children and visitors.

My children and I had settled into our rental house; and as the days became cooler, we began to face the reality of the coming winter. We took numerous trips to the Gold Mine Thrift Store to dress five children for lower temperatures than they had ever experienced before, riding our bikes together to the store and then back home with our bags of clothing.

Another call came from Los Angeles in late October, this time from Mike Hynes. He said that Gerry had been admitted to St. John's Hospital in Santa Monica. The prognosis was no longer positive—the cancer had spread throughout his body. Mike implored me to come and bring the children as quickly as I could. I needed no such plea—Gerry had no other family.

Rosemary had informed me that we would need to move out of our rental house because she wanted to use it for visitors during the Christmas holidays and winter months. I spent no time in packing up the house, having no idea how long I would be gone. In any case,

I knew it would have to be cleared out by mid-December. When he heard the news, Bill Janss generously offered to fly the six of us to Santa Monica in his private plane. It never occurred to me not to feed the children that morning in case of rough air. It must have come as a shock to Bill, a seasoned pilot in a family of pilots, when several of my children utilized their air sickness bags.

Page Jenkins met us at the Santa Monica Airport and took me directly to the hospital. Mike picked up the children and took them to the Morning family's new home in what had once been the garage of my father and mother's old estate. A generation on, my children were taking refuge in the very same place I had lived as a child. I cannot but marvel at the synchronistic circumstances that brought us back to San Vicente. The Mornings showed such deep loyalty and abundant generosity when they welcomed the Cooper children as they came tumbling into their home. The four Morning children shared their bedrooms. My five, plus their daughters Robin, Jody, and Katie, and their son Jimmy, made a total of nine to feed, watch over, to get to appointments like ice-skating routines, and a wide range of school itineraries.

Steve McQueen and his family invited Brant and Christin to stay with them, which gave my two youngest something approximating their former life. They attended the same school as the McQueens' children; then too, there was a busy garage of cars and motorcycles coming and going, and activities provided by Steve for his own children. I hoped it would echo for Brant and Christin a familiar world that could lessen the impact of their father's death.

I reenrolled the children into the schools they had just left; Carlthorp for the three youngest and Lincoln Junior High for Cam and Candy. Kelley had been living with her father on his ferryboat that fall because she was so deeply committed to her ice-skating career that she had begged to stay a year longer to attend her lessons and practice sessions before and after school. She too now became a child of the Mornings. Betty Jane became the taxi cab for all these children's activities.

I decided resolutely to live out Gerry's last weeks or months with him in the hospital. I had him transferred to a room with an adjacent sitting area where I could sleep on the couch. There was no doctor in the hospital who was willing to give him even the slightest chance of survival. Chemotherapy was at that time a largely experimental treatment, known to be as destructive to one's body as it was healing.

In my despair at watching the father of my children die before my eyes, I sought counsel—any counsel—from anyone in the hospital I could find to help me. I was thirty-eight years old, the mother of five children whose father was dying of an incurable disease. There was no rational way for me to accept that this young, virile man was dying, yet that is what I was told, and no guidance was provided to help me deal with the situation. I met with the resident chaplain. Despite my upbringing in the Episcopalian religion, his counsel brought me no peace. Even as my children needed answers and support during this time, I felt that I was being submerged daily in an abyss of grief, and the doctors' serious demeanor offered little hope.

A few weeks into this hospital life, I learned of a *Life* magazine article about psychiatrist Elizabeth Kübler-Ross. She had written a groundbreaking book on the taboo topic of death, *On Death and Dying*. The first highly recognized book of its kind, it dealt with the difficult and impending topics I now faced and contained information and advice on bereavement and the five natural stages of grief. With no one else to go to for support, Kübler-Ross's book became my bible. She came to the rescue just as Adele Davis had become an invaluable resource for me in the 1950s with regard to diet and nutrition.

Gerry wanted few visitors, so we agreed to allow only Mike Hynes, Betty Jane and Vetz Morning, Bob Brandt, Don Bren, Jim Cooper, and few others. I could count them all on the fingers of my two hands. They included a wonderful young woman by the name of Kee Ralphs.

She and Gerry had been together for a few months. I really liked her and felt she was good for him, especially compared to the women he had paraded by us in the past. Kee was smart, pretty, and wise for her age. Though we didn't recognize the connection at the time, I later discovered that she was an heir to the Ralph's supermarket chain Bullock's had bought in 1963; she and I had both gone through the 1964 proxy fight that gave Federated ownership of both. Only later was I able to take the time to ponder the mysterious design of the universe that brings synchronistic relationships like ours together at a time of shared grief.

After one of her visits with Gerry, Kee seemed confused, as if she wanted advice from me. In the hall, she asked rather shyly if she was needed or should come by again. It seemed as if this were all too much for her and she would prefer that the family take over, since we were all here now. She was only in her mid twenties; to have her boyfriend suddenly dying would certainly have been emotionally debilitating. I assured her that I would be happy to have her there whenever she wished to be. I believe Gerry must have released her from any responsibility to visit and she wanted to have that assurance from me as well. Long hours of sleep became Gerry's blessed gift each day, and I took those opportunities to help meet the demands of the children's schedules—schools, activities, and just time to play or be together.

A few days after I moved into the hospital, I received a handwritten note from Page Jenkins, delivered from the ground floor reception desk. He wrote that, because I had returned to my husband, he wanted to cut off our relationship entirely. This came as a total shock to me. I had not yet received any contact from him since my arrival in LA. Page had questioned me on the way to the hospital as to the real reasons for my coming. I assured him that there was no one else, no family member or close friend, who could be there for Gerry and, as our children's father, I owed him my commitment and presence. I was reminded of the way Ric Brown had reacted to my planned move to Idaho. His note was devastating, coming as it did at a time of deep grief when I most needed support. I cried for a while before returning to the hospital room to care for Gerry.

I saw Page once more, much later in life, at a Sun Valley Center for the Arts wine auction. I decided to go up to him and say hello. He seemed embarrassed but introduced me to his wife and the group at his table. With nothing else to say, I returned to my own table, feeling no emotion from the chance encounter except a sense of closure.

Gerry had, in fact, asked me to rejoin him in marriage and wear my wedding ring to honor that commitment. He asked Mike Hynes to open a locked drawer in his office at the lumber company and bring the ring to me, and he vowed to come to Sun Valley with me and the children. I acquiesced to all, knowing that after weeks or maybe months, but more likely only a few days, Gerry would not be content to live in the Wood River Valley. He would need his race boats and cars and his exciting life. There was nothing in Idaho that could in any way excite, interest, or entice him. But at the moment, he needed something to believe in. Although it was obvious he did not have much longer to live, I happily wore the wedding ring in recognition of our love and our years together as a family.

Our apparent renewed connection drew attention from Gerry's brother Jim. He asked me to join him in the hospital hall, where he said that I would be making a big mistake by not re-marrying Gerry right away, as the inheritance and tax ramifications for me and my family were much more favorable for a married couple. I was shocked to be asked to do this. It would have been a continuation of Gerry's and my living a lie. I had moved beyond that now and needed to be true to myself. It would only have been for money.

At Thanksgiving, after a month into the hospital routine, Gerry asked to see his children, so I brought them all there to his bedside. The older ones all scrambled onto the bed to give him a kiss. He looked so fragile that they were afraid to hug him too tightly. Christin was too small to get onto the bed like her siblings and was lifted up, as was Brant. To this day, she tells of her feelings at the time of failing her father in this small way—not being able to climb onto the bed.

Afterward, Gerry told me, "I don't want them to see me this way again." This was for me one of the saddest moments of those six weeks in the hospital. It was so in keeping with Gerry's character but thoroughly impossible to explain to the children. In late December, Gerry struggled by himself to the bathroom, not wanting help, as usual. He fell to the bathroom floor, and I helped him up. As we struggled back to the bed, he said to me, "This is like each day another nail is hammered into my coffin."

Anyone who has watched a loved one deteriorate before their eyes will understand the intensity and stark reality behind such a statement. Every day, he became weaker and more fragile, disappearing like a wave reentering the ocean until it fades into nothingness . . . and yet everything-ness. Looking back, I think of the words of John Cage, words of spiritual consolation: "Every something is an echo of nothing," and Lucio Fontana's idea, "Humanity, in accepting the idea of infinity, has already accepted the idea of nothingness."

On the night of December 4, 1969, Brant's eighth birthday, there was a small party planned at the Mornings' house to celebrate the occasion. I left the hospital to be there in time for dinner. Gerry had been unresponsive for two days. As we prepared to light the birthday candles, the hospital called to say that Gerry's vital signs were rapidly diminishing, that I must hurry to be there before he passed. I rushed over but did not make it in time and just fell apart when I arrived to hear the news that he had died. The finality of it overwhelmed me—and of all days, for him to die on his youngest son's birthday. Brant had been born in the same hospital exactly eight years before. All I could do was return to the Mornings' house to tackle the challenge of telling my children.

They were all asleep when I arrived, so I awaited the morning. We gathered in a circle on couches in the Mornings' living room. There is no compassionate way to tell your children that their father is gone forever. Their reactions varied depending on their ages and developing personalities, each finding different ways to deal with the tragedy—leaving the room, running outside, becoming removed and quiet, crying, or seeking hugs.

Yet, Gerry would never recede from us forever. In fact, his memories as a rogue wave have created for him an infamous and treasured memory for many who knew him. He remains a legend even now. Mike Hynes took over all responsibility for the planning of a memorial service while I immersed myself in the children's schedule. The service was a wondrous event, due entirely to Mike's sensitivity and ingenuity. I was not entirely there, still lost in a world of unbelief.

The service took place in the Glass Church of Palos Verdes on the cliffs above the Pacific Ocean, with the crashing surf below that was always so ironically a part of Gerry's life. The church had been designed by Frank Lloyd Wright's son, Lloyd Wright, who said he wanted to achieve a "delicate enclosure that allows the surrounding landscape to define a sacred space," a place of calm within the storm of life, so fitting for a man whose dream house confronted the immensity of the ocean through walls of glass. The church, also called the Wayfarers Chapel, still commands this daring location.

Mike managed to hire the Robert Mitchell Boys Choir, directed by renowned organist Bob Mitchell, who led the boys in two songs that epitomized Gerry's life and aspirations. The first was "Born Free"; and for a finale, the angelic choir sang a song made famous by Frank Sinatra, "To Dream the Impossible Dream." This final musical epitaph captured all that Gerry was. Tears flowed as the service closed.

There is a benediction in the Wayfarer's Chapel: "May the harmony of sky and water and rock nourish the creation and growth of your inner being as you fare through this life and into the life beyond." The church and choir created the nourishing space for us all as fellow wayfarers on

Gerry's journey. In the chapel, there is another inscription: "Pause for a moment, Wayfarer, on life's journey. Let the beauty of holiness restore your soul." A sacred silence came into each of us that day.

There was no end to what the Mornings did for our family. Gerry's service was followed by a reception at their house for as many friends as could be there. Some had traveled across the country to honor his memory. Piano playing, singing, drinking, and much reminiscing with laughter temporarily took the edge off the day. The following days passed almost blankly, as if we were all in a fog. I began to plan for our return to Sun Valley, but where, how, and when? It was not a simple thing in the 1960s to get to and from the Wood River Valley. Commercial flights were few. I decided that Candy and I would return together first. As the eldest, she could help me clean and prepare the Bradford House in the few days left before the rest of the family arrived. We had to remove all of our possessions before the holidays, so I quickly arranged to rent a Villager I condominium for the two weeks of Christmas.

Candy and I were ready for the other four children's arrival by plane on the only commercial airline then available in Hailey, Idaho—Janss Airways. The children said their sad farewells to dear friends at school for the second and last time. This farewell only added to their confusion and grief over the loss of their father. As much as we want to protect our children from the vicissitudes of life, some of the walls of security and perfection that we erect for them must come tumbling down, just as they had in my own life. We each face reality in our own way. Life is never the way it is "supposed to be." It's simply the way it is. How we cope with it is what makes the difference. Before me now lay a challenge and an opportunity to make a new life for us. My goal was to ensure that this life would be a full, happy, and rewarding one.

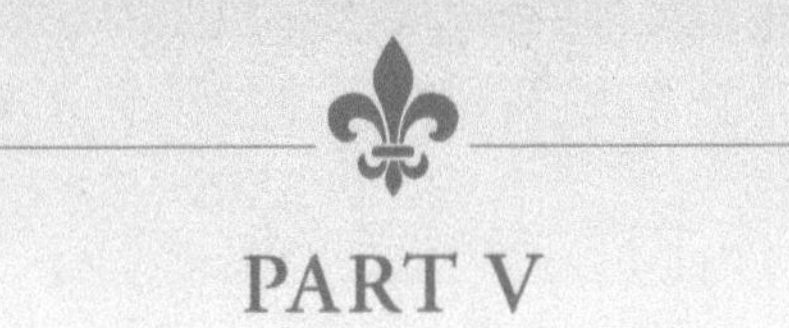

PART V

New Frontiers

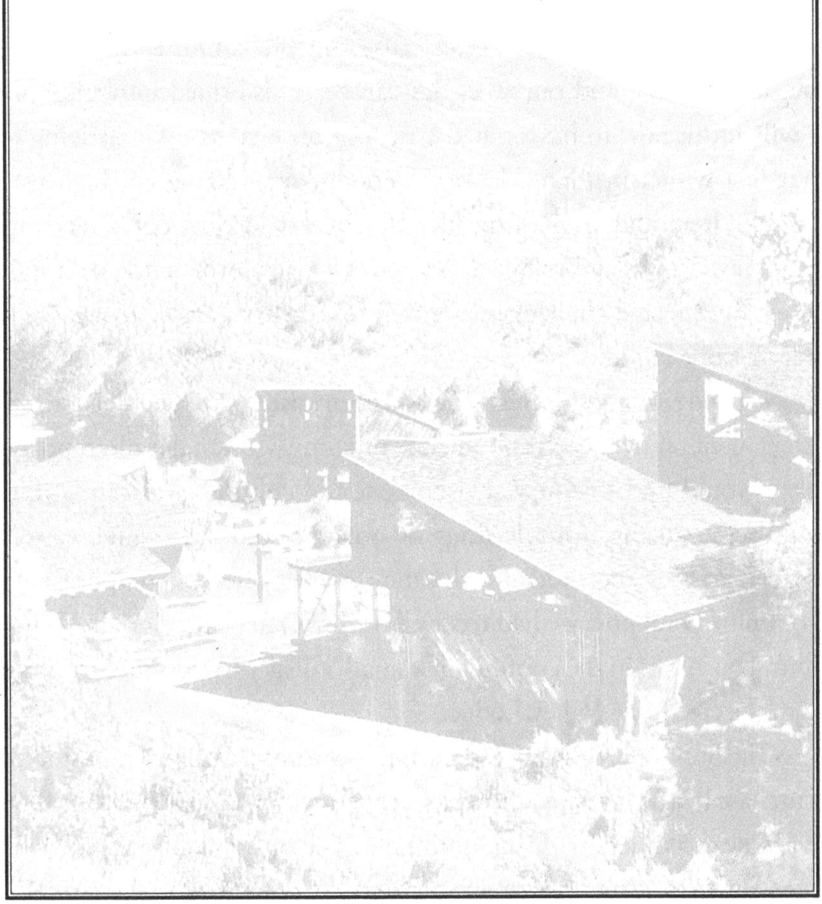

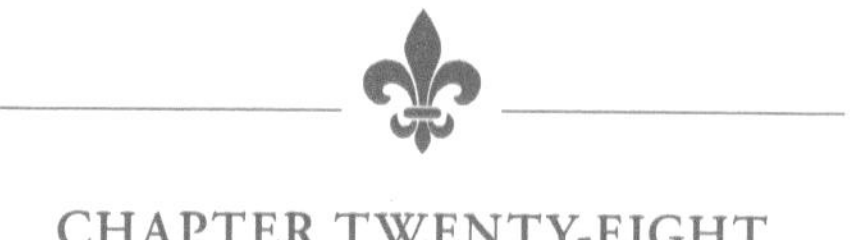

CHAPTER TWENTY-EIGHT

A Year of Trial and Error

As I look back, it seems as though life has a plan for us. We connect the dots in a way that links cause and effect. Our early intuitions become choices, and our struggles can be transformed into triumphs. I will admit now to having had a rush of misgivings upon arriving for our first winter in Idaho. It was a monumental change in the lives of my children, and we had no idea how it would turn out. Those first years in Sun Valley brought a potpourri of new experiences and quite a few unexpected challenges. We were still newcomers from the sunny beaches of Malibu.

I feared that my children, who had been raised with such freedom and excitement on the beach and in close proximity to a major metropolitan area, would find this new environment and cultural landscape stifling and demoralizing. Our feelings of isolation and disorientation were exacerbated by the sudden dislocation we felt after the outpouring of community support we had received during Gerry's memorial. We now found ourselves in the confines of a small Villager Condominium across the lake from Sun Valley Lodge.

The Sun Valley Resort had been under a general renovation since its purchase by the Janss Investment Company from Union Pacific in 1964, with the construction of condominiums and the development of new ski runs and lifts. It was a different era than when I first visited in the 1940s, yet real estate was selling very slowly in 1969, and the area was not yet a popular destination. Ketchum was basically a sheepherding town. There were four stop signs on Main Street and no traffic lights because there was so little traffic. The town felt tiny, surrounded by untold millions of acres of mountain wilderness. Few stores or restaurants stayed open during "slack," the period of time before ski season when many proprietors closed their doors and left town. The Tub Laundromat, operated by Virgie Deckard, was in an old shack on the road to Sun Valley. Virgie washed and folded our clothes for pick-up every few days. Louie's Pizza and Italian Restaurant was situated in an old converted white wooden clapboard church. The Western Café on Main Street in Ketchum served breakfast for the old-timers who sat there with their coffee, cigarettes, and stories in the early morning hours.

Moving to Ketchum had felt like going back in time to 1950. De Costa's was the one and only clothing store in town. The Ketchum Drug Store on Main Street was the center of commercial activity, a veritable emporium selling everything from toiletries and birthday presents to magazines, socks, and underwear. Its soda fountain drew kids on Fridays after school for five-cent ice-cream cones. The Sun Valley Lodge up the road still had an old-world mystique to it, but one could feel the resort's reflected energy, poised as it was on the brink of big changes. During our first summer in Ketchum, I purchased a lot on Bitterroot Road bordering Trail Creek, just below the Sun Valley Horsemen's Center. Lots were a bargain purchase; the Janss Corporation wanted to sell the land to raise funds for further development of the ski resort. Trail Creek curved around our home site.

Perhaps because of the nostalgia I was feeling at that time for my own childhood, I decided to reach out to someone from my youth who had loved and supported me unconditionally yet suddenly abandoned me and my brothers without explanation—Esther Perschnick. I had learned some years earlier that she moved to St. Anthony, Idaho, a few hours' drive from Sun Valley. I looked her up, found her telephone number, and called her. Esther was surprised to hear from me, and there was some awkwardness to our conversation. So much time had passed, and now I had five children. I convinced her to come over for a few days and meet my children.

When Esther came to town, we had fun together, but it was very different from when I was a small girl. I had many stories for her, and she told me about her life. When I asked her why she had left us so suddenly, she confirmed my worst suspicions. My mother had been drinking seriously by then and Esther bravely told her of the danger she posed to her children. My mother was indignant and in complete denial of her illness. She told Esther she was no longer welcome in our household. We had all been traumatized by her departure as children, but now I was mature enough to understand that Esther did not abandon us of her own volition. She had been worried for our safety and courageous enough to speak up for us, even if it meant losing her job and the emotional connection she had to our family. My respect and love for her deepened when I came to understand the fateful choice she had made.

Because my children had recently been through so much with the passing of their father, I wanted to make their first snowy Christmas experience in Sun Valley a memorable one. I shared some ideas for seasonal festivities, but no one seemed to want to participate. I thought we could take some skating lessons together, even though the rink at Sun Valley that fall would be very cold for them after the Santa Monica ice rink. I proposed a horse-drawn wagon or sleigh ride to Trail Creek Cabin for dinner. No one was in the mood for new fun. It was all too distressing, this idea of having a Christmas alone, with just us, in the middle of snow country.

As it turned out, simply enduring the heavy snow winter of 1969–70 was a wake-up call for us all. I grew concerned that my children were becoming downhearted, stranded far from their friends in a condominium complex that was deathly quiet. The first snows came, and then it really began to pile up outside. I tried once again to make plans for winter activities, but to no avail.

I found out, though, that the children had been making plans of their own. When I looked out the window one day, I saw a horse galloping by, pulling a sled with children piled on and clinging to it. It was Candy on her horse, Calazar, pulling the other Cooper children behind. The horse passed by at high speed as the sled crashed against the snow mounds on either side of the plowed path. Children could be seen flying off and beyond into the powder. Certainly, nothing like this had ever happened before in this condominium complex or anywhere nearby. I was relieved and grateful to see that the Cooper spirit was alive and well, even in these new environs.

While we were in Santa Monica for Gerry's memorial service, Candy's horse had been trailered to Sun Valley and stabled at the Sun Valley Horsemen's Center, a short walk from the lodge. I was not forewarned about this inventive skijoring plan. To my children, this was a perfectly reasonable thing to do. No one came by to reprimand them or tell us this was not a permitted use of the paths, so I let them enjoy their fun. Happily, no one was hurt. This would not be the last time they invented a new activity for Sun Valley. Their next adventure would attract an audience that included the tried and true, one and only Sun Valley police officer, the renowned Guy Coles.

Brant, my youngest, came down with the croup on Christmas Eve, and I had to rush him to the Moritz Community Hospital behind the lodge, where Dr. Saviers recommended that he spend the night. I felt as if I were being tested to see just how much anguish I could withstand over my decision to make this move to Idaho. Was it not enough that the children had lost their father just a few weeks ago? Was it not enough that we had moved to a place where they had no friends and no interest in winter activities? We all shared some joy that first year when Santa Claus visited the hospital to see Brant on Christmas Eve. He came in the form of Jack Williams, a local photographer with a very Santa-like countenance. Jack would be our Santa for decades to come, eventually paying visits to my grandchildren as well.

The children were emotionally and psychologically lost and exhibiting justifiable anger over their new circumstances. Their world had been yanked from under them, and now they were living in close quarters in an explosively competitive family atmosphere, taking their anger out on me and each other. After Christmastime, we moved into the larger Star House—so named because of its shape—in the Warm Springs neighborhood for the rest of winter. It was situated below an avalanche chute. As the snow kept falling, we were warned that we might need to evacuate. What surprise might befall us next, I wondered.

An unexpected visitor showed up on the windowsill that winter—a snow-covered stray cat that we welcomed into our home and named "Jacques le Strap" because the white markings up and around his back legs resembled a jock strap—except we realize it wasn't a "he" at all. A few years later, when we were living in our new Bitterroot house, Jacques strayed over to the stables above our neighborhood to visit the male cats and returned to bear us numerous kittens. The children placed all her kittens together on the back of our patient dog Archie, who held very still, never questioning their antics.

That first year in Sun Valley our only car was a Volkswagen bus, not the best winter car. When I needed a second car for Candy to drive to school in the nearby town of Hailey, I accepted the advice of a Ketchum car salesman and purchased a used International Scout. He said this jeep-like junk heap of a vehicle would be an excellent car for winter driving, but we soon found that its unsealed doors and windows left us freezing cold and exposed to the elements. Candy described it perfectly as "a bronze box with no shocks" that bounced sky-high over potholes and up the back roads. It jarred our fillings loose but matched our new frontier lifestyle. The Scout performed admirably, and I felt a certain sense of pride in facing the winter in such a rugged vehicle.

Once we were well into our first school year in Idaho, we began to appreciate the small community that was now our home. Harry Holmes, manager of the Sun Valley Resort, and his wife Gayle introduced us to friends as well as children who were similar in age. There were also Doc Saviers, the Jansses, the Atkinsons, and the Hemingways. Virgie at the Tub and Louie at Louie's Restaurant also became close friends and introduced us to more locals.

The wild, rugged landscape around town became our playground. The children and I joined their classmates for birthday parties at Bald Mountain Hot Springs, near the entrance to Ketchum. We also gathered for parties and quiet floats in "hot springs valley" at Clarendon Hot Springs in Deer Creek. Closer to Ketchum was Frenchman's Bend Hot Springs, which was nothing more than a turnout beside a dirt road with multiple pools among the riverside boulders, eleven miles up Warm Springs Creek past the Board Ranch. About fifty miles north of Ketchum were the Pole Creek hot springs in the Sawtooth Valley, which the children considered to be their own private pool. These hot springs were situated on a ranch owned in part by Clarice and Fred Bleckmann and their daughter Claire, a companion of the Cooper children, who had access to the locked gate.

Ketchum had six gas stations and several bars, including The Casino, where I had had my first drink of alcohol with Sigi Engl during my teenage years. These days, the bars and restaurants are more numerous, and those six gas stations have been replaced by six banks, which reflects the current character of the community. Those early years were a time of living in and with the service industry. Everyone was committed to supporting the community, and we shared a unique rapport. The resort drew young people seeking freedom and adventure in a ski resort town. Young women looking for a place to live and work in Sun Valley were a wonderful source of babysitters for me. When one young girl left, we easily found another. They all became members of the family and remain close friends to this day.

Doc Saviers introduced us to the wonders of the wilderness. He led us on long hikes to lakes in the Pioneer, Boulder, and Sawtooth Ranges, teaching us with unlimited patience to fish and identify wildflowers, even to search for crystal geodes. Doc welcomed us to his cabin at Pettit Lake, one of the few cabins permitted there by the US Forest Service in the early 1970s. The children gained their love of the outdoors and nature on these visits to Pettit Lake and treasured the time they spent there. We had brought Gerry's Hobie catamaran from California, and Doc let us keep it tied to his dock. Whenever the children sailed it, they inevitably capsized under the sudden mountain gusts of wind that fell across the lake. Those wisest among us remained on the dock, watched the boat go over, and then collapsed in laughter.

We soon ventured farther on our own, to Redfish Lake and Devil's Bedstead over Trail Creek Summit and farther, into Copper Basin, staying there in its rustic log cabins. On all of our trips over Galena Pass into the Sawtooth Basin, the children begged to stop at Smiley Creek Lodge for treats at the soda fountain and at the Wampum Trading Post near the lodge. Kelley recalls stopping after a day in the Sawtooths to visit "that old geezer who sold stuff out of that little cabin, things like buffalo robes and turquoise and bone-handled knives and geodes."

One of the advantages of growing up in the Sun Valley community was that young people could benefit from the presence of worldly and well-educated residents who gave their time freely. Author and world traveler Clara Spiegel was known and respected as the "queen of the valley." A noted novelist and short story writer who ventured on safaris to Africa and fishing trips to New Zealand, Clara was the wife of mail-order magnate Frederic W. Spiegel. She was also one of the first guests to visit and ski Sun Valley in 1936.

Clara was precisely the kind of visitor that the resort hoped to attract. She was wealthy, outdoorsy, and socially well-connected. Unlike other celebrities, she was not a short-term visitor to the Wood River Valley, establishing herself as one of the pillars of the town's social life. She built a house to her specifications on a hill overlooking Ketchum and remained there for over forty years, enjoying hunting, fishing, skiing, and horseback riding. A dashing lady who was famous socially and critically acclaimed for her writing, she was talkative, amusing, and respected by all. If you were invited to an evening at Clara's, you felt honored. She was also a good fundraiser and founded Ketchum's Community Library. She was well-known for her community work in the valley from the 1950s until her death in 1997. Clara was a dear friend of author Ernest Hemingway. After his tragic death by suicide in 1961, she invited students to her home to view her Hemingway memorabilia, extensive book collection, and library.

Another of my new friends in town was Ernest Hemingway's son, Jack Hemingway. He was a naturalist, writer, and outdoorsman who took students on guided hikes to identify wildflowers, plants, and animals or gather watercress along the creeks. When Ernest's wife Mary donated money for a permanent primary school location in Ketchum, it was named Ernest Hemingway Elementary.

I felt that I was missing opportunities for my own personal growth during those first years in Sun Valley. I asked Bill Janss during my second summer in town if I could schedule a Personal and Company Effectiveness (PACE) Seminar for the lodge dining room and advertise it through the Sun Valley Resort. Bill liked the idea of offering a program at the resort to supplement the sports schedule—this was a time of drought in the valley for any such mind-expanding opportunities. The seminar was well attended—a great success; requests for more workshops followed.

PACE marked the beginning of an emerging belief in the benefits of positive thinking as a foundation for personal change. I had participated in a number of these workshops in California and had come to know the CEO and staff of the organization well. PACE had been a source of personal growth for me during the Malibu years and a source of emotional growth for the older children as well. My brother Walter came to Idaho to visit and attend the workshop. He returned to Los Angeles with new confidence, and he set a goal to accomplish three things: get a divorce, depart from the insurance business and his dreaded daily drive down Wilshire Boulevard to the office, and move to Idaho. Before he left town, he asked me if I knew a realtor. I connected him with one, and they looked at available properties. Walt found one not yet on the market; he left an offer and soon owned it for $40,000—a cabin on twelve acres, just south of the North Fork Bridge along the Big Wood River.

During one of our first winters in Sun Valley, I allowed my competitive nature to lead me astray. I was halfway toward my goal of becoming a good skier, but new techniques and new equipment had left me years behind. Since my childhood skiing days, I had gone from the Austrian technique to Emile Allais and his jumping turns to Stein Eriksen and his reverse shoulder. Now I wanted to learn the latest technique and decided to take private lessons. A friend suggested that I seek out the admired and handsome young Austrian instructor, Karl Span. We enjoyed each other's company and quickly struck up a relationship that went beyond teacher and student.

I had charged into my new life wanting to fully express my newfound female freedom, and now I found myself in one experience that I never expected to be a part of my Sun Valley life—the clichéd liaison between a divorcée and her ski instructor. One Sunday, I joined Karl and Julie Gorton, another ski school instructor, to charge down a run called Holiday, known for its huge, ungroomed moguls. I was in over my head and well beyond my skill level, but I nevertheless attacked the moguls as though I knew what I was doing. Julie and Karl flew ahead of me; the light was flat, and I did not see the transition to a cat track ahead. I flew off the cat track and one ski planted itself deep into the snowbank, twisting the same hip I had broken as a teenager. Again, I was put into a toboggan and delivered to the hospital, though now it was a real hospital and not just a room in the lodge. It was called the Mollie Scott Clinic. Before I passed into oblivion under anesthesia, I took a moment to wonder if I had abandoned all rational thinking in my wild chase for freedom and adventure.

Doctors George Saviers and Ed Tapper performed the surgery, a complicated operation with numerous screws and plates needed to hold the broken femur together. With six months of recuperation ahead of me, I quickly looked for a total rerouting of interests, commitments, and energies. Peggy O'Neil and Walt and his three children were scheduled to visit us over the Christmas holidays. Despite my being in the hospital that week, recovering from surgery, Peggy and Walt arrived and took care of a total of eight children, providing all the traditional holiday fun and frolick. I was content to be left to brood out of reach of the noise and confusion. Peggy and Walt took a walk on Bitterroot Road one evening that winter and became engaged. They married in 1971 and later moved to Walt's property at North Fork.

Although I was feeling unmotivated, a new personal destiny happened to be awaiting me. An opportunity I had earlier rejected was offered to me once more. He knew of my work at the Los Angeles County Museum of Art and, upon my arrival in Sun Valley, asked if I would be interested in starting an art center there. I had declined, telling him that I was fatigued from nonprofit work in Los Angeles and wanted only to regain a family life with my children.

After my accident, I thought I would also have time to continue writing my thesis for the master's degree in art history I had been working on at UCLA—a goal I had left behind only a few months earlier. I had already finished most of the research. Jim Tobin, a good skiing friend, was then serving as CEO of Scott-USA after his divorce from Rosemarie Bogner. I asked him if he knew of a secretary who could help me by transcribing my research dictation. He recommended Marian French, the wife of Charlie French. They had just arrived in the valley. Charlie worked at Scott, and Marian was as yet unemployed. She agreed to help me; we grew to be close friends over the years. Eventually, she became Bill Janss's personal secretary.

I accepted Bill's invitation to begin an art program of some kind and also went to work on my thesis. I had ample free time to accomplish both and still be that anchor at home with the family. My life was full of purpose again—now intellectual rather than just physical, and inspiring because it involved academia and nonprofit work. I could leave behind the personal doubts and worries I'd had about moving to Idaho and my need for competitive triumphs. I abandoned that role for good and moved into a new mode of thinking about myself. I recall an old saying from that time, "Scars remind us of where we have been. They do not have to dictate where we are going."

My academic path turned out to be short-lived. Once I was once off crutches, I went to see my professor at UCLA and presented him with the first draft of my thesis, "Realism in Trecento Painting." I thought I had done a remarkable job, with all of the proper footnotes and citations. His only comment was that this would never do because I had no German sources, and that those were the most important. He, of course, was German. "But I can't read German," I said.

His answer was to have students do the translating for me. This seemed impossible while I was living in Idaho with no access to a research library. But he was firm in requiring these German sources. I left Los Angeles deflated yet still believing that my novel theory of the influence of realism upon Trecento painting and its continuation into the Renaissance would be an essential contribution to understanding Renaissance art.

I was unwilling to return to Los Angeles, yet I could not continue my research from Sun Valley, so I would have to give up the goal of completing my thesis and master's degree. I realized with gratitude that I had completed six years of art history studies and passed my language and comprehensive exams. I was confident in myself and, most importantly, I now had a broad knowledge of art history to share with others. I would take what I had learned and apply it to the development of an art center for Sun Valley. I would throw all of my energy into joining with my new community in providing educational and cultural opportunities as yet unimagined in the Wood River Valley.

However, there was one detail that I failed to consider upon moving to rural Idaho: the education of my children.

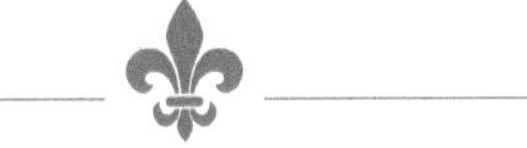

CHAPTER TWENTY-NINE

Lessons from the Wild West

Although the last year in Malibu had been very tight financially for our family, two factors allowed me to send the children to private schools and eventually build a home in Sun Valley. The first was a life insurance policy that Gerry had so wisely taken out on the "risk and reward" life he had been leading. The second factor was my aversion to keeping all my eggs in one basket. The Cooper Lumber Company had been left to me. Mike Hynes, dedicated to the company's future success, was doing a wonderful job as CEO. He loved his work, but I encouraged him to look for a buyer; and as I was the major stockholder, he begrudgingly followed my request. Within a year, another lumber company stepped up to buy Cooper Lumber, and my life was again free of financial worries for my children and myself. This financial freedom allowed me to travel to the children's schools and visit my parents in Los Angeles more frequently.

In Idaho, I was no longer stressed by the frantic drives up and down the Pacific Coast Highway to deliver five children to five different schools, sports, and other extracurricular activities. Yet, I was shocked to find out how far behind Idaho school curricula were compared to those in California. Unable to converse about cows, chickens, and goats, Candy faced a culture shock when she entered Hailey Junior High School to attend ninth and tenth grades. These were major topics in the farming community of Blaine County, and I was no help when she came to me in the afternoon to ask about livestock.

Candy had not wanted to move to Sun Valley. She was happy attending school at St. Augustine by the Sea, where she had numerous friends. That first summer we were in Idaho, she felt "jumbled up," as she said, but was willing to go along with it, thinking Sun Valley was going to be a big, temporary summer camp and that all would return to normal when we got back to "real life" in California. The other four children attended the recently built Hemingway Elementary School in Ketchum. It was overcrowded, with eighth-grader Cameron in the same room with the sixth- and seventh-graders. My well-laid plans seemed to be going awry. It had been my intention to regain our close family ties through shared activities enjoyed together, but now it became obvious that it would be necessary to send the children off to boarding schools if they were to have the quality of education I desired for them. I had only just recreated our family core when I realized that I would soon have to relinquish my dream of staying together.

I at least wanted the children to be content with the choices they made for their education moving forward. I had taken them from California to a situation in Sun Valley not of their choosing, and now I felt strongly that they should control the next big decision of their lives.

Cameron was the first to leave for a distant boarding school. He had been plagued by an unresolved relationship with his father, who never honored him for his gentle personality. His father wanted him to be someone he was not, a youthful mirror of himself. Cameron's frustration about this resulted in a deep-seated anger. He expressed his anger and frustration at home by sitting in the center of the couch in the playroom, slamming his elbows into the girls on either side of him, and changing the channel from what they were watching—usually "Gilligan's Island" —to his favorite show, "M.A.S.H." I would have to stride into the room, pull Cam from the couch, and send him to his room. It happened like clockwork every evening, and only now do we laugh over the memory.

Cam's teacher at Hemingway Elementary, Mrs. Sutcliff, expressed concern about him. She told me of her frustrated attempts to inspire him intellectually. But with so many students of different ages to attend to, she was unable to provide him with much help through that difficult first year in Idaho. The obvious choice for Cam was Lawrenceville School in New Jersey, where both my father and Uncle Bill had studied before going on to Princeton. My uncle had also taught there. With such a family legacy, Cam was readily accepted, and my mother and father were delighted. They had questioned my move to Sun Valley—what they believed would be a temporary move. Little did they know. Little did I know.

Cam and I flew to New York the September he was to enter Lawrenceville. My parents wanted to be there with us and so arranged that we stay with them at the prestigious St. Regis Hotel off Fifth Avenue in Manhattan. My father and mother were monthly guests at the St. Regis and well-known there. By this time, my father was retired from Bullock's and serving on a number of noteworthy boards, traveling monthly to an American Airlines board of directors meeting in New York City. My mother loved her trips with my father now that she was happily alcohol free. During their monthly visits to Manhattan, my mother went to a renowned New York hairdresser and shopped with renewed delight at Bergdorf Goodman's. This was the happiest I ever remember seeing my parents through all the years of my childhood and marriage.

I wanted Cam to experience something of New York on his last night in the city, so we went to dinner on our own and then to a Broadway play. We talked well into the night before falling asleep. I realized that once Cam walked through the door of his boarding school, it would be a jolt to his confidence and a far cry from the freedom he had known all his life. A shock came when the telephone rang loudly at eight the next morning. The voice of my father rang out,

"Where are you? The car is here waiting to take us to Lawrenceville."

Panic! I threw Cam's clothes into his suitcase, dressed quickly, and helped him into his first, just-purchased suit, shirt, and tie. When we reached the lobby, I saw that a long black limousine awaited us. I did not dare express the dismay I felt when I saw this, pretending that all was normal. Like Cam, I had expected a modest car and driver. I suffered for Cam on the drive, knowing how painful it must have been for him to be delivered to his first day at a new school in such a behemoth. It was a disaster. He has never forgotten the embarrassment of his ostentatious arrival at Lawrenceville and his walk with me through the doors into a new world of academic rigor within a regimented schedule. Cameron stayed at Lawrenceville for four years and found good role models while enduring the New Jersey weather, lack of freedom, and intense studies.

Candy, always the rebel, told me that she wanted to go to school in Europe. We checked out several library research books describing available schools in several countries. She decided on the International School of Florence, a little-known and nondescript school in Italy. I contacted them and planned a trip to Florence for just the two of us during her upcoming spring break. She would have culture shock once again in the fall, but this time it would be an expansive new cultural experience that added to her education. She enjoyed it immensely.

Kelley attended Hemingway in the sixth grade, Hailey Junior High for her seventh and eighth grades, and then also decided to attend a boarding school. After reminding me that her sister was in Europe, Kelley chose The American School in Switzerland (TASIS). Brant's school of the moment was Hemingway, and he was very happy with the ski team, but he later became rebellious and desperately sought to escape to a boarding school himself.

Fortunately for Christin, the founding of Sam's School gave her the learning opportunities she most desired. Christin found a home in the skiing world, bonding with other athletes in the Sun Valley Ski

Education Foundation racing program. Competition with her siblings had been a part of her childhood, and she was raised by a father who displayed his competitive spirit at every turn. But one reason she joined the racing team was simply to fit in as a newcomer and make friends. She thrived in these friendships and the racing competition and decided to stay in Sun Valley for her schooling, combining that into what would become a world-class ski racing career.

Over the decades, Sam's School evolved into what is now the highly regarded private school and ski academy known as Sun Valley Community School. The original school was fondly nicknamed for its principal, Sam Hazard. He and his wife Julie and one other teacher comprised the entire teaching staff their first year. The school was the brainchild of Carol and Ed Dumke, generous donors in the area who were committed to its future. But there were no adequate spaces in town for a school, so classes were convened in 1973 in the basement of St. Thomas Episcopal Church on Sun Valley Road. When that was no longer available, Bill Janss provided Trail Creek Cabin as a temporary location. The Community School eventually moved to a permanent campus at the original site of the Sun Valley dog kennels. But that was years later, after the area was developed to provide a campus for the Sun Valley Center for the Arts. The Dumke family's forward-thinking proposal of a private school for the community was supported by the Sun Valley Center for the Arts Board of Directors, which later granted acreage on the campus for the school's first building.

• • •

I was determined to build a permanent home for us in Sun Valley. Upon the recommendation of Bill Janss, I selected a resident architect to design our home. Darryl McMillan was then in town to oversee the projects of David Jay Flood Architects of Los Angeles, the architectural firm responsible for the new Sun Valley Mall and first Villager Condominiums. The simple design included a wooden exterior with a front entrance under a porte cochere. The house's many windows looked out upon Trail Creek. The upstairs contained my bedroom, three children's bedrooms, and a separate study room, reminiscent of the play hall in the Wave House. Downstairs were the two other children's bedrooms, a playroom adjacent to the kitchen, and the dining and living room.

Alberta Harris came to visit us in Sun Valley each Christmas. She had been a part of our family for eight years in Malibu; yet, in those days, a Black woman was an unusual sight in Idaho. We visited the Gold Mine Thrift Store to find her sweaters, coats, gloves, and boots. Proceeds from the store helped fund the Community Library, and this symbiotic relationship created a lasting and remarkable institution. It was not uncommon to find real treasures at the Gold Mine in the form of high-end ski clothing, worn only a few times before being discarded by a departing celebrity tourist. We had fun outfitting Alberta at the Gold Mine. The children adored her and stayed in touch with her for the rest of her lifetime, visiting her in Pasadena in later years.

Life was good—we drew close again as a family, and we came to treasure our new home. The only complaints came during the first winters when the children had to walk up the road in the freezing cold of early morning to catch the school bus on Sun Valley Road. Summers made up for this. Horses and dogs were always present on the property.

And, oh, the horses. While Kelley was dedicated to her skating and Cam was never horse crazy, the rest of us loved horses. Riding opportunities in the valley appeared limitless and wildly adventuresome. It all started with Candy's Calazar, but soon there were three more. For Christin, I purchased from the Hemingway family a stubborn and testy horse named Kokomo, thought to be part mule. Young Mariel Hemingway had told us stories of how they could not keep Kokomo in his corral. They built higher and higher paddock fences, but nothing could contain him. Kokomo continually escaped and had to be retrieved; they tired of this and sold him to us. Christin soon found that Kokomo's prodigious jumping skills were inconsistent. He would happily jump over a six-foot pasture fence but, in a horse show, refuse to jump over two-foot-high rails.

"He was a natural jumper and wanted his freedom," Christin recalled. "But when I got him in a ring to jump, he'd often run full blast as if he were all about it, and then screech to a halt at the last minute and pitch me off. He loved to jump, but only on his terms and when he felt like it."

An Englishman named Barney Beresford, who had retired to the valley, created a small horse stabling and riding arena along Dollar Road at the corner of East Lake Road. The children took riding lessons there for a brief time. Eventually, Katie Breckinridge opened a riding arena in Sheep Meadows, below State Highway 75, and began to welcome riders to beginning English classes. Katie scheduled several horse shows, which included English jumping events, but Candy was always denied entry because she was so advanced in her skills. Katie made progress in training Kokomo and Christin in their jumping routines. But Kokomo still loved to rebel—to shy at fences and throw Christin into the dust. Christin concluded that Kokomo would not change his ways. The mule in him was there to stay.

For Brant, I purchased a pinto pony named Speck. The horse's back was so broad that Brant could hardly mount him bareback. We giggled in the background as he tried to mount, which added to his frustration. Once seated on Speck, Brant's legs extended comically out over the horse's sides. We sold Speck and replaced him with Willy Boy, a small quarter horse that was agile and fast. Brant found barrel racing to be his new challenge and credits Katie for his training in the sport. He entered local rodeo competitions regularly. When the cowboys came through in the fall to round up the grazing horses in Elkhorn Valley, they invited Brant to join them.

The children most enjoyed riding bareback at a gallop. Their favorite track was the grassy airstrip over Saddle Road and along the highway where the Bigwood Golf Course is now situated. At that time, all the roads in the Sun Valley area were dirt roads, so horseback riding was a common means of transportation. Candy and Brant rode to Sun Valley Lake one afternoon to swim their horses and dogs. Cars stopped in amazement, and someone must have called Guy Coles, who drove over to check out the commotion. He stood there for a while and then, shaking his head, just retreated to his car and drove away. Apparently, he could find no legal reason to put an end to their fun.

The Coopers had grown up with few regulations, and now they simply continued to live a lifestyle they had grown accustomed to in Malibu. The boys graduated from Sting Ray bicycles to Honda Mini Trail off-road bikes and then to Yamaha 90 cc dirt bikes, flying over the dirt tracks and obstacle courses they and their companions built in Sheep Meadows. Sun Valley's many trails were open for use with no regulations pertaining to speed or noise. In winter, they loved "hooky-bobbing," a tradition of which I was unaware at the time. It began with Candy pulling a child behind my Jeep Wagoneer on Bitterroot Road, knees bent, hanging on to the rear bumper, sliding in their slickest Moon Boots over new snow. This evolved into the practice of clinging to a rubber raft or, their favorite, a plastic disk at the end of a long rope. These are things a mother never wants to know about.

Brant left our house one summer morning before school and crossed the creek to the Horsemen's Center to feed Willy Boy. "I set my homework down by my side, did the feeding, and when I turned to gather up my papers found that the barn goat had devoured most of them," he said. With the remaining scraps of paper in his hand as evidence to defend his unlikely story, Brant reported to the teacher. She believed him, and so did I.

Corbie Dibble and Gayle Holmes were frequent Western riders at the Horsemen's Center. When Corbie invited us to attend a show in Boise and offered to trailer Calazar, Candy and I accepted because several English jumping events were scheduled. Candy won a number of blue ribbons in the events, a wild and welcome surprise to her. She never expected to win—in California, other horses were more handsome than Calazar, more thoroughbred, and professionally trained. But in Idaho, the judges based their decisions on the skill of a rider rather than the conformation of a horse.

I asked Candy to try out a horse I had admired during a jumping event—a horse that was for sale. Candy forgot to change the horse's name on the entry list and received another blue ribbon for Calazar, but the win was actually on the new horse, Tiny Spender. I was enchanted with the idea of owning a horse again after thirty years, but with what he cost, the horse's name should have been Big Spender. The fact that Tiny had been a racetrack horse appealed to me, and my eagerness to own a horse got the better of me. With little knowledge of the horse's past, I purchased him. After all, my daughter had just won a jumping event on him. He couldn't be too unruly. So back to Sun Valley came our fourth and final horse.

After their gallops on weekends, the children returned to the house for lunch, leaving their horses tied up to the horse rack by the house. The Coopers did not know the word "slow" and we all acknowledged where that tendency came from. One day, as I returned to the stables on the narrow riding trail up and over Saddle Road on Tiny Spender, he picked up the pace, as horses do when heading home. A sage grouse suddenly took flight right in front of us, shooting out of the brush with its noisy grouse calls. Tiny shied and threw me off to one side with my foot caught in the stirrup. Fortunately, my foot quickly freed itself or I might have been dragged onto the pavement and all the way home. I limped to the stable to find him there waiting for me as though nothing had happened.

Had I researched Tiny's background, I might have learned that he was a "cribber." A common habit in racehorses is that they are nervous in their stalls and chew on the wooden doors. Although Tiny had a large pasture in which to roam, he began to bite off the wood on the surrounding fences. The local stablemen were not happy and repeatedly told me so. The Horsemen's Center called one afternoon to tell me that Tiny was injured. I saw the large and bloody gash in his side with a stick of wood protruding. I borrowed a trailer and found my way to a horse veterinarian in Twin Falls, where Tiny stayed for several weeks for surgery and recovery. I began to realize that I was in over my head with a horse that had a nervous tic I would not be able to correct.

Soon enough, though, it was time to sell all the horses. Candy was now at school in Italy, Christin was committed to her ski racing, and Brant was also training with the local ski team. He had joined the ski team because he felt he had done all he could in the rodeo arena and horses were no longer his siblings' primary activity. His friends had all joined the ski team because the schools would let skiers leave for ski training at half past one in the afternoon instead of staying for the full day's classes. Also, as Brant tells me, "Everyone who was cool was on the ski team."

Mariel Hemingway shared some recollections with me recently about those early years when Ketchum was still a very small town where everybody knew one another—the Malarkeys, Coopers, Leggetts, and the Harris and Simpson families. "We formed bonds because we all felt a sense of community with one another," she recalled. "The families that were there in the early days will always have a sense of where we have come from." She called us Coopers the "super cool family" and looked up to Christin in particular, seeing her as beautiful, "insanely smart," an incredible athlete, and also very kind. Mariel said she herself wasn't popular in high school because she was shy, had a high-pitched voice, and was kind of awkward. "People made fun of me, but Christin was always nice to me," Mariel said.

During her junior year, Christin decided that she would venture out beyond the bubble of Sun Valley to Hailey High School, thirteen miles south, to experience what she thought was eluding her—that mysterious reality of local teen life in the Wood River Valley. After being chastened by her public-school experience and missing her more inspiring courses and teachers in Sun Valley, she returned to the Community School for her senior year.

We welcomed Katie Morning into our family for two years. She came to attend school and train with the Sun Valley Ski Team. I was happy to be able to do something for the Mornings after all they had done for my family when Gerry was in the hospital. The Mornings were a legendary ski racing family in California. Sylvester Morning had learned to ski in Colorado and later fell in with skiers at the Sporthaus in Westwood, which was backed by Daryl Zanuck and Otto Lang. The Mornings even got to know my old friends Yves Latreille and Yvan Tache, who befriended me in Sun Valley in 1949 when I broke my hip. These men had come to Los Angeles to open the Sporthaus and trained the Morning children on weekends at Snow Valley.

Three of the Morning children were ski racers, and Katie had learned of our increasingly renowned training program at Sun Valley. Christin was only thirteen years old when she joined the Sun Valley team under the coaching prowess of Michel Rudigoz, who came to the valley to coach the team in 1973. He was a charismatic former member of the French National "B" Team who had taught skiing in the French Alps under the mentorship of Honoré Bonnet, legendary head coach of the French team that produced Jean-Claude Killy. Michel had coached the British men's team for four years, including at the 1972 Olympics in Sapporo, Japan. By the time Christin was eighteen, she was on the US Ski Team with a remarkable career ahead of her, and Michel Rudigoz began honing her skills on the intermountain junior racing circuit.

Due to her extensive ski racing schedules, Christin attended classes only the first and last weeks of her senior year. Sam Hazard had prepared a specialized curriculum so that she could graduate with the first graduating class of Sam's School seniors. But Christin could not receive her diploma until she completed one last course for Sam—Russian Literature. Christin succeeded in her studies while also excelling in sports. Along with many championships, she won a Silver Medal at the Winter Olympics in Sarajevo in 1984 and went on to become an expert ski commentator for numerous women's World Cup Races and seven Winter Olympics. She credits her writing abilities to Sam Hazard's devotion to literature and his wise encouragement in the craft of articulating complex ideas.

Kelley pursued her dreams of being a US rated figure skater, riding daily after school on her beloved balloon-tired bike Blue Boy to the Sun Valley rink. She would have happily spent all day there, including weekends. Her skating friends became her best friends. She took the graduated figure tests, increasingly difficult tests of higher achievement that were required of all competitive skaters.

Ice-skating proved to be our most enduring family activity. As I had always done with new challenges, I took to it with a vengeance and began with dance lessons from rink director Herman Maricich. He was quite the lady's man with all the women taking lessons—and most certainly for those who came from New York to spend their summers skating while in residence at the Sun Valley Lodge. It was at the Sun Valley Lodge skating rink that Anne Janss and I became closer friends. She and Herman introduced me to "patch," the discipline of skating a series of figures within a prescribed circle on the ice. Anne and I met to do our patch figures every morning at eight o'clock. Dance lessons followed, and we practiced our moves during the public session. It was a new discipline that we both enjoyed, and Anne and I together began to test our skill levels by taking the graduated tests.

Kelley wanted to see just how much she had advanced in comparison with others her age, so I agreed to take her to a competition recommended by Herman, a regional championship in Great Falls, Montana, that seemed fairly close by. The fact that I agreed to make this nearly five-hundred-mile drive in the wintertime reveals my ignorance then of western geography. I drove on sheet ice nearly all the way, with children squirming and wrestling noisily in the back of the car. Brant and Christin wanted to have some companions along, so I unwisely included the young Tobin children. Once I realized how dangerous the roads were, I nearly turned around and went home, but Herman was expecting Kelley to participate as one of Sun Valley's infrequent competitors.

Arriving at the motel in Great Falls brought no comfort as the bored Cooper children found anything and everything they could do that would be off-limits. This included throwing water balloons off the room deck onto cars below. The motel manager called me to the front desk. To my embarrassment—and for the first time in my parenting life—I was asked to control my undisciplined children. The entire trip had been a big mistake. In hindsight, I realized that I should have left all the children but Kelley at home with a sitter. I had imagined a fun outing in a new western town; but the trip was a disaster, and I was at wits' end.

Driving to the first morning of the competition, Kelley made some flippant comment about my mood and level of patience, and I just lost it. I threw my hand across the front seat of the car and hit her on the mouth, causing it to bleed. There was still a blood mark on her face when we arrived at the rink and Herman looked at me with a questioning glance. I admitted to Herman what I had done. I was demoralized in so many ways: failure in parenting, failure in anger management, failure in stress level control. You name it—guilty and ashamed. I wanted to cry somewhere, anywhere, all by myself, but that was not possible. I have never forgiven myself for that outburst and loss of control.

The original promise I made in 1969 that Kelley could train in both summer and winter proved to be a drastic misconception and failure. What I did not know then was that a competitive skater cannot train on frozen outdoor ice in the winter months. Practicing patch figures consistently is impossible with changing temperatures and the resulting change in the quality of the ice. And then there was the added problem of the many layers of clothing required in the winter, making jumping practice impossible.

One day, during a personal competition with one of the ice show skaters, Kelley wanted to see who could make the highest and longest axle jump. She landed badly, twisted into a fall and fractured a bone in her leg. She required a cast and was prohibited from skating for the next six months. In addition to this setback was the lack of competitive ice-skaters in the winter in Sun Valley. As a result, Kelley lost her motivation to practice, and her desire dwindled into a total lack of interest. There was no one against whom she could compare and judge herself as she skated all alone on the ice. Kelley's desire that fall to attend school abroad brought her skating dreams to an end.

My mistaken belief that I could provide an ice-skating future for Kelley added one more blunder that haunted me about my decision to move my entire family to Sun Valley. The negatives were mounting, and I hoped that some positives might yet surface to outweigh them. I had no one to blame but myself. I could not yet foresee a decision in the not too distant future that would again affect the children, adding even more to their disappointments—my decision to remarry.

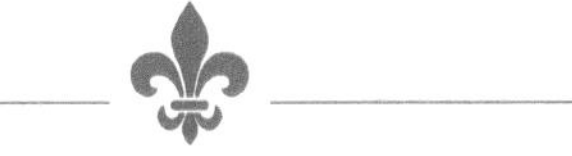

CHAPTER THIRTY

The Soul of a Community

"The purpose of art is washing the dust of daily life off of our souls."—Pablo Picasso

The founding of the Sun Valley Center for the Arts paralleled the start of a new era at America's legendary Sun Valley Resort. The Union Pacific Railroad Company under Averell Harriman had established it as the first destination ski resort in the United States in 1936, drawing celebrities and the rich and famous from around the country and around the world. But by the late 1960s, the company had discontinued rail service through the Wood River Valley. Some thought the once grand Sun Valley Resort had seen its day as other more modern winter resorts were springing up around the country.

Ed and Bill Janss were third-generation owners of a family-run company founded in Southern California by their grandfather, Peter "Doc" Janss, in 1895. Although I only knew Bill and Anne Janss indirectly through my work in the Los Angeles art community, my family and the Janss family had connections that reached back to at least 1911, when Doc's son Harold Janss married Arthur Letts's daughter Gladys. Letts was the founder of the Bullock's retail empire that my grandfather, PG Winnett, and John G. Bullock took to new levels with the art deco masterpiece building known as Bullocks Wilshire. The Janss Investment Company handled some of Arthur Letts's more substantial real estate developments and helped shape the city of Los Angeles over many years.

Bill became an expert ski racer. He won a spot on the US Ski Team for the 1940 Olympics, but the games were cancelled that year because of World War II. By the 1960s, the two Janss brothers were in charge of a company that had developed Los Angeles's Canoga Park and Westwood Village and Arthur Letts's 3,300-acre Wolfskill Ranch, a portion of which became home to the University of California. By the mid 1960s, the Janss brothers turned their considerable resources and expertise toward the development of winter resorts, beginning with Snowmass at Aspen, Colorado. Within a few years, Union Pacific called on them to see what to do with the aging and somewhat remote Sun Valley Resort in Blaine County, Idaho. The Janss Company surveyed the resort and its amenities, calculated that it would take about $6 million to modernize and expand it, and then bought the resort for about $3 million. By the time I came to the valley with my children, Bill had bought out his brother Ed and was now the sole owner and CEO of a resort that had achieved a glamorous mystique during a bygone era.

Bill sold about twenty-five hundred acres in the nearby Elkhorn area to the Johns Manville Corporation for development, retaining a 15 percent interest in the property there. His goal was to use proceeds to modernize the resort. There were still about 350 union workers at Sun Valley Resort at the time of the purchase, left over from the Union Pacific days: lift operators, mechanics, plumbers, groundskeepers, bus drivers, and so on. These union members were unlikely to allow for a change to their status quo.

Hired to wash dishes at the employee cafeteria, twenty-four-year-old Wally Huffman, from Eugene, Oregon, quickly worked his way up the chain of command. Sun Valley Resort became his lifelong career, and he eventually served for many years as the resort's general manager. Like Bill, Wally had also attended Stanford University, but he had to expand his studies to *Old Mr. Boston Official Bartender's Guide* for his next position as manager of the Boiler Room, a subterranean night club under the lobby of the Sun Valley Lodge. The club had in fact been a boiler room, supplying steam heat for the lodge above. Wally gathered and installed old pipes and other recycled relics for the club's décor. During the process, he ran into trouble with old union workers who still had a grip on operations at the resort.

Dave Sherritt, the head of the house mechanics, was not eager to share the location of breaker boxes, pipes, or other important details with a manager who had only been on the job a few months. Wally found a way to get the much older men to work with him. He offered the mechanics the job of guarding a beer cooler behind the lodge during the afternoons. "I told them that there was no security to protect the beer, and would they please make sure it was safe," Wally confided. "They protected the beer alright. After that, I had no problem getting anything from them."

Union Pacific employee strikes held the threat of bringing operations at the resort to a halt. Old-timers who were willing to come out of the woodwork to run the lifts had to be found. When Earl Holding took over as owner many years later, said Wally, it came as no surprise when he fired everyone and then hired people back just to get rid of the union influence. One day shortly after Wally was on the job, a man came down the stairs to the Boiler Room carrying two large stereo speakers with bright lights on them. The new-fangled speakers were the latest thing, engineered to change colors to the beat of music.

"It was Bill Janss, and that was the first day I met him," said Wally. "We hooked up the speakers and from then on we called him Mister Feel Good. The thrust of Bill's efforts was to build a perfect resort centered around the best ski mountain that could be created, including opportunities to ski. Free ski passes were provided for all teachers in Blaine County, all nurses, and all resort staff. There was a tremendous feeling of gratitude at the time by all who worked and played in the Wood River Valley. No one was flagged for not appearing for work on a powder day. Bill was a good guy, and these were his gifts to the community."

The eaves of the Sun Valley Lodge used to collect huge icicles, and staff installed plywood over some of the first-floor windows to protect them from falling ice. Bill parked his Porsche sports car near the Boiler Room entrance at just the wrong spot one day, and one of the huge slabs of ice fell onto his car. Mister Feel Good could not have been pleased about the damage to his prized automobile, but at least the Boiler Room turned out to be a smash, drawing a crowd of locals, visitors, and celebrities who wanted to drink Dirty Mothers (vodka, Kahlua, and cream) and do the Gator Dance, rolling on the floor and kicking in the air, often winding up in a big pile at the end of the night. "What people did not know was that the sewers backed up four or five times a week in the lodge back in those days," said Wally. "We worked cleaning that dance floor many nights just in time for the crowd."

Indeed, Sun Valley entered a new era of excitement and intrigue. Several members of the Kennedy family got wild at the Boiler Room. The Carpenters played there when they were just starting out as a band. Famous crooner Andy Williams and his wife Claudine Longet danced along in the crowd. They had released a smash version of Burt Bacharach's "The Look of Love," together. A few years later in Aspen, Claudine was arrested for shooting Spider Sabich, probably the most famous skier in the country at that time. Wally recalled some events that I was not privy to, including the wet T-shirt contests. "You have to admit they had their points," he cracked.

During the 1970s, there were two fires in the Sun Valley Lodge. Bill told me that fire chief Oliver Dibble doubled the harm to the lodge's upper stories by leaving fire hoses shooting into the rooms for longer than was necessary, causing extensive water damage.

Sun Valley was never an easy place to get to. United Airlines employees held a strike back in its early days of service, hindering access to the resort. People were used to driving into the Wood River Valley, so Bill's Janss Airlines didn't last very long. Despite the general wildness of the place, Bill had hopes of building an arts and culture center that would rival the Aspen Institute, on whose board he had served. When I first arrived in town, Bill asked me if I would be interested in establishing such an organization. The idea was tossed around for a while, but I doubted whether it could succeed.

"The Janss brothers say the Sun Valley of the future will be a cultural headquarters, an intellectual watering hole," reported *Sports Illustrated* in 1965. "That it will borrow from the Aspen Institute program in offering seminars and institutes as mental challenges for business-weary executives." But it was plain to see that Idaho was not Colorado and Sun Valley certainly was not Aspen. The Aspen Institute for Humanistic Studies had quickly become a world-renowned gathering site for leaders from all professions—business, politics, government, and academia. It became recognized as an international nonprofit think tank and nonpartisan forum for leadership initiatives and the exchange of ideas and values. The Aspen Institute's immediate success was due not only to its numerous workshops, forums, and conventions, but also to its presence in a resort with established amenities. The locale also boasted the Aspen Music Festival, which ensured the continued presence of artists, musicians, and patrons.

By contrast, the population of the Wood River Valley in 1970 was said to be comprised of cattle ranchers, sheepherders, hippies, ski bums, and vigilantes, all of them at odds with one another and, I assumed, not at all interested in the arts. The Sun Valley Resort was not prepared for large gatherings. It had no adequate conference center and few facilities, hotel accommodations, or restaurants. I told Bill that the Aspen scenario was not even a remote possibility for Sun Valley and stressed to him that a cultural center would only succeed if it were grounded in the needs and interests of the local community—seeded in its roots and not the product of a superimposed ideal. It would have to begin where there was enthusiasm and receptivity. For me, support for the arts could never be an elitist enterprise. I believed strongly in the importance of bringing the arts and an arts education to young people. This is where the primary effort must be. In Los Angeles, such an effort brought school buses full of public school children on the opening day to the new Los Angeles County Museum of Art.

Throughout my life, my work has been based on the belief that an art education is of essential importance to the betterment of humanity. This sounds like a grandiose predication, but it is simple in its rationale—an education in the arts through the exploration of creativity produces more self-actualized, sensitive, and well-rounded people.

The arts can be seen as the soul of a community, and even the humblest of creative endeavors can yield unimagined success. I recalled Pablo Picasso saying that art's purpose was to "wash off the dust of life," an idea that inspired me during the early days. The Wood River Valley was primarily a physically centered place for skiing, rodeo, hunting, and wrangling. During our early discussion about an arts center, Bill, Anne, and I agreed that an arts center must make available equally important opportunities that would encourage creative expression. We believed that an arts-and-humanities-centered enterprise could provide new avenues of personal expression for young people and that we could accomplish this by inviting renowned teachers and artists to mix closely with the local community.

When I learned of an educational program available through the federal government that funded the arts in rural areas, I immediately applied. Because we had an entire school district without arts funding, we instantly qualified. We received the funding for three years. Those funds would only provide a portion of the operating budget and therefore would need to be matched. After a few years, we would be increasingly dependent on fund-raising to continue. My next hurdle was to complete an application to the IRS for certification as a nonprofit. The requirements included bylaws in support of a mission statement, a board of directors, and a viable source of funding for the first three years. This last requirement meant that a budget and a funding source had to be identified.

In the early 1970s, nonprofit fund-raising was a challenge in the Wood River Valley, and I could not have succeeded without the support of the Janss Foundation. There were few potential donors then residing in the area and even fewer Sun Valley residents outside the Wood River Valley with an appreciation of the arts. The IRS stipulations required that the majority of funding come from numerous smaller donors, rather than one larger one. I began a fund-raising campaign—not a new enterprise for me, but never my favorite task.

My original board of directors was small, but it met the requirement. I served as chairwoman; and Rene Meyer, who also served as the financial administrator for Sun Valley, joined us. Anne Janss and Henry Hopkins also agreed to be board members. Henry was a perfect choice for a board position as he was an Idahoan with a background as director of education for several museums with a track record of delivering youth arts programs. Our budget included nothing for paid staff and a facility. Bill agreed to let us use whatever resort spaces were not in use and could be vacated in the summer months. We ended up taking over much of the resort complex for our programming.

With our initial grant funding, we started an art program at the Hemingway School. This was our first trial curriculum, and the teachers were open to the addition. Judy Atkinson, of the local grocery store family, had already started an after-school painting program at Hemingway, and she welcomed our provision of art supplies and an increased diversity of media. I enlisted volunteers in the community who believed in our mission and were also working artists. Judy Atkinson taught multimedia; Marilyn Frasier, weaving; Gordon Webster, ceramics; and Mary Rolland, painting. The response was so positive and immediate that we were asked to offer the same curriculum to other schools in the Wood River Valley the following year. We added photography for Wood River High School, taught by photographer Robert Ketchum, who had just arrived in the valley to ski and practice his art.

From this tentative beginning, the Blaine County School Art Program would ultimately be recognized as one of the most highly successful programs of the Sun Valley Center for the Arts (now known as the Sun Valley Museum of Art), offered through what we called our Satellite Learning Center. In just a few years, the program involved some fifty children from county schools who were bussed to our campus every afternoon to experience expert instruction in a diversity of disciplines otherwise unavailable in Blaine County. Now, we were not only being approached by all the local schools to present our art curriculum but were also being asked to offer the same workshop disciplines to the general public.

The title of our organization at its founding in 1970 was the Sun Valley Creative Arts Workshops. We received our IRS nonprofit status in 1971. That summer, we opened for student registration in the gift shop at the end of the Sun Valley Mall. This was our first physical space, rented for a minimal fee from Sun Valley Company, but it would not be our last. Mary Rolland, an innovative and respected local painter, organized the front space of the shop as a gallery of changing art exhibitions to display our growing crop of local artists. She proudly called it the Potato Gallery, but it was more familiarly known as the Elkhorn Gallery. The remaining space was reserved for our offices. Marian French, who I had hoped would work as secretary for my dissertation, proved indispensable and became our first paid staff member.

During my first years in the Wood River Valley, I also participated in local government affairs. I received a call from rancher Nick Purdy, inviting me to join the first Blaine County Planning and Zoning Commission, which he was organizing at the request of the county commissioners. I accepted the invitation, eager to learn something new, recognizing that volunteers were scarce in the valley.

Bud Purdy, Nick's father, was a true leader in the ranching business. Born in Nebraska, Bud and his brother Bill were sent by their mother from Redlands, California, in 1928 to work on the family ranch near Picabo, forty miles from Sun Valley. The sheep ranch was owned by Bud Purdy's grandfather, W. H. Kilpatrick, who had organized a team of one thousand men and three hundred mules to lay the rail line from Shoshone to Bellevue, Idaho Territory, in 1883. Bud hunted ducks and fished with Ernest Hemingway after the writer came to the valley in 1939, sharing his knowledge of all the best hunting spots in the Silver Creek area, where Purdy's ranch dotted the land. This friendship was one reason that Hemingway eventually moved to Ketchum in 1959, a move that helped put Sun Valley Resort on the map.

The Blaine County Planning and Zoning Commission consisted of five people who met one night a week. The work was fascinating; but when we began, none of us knew anything about how to plan for the county's future. We immersed ourselves in research and studied the comprehensive plans of counties similar to ours in size and demographics, discussing at length what we thought might be applicable. Our work involved delineating where commercial and residential zones would exist between the various municipal boundaries in the Wood River Valley and farther south.

The planning for development of county lands would have far-reaching consequences, so we were diligent, meeting from seven in the evening until as late as two in the morning. The reason these meetings lasted so long was that we all came from different backgrounds—cities, farms, rural areas, and small towns—so the discussions entailed a variety of opinions. One issue on which we easily agreed was that the recreational vehicle parking sites alongside Highway 75 north of Hailey and south of the East Fork Bridge had to go. This type of use would no longer be permitted in the comprehensive plan for that area.

I worked on the planning and zoning commission for three years and gained valuable experience in consensus-building among a mixed group of stakeholders. These meetings and the issues we worked through provided me with an introduction to the specificity and implications of land use planning and the need for compromise. The experience would ultimately serve me well during another chapter in my life that centered around environmental conservation, when I was invited years later to join the board of The Nature Conservancy, a position that would take me to places I could not have imagined.

By summer 1972, the Sun Valley Creative Arts Workshops were receiving a multitude of requests for a broader selection of arts disciplines. Filling this need required more space for workshops. With my newfound understanding of land use planning, I decided to approach Bill Janss with our need to grow. I gathered the courage to go to his office, certain by now that he had grown weary of my requests. I had earlier expressed interest in a deserted and obsolete sewer plant as a location for a glassblower named Craig Zweifel, who had come to me with the idea of teaching his craft locally. I wanted to provide Craig with space for his own use in a mutually beneficial arrangement that was becoming common between us and our artists and teachers.

Bill took me for a drive to the Sun Valley Horsemen's Center and as we stood by the sewage plant, he made a wide, sweeping gesture that I will never forget. I cherish the memory. "You can have all of this land," he said with a flourish. At the time, I did not comprehend just how much land that was, but it turned out to be close to seven acres of prime Sun Valley real estate.

Of course, it wasn't as though real estate developers were pounding down the doors to make land purchases at that time, and I am not sure the land had any other potential uses. With a nonchalant shrug of my shoulders and no real appreciation for what had just happened, I simply welcomed the gift and set out to create what would become the Sun Valley Center for the Arts campus.

While working at this new location, Craig Zweifel gained considerable fame in his craft within just a few years. He was only the first of our working and teaching artists who went on to have extraordinary careers. Also on this land was a shack that had previously served as a kennel for the Union Pacific sled dogs that provided winter sleigh rides. I asked Gordon Webster to take it over. Not only a professional ceramicist, he also worked in construction. Gordie and other volunteers assumed various development responsibilities. More buildings followed the ceramics studio. The campus was taking shape.

Another spot I had commandeered for use in the summer months was Dollar Cabin at Dollar Mountain, the learning hill for beginning skiers. This is where the first of our photography workshops took place. Robert Ketchum came to Sun Valley fresh out of college, hoping to find a job that would give him the freedom to ski. To afford a lift pass during his first winter in town, he taught photography at the Bald Mountain Hot Springs Motel. At night he ran the light show in the Boiler Room. My daughter Christin took one of his workshops. She recently found some of Robert's writing about those early days in his career.

"Glenn Cooper asked me to teach photography at the newly founded Sun Valley Creative Arts Center during the coming summer months," he wrote. "There is, as yet, no photography darkroom constructed, so Glenn Cooper secures Dollar Cabin for us, which I transform into a classroom and darkroom using duct tape and tarpaper from the nearby home construction sites. Dollar Cabin is the winter lunch café for those that ski Dollar Mountain, so it has numerous benches and tables, as well as two large bathrooms that became our darkrooms."

Robert convinced me that he had too many children mixed with adults taking classes and suggested that I hire a high school friend and fellow photographer to teach a children's photography workshop. "Dollar is truly a ski 'shack,' and the darkroom bathroom floors had tile and drains, so kids could get really involved with their work and it was still easy to clean up," he wrote.

Robert went on to become one of the country's most well-known and respected photographer-environmentalists. With over four hundred one-man and group shows, his photographs are in major museum collections all over the world. His books have been published by Viking Press and Harry N. Abrams, Inc. Aperture Foundation alone published seven of his titles. In 2001, he was named "Outstanding Photographer of the Year" by the North American Nature Photography Association and Outstanding Person of the Year 2000 by *PhotoMedia Magazine*. *Audubon* magazine listed Robert Ketchum as one of the one hundred people who shaped the environmental movement in the twentieth century.

News spread across college campuses about the excellence of our teaching staff, drawing even more students. The proximity of the arts center to Sun Valley Resort, with its mountain scenery and recreational advantages, was enticing, of course. But if we were to continue growing and meeting new demands, we needed housing. This was a manageable challenge only because Bill let us use the resort's dormitory rooms in the summer after the ski instructors departed. We also found space in Ketchum motels. Students joined together to rent houses in town, made available after the skiers and tourists departed. At that time, Sun Valley was not considered a viable summer destination resort, and the local motels were delighted to have the extra business.

We were managing with no additional paid administrative staff, just myself and Marian French working full-time in the office. Instructors were paid for their classes from tuition fees, and the formula seemed to be working. During the winter, we had some time to regroup and make further plans. Skiing was central to the culture in Sun Valley, and I was pushing myself to get better. That bright, sunny day of January 22, 1973, might have been a day of celebration for all that was coming together for the resort and the arts center, but that's not how it turned out. Instead, it began with a phone call from Anne Janss, who wanted to go helicopter skiing in the deep snow of the mountains high above Sun Valley. Bill would not be joining us.

I grabbed my rarely used metal Head skis, the only powder skis made in those days, and met the group at the helicopter pad not far from Sun Valley Lodge. We were given some basic instructions before boarding the helicopter, then it lifted off and flew north, up the Trail Creek drainage, rising above steep hillsides that fell away on both sides. Our guides assured us that the selected slopes had been dynamited earlier that morning to dislodge any potential avalanches and then skied by guides for safe measure. Everyone realized that there remained an inherent danger in what we were doing.

The helicopter settled onto the top of Balcom Ridge, about seven miles northeast of Sun Valley. Forest Service official Butch Harper and ski guide Roger Bergdahl led our group of about ten people, including Peggy and Sam Grossman, a couple I knew from the San Onofre Beach Club in California. The helicopter sped away in a blast of white wind and left us alone on the quiet ridge to begin our first run.

I fell several times while trying to keep up with the more seasoned skiers in the group. On the third run, I asked Roger if he would help me, suggesting that he follow me and give me some tips. He agreed to my request as the rest of the group tracked across a gully ahead of me, one after another, settling in a row on the opposite ridge. Butch went after them to bring them back. Suddenly the entire mass under them slipped loose, and everyone was swept into the cascading snow and debris of an avalanche. Butch saw what was happening and quickly jumped into a tree on the slope, perhaps saving his life. The tree bent over under the force of the slide and then popped back up with Butch still clinging to its branches. I remember looking down at my skis. I was standing so close to the slide that snow from the avalanche had collected on top of them.

Butch immediately yelled to anyone who could hear him to form a line at one end of the mass of snow and debris. We removed our ski pole baskets and slowly skied across the debris in a line, driving our poles deep into the snow in the hope of finding survivors. One man from New York had a hand above the snow and so was rescued. Others were able to dig themselves out. All were found, except Annie, with whom only moments before I had been chatting excitedly about our day. I plunged my pole deep into the snow, horrified that I might strike Anne's face. Butch told us we had only twenty minutes to find her before she suffocated, so we worked in a panic to locate her. The guides used their radio telephones to call the hospital for help.

We found out later that Anne had received a blow to her skull; most likely, she hit one of the trees in the middle of the slope. It was a small consolation that she had been knocked unconscious and did not suffer a prolonged death. We also learned that avalanche radio transceivers, used in the back country to locate avalanche victims, had been ordered by the Forest Service and were due to arrive only a few days after the tragedy.

Still in shock from the avalanche, I made my way home to Bitterroot Road. Don Bren came immediately to my house to console me. He kept me company for the next few days, until we attended the memorial service together at the Opera House. Bill sat in the front row with his children—Susie Ferguson and her husband, Dr. James Ferguson; Mary Janss Daenzer; and the youngest child, Bill Jr. I knew his children would remain with Bill for a few days, so I waited to call or visit.

A pall fell on the community of Sun Valley, and no one was sure what would happen next. Surely Anne Janss, if anyone, should have been protected from a tragedy like this. But no one seemed able to even speak of the tragedy that now lay heavy on everyone's heart. It struck at the very soul of our community. There were many tears, and others of us were simply in shock. Our sense of security in the mountains was shattered. There was a feeling of emptiness and despair throughout the town and the resort. That emptiness is often the hardest feeling to bear.

After the memorial service, we slowly began to piece our lives back together. I finally gathered the courage to call Bill and ask how he was doing. "You must be feeling lonely," I said. "Let me know if you want someone to share it with." I had never socialized at the Jansses' home, but we had all been friends for many years. Anne was quiet and rather shy but had always been supportive of my work in town. "Why don't you come by for a glass of wine sometime," Bill managed, and then hung up.

Tragedy knows no boundaries when it comes to wealth or privilege. Bill had lost his sister many years earlier in an automobile accident. He and Anne had suffered immeasurably when a barn used by their children caught fire in California. After the children were found safe outside, their three-year-old daughter ran back into the burning building to retrieve her favorite doll. Anne ran into the flames to find her. Bill stood yelling for her not to go in, but a mother's courage can be irrational in such a circumstance. Despite being pregnant at the time, Anne ran up the stairs and through the burning rooms, catching fire herself as she searched for her child, to no avail. Moments later, she was screaming from an upper story window to her husband below. Bill shouted at her to jump for her life, and she fell to the ground, badly injuring herself. Anne lost both her daughter and her unborn child that day and was covered in burns over much of her body. Her emotional scars never healed.

When I visited Bill at his home, we talked about our families, about loss, but eventually also about the things that had brought us all together as friends years before in Los Angeles. We talked about wine, about art, and about his plans for the future of the resort. The tragedies of our lives never leave us; but sometimes, through our wounds, people can form the strongest of bonds and learn to love and trust one another completely. I went to Bill to console him during his deepest loss and never left his side for the rest of his life.

CHAPTER THIRTY-ONE

The Sun Valley Center for the Arts and Humanities

People in town gossiped about how much time Bill and I were spending together. After all, we had become inseparable. Rather than try to dispel the rumors, Bill proposed that we get married the following summer of 1973. I accepted immediately, aware that our honeymoon would fall within the busiest time for the art workshops.

"That will be the time of my greatest responsibility, when several hundred students will be arriving for registration," I told him.

"Well, hire someone!" he replied decisively. Bill's declaration, perhaps an ultimatum, set in motion new considerations that would ultimately create a dynamic staff to propel the new arts center forward.

I had been living in Bill's house only a few weeks when I told him that I felt like a third wheel there. The maid seemed to be everywhere, doing everything. Bill's children hired her after Anne's death so that he would not have to prepare his own meals. I assured him that I could handle all of the meals though we should get someone in to clean occasionally. The maid fired me an angry look upon her departure, knowing that I had been the one to usurp her position as mistress of the house. I wanted no in-house helpers because I was loathe to create one of the more painful situations of my childhood, when a house man held sway over my mother. Of course, Alberta had been like a member of our family—one of us—and that made all the difference.

Bill's house was overpowering, as though it had been designed for parties. It was more of a museum than a home. The approach was along a winding entrance off Trail Creek Road that passed what Bill called "the Kinderhaus," a cabin that contained the only bedrooms for my children. Farther on and across a bridge over Trail Creek was the main house, situated within seven acres of untouched woodland on the valley floor. Despite its being only a short drive from town, the home was in a world of its own. The front windows faced Bald Mountain. The backyard faced Bill's delight—a large pond filled with rainbow trout. He loved to create a turbulent feeding frenzy in the pond by tossing the fish bread loaves left over from the lodge.

The house was no doubt designed to exhibit the large paintings in Bill and Anne Janss's impressive art collection. The entry was through a heavy, carved wooden door that led down two steps into an expansive, two-story hallway. The walls were hung with the finest examples of abstract expressionism, including the works of Sam Francis and Hans Hofmann. The living room fireplace was flanked by a Robert Motherwell painting on one side and a Franz Kline on the other. The room was furnished with deep, black Mies Van Der Rohe leather chairs. Across the room was a large dining area centered around a sturdy table collected from a medieval European monastery and surrounded by sixteen antique chairs.

A staircase led to a second floor that housed an extensive library of rare books: poetry, historical writings about the California Sierras; and a rare and valuable collection of the photographic works of Edward Curtis, which had been gifted to Bill by Mary Curry Tresidder and Donald Tresidder, the fourth president of Stanford University and president of Yosemite Park and Curry Company. On the walls of the master bedroom were more paintings, including a large Arshile Gorky and a Jasper Johns. The linen closet was so large that Peder Monsen would joke that he slept in there whenever he stayed over.

Such luxury. Such exquisite art. And yet, despite our love for one another, all was not well in our home. When our children gathered altogether in the dining room, they tended to sit at the far end of the monastery table, away from us. They spoke among themselves, glancing back at Bill and me with quiet disdain. We didn't know whether this were an example of "misery loves company," or "there is strength in numbers," but there it was—a palpable expression of their collective dismay about my decision to marry and the uncomfortable situation that had been imposed upon them.

In addition to the tragedy that had befallen Bill and his family, the responsibility for operating the resort continued to lie heavily on his shoulders. I came to understand that it was like running an entire town. There were numerous businesses and concessions to operate, both on and off the ski mountain, commercial and residential developments that would secure the resort's future, a web of regulatory agencies to navigate, and hundreds of employees at the resort who had to be managed while moving forward. But I too now faced the responsibility of running an organization that was growing by leaps and bounds, and I had to consider delegating some of my leadership responsibilities if I was going to marry Bill in June.

I thought back to the previous summer, when a young man named Jim Belson had stopped in Sun Valley while on a camping trip around Idaho. He stayed for a night at the lodge, primarily, as he later confessed, to get a shower. While walking through the resort, he saw a poster announcing our Sun Valley Creative Arts Workshops and inquired at the front desk of the lodge if a meeting could be arranged with the head of the organization. I answered his call and we lunched in Gretchen's, a restaurant adjacent to the lodge. He told me of his background in filmmaking and literature studies; he said he was interested in spending a few months in the valley to lead a workshop and that he might one day be interested in working for a nonprofit organization. I responded that we had no paid positions for teaching and that I could not guarantee him a reliable paycheck from tuition fees. He replied, "Money isn't everything, but I will be in touch."

One thing that interested me about Jim Belson was that he was a native Idahoan, having grown up a couple of hours to the east, skiing in Sun Valley every winter, and attending the Idaho Grower Shippers Association's annual convention there every summer with his family.

A year later, the workshops were thriving, so I called Jim Belson and invited him to meet with Bill and me in Sun Valley. We learned that he was finishing a graduate degree in comparative literature with a dissertation on film and the novel at the University of Southern California. Because of his academic credentials and appreciation for the region—and his willingness to make the move with his family—I offered him the position of executive director. I had no idea at the time what significant achievements this hiring would manifest for us, but I was thankful that the Janss Foundation agreed to provide the first year's funding for Jim's salary.

As a graduate student at USC, Jim had created the first interdisciplinary undergraduate program combining drama, music, comparative literature, cinema, and graphic arts. The "Semester of the Arts" he created at USC was given the Dart Award for Academic Innovation, the first time that award had been presented to a student rather than a professor. Jim would bring a diversity of disciplines to expand the mission of what soon became known as the Sun Valley Center for the Arts and Humanities. His interdisciplinary vision would open up new areas of study through the cross-fertilization of academic curricula that had until then been separated from one another. His goal was to create a new synthesis where, for example, dance students could interact with photography students or historians with filmmakers.

• • •

In June 1973, Bill and I were married at Flossie Janss's house in Thousand Oaks, just a small gathering of friends and family. Bill's grown children were no happier about our wedding plans than mine. They feared, no doubt, that they would be given no time or place in our—Bill's and my—new life together. I was adding a wife and five children into the already challenging business enterprise that was Bill's life. I needed to find a means of bringing comfort and making peace among eight children who had been thrown together in a way that none of them could have imagined or desired. Susie, Bill's oldest at twenty-eight, was married to psycho-pharmacologist James Ferguson. They lived in Salt Lake City with their one-year-old daughter Cassandra. Mary, twenty-five, was recently divorced from her Sun Valley husband and remarried to Frank Daenzer. They lived in San Francisco with their first child. Billy Janss Jr., twenty-three, was in the midst of his studies at UCLA School of Medicine.

Don Bren invited Brant to his house in LA for the wedding weekend; his own boys, about Brant's age, had often played with him at our home in Malibu. He believed this would be the happiest place for Brant and that he might possibly forget why he was in Los Angeles. Brant was decidedly against my relationship with Bill; when Don came to dress him in a shirt, tie, and suit jacket for the wedding, Brant struggled and ran away. Don had to physically carry Brant to his car to drive him to the wedding. Even then, Brant refused to come in to the ceremony, sneaking in out of curiosity, but hiding in the back among the guests. When the minister asked anyone opposed to our union to speak their minds, Brant raised his hand to speak as if he were waiting for the teacher to call on him, only lowering it when his siblings gave him dirty looks.

Our honeymoon was neither restful nor inspiring. We traveled to Norway on the invitation of a longtime friend of Bill and Anne's named Peder Monsen, who reserved a prized stretch of some Norwegian river each year during the salmon run. It was apparently a great honor for anyone to be there. Thanks to the Scandinavian midnight sun, it was light the entire time, so we ventured to the river around ten o'clock at night and remained there until four in the morning. For me, this ordeal involved trying to cast out tackle that was so heavy that I could never get it far enough out into the river to tempt a fish. I gave up and curled up in the grass to watch the others, often dozing for lack of sleep.

At about three in the morning, we all met in a small shack and began drinking straight aquavit, washed down with beer—not water, but beer. At five o'clock, we left the river for our hotel room, where I quickly fell fast asleep. In the morning, we arose for a smorgasbord brunch, only to return again that "night" to the river. And so it went. No sleeping, no sightseeing. Fishing, drinking, eating and fishing, drinking and eating again. The joy of the trip rested simply in being with Bill, without our usual responsibilities to attend to. We eventually left Norway for Denmark, where we enjoyed the grand city of Copenhagen—sleeping, eating, sightseeing, and no fishing—just the two of us.

Upon our return to Sun Valley, Bill informed me that he would be leaving soon to enjoy two weeks at the Bohemian Club. Based in San Francisco, this exclusive men's social club was a bit mysterious. Bill provided no details but said it had been formed in 1872 by a group of prominent artists, journalists, businessmen, and military leaders. "What?" I asked him. "You are going right away to some Boy Scout camp this first summer right after our marriage?"

I soon learned how important these retreats were to him each year. They involved a great deal of ceremony, theater, and presentations geared toward enlightenment and relaxation. Bill, who was always fond of costumes, must have been drawn to these theatrical entertainments. Oliver Wendell Holmes and Samuel Clemens had been honorary members back in the day. When Oscar Wilde visited the club in 1882, he reportedly said, "I never saw so many well-dressed, well-fed, business-looking Bohemians in my life."

I decided that I too needed a retreat from the "busy-ness" of summer and all the demands of the nonprofit events I was becoming increasingly involved with. I bought what I called the Last Resort Ranch, a parcel of remote land at Fourth of July Creek, five miles north of Salmon, Idaho. For thirteen years, I went there each summer to seek rejuvenation in the best way I could imagine, through isolation. The first thing I did when I bought the place was pull out the telephone and television wiring. It was pure bliss and tranquility. My children would arrive and complain about having nothing to do. I pointed out that there were myriad outdoor chores, including weeding in the garden. They could even read a book.

Upon finishing his doctorate, Jim Belson moved to Ketchum to take over the arts workshops. I believed in him, but his leadership skills were as yet unproven. He arrived in time for registration, about the same time I left for my honeymoon. I feared that he would never forgive me for deserting him amid the chaos of his first days on the job. He taught two courses of his own that first summer—Creative Writing and Masterpieces of Cinema, both drawn from his recent university studies. Significantly, he was able to get Idaho State University credits for many of our courses.

Jim believed that the organization should have a broader mission, and he expanded our efforts to attract prominent artists to teach and work in Sun Valley. This approach began to draw students from all over the world and eventually established Sun Valley as a cultural center well into the future. I welcomed his innovative ideas and gave him the freedom to expand our original mission, certain that his approach would prove successful.

During the summer of 1974, Jim founded several groundbreaking new programs. "The Wilderness Art Project" produced new work while providing encounters between artists and students within the natural open spaces of the Sun Valley region. Sun Valley Center/University of Southern California Humanities Institute combined the center's teachers with USC professors to offer courses such as Writing, Afro-American Literature, Film and Literature, and Masterpieces of World Literature. The advent of Jim's leadership brought immediate and rapid growth for the organization. He proposed that we change our name to Sun Valley Center for the Arts and Humanities, pointing out that the original title was too parochial and that the arts are, by definition, "creative." As an Idahoan, Jim felt he could get away with this more easily than a non-native; he wouldn't be cramming culture down the natives' throats—he was an Idaho native, himself. The name change was made official in 1976.

Jim also founded the Sun Valley Seminar on the Western Arts and Humanities in 1974, with an annual conference that took place over the next eight years called the Institute of the American West. These gatherings convened Idaho and other Northwest senators and congressmen with people from the National Endowment for the Humanities (NEH) and notable art museums, including my friend Henry Hopkins, who was then serving as director of the San Francisco Museum of Modern Art. The institute eventually drew numerous scholars of Western literature, art, film, mythology, archaeology, and paleontology. The center was on its way to becoming a major player in the field of humanities in the Intermountain West.

Jim Belson and I interviewed prospective paid staff members, inviting candidates to town and giving them a room in the Sun Valley Lodge for several days to let them get a feel for the surrounding area and the center's potential. When Robert Ketchum chose to move elsewhere with his career, Jim made his first hire, bringing photography instructor Cheri Hiser on board. She had been teaching at Anderson Ranch in Snowmass, Colorado, where in 1968 she founded the Center of the Eye (COE) photography workshop, considered one of the most influential such programs in the world at that time.

Cheri was recommended to us by Ansel Adams, whom Bill had met and become friends with when he acquired some of Ansel's Yosemite National Park photographs. Cheri brought us immediate recognition and increased credibility. Her presence led to the construction of a new building on our campus dedicated entirely to photography. She, in turn, recommended Peter de Lory for her photography department and Jim Romberg to teach raku and head up a ceramics program.

The establishment of these first two departments began an explosive period of growth for the center. Such accomplished artists were able to attract others. Photographers Jerry Uelsmann, Linda Conner, Duane Michals, Frederick Sommer, Lee Friedlander, Mark Klett, and William Wegman came to the campus. The well-known ceramicists in Sun Valley at that time included Paul Soldner, Don Reitz, Richard Shaw, Mary Frank, Jenny Lind, and Robert Turner. In the painting and printmaking departments were Terry Allen, John Buck, Ted Villa, William Wiley, and Otto Piene. Karen Vanderpool taught weaving.

David Wharton headed up the graphic arts programs. Kiowa writer N. Scott Momaday participated in one of David's classes as an artist. James Turrell also came to the center during those years. The artist Christo came to town, and we all laughed over his grandiose proposal to cover Bald Mountain in colored sheets. Many teachers and students from the center's early days went on to their own successful careers, such as Tina Barney, a student in photography, and painters Ted Waddell, Sheila Gardner, and Mary Rolland.

Marian French, with her strong administrative skills, served as our head of performing arts. She initiated a drama workshop under Ben Tucker, a drama teacher at The New School of Social Research who had been recommended to us by Michael Engl. Tucker became our theater director. He offered mime, production, and acting technique classes. Following Tucker, there was Vincent Downing; within a few years, Walt Jones took over. Walt had been a drama teacher from Yale who convened his classes in Dollar Cabin. Walt Jones and Meryl Streep had been in the same Yale graduating class in drama. Mariel Hemingway and the Cooper children were among the drama students in Walt Jones's first Summer Improvisation Workshop. Through these connections, my daughter Kelley had the opportunity several years later to dine with Meryl Streep and Walt Jones while visiting Yale as a potential student.

For two summers, Mariel Hemingway joined other young thespians at the workshops at Dollar Cabin. "I had never done Shakespeare before," she said about that time in her life. "We learned from Walt Jones about iambic pentameter and all the different ways people had translated the bard. He taught us how to speak the lines as ordinary people would . . . when they were talking, how to make the dialogue real."

Mariel's first acting role was to play the humble dormouse in the Sun Valley Community School's production of *Alice in Wonderland*. "I wanted the part of Alice, but I didn't quite get that part," she recalled. "But in my role as dormouse, I fell to the ground dramatically and thought I was just brilliant."

Mariel landed her first acting job in the film *Lipstick*, alongside her big sister Margaux, who recommended her for the role. She later took on a lead in the Community School's production of Lillian Hellman's *The Children's Hour*, about an all-girls boarding school. "I never planned on being an actress" she told me recently." I wanted to be to be an architect, or go into marine biology, which was odd since there was nothing resembling an ocean in Idaho."

The center was making many social contacts at that time—too numerous to take advantage of them all. Through friends, we were introduced to Bella Lewitzky, who in 1946 had founded Dance Theatre in Los Angeles. She was subpoenaed in 1951 by the House Un-American Activities Committee to answer questions about suspected communists active in the art world. She reportedly said, "I'm a dancer, not a singer." She later worked in the film industry and eventually founded the Lewitzky Dance Company in 1966, one of the leading international modern dance companies of the era. Through Bella, we were able to get Dance L.A. to come for several summers, using an old Quonset hut on Trail Creek Road for its classes. Performances were held in the Sun Valley Opera House. For both spaces, it was necessary to install the special flooring required for dance.

It was clear to all of us who relished our growing successes that without the support of the Sun Valley Company, and Bill Janss in particular, there would have been no arts center in Sun Valley. Belson referred to the symbiosis between the center and the Sun Valley Resort as an "ecology of spirit" that integrated mental, creative and physical activities; photography and fly-fishing; ice-skating and theater; horsemanship and ceramics. How wrong I was to assume that Sun Valley and the surrounding community would have no appetite for the arts.

Not everything we tried turned into an instant success. I invited the Boise Philharmonic to come to Sun Valley for two weeks one summer. Bill allowed us to use the opera house in the late afternoons, as long as the performances did not conflict with the scheduled movie times. I happily set about arranging housing for the musicians and their families, to ensure they enjoyed their two-week "vacation." As it turned out, they were the only ones delighted and grateful; nobody else showed up for the concerts. Who would want to stop their fun outdoor family activities and come into a dark theater while the sun was still high in the sky?

Bill was so amused with my failure that he teased me, saying "smarty, smarty had a party, but nobody came." I was trying to do too much too quickly and responding with too much eagerness to fulfill the multitude of requests for new arts programs. Several years later, Carl Eberl began a successful symphony performance outdoors on the Elkhorn Plaza. This small beginning under a tent slowly evolved over the years into the professional Sun Valley Summer Symphony, which is now attended by thousands in the extraordinary Sun Valley Symphony Pavilion, provided by the Holding family, who in 1977 purchased the resort from Bill.

Jim Belson knew we needed a voice, and that voice became the *Sun Valley Center Magazine*, which we published for a few years. It featured many articles about resort and recreation operations, but it also covered the emerging education and arts opportunities provided by the center. The Sun Valley Company was eager for us to take on the magazine and trusted us to use it to present Sun Valley to the outside world.

The May 1974 edition of *Sun Valley Center Magazine* welcomed new teaching staff and listed more than sixty arts workshops, humanities seminars, and performing arts events. These included glass crafting, weaving, leather craft, literary arts, environmental workshops, and children's workshops. The center's new building complex on Trail Creek, below the Horsemen's Center in Sun Valley, provided a nexus for our operations, with some workshops continuing through the winter. Two years later, an article in the magazine quoted Jim Belson as he summed up the ongoing mission of the organization, which Bill and Anne and I had initially formed years before:

> The Sun Valley Center for the Arts and Humanities is a unique, nonprofit educational foundation serving the creative, intellectual, and cultural needs of the community of Sun Valley and the worldwide community of artists and scholars. The center's uniqueness derives from its origins—a center born of the irrepressible need for a mental and spiritual "balance" in an area well established as one of the country's finest centers of physical activity and instruction. The Sun Valley Center provides the creative equivalent and necessary complement to Sun Valley's physical sports orientation, just as, within the Center itself, the humanities, disciplines of "humane study," provide a natural and necessary complement to the arts, disciplines in which the total human being may involve and express himself.

I could never have envisioned at the outset just how widely known the center would become. Our dream was now a reality. The center served as a working model for American art historian Bernard Berenson's inspired belief that "all the arts, poetry, music, ritual, the visible arts, and the theatre must singly and together create the most comprehensive art of all: a humanized society, and its masterpiece, the freeman."

To guarantee our future and continue to attract artists and scholars from around the world, the center's board of trustees needed a daring but justifiable building campaign. Real estate was beginning to sell in the area, and new homes were being built. New residents as well as locals appreciated the presence of culture and the arts, all of which brought new donors to our support. We had already spent our building fund remodeling the ceramics building and constructing the photography and multiuse buildings. The latter was used both for our administrative offices and a variety of workshops: drawing, painting, sculpture, weaving, and even printmaking—after we purchased a printmaking machine—which permitted us to undertake lithography and silkscreen processing.

Our next project would be a joint venture between the center and the Ketchum-Sun Valley Community School. This building would be the largest structure on the center's growing campus and provide classrooms and seminar space for both the center and the Community School, as well as office space, an art gallery, and an auditorium. As a result, Community School students could avail themselves of world-class art instructors.

The Sun Valley Center for the Arts' original major donors were Edmund and Carol Dumke's Ezekiel R. and Edna Wattis Dumke Foundation, and Michael Engl's Peggy Engl Trust. The Dumkes were the idealistic donors behind Sam's School, which became the Community School. They also provided the funding for the center's iconic photography building. Michael Engl supplied significant funding as well as innovative programming in the arts and humanities, thanks to his wide circle of connections in academia.

Michael is the son of Sigi and Peggy Engl, the couple who served as chaperones for me during my Christmas visits to Sun Valley in the late 1940s. Peggy had been a beneficiary of Harlow and Bruce Bundy of the Bundy Manufacturing Company, a predecessor of International Business Machines, or IBM. The Peggy Engl Trust had accumulated family wealth through the Bundy family and its early ties to the company. Peggy was the daughter of Margaret Bundy Scott, for whom the Mollie Scott Clinic in Sun Valley was named, and the wife of John Scott. The Peggy Engl Trust passed on to Michael after her death in 1972.

Michael had been a resident of the Wood River Valley since his early childhood, but he lived in New York City much of the year. He attended Williams College and went on to graduate studies, receiving a degree in Elizabethan literature from Yale University and another from Columbia University in nineteenth-century English literature. He joined the center's board in its early years and timed his visits to Sun Valley to coincide with our board meetings. While studying at Columbia, Michael organized and taught classes for high school students at The New School for Social Research in New York City. He later accepted a position at The New School as assistant dean and chairman of the visual communications department. The New School was founded in 1919 with an original mission dedicated to "academic freedom and intellectual inquiry and a home for progressive thinkers."

Although we had support from these major donors, we also needed to create a fund-raising event that would attract a wider circle of supporters and continue to produce enthusiasm for the center. Molly and Donn Chappellet invited me to come for a visit during the spring Napa Valley Wine Auction, an event that was gaining notice as a means of support for nonprofits in the area. Molly and Donn were crucial early supporters of this event, giving generously of their wines. Molly served twice over the years as event chairwoman for the Napa Valley Wine Auction. I watched the auction with amazement as wine lots were sold throughout the evening at enormous prices far beyond their value. The combination of wine, entertainment, and good-natured cajoling had a way of loosening donors' checkbooks.

I decided to schedule a wine auction of our own and returned home to meet with John Beaupre, then owner of the Ore House, a restaurant on Sun Valley mall, and a wine connoisseur. I told him of my plans and my desire to get the auction on the calendar for that summer. He wisely guided me away from rushing into the event, warning me that it would take an enormous amount of time to organize. Indulging in the fear that some other organization might get the idea and run with it, I announced our wine auction in Idaho newspapers for the following summer. Our networking began right away. Molly and Donn were able to open doors for us with other vintners in the Napa Valley area. We received donations far beyond my expectations. I made several trips to Napa during that year to meet with donors and initiated friendships for the center that have ensured their support to this day.

The first Sun Valley Center Wine Auction, held on the grassy area of the campus by Trail Creek on a lovely sunny afternoon in July 1981, was a flop. Nobody came, and nobody bought. Well, almost nobody. There were maybe twenty-five attendees, all of whom had contributed their very best wines from their cellars. "Smarty, smarty had a party, but nobody came," Bill said again, teasingly. All we could do was buy each other's wines, with the intention of placing them up for sale in the next summer's wine auction. Although little money was raised, it was fun and memorable as the valley's few wine enthusiasts gathered in devotion to the red elixir.

For our second summer's wine auction, I convinced artist friends Don Nice and Billy Al Bengston to design custom labels. I expected these labels to add greatly to the prestige and value of the bottles. I convinced Don Bren to donate a number of cases of wine he had already purchased earlier that year from Donn and Molly's Chappellet Winery, bottles that were as yet unlabeled.

I gathered a few female volunteers in a garage one afternoon before the auction to tackle the job of applying art labels to the bottles. How hard could it be? We had the bottles, the labels, and the glue. But we also had a box of the foil wrappings that had to be wrapped around the bottle tops. We opened a box, and there they were, lying in a neat, flat stack of wide circles. They obviously needed somehow to be shrunk over the top of the bottles. With only hours to go, I was in a bit of a panic. I called Donn, who told me, in his calm voice, just what to do, "Oh, just go get some hair dryers and hold the hot air heat over them and they will shrink down over the bottle tops."

This was female technology familiar to us. Quickly, we all ran home to get our hair dryers and then got busy. From such humble beginnings, the Sun Valley Center for the Arts Wine Auction grew exponentially in the years that followed. It now raises up to $1 million annually for operations and programming and by 2021 had provided over $1 million in funding for children's art programs and scholarships. The wine auction guarantees that 100 percent of Blaine County students are able to participate in multiple arts education programs every year. Generous donations underwrite free and reduced-cost arts education programming and provide scholarships for students and local educators, serving more than four thousand students from kindergarten through high school.

The Sun Valley Wine Auction is consistently ranked among the nation's top ten charity wine auctions by *Wine Spectator* magazine. During its three-day July festivities, more than five thousand people attend myriad events, ranging from the Wine Auction Gala to a dozen or more intimate Vintner Dinners at private homes with guest chefs preparing multicourse, wine-matched feasts. Now, when the center has a wine party, everybody comes. In those early years, I took on the task of gathering donations vigorously; and Bill used to joke that, when friends saw me walking down the sidewalk, they crossed the street to avoid yet another fund-raising request.

I suppose Sun Valley's glamorous history made it inevitable that the center's programming would eventually involve the film industry. Hollywood was in the midst of change in the 1970s, and scholars were poised to reinterpret the films that had helped shape the American zeitgeist. Under the center's auspices, Jim Belson proposed a series of programs that came to be called the Institute of the American West. Its first program, sponsored by Levi Strauss & Co. and the NEH, was "Western Movies: Myths and Images." Scholars and writers of the American West came together with an impressive roster of names from the entertainment industry—including directors such as King Vidor, Henry King, and Delmer Daves—holding seminars and screening films. Among these was the premiere screening of Clint Eastwood's revisionist Western *The Outlaw Josey Wales*, with Clint himself in attendance. The six-day conference was well attended and successful.

Film history and Western history were only one aspect of an institute that would eventually include studies of the Western environment and the Western novel. The initial focus on film was driven by the fact that nowhere in the West were early Western films being shown as a historic collection. As a natural humanities complement to arts programming, the institute scheduled symposia and seminars on subjects relating to these films and the American West. The mission was to combine the art of film with the scholars who wrote about them, bridging various and changing perspectives on Western films within contemporary academic conversations. The events were illuminating, in part because of the mix of renowned Western actors who arrived—including Tim McCoy, Clint Eastwood, Iron Eyes Cody, Chief Dan George, Peter Fonda, and Warren Oates. They were joined by some of the most well-known directors, editors, and critics of the day.

Jim Belson and Michael Engl produced this event with help from George Gund III, a Sun Valley Center board member active with the San Francisco International Film Festival, and Howard Lamar, Yale professor of American history. Thanks to Michael, William Everson, author and New York University-The New School film history instructor, also provided major support and expertise.

Michael had grown up a true Sun Valley local. In the late 1940s, he was delivered each day to kindergarten at Sun Valley's Trail Creek Cabin. By the 1970s, he was in a position to bring cutting-edge ideas and progressive thinking to rural Idaho. His time at The New School for Social Research coincided with the development of a radical new technology known as video, which enabled filmmaking with portable, handheld devices. Students then were researching how these cameras were being used to cover protest marches in New York City.

Michael invited William Everson to participate in the center's Institute of the American West. Everson was at that time organizing classic Hollywood film programs every Friday and Saturday that sold out in The New School's five-hundred-seat auditorium. Everson was also serving on the faculties of New York University and its School of Visual Arts. He maintained a vast collection of films, including an archive that was especially deep in Western films. His collection was well-known worldwide, and his "storage" facility was a subject of amazement for Michael, who described it as "a six-room New York apartment, each room and closet stacked to the ceiling with thirty-five-millimeter film canisters, askew and ready to tumble at any slight misstep." The furniture in Everson's apartment consisted of rows of well-worn movie theater seats.

Everson had long served as an archive consultant to the American Film Institute. He had published a dozen books and lectured all over the world while organizing cycles of films at such significant venues as the Museum of Modern Art in New York, the National Film Theatre in London, the Royal Film Archive in Belgium, and the George Eastman House in Rochester, New York. Everson's support for the center's film programs, along with our access to his film collection, brought immediate credibility to the center's film festival. His dedication to film history drew the attendance of recognized editors, authors, producers, directors, cinematographers, screenwriters, actors and actresses, curators of film, and professors in the history of the Western film genre.

Following the premiere of *The Outlaw Josey Wales*, the center benefited from a fortuitous visit by scholar and writer Alvin M. Josephy Jr. He first came to the valley to visit his daughter Diane, who was about to marry rancher and Idaho state senator John Peavey. Born into the Knopf publishing family, Alvin Josephy became a noted journalist, historian, editor, and author of books about Native American culture and history. His influential work, including significant writings about the Nez Perce Nation of Northern Idaho, led to sweeping changes in federal policy with regard to native sovereignty and self-determination. Josephy was then serving as the editor of *American Heritage Magazine* and was author of a compendium titled *The Indian Heritage of America*.

Josephy's visit to Sun Valley was followed by a cover story in *Atlantic Monthly* that included a glowing reference to a "renaissance in the West," with several paragraphs devoted to the Sun Valley Center for the Arts and Humanities' cultural impact on the region. The article was written by Wallace Stegner, who interviewed Jim Belson in the Potato Gallery and later wrote in an ironic tone about how the Sun Valley Center was "determined to bring art and ideas into the isolated and half-educated hinterlands."

Josephy proved invaluable to the institute and its programs through his contacts with journalists and academic professionals who would later attend and lead our seminars. This critical look at American culture continued for a number of years. In 1977, "The American Hero: Myths and Media" conference grew directly from ideas introduced the year before. It drew a wildly diverse group, from civil rights leader Julian Bond and lawyer William Kunstler to writer and comedian Paul Krassner. Counterculture acid guru Timothy Leary attended, as did feminist activist Kate Millet and actress Lindsay Wagner, known for her portrayal as the lead in The Bionic Woman. Rob Reiner and Tom Laughlin (aka Billy Jack) came, as did actress Penny Marshall, not to mention respected and outspoken writers, producers, and historians on the subject of American heroes, including Leslie Fiedler, Greil Marcus, and Richard Slotkin.

The 1978 conference, "The Writer and the West," drew a similarly eclectic mix of authors and speakers who examined timely issues in the real American West—"Who Owns the Rain?" about water problems now and in the past; "The Western Detective"; "Indians, Whites and Western Lands"; and finally, "That Awesome Space," an exploration of Western photographers, filmmakers, and writers. The programs were so well received that we needed to hire a full-time conference coordinator. Richard Hart filled the role and later became the director of the Institute of the American West as a separate program from the center's other humanities programs.

Under Hart, the annual institute program, supported by Levi Strauss, NEH, and state-based humanities programs, focused on federal Indian policy, western parks, and artist's conceptions of western space. The institute did a number of projects with individual tribes, such as the Shoshone-Piaute Tribes of Duck Valley Indian Reservation and the Zuni Pueblo people. These projects brought the institute national acclaim and helped Hart's later career, which involved working with many western tribes. The annual conferences resulted in numerous publications, as well as National Public Radio and Public Broadcasting Service (PBS) programming.

As was usually the case, we benefited considerably from well-connected friends in our areas of programming. I was fortunate to have met Evelyn Haas when I served with her on the San Francisco Museum of Modern Art Board of Trustees; consequently, I met her husband, Walter Haas Jr., through the museum. Walter had succeeded his father, Walter A. Haas, as CEO of the family-owned Levi Strauss & Co. Our request for the company's sponsorship of the institute and its annual conference was enthusiastically embraced. The conference was a perfect match for their iconic Western product. Bud Johns, then director of corporate communications for Levi Strauss, had the company design original posters announcing the conference. These posters are still treasured as collector's items.

Sponsored originally by Levi Strauss and the Peggy Engl Trust, our film conferences eventually included a long list of sponsors, including Bing Crosby Productions, Budget Films, Cinema Five, Columbia Pictures, MGM, New World Films, Paramount Pictures, Specialty Films, Twentieth Century Fox, and Warner Bros. Pictures. The National Endowment for the Arts (NEA) also provided considerable conference support.

The Institute of the American West's Western Film Conferences became such a draw that our "Western Movies: Myths and Images" and "American Hero: Myths and Media" programs spawned PBS films, shot on location in Sun Valley and shown nationally in 1978 as *The Reel West and You're Not a Hero 'Til You're Sung.* Jim Belson organized the taping of these documentaries during the conferences using a video crew from KCTS, Seattle's PBS station.

Although the Institute of the American West continued to grow in influence and impact over the years, a number of contributing factors led to increasing financial challenges for the center itself. The number of students coming to study in Sun Valley had been decreasing, due in part to the increasing popularity of Sun Valley as a destination resort. It became more difficult for students to find affordable places to stay. As more tourists began to flock to the valley for summer recreation, the motels in Ketchum were delighted to be able to raise their prices.

Another factor was a marked shift in academic priorities. Parents became less eager to support educations that might lead to a professional art career but instead steered their children back to traditional academia in hope that they would land jobs in the new field of high tech. Much of the burden of these changes fell upon Jim Belson, who had successfully guided the evolution of the center to such high recognition. He was eager to continue moving ahead with even more ambitious plans to justify our growing reputation, but the board voted instead to hire a new director, David Griffith, who would manage with tighter financial discipline and perform admirably in the position.

In 1978, Jim was given a lesser title and agreed to serve another year, but he told us that he intended to look for a position elsewhere. He remained in the area for several years, filming documentaries with Jim Dutcher about the Sawtooth wolf pack, but in 1980 he returned to Los Angeles to further pursue documentary film work.

The center's board also recognized that the campus building complex we created would no longer have the support it required and instead would have to become part of a new vision. In 1978, with the encouragement of Ed Dumke and Michael Engl, the center announced the prospect of selling the campus to the Community School. The boards of both organizations met this proposal with approval. Michael was board chairman of both the center and the Community School at the time. The sale took place in 1982, and the center opened new offices and galleries at a number of locations before settling in 1986 into its current location at 191 Fifth Street in Ketchum. On the entrance to the building is a sign that reads, "The Janss Building," in recognition of Bill and me and our early support.

The center, now called the Sun Valley Museum of Art, has remained true to its original mission and is still nationally recognized for its unique multidisciplinary programming. The visual arts, performing arts, education, and humanities directors organize three or four multidisciplinary projects each year around timely themes and topics from multiple perspectives. The exhibitions, concerts, lectures, and classes for each year all relate to one theme. The center organizes many of its own exhibitions, highlighting contemporary and historical work by artists both internationally known and at the beginning of promising careers. The museum's annual lecture and performance series bring distinguished performers and provocative writers and thinkers to the area.

These exhibitions are often so impactful that the shows are invited to travel to other venues, but I believe the organization's most important legacy is its continued educational outreach within the local Blaine County School District. Many of the visiting performers, writers, and artists who participate in the museum's programs also visit the schools. The museum offers after-school classes in English and Spanish, both within the classroom and at other facilities. These offerings are free of charge to elementary and middle school students, and a variety of scholarships are offered to students and teachers.

I have long since been "out of the loop," so to speak. The last time I attended our wine auction fundraiser was about ten years ago, for the center's fortieth anniversary, along with Molly Chappellet and her sister Luanne Wells. The auction had grown into such an enormous and successful event, attended by the new Sun Valley elite, that we hardly knew anyone there.

Many nonprofits followed the Sun Valley Center for the Arts' groundbreaking efforts. The Potato Gallery that we first commissioned in 1971 was the first commercial arts gallery in the area. It has now spawned more than forty other galleries and a lively local art market. Sun Valley Resort now has an impressive symphony pavilion that hosts the largest free symphony in the United States. Ketchum has the Argyros Performing Arts Center, and arts advocates willingly proclaim that they look now to the Wood River Valley as the center of Idaho arts and culture.

Throughout those extraordinary early years of the Sun Valley Center for the Arts and Humanities, the Sun Valley Company was able to provide a significant portion of our financial needs. By the mid 1970s, however, the resort was facing financial challenges as Bill struggled to expand his vision for the resort.

CHAPTER THIRTY-TWO

A Vision Under Challenge

Bill faced continuous challenges while he worked to modernize the Sun Valley Resort. In the earliest years, he shared an office with company president Harry Holmes in the Quonset hut, always tripping over Harry's 120-pound Great Pyrenees dog Studley, who slept in the hallway. Bill wanted to spend money on the mountain. That's what it was all about for him, but Harry did not agree with this priority.

Bill created the Duchin 9000 restaurant on top of Baldy Mountain from an old ski patrol shack. It became a place for local skiers to get together and have lunch. He eventually developed and opened the entire Warm Springs side of Bald Mountain, which had been out-of-bounds skiing before he took over. Soon after buying the resort, Bill had influenced the Sun Valley Ski Club to disengage from the responsibility of funding the Sun Valley Ski Education Foundation, making it possible for this organization to become its own nonprofit organization and thrive well into the future. As a ski racer, Bill knew this was the right decision. The foundation is a tremendous success today, training top athletes who regularly compete in major competitions around the world, including the Winter Olympics.

My brother Walt went to Bill's office one day with a proposal to start a Sun Valley Nordic School with Leif Odmark. Walt said the concession would be funded equally by the partners and requested the use of an old building utilized in the summer by golfers to access the golf course. Bill agreed to the request, knowing it would be a good winter use for the building.

Leif was the glamour guy of Nordic enthusiasts. He served as director of the program and was the most desirable first choice for private lessons as an instructor. Walt taught the group classes, taking groups on all-day trips as far afield as Galena Summit, Prairie Creek, and Redfish Lake in the Sawtooth Valley. Occasionally, a local helicopter pilot flew Walt and his skiers to areas around Hyndman Peak in the Pioneer Mountains or even as far as Copper Basin. Walt also organized the tiki torch nighttime ski tours to dinner at Trail Creek Cabin. After several years, when the Nordic School was well on its way to success, Walt sold his half of the partnership to Leif. In the summer months, Walt enjoyed the outdoor work of landscaping and became the treasured gardener at the Perry Gardens, a property up Clear Creek Canyon along Highway 75 that was well-known for its floral extravagance. Walt and Peggy eventually purchased a farm in the Hagerman Valley and left the Wood River Valley to live and work there.

Because so many of Bill's ideas didn't sit well with Harry Holmes, Bill eventually chose to let him go. I ran into Bill on the Sun Valley Mall after the firing and found him distressed but also relieved. Harry was a great friend to everyone, but he had never been a skier, so he didn't understand what Bill was trying to do. Harry saw his role as honorary, rather than as a working company president. He and his wife Gayle enjoyed holding parties and entertaining people at the resort's expense. Their aims were primarily social, so Harry was just never a good fit for Bill, who had serious goals that he wanted to achieve. Initially, Harry and Gayle were upset by the dismissal, but then Harry went on to become manager of the prestigious Pebble Beach Golf Club.

I met Cecil Andrus through friends of Bill and Anne Janss sometime before Cecil was elected governor of Idaho in 1970. I remember telling him that I had come to Idaho looking for a friendly rural area to raise my kids. Much later—in 2018—in a discussion with Cecil, he recalled for me the days when Ketchum was nothing more than what he described as "a little rural cow town of miners and cowboys." Averell Harriman had given the place a reputation for skiing, he said. But it wasn't the place that it is today. "You helped to create a sophistication that did not yet exist in Sun Valley," Cecil said. "During the years of Bill and Glenn Janss, Sun Valley became a hub where people of national and international significance spent time together. It was no longer just a sheepherding town."

Cecil reminded me of the work Bill did to get new legislation passed in the Idaho state house that would permit the development of condominiums in Sun Valley. Bill saw condos as a solution to an employee housing shortage, but state law did not yet allow common-wall dwellings to be owned separately, even though other states had allowed it. "The law was eventually passed with help from attorney Lloyd Walker in Twin Falls," said Cecil. "And soon there were premanufactured condominiums in building sections that could be seen on trucks coming down Highway 75 to the resort."

Bill promoted Wally Huffman to vice president and director of recreation. He oversaw numerous employees on Bald Mountain and at the golf course and ice rink. There were small sailboats cutting across Sun Valley Lake in those days—with beginner boat renters sailing uncontrollably into one another—and an archery range out on the soccer field, which is now the lawn by the symphony pavilion. Activities such as these were eventually curtailed by liability concerns.

Wally felt that he had the best job in the world. He worked closely with Bill, who spent many hours skiing on the mountain. Wally soon found that Bill was actually at work while on the slopes, looking for problems and seeking out ways to improve the skiing experience. His goal was to make Sun Valley a premier skiing destination.

"He would arrive back at his office for a meeting with his managers, wearing a list of chores and ideas he had written in ink on the back of his hand," said Wally. "He would roll up his sleeves at our meeting; and if his list went as far as his elbow, we knew it was going to be a long evening and we were in deep shit."

Wally learned about the history of the resort, how the first chair lifts had been developed there, and how the first year of skiing in 1936 turned out to be a bust. Although Count Felix Schaffgotsch, who first scouted out the valley for Averell Harriman, had heard from someone that the valley was always steeped in snow, it was also situated on the edge of a desert. "That first year, the company had to bus people to Galena Summit to find snow," said Wally.

Tennis was booming in the early 1970s, and Bill was an avid tennis player, as was I. We spent time at many tennis clubs, including the Silverado Resort in Napa Valley and John Gardiner's Tennis Ranch in Carmel after we were married. Bill sent Wally around to these upscale tennis destinations to learn how to set up a tennis operation. Wally received good advice from Tom Stowe at Silverado. First off, he asked Wally, "Are you charging for tennis?"

It turned out that Sun Valley was giving away court time for which other centers were charging eight dollars per hour per person. Changes were made quickly, but it was painful for regulars. Nevertheless, tennis in Sun Valley grew, and Wally was directed to build more courts. Rod Laver, Chuck McKinley, and other greats were invited to play exhibition matches at the Sun Valley courts and in Elkhorn.

Bill had built the commercial mall between the Sun Valley Lodge and the Sun Valley Inn back in 1966. Designed by David Jay Flood, it looked exactly like his Camino Real development in the Bay Area. Flood went on to design for numerous ski resorts. In 1970, Bill had sold twenty-five hundred acres of land in the Elkhorn area for development by the Johns Manville Corporation, retaining a 15 percent partnership in the properties. "That was the only year Bill ever made money in

Sun Valley," said Wally. "He got about $3 million for the land, but then turned around and reinvested it back into the resort. He built lifts on Baldy and remodeled the Sun Valley Lodge, among many other projects."

The original 1936 Sun Valley Lodge design had been based on old plans for Union Pacific Railroad stations, except that the concrete forms were designed to make the walls look like stacked logs. Only the Sun Valley Inn and Sun Valley Opera House had an Austrian look, primarily because skiing came to America through the Austrians. In fact, it also came to America through the troops of the Tenth Mountain Division, US Army, during World War II.

Ketchum engineer and Tenth Mountain Division veteran Phil Puchner happened to live downhill from one Janss-era project. In 1973, Bill decided that a swath of trees had to be removed from the bottom of Baldy to connect Greyhawk run to the Warm Springs lifts. Puchner owned a house below the soon-to-be ski slope, and when the trees came down—thousands of them—he sued the resort, claiming that the tree-cutting put him in danger of an avalanche. For a while, the Puchners were furious at the resort, but Phil's wife Ann became a big supporter of the Sun Valley Center for the Arts in the years that followed, and this helped smooth things out.

After the trees were felled, Bill came to Wally and told him rather sheepishly that matters were even worse than he had imagined. The trees were on land that he did not yet own but only had an option to purchase from the Capozzi family. "He told me I would have to help him figure out a way out of the mess," said Wally.

The Capozzi family had developed the International Village in Warm Springs. For some reason, Wally was convinced they were part of the East Coast mafia. When he called Herb Capozzi, he was told that the family would be in town for ski season; he inquired whether they could try to work something out at that time.

"In December, I went to the Capozzi house, and Herb answered the door," said Wally. "Standing next to him was the most beautiful woman I had ever laid eyes on, except for the other twenty more beautiful women inside at the party. We were popping drinks and talking, and finally I asked what could be done about the forest we had cut down on his property. Herb said it would all be okay if the resort were to give the Capozzi family, including all the brothers and their families, ski passes for life. And that was the end of it. Bill was all too happy to oblige."

By 1974, it was apparent to Bill that the mountain required snowmaking equipment to ensure a Christmas ski season. He approached Tom Corcoran, a fellow Olympic skier who founded the Waterville Valley Resort in New Hampshire, to get his opinion. "Tom said 'Bill, you are out of your mind,' thinking such an expense would be unnecessary," Wally recalled.

Bill then sent Wally to Hunter Mountain Resort in upstate New York to meet with the Slutzky brothers, Israel and Orville, who had pioneered snowmaking technology there. Wally hired an engineer and cowrote a thirty-five-page feasibility study on snowmaking. The last sentence of the report concluded that, in Wally's opinion, there was no need for snowmaking on Baldy. "Bill told me that, except for the last sentence in the report, it was the best study he had ever seen," said Wally.

At first, Bill's idea to install snowmaking equipment was met with community concerns over taking water out of Warm Springs Creek. Yet, Bill knew that snowmaking was essential for the resort's success. People questioned snowmaking for about ten years, remembered Wally. After a few bad snow years, it was seen for the necessity that it was. It saved the resort. Later, when the Holding family came along, they covered the entire mountain in snowmaking facilities at great expense.

There were times when Bill grew frustrated during the new era of environmental restrictions. Even as ski resorts were growing in popularity, environmentalists pushed back against expansion into forested areas. Prior to 1970, there were fewer regulations. Restrictions that were implemented under the National Environmental Policy Act (NEPA) of 1969 added numerous challenges. The resort's leases were complicated because 60 percent of Baldy was on US Forest Service land and 40 percent on US Bureau of Land Management Land. Land alteration permits could take two years to complete. "Back in the old days, if a tree was in the wrong place, it would just get cut," said Wally. "When the restrictions were tightened, Bill would joke, 'Hey, go get me a bucket of copper nails,' which we all knew would poison a tree and take care of the problem."

There were many times when Bill and I ventured out for respite into the millions of acres of true wilderness that surrounded us. For a time, John McCaw owned the Middle Fork Lodge, a remarkable property on the Salmon River surrounded by more than 2 million acres in the middle of the Frank Church-River of No Return Wilderness. When Bill turned seventy-three, John and Ann McCaw invited us to celebrate at the lodge, which could only be accessed by private airplane. Our guests included Don and Judy Atkinson, Pete and Becky Smith, Lynn and Tim Harris, and Barbara and Mike Wallace.

The Middle Fork Lodge is one of the few private lodges on the Salmon River's Middle Fork, with manicured lawns connecting the cabins and the lodge along the river. Deer and elk often stand unperturbed on the edge of the runway as you land. The remoteness is tangible, surrounded by twenty-five hundred square miles of wilderness. The US Forest Service airstrip allows access to the lodge, or guests can arrive by boat or after a two-day pack trip. The original property was homesteaded by two trappers: James Voller and Michael McNerney, known as the "Buckskin Boys."

The lodge was for us the perfect combination of isolated luxury and wilderness adventure; we were able to hike, fish, swim, or just relax, play games, and participate in the home-cooked ranch feasts at a long table set up on the grass in front of the lodge. This retreat from our complex and challenging lives provided an essential sanctuary. Our friendships deepened, as they always do in the wilderness, with no distractions and plenty of leisure time to hear one another's stories. Those days of relaxation in the wilderness with close friends were a respite for Bill before he headed back to the office to complete his commitment to a vision for Sun Valley Resort in the midst of increasingly turbulent times.

CHAPTER THIRTY-THREE

Royal Mischief

Brant was eleven years old going on fifteen when his older siblings departed for their various boarding schools. The youngest of the siblings, he had been enticed by them into an imagined maturity. He was also angry, feeling deserted by the loss of his father and by his siblings who were now off discovering their own worlds. Brant was estranged and envious, but also defiant. After seeing his brother Cam brushing his hair from right to left, he decided that he would brush his hair from left to right, and he has continued the practice to this day.

Brant used rudeness to take out his unhappiness on Bill and me. One day, I was so exasperated by his belligerent behavior that I offered him the option of going away to school. He leapt at the chance to be anywhere else, surely imagining that some mysterious happiness, which his siblings had already found, awaited him elsewhere. Once again, I took one of my children to the Community Library to research boarding schools. Brant liked one in the Southwest, and I consulted Sam Hazard on its reputation. Sam frowned and said, "Definitely not. That is the school for the decadent and disreputable."

Such a definitive statement from Sam meant the end of that possibility. He suggested Eaglebrook, a preparatory school for Deerfield Academy in Deerfield, Massachusetts. It proved to be just the right school, and the timing was good. Brant was still quite impressionable.

In Deerfield, he found male mentors who became father figures for him during the two years he spent there from age thirteen to fifteen. He returned home for his first Christmas vacation a perfect gentleman, opening doors for me and pulling out my chair at the dining room table. I convinced the others not to laugh at him but instead to appreciate our newly conditioned family member.

When we first visited Deerfield with Brant to consider it for his next school, the headmaster indicated how happy they were to have a ski racer join their student body. I took one look at the rope tow on their short, flat hill and said nothing. I knew that Brant would scoff at that suggestion, having been in training to race with the Sun Valley Ski Team. And that is what happened. He took one look at the tiny ski hill and joined the wrestling team.

Brant found himself in the same dormitory as the King of Jordan's two sons, Abdullah and Faisal, and their two ever-present security guards. The guards, only on duty during the day, had their own apartment in town. Once the dormitories and classrooms were in lockdown, they could retire for the night.

Brant became close friends with Abdullah, the brother closest to him in age. He extended an invitation for the two brothers to visit him in Sun Valley, and they came for a week, along with an entourage that included their mother and four security guards. The former queen, who retained the title of "Her Royal High Princess Muna al-Hussein," had married their father, heir to the family legacy of the Hashemite Kingdom of Jordan, in 1961 and divorced him in 1971. To us, she was simply Toni Gardiner, known in England as Lady Antoinette Gardiner, the mother of four of King Hussein's children—Abdullah II, Faisal, and their younger twin sisters, Aisha and Zein.

Their visit was a novelty for Sun Valley. Although accustomed to celebrities, the resort was not prepared to provide protection for the family of the future King of Jordan, who fortunately traveled with his own security. Toni Gardiner was the daughter of a British Army officer. She reportedly had met King Hussein while on location as a secretarial assistant for the filming of *Lawrence of Arabia*.

Two of the security guards were with the princess and two were assigned to the boys. The guards, who had their own Sun Valley Lodge apartment above the royal family, were kept busy; the boys had mischievous fun in mind in the wide-open landscape of Sun Valley. Brant encouraged the boys to "ditch" the security guards, and they sped off on bikes at their fastest, easily outdistancing the guards. After they were recovered, all three were severely scolded, but the royal boys felt smug, clever, and masterful for having gone on the run.

On the Fourth of July, Brant acquired a string of firecrackers. He and the boys hid in the bushes and lit them. A noise sounding very much like gunfire exploded on the lawn; and the security guards, who had been playing cards nearby, ran out and rushed toward the bushes with guns drawn. The guards were livid, took away Brant's lighter, and scolded all three boys again. After that stunt, they decided to "cool it" and hang out at the ice rink and bowling alley. But it must have been novel fun for the royal boys to enjoy some Wild West freedom and successfully create a ruckus.

Brant then visited the brothers in Jordan. The Royal Palace was impressive, he said, but not anything like the castle he had anticipated. It was more like a large Beverly Hills celebrity home on top of a hill. Yet, the entrance was outfitted like a military base, and they entered through a series of locked gates with armed sentries saluting as they passed. Brant was allowed to join the two brothers on a visit to a military base shooting range. They started with small pistols and then graduated to shotguns, an AK-47 and M16, and finally the chance to sit in artillery trucks pretending they were shooting at the enemy.

Wanting to spend time with his sons and their friend, King Hussein took two trips with the boys. The first trip was to Petra, the ancient city hewn from rock cliffs. The second trip was overnight to the city of Aqaba, in southernmost Jordan at the northeastern tip of the

Red Sea, bordering Israel. They traveled in black, bulletproof Mercedes limousines, the king in one, Abdullah in another, and Faisal in a third, with one armored truck ahead of the convoy and another bringing up the rear. King Hussein's brother was next in line for the throne and did not want Abdullah to be heir to the throne, Brant told me, so extra precautions were taken for Abdullah's safety.

While Brant was still at Eaglebrook, we were able to spend time with him in New York. Some years earlier, Bill had joined the Johns Manville Corporation Board of Directors following the company's purchase of the adjacent Elkhorn Valley. The board met monthly in New York City, so Bill and I had regular opportunities to be in the center of the art world. These were years that Bill was adding diversity to his art collection, selling his American Expressionist works for American Modernists of the earlier twentieth century. Every spare minute was spent dashing from gallery to gallery. For the second time in my life, I found myself on a search for hidden art treasures.

For us to see Brant on these trips, Eaglebrook School would deliver him to the Greenville, Massachusetts, bus depot for a two-and-a-half-hour ride to the downtown New York bus terminal, where I would meet him. We always stayed at the Park Lane Hotel for its view of trees and access to the park. Brant loved these excursions alone to New York; and in hindsight, I am grateful that in those days such travel was safe for a child. His favorite restaurant was Benihana, just two doors away from the hotel, so we took him there often for the grand performance they put on while preparing our meals. Bill knew that a fine French meal would be wasted on Brant.

After two years at Eaglebrook and yet another lengthy analysis of school choices, Brant chose to go to Hawaii Preparatory Academy. The school had a serious enough sounding name, but its location in paradise made me doubt just how serious the academic challenge could be. Since I had taken a trip to Italy with Candy to look at schools, Bill and I also decided to also take the trip with Brant to Hawaii to assess this new school. It had all the indications of being worthwhile, with high scholastic standards and an extensive offering of sports and extracurricular activities. The location near Kona meant Bill and I could occasionally enjoy the warm and balmy breezes during a break from the winter months in Idaho. And we did just that. We were delighted to stay at the Mauna Kea Hotel, enjoying grand buffets, snorkeling, and searching for turtles in kayaks. The only challenge for me was watching my son compete at his chosen sport of wrestling. As he faced off with a grimace against brawny Polynesian boys, I dutifully watched and cheered him on. It was the right school, and Brant thrived there, even serving as student body president his graduating year.

CHAPTER THIRTY-FOUR

Iran Synergistic

While governor of Idaho, Cecil Andrus recognized that Bill was under challenges at the resort and thought we would benefit from a diverting adventure he was leading to the Middle East in 1976. He invited us to join him on a trade delegation to the Persian kingdom of Iran, a trip that would surely provide us with a fresh perspective. The delegation consisted of Cecil, Senator James McClure of Idaho, and about a dozen prominent Idaho businessmen and some of their wives. Harry Magnuson, Jack Simplot, and Jack Hume were among those invited. Bill was asked along as a businessman and to personally advise Mohammad Reza Shah Pahlavi and his advisors on a ski resort the shah wished to build. The shah had visited Sun Valley several times and was taken with the sport of skiing. Iran had elevations, terrain, and climate similar to Idaho's—it was a country with plenty of snow but only one very small ski-worthy hill. Bill believed he could help jump-start the skiing industry in the country or at least provide some helpful ideas on how to develop a worthwhile ski resort.

The stated purpose of the trip was to introduce the idea of sharing industry and trade contracts—especially in agriculture—between Iran and Idaho. The title for the trade mission was "Iran-Idaho Synergistic, 1976." The term synergy, then in vogue, meant a collaboration between two organizations that would yield more than the sum of their parts.

"I had no real idea what the word 'synergy' meant at the time," Cecil confessed to me recently—that is, until we all sat down to eat at the United Nations the night before we flew to Tehran.

The Iranian ambassador to the United States, Ardeshir Zahedi, had attended Utah State University. He knew about Idaho and had instructed his staff to prepare a lavish dinner for the delegation at the United Nations headquarters. The hors d'oeuvres included an Idaho potato filled with Iranian caviar from the Caspian Sea. "See that?" someone said to Cecil. "That's synergy!"

Our group stayed at the Royal Tehran Hilton. Some of the women on the street wore traditional hijab coverings; but otherwise, Tehran appeared to be more modern than I expected, perhaps due to the shah's westernizing influence. A group of the men from Idaho joined Cecil for meetings with the shah and his ministers. The shah pointed out that Iran stood at the soft underbelly of the USSR and that military aircraft, bombs, and artillery were needed to protect the region from communism. When Cecil met with the shah privately, he found that the Iranian leader was more interested in security than agriculture. "The shah was obsessed with weapons and did not want to talk about anything else, such as the need for the creation of additional food sources for his people," Cecil said.

During a meeting with agricultural leaders in Tehran, Jack Simplot suggested growing potatoes in the region. He pointed out that the soil and climate were ideal and that Idaho could provide the necessary potatoes and fertilizer. The Americans were told that rice was the preferred alternative and that Iranians occasionally used only very small potatoes in cooking stews. Cecil said Jack grew flustered when his brilliant solution to their food needs was so unexpectedly dismissed. "Jack said, 'Well, Jesus Christ. You have a knife, don't you?'" Cecil recalled. "'Just take a big Idaho potato and cut it up into tiny pieces, like this,'" and Jack gestured with his hands to show how to cut a potato. Mortified, Cecil realized it was time to get out of there.

Bill and I met Betty and Jack Hume for the first time on this trip. Jack was a prominent businessman from San Francisco who had founded a remarkable business in Blackfoot, Idaho, called American Foods, a processing and product company for potatoes. The business still flourishes under the management of his son, George Hume.

It took only a short conversation to know that the Humes would be ideal and compatible traveling companions. They too relied on a general lack of planning, a sense of humor, and a willingness to just set out on a spontaneous adventure in an unfamiliar country. This is the way Bill and I liked to travel, and we trusted that there would be wonderful experiences ahead for the four of us. It was the beginning of a lifelong friendship.

The ancient history of Persepolis was astounding and, as it turned out, provided a broad perspective on the tumultuous events that would soon take place in Iran. The earliest remains of these magnificent ruins dated back to 515 BC and the Achaemenid Empire. Cyrus the Great first chose the site, but it was his son Darius I who built the palaces and the expansive fortified terrace upon which it rested. The palace complex became so vast under Darius's new branch of the royal house that Persepolis for some years served as the capital of Persia.

As we spent the day among these ruins, we recognized why the giant terrace of 125,000 square meters, which dominated the ruin complex, was so noteworthy to archaeologists. The eastern side was actually cut from and emerges out of the adjacent Mount Rahmet. Most amazing to me was the dual stairway to the terrace. Called the Persepolitan Stairway, its 111 steps were built symmetrically and rose off the western side of the great wall. The shallow risers of the steps are believed to have been created to allow dignitaries to maintain a regal appearance when ascending.

Alexander the Great invaded the Achaemenid Empire in 320 BC and allowed his troops to loot Persepolis. In 316 BC, Persepolis was still the capital of Persia but as a province of the Macedonian Empire.

The city gradually declined, but its ruins remain, evidence of a once-glorious empire. For this reason, Persepolis remained a key palatial complex for later empires as well, even though it was a remote place in an alpine region, challenging to access. UNESCO declared the site of the ruins of Persepolis a World Heritage site in 1979, just three years after we visited those historic ruins and during the height of Iran's Islamic Revolution. It would seem that the shah's obsession with weapons was not entirely unfounded.

Our most remarkable adventure was to Isfahan, the second most populous area after Tehran. The city had flourished between AD 1050 and 1722, serving as the capital of Persia; at one time, it was one of the largest cities in the world. Isfahan is particularly well-known for its fine examples of Islamic-era Persian architecture, as can be seen in its numerous, still-extant palaces, mosques, and minarets. We had earlier been advised that it was now famous for its carpets.

The day after arriving, we ventured into Isfahan's wildly busy and crowded bazaar, the largest in the country. In my experience, it can only be compared to the expansive Grand Bazaar located below the streets of Istanbul, Turkey. We quickly tired in the heat of the day and were ready to return to our hotel when a man in fine Persian garb approached and said in broken English, "You see carpets?" He had readily identified us as tourists—Americans, no doubt. We all shook our heads in unison because we did not know this man or where he might take us. He persisted, and the men in our group decided that it would be interesting to follow him.

We trailed him along narrow, empty streets—no people, no cars. As the streets became narrower still, I grew concerned. The buildings were taller and closer together; this was clearly a residential area. Women in Iran were at that time not allowed to look out of their windows, but we could see them peering at us from behind shutters. We must have walked another half hour before the man leading us rang a doorbell on the ground floor of a shuttered building. A regally robed Persian man greeted us and left to announce our arrival.

Out of the depths of the hallway stepped an old man of noteworthy build and dress, with an undeniably autocratic dignity, decidedly the "master" of the establishment. He led us into a room so outlandish that we could not contain our giggles of astonishment and invited us to be seated on pillows along one side of a room that had walls covered in gold, so overwhelming in brilliance that I had to close my eyes until they became accustomed to the refracting light. The magnificent atmosphere produced in us a great sense of excitement and anticipation.

We were offered hot tea on small trays set before each of us by this maestro, as I came to call him. It seemed that, with his careful movements, he was leading a symphony, and his numerous attendants kept perfect step. He eventually asked us what we would like to see, and of course we did not have a clue, so he began the performance by instructing one after another of his men to enter carrying heavy and elaborately designed carpets, which they competently spread before us.

We were overwhelmed and confused by the beauty of these carpets, some centuries old, some recently woven. In excellent English and with limitless patience, the maestro explained the diversity of what he was showing us, the differences in the thread counts, designs, and colorations created by the different tribal traditions of Persian carpet weaving. Nowhere else in my lifetime have I experienced such an overwhelming sales performance. And it worked. Bill became entranced by this well-educated man who could provide in-depth answers to his many questions.

The Humes were astounded as Bill bought carpet after carpet, getting up to examine each one when our host described its importance and historic value. I was not surprised. As a man dedicated to the arts, Bill was known for his intensive research and evaluation of any purchase he ever made. He asked me for my opinions, and I willingly gave them. It was indeed an educational and unforgettable event for all of us. Bill ended up selecting twenty carpets, maybe more, for our home and as gifts for all of our children. Hours after we arrived, it came time to decide on a method of payment. The host tallied the expenditure and wrote the substantial total on a piece of paper. Bill told him he would wire the funds when he arrived home, and the host assured him that he would then send the carpets to America.

What remains extraordinary about this experience is the trust exhibited between these two individuals. The Humes and I had a hard time believing that the carpets would ever arrive, but Bill never had a doubt. The two men had developed a quiet, personal relationship and a deep understanding and commitment only they could comprehend.

Bill wired the money when we arrived home; six weeks later, the carpets arrived just as we had last seen them, individually rolled up and wrapped in heavy paper with JANSS written on the back with a black felt pen. The maestro surely must have been one of the most successful carpet traders in the history of his family's business. He had inherited and perfected his dramatic sales performance over generations. We were fortunate and grateful to have taken the opportunity and felt honored to have experienced those incredible and unforgettable hours in his golden showroom.

My children and I are still enjoying the carpets as we tread through our homes each day. They were kept until passed along in what came to be called our "bazaar room," a large closet filled with many exotic treasures purchased on our frequent trips to foreign lands; we enjoyed the carpets for many years and then enjoyed passing them along to future generations in our family.

The Idaho-Iran Synergistic trade delegation was less than successful, but it may only have been a matter of bad timing. It was hoped that Iranian officials would gather a delegation of their own to visit Idaho, but this never transpired. Cecil told me that the trade mission ended with very few financial prospects. Idaho irrigation equipment may have been sold to Tehran, including some pumps and pipes, but little else came of the trip from a trade perspective. We couldn't know that within two years the shah and his family would be overthrown by religious fundamentalists, setting our two countries into a conflict that exists to this day.

Cecil, always curious about history and culture, had an audience with Pope Paul VI in Rome on the way back to Idaho. His straightforward view of the world is always refreshing. "I am not Catholic," he said. "But I have great respect for the popes. Everything would have been fine and we'd all still be together in one church if the popes had listened to Martin Luther when he nailed his message to the door of the church."

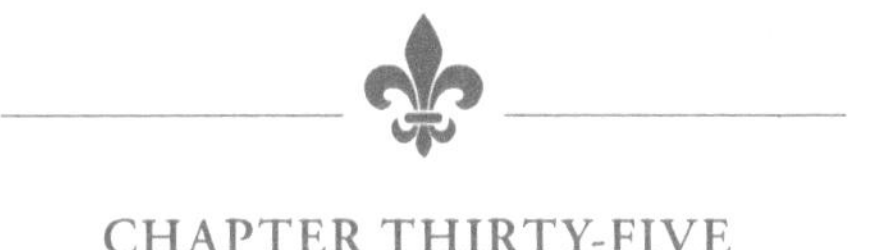

CHAPTER THIRTY-FIVE

The Centennial Commission

Cecil Andrus was governor of Idaho from 1971 to 1977, and then served President Jimmy Carter as US secretary of the interior from 1977 to 1981. He ran for the state's highest office again in 1986 and served as governor for another eight years, to 1995. With a total of fourteen years in office, Cecil is the longest serving governor in Idaho's history.

In 1989, it came time to plan a celebration for Idaho's centennial, and naturally Cecil was chosen to be leader of the Idaho Centennial Commission. His charisma and love for the state translated into remarkable support for numerous initiatives to help define Idaho's history. "As I traveled the state during our Centennial year, it was impossible not to be caught up in the enthusiasm," Cecil later wrote. "Everywhere I went, people were finding a new sense of pride in their state. It was the kind of pride that comes from understanding how fortunate we are to live in Idaho and to be able to call ourselves Idahoans."

Cecil asked me to serve on the Centennial Commission and to chair the Lasting Legacy Committee, one of the commission's twelve standing committees. I accepted this as an inspiring opportunity to serve my state. Eventually, more than two hundred people served on forty state committees and subcommittees for the Centennial

Commission. It was made up of Idaho's most knowledgeable and dedicated citizens. We were expected to attend meetings at the capitol building in Boise, travel the state, and give thoughtful consideration to hundreds of proposals to commemorate the event.

By the end of 1990, the committees had provided financial support for 240 projects and events and funded endorsements for many more. Centennial programs included the Idaho Heritage Trust, the Centennial Trail from Nevada to Canada, and a state park priority study to identify 150 potential new parks. Dozens of smaller programs proposed environmental conservation, historic re-creations of early explorations, and many local arts projects.

Although Cecil dealt with the broad overview of events and planning, Harry F. Magnuson, the appointed chairman, and I were called to serve the commission in a more hands-on capacity. That, of course, meant fund-raising, but it also involved considerable work to identify likely sites for historic preservation. The commission originally sought $100,000 per year for five years to undertake the work, but an Idaho Centennial license plate and other donation sources brought in more than $8.5 million. Every centennial license plate sold continues to bring in twenty-five cents for the Idaho Heritage Trust, an organization that I chaired for a number of years.

I agreed to help with the organization of the Lasting Legacy Committee because I was interested in identifying and preserving the architectural history in many small towns across Idaho. A Union Pacific Railroad engine and train cars were commissioned to travel the state in celebration of the centennial. Cecil told me later that it was the public enthusiasm we generated that led to recognition of the Idaho Heritage Trust as a permanent, state-supported, honored nonprofit.

"The Centennial was more than simply a birthday celebration. It was an opportunity for all Idahoans to join in a common cause and show their pride and affection for both the state and the people," Harry Magnuson wrote in 1991. "For much of Idaho's history, we have found ourselves separated by either geography or a variety of other differences. With the Centennial, those divisions have melted away . . . the success is not so much a testament to the work of any single group or organization as it is a tribute to the efforts of all Idahoans who so readily accepted Governor John Evans's charge that they become a 'committee of one million' to celebrate the Centennial." Evans served as governor from 1977 to 1987.

It was an honor to serve under Cecil Andrus. In his public life, he was noted for his dedication to environmental conservation. An Idaho wildlife preserve established in Washington County, Idaho, in 1993 was named the Cecil D. Andrus Wildlife Management Area in his honor. In 2018, the White Clouds Wilderness near Sun Valley was renamed, also in his honor, as the Cecil D. Andrus-White Clouds Wilderness.

Cecil knew the importance of political compromise in making things happen. Working across the aisle had succeeded during the creation of the Sawtooth National Recreation Area and the Frank Church-River of No Return Wilderness, iconic conservation areas near Sun Valley that define central Idaho. In 1988, Cecil and Senator Jim McClure put together a wilderness bill for the entire state of Idaho, but partisan challenges caused this compromise bill to fail in the legislature. As Cecil expressed it to me, "The Democrats thought I was selling out to the lumber industry. The Republicans thought Jim, a Republican, was selling out to the posy sniffers."

It was probably my reputation as an organizer that led to my appointment as chair of the Lasting Legacy Committee, but never before had I not personally selected the board I was chairing. I suddenly found myself with a committee of twenty-nine members, many of whom I did not know. It was a novel challenge to manage these unfamiliar yet strong and competent voices, who came forward to propose what each believed should be the most important lasting historical legacies for future generations. These committee members represented all areas of the state, and I soon learned that many true friendships would result from this new challenge. Relationships provide the most treasured memories from public service. The Lasting Legacy members that represented Blaine County were Terry Ring, owner of Silver Creek Outfitters and a chairman in the early years of the Idaho Nature Conservancy; Toni Smith, board member of the Sun Valley Center for the Arts and the Community School; Bill Vanderbilt, an active community supporter; and Guy Bonnivier, executive director of the Idaho Nature Conservancy. I hoped for strong support for legacies of conservation from these individuals.

Over the years, the Idaho Heritage Trust has provided millions of dollars and untold hours of technical preservation expertise to communities across the state, helping to preserve hundreds of buildings and landmark properties, most of them in small towns. Notable projects include the Cataldo Mission in Coeur d'Alene, the Panida Theater in Sandpoint, and the Ore Wagon Museum in Ketchum. I made a trip to Silver City to explore the mining town's history and help identify buildings there for preservation.

Harry Magnuson and Marty Peterson served as chair and cochair of the Idaho Centennial Commission. Born in Wallace, Magnuson became a legendary business leader and philanthropist in the Northwest. He never forgot his beloved hometown roots; he is most remembered for his leadership in the battle from 1970 to 1986 to save Wallace from state and federal highway officials who planned to route Interstate 90 through the center of the town.

Magnuson sued the Federal Highway Adminstration and the Idaho Transportation Department, alleging that they had failed to file an environmental impact statement. A federal judge concurred, entered an injunction, and halted the waiting bulldozers. Magnuson then secured inclusion of the entire town of Wallace on the National Register of Historic Places, creating insurmountable "roadblocks" to its destruction. As a result, historic Wallace was preserved and overhead freeway routing bypassed the town. A grateful citizenry dedicated the original routing of I-90 as "The Harry F. Magnuson Way."

It was Harry's "way" that so dominated the Centennial Commission. I revered him and his easy Idaho style, his openness, fun and merry personality, winning laughter, humility, and gracious hospitality. He appeared to be almost shy, but within his apparent reticence was a keen listener with a strong and decisive personality. Several meetings and social gatherings were scheduled at his home on Lake Coeur d'Alene. His leadership was reserved, accepting, and thoughtful as he patiently withstood the barrage of requests from passionate and caring Idahoans.

Gaetha Pace is the person who succeeded me and worked tirelessly over many years to carry forward the mission of the Idaho Heritage Trust. She grew up in rural communities in Nevada and South Dakota before coming to Idaho, where she gained valuable administrative experience working as special assistant to Governor John Evans. She was then chosen by John S. Chapman to serve as executive director of the Idaho Arts Commission for three years. In 1989, I invited Gaetha to lunch and asked her to help out with the Idaho Centennial Commission. Gaetha knew who I was from my work in the arts and agreed to take a job helping me with fund-raising. After the Idaho Heritage Trust was established, she was soon hired as its executive director.

The trust was created by the Lasting Legacy Committee for the purpose of carrying on its mission after the centennial. To help fund it originally, we created a "Truck for Art" mobile art gallery and companion book featuring paintings and sculptures by Idaho artists. I used my donor contact lists and went to work, raising over $1.2 million, an endowment that has continued to grow. The trust was initially formed to include natural resource conservation, but Idaho legislators, including Representative Mike Simpson, didn't believe voters would support a quasi-state fund that would take more land off the tax rolls. As a result, the trust refocused its efforts on historic preservation. Gaetha added her own ideas for generating donations.

"I felt the only way the trust would survive would be to have projects in every corner of the state, and this would only happen if we listened to people and found out what we could do for them," said Gaetha. She hired Oregon architect Frederick Walters, who had expertise in historic preservation. He and Gaetha would show up in a rural town for a meeting organized by Harry Magnuson and ask the locals, "What would you want to be here in 2090 for your great grandchildren?" Meanwhile, I worked as a fundraiser to make sure the trust would survive. I stepped down in 1993, after several hallmark projects were initiated or completed, projects that often focused capital on preserving Idaho's frontier heritage.

The Idaho Heritage Trust went to work right away in partnership with the Trust for Public Land and the US Forest Service to preserve Campbell's Ferry, a cabin and ranch that sits high on the canyon rim over the Salmon River, within the Frank Church-River of No Return Wilderness. This eighty-five-acre property had been used by William Campbell since the 1800s to provide ferry service to miners and packers on their way to the Thunder Mountain gold mine.

Frances and Joe Zaunmiller lived in this remote "primitive area" cabin for forty years, operating the ferry while Frances wrote newspaper columns about life along the river. She became famous throughout Idaho for her weekly columns in Grangeville's *Idaho County Free Press*. For thirty-one years, she wrote about subsistence living, surviving solitude and hardships amidst the rugged beauty in the Salmon River Canyon backcountry. "Frances wrote consistently about life in the back country but also advocated with Cecil Andrus against shooting elk from aircraft," said Gaetha. "The forest service wanted to destroy all those cabins along the river, but many people didn't want to see them go."

A coalition of nonprofit organizations worked to stabilize the cabin; then they wrote a cooperative agreement to restore the homestead, put protective scenic easements on the property, and resold it to conservation buyer Doug Tims. Today, the ranch stands as an enduring example of early Idaho river life during the mid twentieth century.

The trust then kicked off a large project that became emblematic of the kind of programs it would offer over the years. Working in partnership with the Chesterfield Foundation, the trust helped to preserve the nineteenth-century Mormon outpost of Chesterfield on the Portneuf River, which was abandoned when a railway bypassed the town. About twenty tall brick houses and log structures were preserved there for posterity and now operate as a tourist attraction. Chesterfield was the hometown of Western author Frank Chester Robertson. The trust then worked on the preservation of Enders Hotel in Soda Springs, and numerous other rural projects around the state.

Gaetha worked with many other organizations in Idaho to keep costs down and so avoid eating into the endowment. She traveled up to twenty-five thousand miles in a year, speaking at rotary meetings and luncheons, and, above all, listening. The trust held workshops across the state to train locals in a variety of skill areas, including how to preserve headstones, organize museum collections, and create historical interpretations. They helped protect a Bureau of Indian Affairs girls dormitory in Salmon from demolition. Lemhi Shoshone youths had been housed there in the early 1900s, until the tribe was forced from the town and tragically marched all the way to the Fort Hall Reservation near Pocatello. Today, the building is used as a Grange hall.

The trust faced opposition from some for a conservation plan on the Shoshone-Bannock Fort Hall Reservation. Some thought the Lincoln Creek Day School there held a painful legacy worth forgetting. "The elders remembered it as a place where kids would be taken away from their families and stripped of clothing and other family artifacts that were thrown into a pit," Gaetha said. "In the pit was layer after layer of this painful legacy. The people had for many years been having a quiet fight with this history, although by this time it had become more of a community center. It had been vandalized and was no longer structurally sound. A young person came to me and asked about preserving it. We found money from foundations and told them how to do it, helping them identify further funding to complete the project."

The trust worked to save railway depots, theaters, rural schools, cabins, and ranger stations—hiring consultants instead of using staff. Masons, document conservators, and log cabin specialists joined the trust for a project. An expert in mid-century lighting was brought on for one project. A theater specialist was hired to preserve the Panida Theater in Sandpoint. "In Hagerman, a young man wanted to save the family barn," recalled Gaetha. "Fred said he should just hook a tractor onto it, straighten it out, and then put back the supporting structures that had been taken out when the family changed its use years before."

Well-heeled donors also came into play. John Chapman, who had hired Gaetha for the Idaho Arts Commission, reached out to a member of the Du Pont family for help in preserving buildings in Silver City that had ties to the family's history. Senator Larry Craig facilitated the use of funding from the Lewis and Clark Trail Committee for projects along the Lewis and Clark Trail. Some projects could take as long as take twenty years to complete. By 2017, the Idaho Heritage Trust had funded more than four hundred projects totaling over $3 million in grants and technical architectural, engineering, and conservation advice in every Idaho county. The trust awarded more than 66 percent of its grants to communities of five thousand residents or less.

Another important collaborator during this time was Marty Peterson, who in 1970 had been working for Senator Frank Church in support of gubernatorial candidate Cecil Andrus. At a meeting in Sun Valley about the proposed establishment of the Sawtooth National Recreation Area, Marty struck up a conversation with Mary Hemingway, Ernest Hemingway's fourth wife, who lived in the Hemingway House in Ketchum. At the time, Andrus was running a campaign against incumbent Governor Don Samuelson that centered on opposition to a proposed molybdenum mine at the foot of Castle Peak in the heart of what is today the Cecil D. Andrus-White Clouds Wilderness. Samuelson supported the mine. Andrus strongly opposed it, and it was ultimately denied.

Idaho US Senator Frank Church had sponsored the Wilderness Act of 1964, which eventually set aside 9 million acres for preservation as areas where "the earth and its community of life are untrammeled by man, where man himself is a visitor who does not remain." Cecil told me recently about those years of bipartisan support and communication, which appear to be remote from today's political discourse. "We knew how to disagree without being disagreeable," he said. "The environment may have been controversial, but no particular political party thought they owned it all."

The passage of the Wild and Scenic Rivers Act in 1968 and the Central Idaho Wilderness Act in 1979 led to the establishment of the Frank Church-River of No Return Wilderness. At 2.4 million acres, it is the largest contiguous federally managed wilderness in the continental United States.

The Hemingway Family legacy had an impact on history, culture, and conservation in Idaho. Ernest Hemingway first began spending time in the Wood River Valley in the 1930s. *For Whom the Bell Tolls* was partially written during his stay at the Sun Valley Lodge with then-girlfriend Martha Gellhorn. He returned with his sons in the 1940s to hunt, fish, and escape the hoopla. He left and then returned after ten years with his fourth wife, Mary. Together, they purchased a sturdy, plastered three-story home on a dirt road overlooking the Big Wood River in north Ketchum for $50,000. This is where the great writer, after bouts with severe depression, ended his life with a shotgun in 1961.

Known as the "Topping House," the home had been built by Henry J. "Bob" Topping, the heir to a tin fortune who had been eighty-sixed from the Sun Valley Lodge for unruly behavior. Bill told me that, in addition to other activities, he had been caught running naked through the lodge. Rather than leave town, Topping opted to build a "lodge" of his own. The building he sold to the Hemingways bears a striking resemblance to the simulated stacked-log appearance of the Sun Valley Lodge because it was crafted using the same concrete forms.

The house was turned over to The Nature Conservancy in 1986, at the time of Mary's death. Mary intended for the home to serve as a library and nature preserve and endowed a sum for upkeep that recently amounted to about $15,000 annually. She knew of The Nature Conservancy through her stepson Jack. For many years, TNC used the house as a regional office, more than doubling the bequeathed amount for yearly maintenance.

The Hemingway House was rarely visited by the outside world, other than an occasional private tour. We did, however, use it for board meetings and TNC fund-raising gatherings that provided special tours. The house was left to The Nature Conservancy in roughly the same condition it had been in when Mary and Ernest lived there in the late 1950s. Mary's wardrobes still hung in the closets. Photographs, books, and memorabilia remained on shelves and under glass on tables. The John F. Kennedy Library had earlier combed through the residence for important memorabilia and texts but left in place mounted African hunting trophies, a bullfight poster featuring Hemingway's friend Antonio Ordóñez, and personal photographs from Hemingway's colorful life.

In a hallway of the home still hangs a painting Waldo Peirce did for Hemingway in 1959 as a birthday present. In it, two men are skinning a bull after a Spanish bullfight, with "Bon Appetit" painted in broad strokes at the bottom. A collage of photographs from Cuba and elsewhere include the great writer standing on the back of a boat, buck naked, with his manly buns to the camera. Even after years under TNC ownership, the house continued to give up treasures that

Ernest and Mary had tucked away here and there. Only a few years ago, Marty Peterson found behind a stack of books what appeared to be a flyswatter but was later identified as a bull's tail, probably given to Hemingway by one of his matador friends in Spain in 1959. About that time, a collection of wine glasses was found in a linen closet. Peterson identified them as matching glasses at Hemingway's Cuban estate. They were identified as fine glass works from the island of Murano near Venice.

Marty was called in recently to identify a rolled-up watercolor painting that was discovered in a closet. It turned out to be a painting by Ezra Pound's wife, Dorothy Shakespeare, dated 1926. The painting by the great poet's wife reaches back to an earlier era in the life of Hemingway. After World War I, Pound was a mentor to Hemingway in Europe, where they spent time together with Gertrude Stein, F. Scott Fitzgerald, James Joyce, and others. In A Moveable Feast, Hemingway described giving Pound boxing lessons in exchange for lessons about writing and literature. He wrote that Pound taught him to "distrust adjectives as I would later learn to distrust certain people in certain situations." Hemingway also expressed admiration for the paintings of Dorothy Shakespeare.

"That painting of Dorothy's is still in the house and is the most valuable painting in the place," said Marty, at a recent gathering to celebrate the transfer of the Hemingway House to the Community Library in Ketchum.

Ezra Pound was arrested for treason after World War II. It just so happened that he was born in Hailey, thirteen miles from the Hemingway house in Ketchum. Only a controversial plea of insanity kept Pound from standing trial and, perhaps, hanging. After spending twelve years in St. Elizabeth's Hospital for the insane in Washington, DC, he was released in 1958, with the help of Hemingway, Robert Frost, and Archibald MacLeish. Pound spent his last years in silent exile in Venice, Italy, apparently unrepentant about his fascist loyalties.

The history of Pound's career as a Modernist poet and mentor was supported by the Idaho Heritage Trust when funding came through to preserve his birthplace in Hailey, which is now operated under the auspices of the Sun Valley Center for the Arts. Both the Pound House and Hemingway House are on the National Register of Historic Places.

The Nature Conservancy board had long desired to make the Hemingway House more accessible to the public. In the early 2000s, Hemingway's granddaughter Mariel served on the Idaho Hemingway House Foundation board as co-chair. The board proposed that the house be open for tours, but a handful of well-heeled neighbors, concerned about their privacy, protested so vehemently that a threatened lawsuit made news both nationally and internationally. The Nature Conservancy had no choice but to back down, so for many years the home was only available for occasional private tours. Salman Rushdie had signed the guest book, as well as the artist Dale Chihuly and several other lucky scholars, donors, and friends. Now that it is owned and maintained by the Ketchum Community Library, students and writers in residence can visit and the literary legacy of Ernest Hemingway in Idaho can be shared for generations to come.

The Idaho Centennial Commission and its Lasting Legacy Committee enhanced the visibility of historic sites throughout the state, which resulted in numerous publications, and inspired more local initiatives and community pride than we will ever know. *The Idaho Centennial Wish Book* of 1988 provided early information on projects throughout the state that had been selected for funding. The American Library Association placed this book on its 1989 Notable Documents List. Under the commission's auspices, the State Parks Priority Study was able to review 150 potential future park sites in virtually every corner of the state. A significant selection was the Land of the Yankee Fork State Park, featuring a historic mining district in Custer County, as a tribute to the Idaho Centennial.

One commission project that proved exceedingly difficult to

manage was the selection of the route for the Idaho Centennial Trail. Although there was agreement that the trail would run from the Idaho-Nevada border north to the Canadian boundary, there were a multitude of concerns and ideas from government agencies and interest groups, and negotiating these differences was a major accomplishment. The selected 900-mile route can take months to travel or hike, and few accomplish it.

A "Take Pride in Idaho" program was initiated by the commission under the auspices of the Lasting Legacy Committee. We were to administer the awards program for this initiative in 1990. Significant to the success of the program was the desire to provide public recognition for organizations and individuals whose achievements so often go unnoticed and, in this way, to encourage more statewide volunteer support. During the first three years of the program, nearly one hundred awards were given for such diverse projects as books, historic preservation, wildlife habitat preservation, and lifetime achievements.

Since the centennial, the program has continued under the auspices of the Idaho Heritage Trust, perhaps the most significant and far-reaching of the Lasting Legacy Committee's projects. The trust was established specifically to find and fund projects key to the preservation of Idaho's heritage. In an unprecedented move, the Idaho Legislature eventually recognized the trust as a private entity entitled to carry out state heritage preservation.

In one of the books written about those years, I am quoted as saying, "The passage of that legislation was the high point for me of the entire Centennial. It was not only a tremendous boost for the trust, but also an indication of the public leadership shared in the commitment to help preserve Idaho's heritage."

The Idaho Centennial Foundation, along with a number of leading citizens and Idaho corporations, made support of the trust a high giving priority. The foundation also transferred the trademarks of the Idaho Centennial license plate design and the Celebrate Idaho logo to the trust. Idaho's state motto of *Esto Perpetua* (Let it be Perpetual) is emblazoned in the work of the Idaho Heritage Trust. The trust's Lasting Legacy projects will ensure that Idaho's second century of statehood will live up to its motto. After the centennial committees dispersed, I continued to chair the Idaho Heritage Trust for a number of years. It was an honor for me to have been selected for this role in preserving Idaho's history.

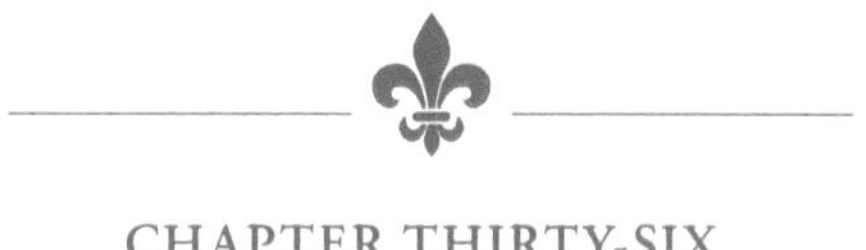

CHAPTER THIRTY-SIX

American Realism

On one of our trips to New York for Bill's monthly Johns Manville Corporation board meetings, an extraordinary and consequential circumstance opened up for me, one that would provide me with an unanticipated opportunity to leave a lasting contribution to the world of art. For many years, I had been making occasional art purchases based on my own tastes. Bill, too, had been collecting over the years, primarily modernist works. When in New York, we always spent several days visiting our favorite art galleries. Bill came to appreciate my art history background and depend on my guidance for purchases based on the acumen I had developed in Los Angeles for assessing the significance of a piece of art in the historical oeuvre of a particular artist.

One morning, we walked into a Madison Avenue gallery that specialized in modernist paintings. Bill went straight to the back to join the owners for a prearranged meeting in a private room while I lingered at the entrance to talk to the receptionist at the front desk.

I happened to glance down and notice a book on her desk, *Realist Drawings and Watercolors: Contemporary American Works on Paper,* by John Arthur. I recognized the painting displayed on the book's cover as one that I owned. I knew the artist, Carolyn Brady, and found it interesting, even very curious, that this book would be in a gallery that did not specialize in such contemporary realism. As I leafed through the book, I was shocked to find that I owned about a quarter of the works featured in its pages and recognized immediately the works of most of the other artists. I had considered purchasing almost all of them over the years.

I joined Bill in his meeting as he contemplated some of the finest examples of the American Modernist movement—Henri Matisse, Alfred Stieglitz, Charles Sheeler, Georgia O'Keeffe, Robert Henri, Marsden Hartley, Arthur Dove, and Charles Burchfield. As we exited the gallery, I could hardly contain my excitement. I tugged on his sleeve and announced, "Bill, I am an art collector, and I didn't know it."

This unanticipated consequence of my passion for art had never been a goal. Since my daily expenses were now covered by Bill and I had already set aside college funds for all five Cooper children, I continued spending occasionally on art. I considered this to be a fun pursuit while accompanying Bill on his gallery visits. Now I could see that I might as well take the pursuit more seriously and become an acknowledged collector.

It turned out that I had been collecting works under the genre of American Realism, a popular movement under way at that time and of great interest to gallery owners and collectors. The first painting I had ever purchased fell into this category—a very loose, painterly depiction of trees by Paul Wonner. He and other Bay Area artists represented the West Coast counterpart to the American Realism movement on the East Coast. Richard Diebenkorn and Fairfield Porter had led the way by defying the dominance of Abstract Expressionism and continuing to paint representational works. But realism reached back much further than this. Fairfield Porter opens one of John Arthur's books with a quote from Pablo Picasso, an early master of realist depictions, on the great tradition of representational art as opposed to abstraction: "Actually, that's the best part, pictures full of literature, rotten with anecdotes, that tell stories."

American Realism is generally ascribed to a movement in the latter half of the twentieth century, but it was actually a continuation of a longer tradition within the history of American art. The 1980s resurgence of interest in realism was due to numerous artists I had come to appreciate, whose works had kept it in the public eye. Their art formed a resistance to critical interpretations that had overlooked so many realist treasures over the previous several decades. During the 1950s and 1960s, an influential segment of the art establishment began to regard the tradition of representational art as backward. It was proclaimed to be "retrograde" and not deserving of attention—not innovative or creative enough. The tradition of figural elements in the visual arts was being discarded as uninteresting, and so this representative tradition was ignored in favor of abstraction, specifically Abstract Expressionism.

American Realism captured and honored the social reality in the lives of ordinary people. The movement began in the mid nineteenth century in literature, becoming an important avenue of visual depiction in the early twentieth century. American realist works in all media attempt to depict what is real rather than ideal. Yet, the newer generation of artists did not always appreciate such early realist painters as Thomas Eakins, Winslow Homer, Childe Hassam, Mary Cassatt, and John Singer Sargent. These artists had continued a tradition that once captured the American zeitgeist. The new mission for realist painters was to create works depicting city life for a population that was now more urban than rural.

In the early twentieth century, the United States was emerging into a time of exuberant industrial, economic, social, and cultural change that took place in the midst of a wave of European immigration, growth, and prosperity. Artists wanted to depict this moment—this "now"—and they exalted the ordinary feelings and textures of American city life. These circumstances influenced their innovative work, its texture, color, and subject matter. They were no longer interested in fantasy but in the reality of the moment. In this way, they introduced a new modernism and created the core of what came to be called American Modernism in the visual arts. The groups of artists who created this movement were called the Ashcan School and The Eight.

The Ashcan School was made up of New York artists who captured the feel of New York City. They preferred to paint portraits of lower-class immigrants rather than the high-society inhabitants of Fifth Avenue. They depicted tenements, alleys, slums, and the taverns of the working class. These were the original heroes who influenced the mid-century revolution that I was now representing. They included George Bellows, Robert Henri, Everett Shinn, George Luks, William Glackens, John Sloan, and Edward Hopper. They provided the background into which the next generation entered, the generation whose work I was currently collecting.

I sought to include not only the well-known artists at the time, such as Georgia O'Keefe and the more contemporary Edward Ruscha, but also those who were newly emerging from their "underground" studios because they now felt safe painting what they most valued. I use the word underground because they had been working in a time when no art journalists or critics wanted to write about them and few gallery owners supported or represented their work. Suddenly, New York was awash with these art dealers because they realized what was happening in the rest of the country and rushed to represent the best of these realist painters. Collecting them at this time also became a passion for me.

The range of artistic diversity was overwhelming. During the 1980s, in the prime of the movement, I set the goal of applying my time, money, and eye to building a collection that would justify the historical significance of the movement. In the process, I created one of the largest private American Realism collections of the twentieth century.

At first, I had to move slowly because of the sheer diversity of what had come to currently represent the term "realism," a word that had suddenly reentered the art vocabulary in the 1970s. To art historians and critics, realism had always been an academic tradition, but now there was a deluge of new labels: magic realism, painterly realism, photo realism, new realism, superrealism, sharp-focus realism. Eventually, I wanted to include all facets of the movement and ensure that the entire range of contemporary realist categories was represented. I also decided that everything in my collection would be "works on paper."

My own sensibility reflected a preference for the styles of more naturalistic and flowing compositions, a style that was associated with painterly realism. I realized that abstract art could bring huge prices at auction, but my emotional response had always been contrary to this. My loyalty has always been to an artist's personal and skillful response to an actual landscape or subject. I was not drawn to the expressionist art of Jackson Pollack, Franz Kline, Robert Motherwell or Jasper Johns.

Collecting and presenting this movement in realism became a mission for me. I visited as many artist studios as I could over the years, learning from the immediacy, wisdom, and eye of the painter. The artists' personal perspectives gave me a better understanding and appreciation of their style and its connection to the subject matter through their choice of paint distribution, color, and composition.

With the support of my longtime friend Henry Hopkins, my mission to exhibit a major collection became a reality. In the 1980s, Henry was executive director of the San Francisco Museum of Modern Art, and I was a member of its board of trustees. Henry introduced the possibility of mounting an exhibition of my collection. Following my excited approval, he then proposed the idea to the museum board. It was approved unanimously, and the dates were selected: November 7, 1985, to January 12, 1986.

Henry's established reputation and the expansiveness of the collection led to a book published by Harry N. Abrams, Inc. of

New York, titled *American Realism: Twentieth-Century Drawings and Watercolors from the Glenn C. Janss Collection,* a significant hardbound book that included about 250 reproductions of paintings and drawings. It included famous works from history that illustrated the book's essay by noted historian Alvin Martin, who was an associate professor of art history at Southern Methodist University in Dallas. Martin's introduction was a historical review of realism that began with Paleolithic art. He titled his essay, "Facing Reality: Twentieth-Century American Realist and Realistic Drawings in Perspective." I welcomed this inclusive history of the many facets of realism that evolved over centuries into the modern era. Henry wrote the foreword. In the introduction, "A Collector's Perspective," I wrote:

> Collecting is an art. It requires the nurturing of many of the same creative talents that must be developed by the artist. The collector also confronts the "tabula rasa" of the artist . . . an untouched smooth tablet. The artist faces his prepared "tabula" with concern, uncomfortable with its emptiness and with what he alone is responsible for. Collectors face their empty walls with a similar concern . . . that what is to be placed there will be meaningful. The collector and the artist ask many of the same questions and seek the same answers. The artist must ultimately confront the tablet and make either intuitive or conscious choices. As he develops and matures, he will care less and less about what the world thinks of his art and will create for himself with confidence; so it is with the collector.

Henry organized the schedule for a traveling exhibition that ran for two years and included such well-known sites as the Akron Art Museum in Ohio and the Madison Art Center in Wisconsin. We also scheduled exhibitions at many smaller college and university museums for the benefit of their art departments' emerging artists. I scheduled two years of travel to coincide with as many of the venues as possible, giving talks to the public as I toured them through the collection.

An unanticipated consequence of my collection came during this period of my life in the form of an eye-opening visit to museums in Moscow, USSR, during the height of the Cold War. Because of the collection's depth and breadth, I was invited by Tom Armstrong, then director of the Whitney Museum of American Art in New York, to join the Drawing Council, a group of professionals who were responsible for deciding which works were selected for addition to the Whitney Museum's drawing collection. Tom became a close friend. He knew my Aunt Dougie, who still resided on Park Avenue in New York. Both had summer homes on Fishers Island, an exclusive retreat at the eastern end of Long Island. That was where Tom could be his creative self, within an expanse of private floral gardens populated with exquisite sculptures. When Bill and I visited Dougie, we also enjoyed these glorious gardens with Tom.

The Whitney Museum Drawing Council invited Bill and me to join them on a trip to the USSR, with Tom as our leader. The trip was planned around a viewing of the great works of art that had been sequestered there since World War ll. During the mid 1980s, Moscow was under the strict rule of communism. People wore drab, colorless attire, and we walked past many long lines of people waiting for access to groceries and everyday necessities. The city was depressing. Few people seemed to have the time or interest to visit museums, and we found them nearly empty.

Our hope was that we would feel uplifted in the presence of these great works of European art that had been brought to Moscow from the allied countries during the war, ostensibly for safekeeping. It was a shock to all of us to instead experience the terrible condition of the paintings and the museum. There was no lighting on the paintings, and they had not yet been cleaned or restored since the war. They were musty, bleak, and often unrecognizable. From behind the stanchions and rope barriers, it was impossible to know what was before us. We were disappointed and sad to see some of the most important masterpieces in the world in such poor condition. The French Impressionists, including several Monets, and the Renaissance portraits, including several Rembrandts, were difficult to appreciate in the dim light. This excursion served as a stark warning to me. This is what can befall a priceless collection of artworks when governments do not prioritize their value and work to maintain them for future generations.

The hotel where we stayed was equally bleak. We were all assigned to the same floor and the same restaurant on that floor for dining. Although there were other restaurants on other floors, we were not allowed to socialize outside of our group. We were all served the same dull meal and conjectured amongst ourselves what we might be eating, as it was similarly unrecognizable. When Bill and I checked into our room, we found it very dirty and at once tried to find the hidden Cold War surveillance cameras.

The elevator was from another era. If it came at all, it was already full of people from stopping at every floor below us. We were lucky if dinner was not cold upon arrival. Tom's unique sense of humor saved us. He had planned ahead to provide a final dinner that would be our crowning, positive memory of the Moscow trip. He had carted with him an assortment of wind-up mechanical toys, animals, trucks, cars, and robots. After dinner, we spread out on the floor with our toys and wound them up for races. We went to war as our toys wrestled and jostled with one another. The remaining dinner guests in the restaurant must have thought the Americans had gone mad, and they exited rapidly without laughter or interest, in obvious disdain for our childish behavior. Perhaps they hoped we would all go to jail for disturbing the peace.

We took a side trip to St. Petersburg, where restoration was under way on the famed palaces. The whitewashing and gilding there provided relief against the constant grays of Moscow. When we took off on our flight from Russia to Norway, I was shocked when all the passengers began to clap and cheer, but our group joined in the spontaneous expression of distaste for what we had all experienced and our joy at finally being on our way back to the freedom we cherished.

Our return to New York was a return to sparkling, amply lit galleries and smiling, welcoming gallery dealers. The galleries I frequented most at that time were those supporting the traditional and emerging realists: Fischbach, Allan Frumkin, Forum, Alexandre, Kennedy, Brooke Alexander, Marlborough, Schmidt-Bingham, Hirschl-Adler Gallery, and primary among them, the Nancy Hoffman Gallery. Nancy Hoffman was an enterprising gallerist ahead of her time. She was the first to make the novel and courageous move to the area of Soho in lower New York. Numerous galleries followed, and Soho soon became a prime location for contemporary galleries and a destination for tourists seeking the latest in apparel, crafts, artisan shops, and restaurants. Visitors came in droves to experience the wave of art galleries that had overtaken this area of lower Manhattan.

Bill and I had discovered the Nancy Hoffman Gallery while tracking the work of an artist named Joseph Raffael. We became so enamored with Raffael's painterly stylization of fish and landscape scenes that Bill bought one of his largest works to cover an entire wall in our living room. Titled *Waterfall*, it could have been mistaken for an abstract work because the cascade was painted as a mass of white bubbles against blue—a classic example of painterly realism.

After my American Realism collection's two years of traveling exhibitions, I decided to respond to an enticing proposal from Dennis O'Leary, then executive director of the Boise Art Gallery. He asked if I would display my collection for a term of ten years in order for the gallery to meet the "permanent collection" requirement to achieve national certification as an art museum. I agreed to this and also agreed to gift the gallery a specific number of artworks to meet another of the certification qualifications. I was elated with this agreement; it meant that I could again, and in a new way, provide art for a community. As a result, the Boise Art Gallery received certification from the American Alliance of Museums and became the Boise Art Museum, meeting or exceeding national standards of operation in all areas, including educational programs, a library, and a permanent exhibited collection. Henry Hopkins wrote of my collection in his forward to the catalog:

> The Glenn Janss collection of American Realist drawings and watercolors, now numbering more than three hundred works, is possibly the most comprehensive gathering of this material in private hands. Ranging from a turn-of-the-century Edward Hopper drawing to a recent Edward Ruscha, the collection presents a wide variety of subject matter, techniques, and philosophical attitudes. Although comprehensiveness is in itself a virtue, the primary virtue in this grouping is its particular complexity, which reflects the passionate and single-minded vision of its collector, who looked for the special and sometimes unique qualities of an individual drawing or watercolor within the accepted body of work by a given artist. The result is a rich crazy quilt of images, including portraits, landscapes, still lifes, and interiors of large and small scale. The works of the most renowned artists mix easily with works by artists of lesser reputation.

I was grateful for Henry's professional acknowledgment. Many of the artists included had not yet been recognized for their talent, courage, and innovation; and this added to the collection's diversity and complexity. It was an honor for me to celebrate all of these artists, the well-known and the unknown together, and to be able to gather in one place so many examples in the great tradition of American Realism.

I had started out collecting many of these artists when a piece of work could be acquired for only a few hundred dollars. The collection was now worth far more than the sum of its parts and had a permanent home for public viewing. This marked the culmination of interests and desires that I first formed during my studies in college. I could now see that it had all come together, from art history studies to leading the LACMA Docent Council and onward to the establishment of the Sun Valley Center for the Arts. This legacy became a reality as the result of patience and a commitment to the mission of bringing art to a new audience.

It is worth saying to anyone who wishes to purchase a piece of art that the artist has already confronted the canvas with a sense of trepidation. And so it is with a collector. But as she proceeds over the years, she will begin to trust her intuition and care less and less what the world might think.

CHAPTER THIRTY-SEVEN

Turning the Tide

While Bill faced ongoing financial challenges in Sun Valley, a rumor began circulating that the Walt Disney Company was interested in buying the resort. This rumor was not entirely unfounded as Disney had begun sending representatives to Idaho in 1973. They asked Bill many questions about the resort's operations, its staffing requirements, and business plans. They even asked about the resort's new wastewater facility. I was in the process of turning the old one into a glassblowing studio for the Sun Valley Center for the Arts.

Lilly and Walt Disney had been family friends for as long as I could remember. Lilly, always friendly and affectionate, was from a small town on an Indian reservation in Northern Idaho. Their daughter Diane attended the Marlborough School when I was there, although she was several years behind me in classes. My brother Peter was closer with Diane; they later attended Stanford together. By the mid 1970s, Diane Disney was married to Ron Miller, a Disney company executive who spent a fair amount of time in Sun Valley. I suspect that the Sun Valley Company board might have been interested in selling at that time if the price was right.

Wally Huffman recalled seeing Disney CEO Card Walker skiing down the Flying Squirrel run on Warm Springs on man-made snow during an especially bad snow year. Card fell, injured his knee, and spent much of the afternoon sitting in Warm Springs hut, fuming. Wally was convinced that this was the moment Disney lost interest in Sun Valley, but the actual situation was far more complex and had to do with a place called Mineral King, a subalpine glacial valley in the southern part of Sequoia National Park in California.

Skiers knew that this pristine area had the potential to become one of the greatest ski resorts in America. Several developers had been circling it for years, as environmentalists fought to protect it. The area had been the location of a mining boom town at one time but was now designated a Primitive Area and therefore under federal jurisdiction.

My old friend and architect Harry Gesner was part of one design team organized and funded by our mutual friend Bob Brandt to win the development bid. Harry was flown into the mountains in a helicopter and took sample runs down what could be potential ski slopes. His team presented plans to the US Department of Agriculture's office in San Francisco, vying with six other interests for the development rights at Mineral King.

Their plan would have placed the resort in the center of three twelve-thousand-foot peaks, with several alpine lakes and an entire river from which to draw enough hydroelectric power to run the resort. Harry's team had an ambitious plan that would prohibit automobiles and instead build an electric train to take people and supplies thirty miles into and out of the area. A fifty-six-foot trailer displaying the project's designs with drawings and presentations was towed to Mineral King Village and later sent to Washington, DC.

Interest in the area was high. Harry said that Bob Brandt got a call one day from a man in Washington, DC, who claimed to be the president. Bob thought it was his friend Gerry Cooper, joking around. "Come on, Cooper. Stop screwing with me. I am a busy man," Brandt responded.

"No, this really is the president," said John Kennedy. "What can you tell me about Mineral King?"

In 1965, Walt Disney Company had presented plans for Disney's Mineral King Ski Resort and won the bid over the other developers. The US Forest Service awarded a preliminary permit, giving the company three years to complete a satisfactory plan, the next step being a permanent thirty-year permit. Disney's plan was for a $35 million year-round resort that would have an estimated 2.5 million visitors annually—800,000 of them from out of state—with the first full year of operation in 1976. A controversial access road to the ski village became a major sticking point. After Walt Disney died in 1966, the Sierra Club announced its opposition to the project and began a widespread national campaign to fight the resort with a coalition of preservationists.

The bad press came at a time when Walt's brother Roy was planning and building an enormous entertainment complex in Orlando that would become Walt Disney World. By 1973, the Disney Company appeared to be losing interest in the Mineral King project, especially after an environmental impact assessment was ordered, yet Disney representatives continued to fly into Sun Valley, which led many of us to think that Disney might step up with an offer to purchase it instead. After Bill had spent so much time working with them on the details of the resort's operations, our hopes were up.

By then, Bill and I had plans to sell our home and build a new one together on Back Pay Way, one we would feel we had created jointly and which would establish a new beginning for us. Just before we placed the property on the real estate market, we hosted one last elegant multicourse catered dinner in our dining room. It was planned for the esteemed group from the Disney Company, including Card Walker and Ron Miller. Everyone was talkative. There appeared to be a joining of minds, with toasts of gratitude to Bill and Sun Valley for their welcoming openness to valuable information about the resort over a number of years.

I sat next to Ron Miller, and we talked at length about the Sun

Valley Center for the Arts. He convinced me that it could be generously funded as a summer campus through the California Institute of the Arts, of which Disney was a major supporter, and seemed excited to support the center with Disney funding. I was ecstatic to think of the increased notoriety and donor support that would bring us, virtually guaranteeing the center's future. I would no longer need to be the major funding solicitor and guarantor of the center's stability.

The next morning, Bill received the definitive call from Card Walker onboard the Disney plane, just before it took off for LA. Card stated simply, as if reading from a prepared statement, "Walt always started every enterprise from scratch, from the ground up, so Sun Valley could never be an option for Disney Company as this would not be true to his legacy."

Bill and I were devastated. All of his efforts over the last few years had brought him nothing but despair. We realized at once that they had only been investigating us as a model of a renowned ski resort under single-family ownership. Walt Disney was once quoted as saying: "When I first saw Mineral King five years ago, I thought it was one of the most beautiful spots I had ever seen, and we want to keep it that way." To Walt, this meant creating a self-contained alpine village designed to preserve the natural beauty of the Mineral King Valley, similar to what had taken place in Sun Valley. The Disney Company had been gathering information to further support their development planning and hoped-for development rights at Mineral King. In the end, the environmentalists who treasured the area won out. All development plans were abandoned, and Mineral King was preserved forever in 1978 as part of Sequoia National Park.

• • •

Our house sold readily to casino tycoon Bill Harrah and his wife Verna. There was only one drawback. They wanted occupancy within a month. This deadline brought sleepless nights for us and the exhausting chore of packing up what were for me strange belongings from Bill's earlier marriage that included precious china, glassware, entertainment place settings and serving dishes. Bill needed to decide which of his children would receive each item, and what would be given away or sold. In those days, such things would have been given as lavish wedding gifts and only used if a household kitchen and pantry had servants. We had no need for them.

After Bill's house sold and while we were waiting for our new house at Back Pay Way to be built, we moved into one of Bill Hewlett's Lodge apartments. Bill left the apartment on a warm spring day in 1978 to cross country ski the nearby golf course track, unaware that our lives were about to change forever. I recall that he had the wrong wax and the trail was sloppy with heavy, mushy snow. He struggled through it and then returned to take a hot shower, eat, and nap on the couch—all no-no's after intense exercise. He yelled to me to come help him up, to free him from the "elephants on his chest"; then he got up briefly and fell over, unconscious. This had every appearance of a heart attack, and I ran to call the hospital.

The ambulance was there within minutes. After he recovered, we went to Santa Monica for him to check in with his heart doctor at St. John's Hospital and undergo some tests. Bill was told that he now had a serious heart condition and must be more cautious and aware of his cardiovascular health. Thus began a period of years during which Bill faced increasing health challenges; he and I could no longer take for granted our time together. I have no doubt that the stresses and disappointments of the previous years contributed to his condition.

While we continued working on the architectural plans for our new house, we moved into one of Bill Hewlett's Sun Valley Lodge I condos for two interim years. Not long after the Harrahs bought our home, Bill Harrah went to the Mayo Clinic to have surgery for an aortal aneurysm and died two days later. Following her husband's death, Verna became a friend and confidante of ours, and she relied on us for counsel and advice. She didn't know anyone else in Sun Valley at the time, so we tried to make her feel comfortable in the community.

Bill Harrah opened his first bingo operation in Reno in 1937. By the time of his death in 1978 at age sixty-six, he had created perhaps the biggest star-studded gaming enterprise in the world, as well as other companies that continued to grow in profitability well after his death. Nevertheless, I could not help feeling sympathy for Verna. She had worked in a casino as a waitress before marrying its wealthy owner and then inherited a fortune beyond her wildest dreams. When her husband died, she naturally felt that others were more interested in her money than her friendship.

Verna was shy, naïve, and deeply compassionate. During her years in Sun Valley, she became a beloved companion to many local residents and was known for her willingness to help those in need. As she gained confidence, Verna set up foundations for rape victims, funded medical research, and even worked to bring peace between the United States and Russia. But when we first knew Verna, Bill and I took her on trips with us and were amused by her naivete. In San Francisco, she wanted to spend all of her time shopping for clothes. I would leave her surrounded by a host of saleswomen fawning over her in a dressing room filled with fancy evening clothes. Verna could never make up her mind. When I returned to say it was time to move on, she would insist that I choose for her or she would just buy everything on display. The flight home would be filled to the brim with boxes.

At least this was safer and lighter cargo than the cases of wine transported in those days from the Chappellets' vineyard. The Chappellet and Cooper families had become such close friends in the 1960s in Malibu that I wanted the same close relationships to continue after our move to Sun Valley and my marriage to Bill. Donn Chappellet and Bill hit it off right away because of their mutual respect for each other's business successes. We frequently flew in Bill's plane to enjoy a weekend at the vineyard with the Chappellets and then returned to Sun Valley with choice wines. On one of these visits, Donn proposed that Bill purchase a piece of a property in the midst of their acreage that was coming up for sale. Donn was eager to continue harvesting grapes on that property, which he hoped would be permitted by a willing owner such as Bill.

Both Donn and Bill were visionaries, and Bill appreciated Donn's long-range vision for his vineyard—producing the best wines in the Napa Valley. Bill bought the property, and for a number of years we enjoyed the visits there even more as we toured the vineyard and were educated about the wine-making process. The Chappellet Winery was designed by prominent Los Angeles artist Ed Moses together with Molly Chappellet. Along with a structural engineer, they created a triangular, high-roofed building that dominates the vineyard like a fortress. Donn built a wine cellar that was nestled deep into the hillside near their house. Since he now wanted to serve only Chappellet wines, he offered us, at a bargain price, the other exceptional wines in his cellar that he had collected over the years to develop his palate and knowledge, including classic French Bordeaux and Burgundies from all the best years.

Back in Sun Valley, we planned a deep wine cellar of our own under our new house on Back Pay Way. Bill and Donn would drive to the Napa Airport with their cars full of cases of valuable wines and load the airplane to its brim. I was not yet a seasoned passenger who was comfortable flying in a small private plane. As we crossed over the mountains and desert on our way back into Idaho, I worried that the plane might crash and I would be found in the desert surrounded by broken wine bottles as a final legacy for my children to ponder.

Verna eventually connected to a lifestyle of fame and fortune and grew more comfortable in the freedom of her new circumstances. She bought an enormous and expensive home in a celebrity-filled area of Beverly Hills and became a film producer. We learned that she had partnered with music producer Quincy Jones, but Bill and I eventually lost track of her. Our old Sun Valley house sold yet again, this time to

Keith and Mary Kay McCaw.

During this period of upheaval, I was proud to be included by Bill at Sun Valley Company Board of Directors meetings. We met around a long table in the Sunroom at Sun Valley Lodge. The meetings were fun, not like other board meetings I had attended. Ideas were free flowing, debated, and either referred to future agendas for further research or discarded as unpromising. The meetings were never boring because they did not include a lot of budget reporting. In hindsight, perhaps someone should have paid closer attention to the spending of capital. But at that time, all thoughts were positive and visionary.

The board focused on testing ideas and envisioning big plans for the resort; conversations ensued about which new lifts would be purchased first, what new runs in the Warm Springs area should be cleared, how many new tennis courts were to be built, what new restaurants or shops were needed, and what condominium complexes needed approval next for design and construction. Many of these developments were considered necessary to make Sun Valley a summer resort. The Sun Valley Company's board consisted of an impressive group of individuals: Joe Leggett, Billy Janss Jr., Carl Burke, Spencer Eccles, Ralph Davidson, and Donald Bren.

Joe Leggett was the first manager of Sun Valley after the Janss Investment Company purchased it in 1964. He was at that time vice president of the Janss Company, which was based in Thousand Oaks, California. The Leggett family moved to Sun Valley in 1964 and resided there for one year following purchase of the resort from Union Pacific. Joe had never been on a pair of skis but was skilled in finance. He also had a wonderful sense of humor. Actor Bob Newhart once said of him: "Mr. Leggett is the funniest comedian who ever became a certified public accountant."

Leggett's was temporary until Harry Holmes filled the post in 1965, but Joe remained a respected and essential member of the Sun Valley board as the representative of the Janss family's investments.

In 1967, Bill and his brother Ed split the Janss Investment Company between them, and Bill subsequently bought Sun Valley in 1968 from the family corporation.

Board member Carl Burke was with the Boise legal firm of Elam & Burke. Billy Janss Jr. was attending medical school at UCLA. Spencer Eccles, whom everyone called Spence, was from a legendary banking family. He is the grandson of David Eccles, the well-known Utah financier, banker, and industrialist. Spence was working at the time for his uncle, George Eccles, president of First Security Bank. Spence would carry on the legacy of his banking family with great success. He was also a ski racer, like Bill, and as friends they held a shared a vision for Sun Valley Resort.

I personally recommended to Bill the other two members of the board, Ralph Davidson and Don Bren. They were old friends of mine. Ralph had been a childhood partner in doubles volleyball at the Santa Monica Beach Club. Don was a close childhood friend. Our friendships had been renewed through Janet Leigh and Bob Brandt when they all became frequent visitors to the Wave House in Malibu.

Although I knew Ralph and Don socially rather than through business connections, I was familiar with their successful careers. Ralph was in the midst of a thirty-three-year career with Time, Inc. having started there in 1954 as an advertising salesman for *Life* magazine. He was publisher of *Time Magazine* in the 1970s, when he served on Bill's Sun Valley board, and was later appointed chairman of the John F. Kennedy Center for the Performing Arts. On trips to Washington, DC, Bill and I stayed with Ralph and his wife, or with US Supreme Court Justice Byron White, whom Bill met when he came to the rescue of a man who had fallen on a run at Snowmass, the Colorado ski resort founded by the Janss Investment Company.

One day while skiing, Bill came upon a man lying crumpled on the ground, skied over to him, and found he had a dislocated shoulder. Bill helped him down off the mountain to first aid. The man looked at Bill and said, "You just saved me. Thank you. My name is Byron White." Afterward, they became close friends. When Bill and I visited Byron and his wife in Washington, DC, we enjoyed quiet dinners with these fine people. In those days, they didn't have security, and he would have been hounded by the public if we dined out.

Don Bren had been a constant in my life for many years. His parents and mine were friends, and I reunited with his mother again during my Sun Valley years. She was a part of the celebrity world inherited from Union Pacific in the first years of Janss's corporate ownership. Don's father, Milton Bren, was a successful movie producer. His mother Marion was a prominent civic leader in Los Angeles. They divorced in 1948, and Milton married actress Claire Trevor. Marion married steel magnate Earle Jorgensen. Bill and I saw them socially for many years.

Don Bren was such a dedicated skier that he tried out for the 1956 Olympic Team but did not make it because of an injury. After serving in the Marine Corps, he began his business career at age twenty-five, building homes in Orange County, California. In 1963, he and his partners purchased eleven thousand acres that were developed into Mission Viejo. International Paper bought Bren Company in 1970 for $34 million, selling it back to Don two years later, following the recession, for $22 million. With the proceeds, he and a group of investors purchased the 146-year-old Irvine Company in 1977. By 1983, he was the majority owner of the firm and chairman of the board. The Irvine Company now owns more than 115 million square feet of real estate, encompassing hotels, marinas, golf courses, sixty thousand apartments, over forty shopping centers, and five hundred office buildings in its property portfolio; and it continues to grow.

"Bren wields more power than Howard Hughes ever did, probably as much as any man in America over a concentrated region," reported the Orange County Weekly in 2005. In 2008, Business Week named him one of the top ten philanthropists in the nation, with more than $1 billion in donations to causes in education, conservation, and research.

Don was listed by Forbes as the wealthiest real estate developer in the United States and the thirtieth richest American in 2015.

I cannot help but muse that if Sun Valley had become an option for purchase only a few years later, Bren Company would have been well enough established for Don to have followed his love of skiing into the development of a major resort for the nation. However, I recall a conversation Don and I once had in Sun Valley about this possibility, and he commented, "I would never again be able to enjoy skiing here."

It is true that most of the leaders of industry that come to Sun Valley do so to escape business rather than do business. Don continued to enjoy skiing in Sun Valley, eventually buying a large ranch near Hailey up Deer Creek Canyon, which has been preserved against development through conservation easements.

During the early 1970s, Sun Valley Resort department heads served as vice presidents of the company and were also included at the board meetings to present their reports. At the time, they included Executive Vice President Rene Meyer as director of administration and accounting, Wally Huffman as director of recreation, Phil Conger as director of real estate, and Keith Whitfield as director of hotels. With such a talented bunch, it seemed that Sun Valley's future was bright indeed. And with all of the funds that had been invested in Sun Valley, it was no wonder that the resort was becoming more well-known, real estate was selling, and skiers were showing up in greater numbers.

A significant investment had been made over the years to turn Sun Valley into a year-round resort. In addition to millions of dollars spent on the Bald Mountain ski area, there were new tennis courts, a golf course, restaurants, and a shopping mall between the lodge and the opera house. Without the expensive new snowmaking system, the resort would not have been able to open reliably on Thanksgiving Day. And yet, as owner, Bill still got a lot of flak from some of the locals. Ketchum was a small town that didn't want to see change. Perhaps the local *Idaho Mountain Express* would have been critical of anyone running Sun Valley, and they were certainly critical of Bill. Perhaps that just came with the territory. I told Bill he should simply not read the *Mountain Express*. Sureley the locals would have objected also if Disney had purchased the resort, expecting to see Mickey Mouse and Donald Duck walking around the lodge.

Bill faced numerous challenges during this period. There were two airline strikes that slowed commercial air traffic into the valley. Union strikes by a mechanical workers union and a bus drivers' union hobbled operation of the resort for one winter season. Bill had to find construction workers, or anyone else, to operate the ski lifts. Two fires in Sun Valley Lodge posed further setbacks. Bill couldn't understand why everything was going against him.

In addition, a recession hit in 1974 that was exacerbated by the OPEC oil crisis, which sent the price of gasoline higher than anyone had ever imagined it would go. There were also a number of very bad snow years. The economic stagnation that hit the country and other parts of the world economy lasted until the 1980s. With our deep love for one another, Bill and I remained confident and courageous together through those challenging years. Sadly, it was only a matter of time before Bill and the board realized there was no other option than to continue looking for buyers. Few people knew just how precarious the situation was. Some remained loyal and willing to come to our aid, while others sought to take advantage of the situation.

One of the housing projects presented for approval at the time was Wildflower Condominiums. The individuals proposing the project were developer Chuck Dwight and realtor Dick Fenton. They planned to build the most luxurious Sun Valley condominiums to date. Bill's earliest condominiums in Sun Valley were simple Boise Cascade prefab drop-in-the-spot models. Bill was delighted to have someone else offer to finance condominium construction. Although eager for more housing in the area, he preferred to spend the company's limited capital on his long-range vision for the ski mountain.

Chuck Dwight and his wife Sherri worked their ways into our lives, becoming close friends. They were fun, and they introduced us to their friends, including singer and film star Paul Anka and his wife Ann. Paul proposed to Bill that he open a restaurant in Sun Valley and assured him that he would be there to sing on weekends. Chez Paul, as it was known, was on the lower story of the dormitory building for ski instructors, just off of the mall and across from Elkhorn Gallery. It was wildly successful and booked weeks ahead. A French chef prepared innovative cuisine that was a novel departure from Sun Valley's typical Austrian-oriented fare.

Paul and Ann owned a condominium in San Francisco that they offered for our use at any time, so we traveled there frequently with the Dwights in Bill's plane. Life could not have been any more fun or happy for us at the time. Paul even invited us to one of his concerts in New York City, providing us with hotel accommodations and a limo to the concert, welcoming us backstage to socialize with the inner entertainment circle. In the spring of 1975, we planned a ski trip to French resorts with the Dwights, followed by a few days in Paris. Our stay was cut short when I was called home to California by my brother Peter because of my mother's impending death from esophageal cancer. This was a tragic turn of events for her, after eight years of sobriety.

We flew on the supersonic Concorde jet to get back quickly. Despite the tragic purpose of our four-hour flight, or perhaps because of it, we consumed free champagne and gourmet food continuously during our trip to Los Angeles. I spent a day with my mother when I returned. She was unable to speak because of the cancer in her throat and the equipment used to keep her alive.

As we flew back from Paris, I recalled the time many years earlier when my father had asked me to travel to Paris with my mother so that he would not feel guilty leaving her home while he went duck hunting. My mother wanted to remember spending time in France when she was much younger and free. I was afraid to join her because of all the miseries I had been through with her in my youth when she was still drinking. But I acquiesced. We went to Notre Dame Cathedral and to the museums, but I was a nervous wreck the entire time. I did take pleasure in showing her many of the earliest Christian churches in small towns outside of Paris.

My mother and I had grown closer after she found sobriety. She came to Sun Valley after I first moved there. It was a novel and rustic experience for her and the first time in her life she had worn pants. Back in Los Angeles, we had continued to shop together from time to time at Bullocks Wilshire. I often took my children and some of the grandchildren to visit at my mother's small Trancas beach house in Malibu. I had to explain to them that she wasn't exactly used to dealing with small children and they should not run around and scream or yell as they usually did.

By the time my mother was struggling through her last days, we had put all of our hardships behind us, much of which she surely no longer recalled. Within two weeks, my mother died. Peter organized a ceremony for her at Forest Lawn Cemetery. A few weeks later, I visited my father and found him totally devastated, at a loss after my mother's death. The two of them had finally found each other again after so many difficult years, during which he had suffered through her alcoholism while working hard to prove himself in the Bullock's hierarchy, only to lose so much during the proxy fight. My father was bereft without his wife, and within two years he also died, perhaps from loneliness.

I cleared out my mother's possessions but found very little left of her prized jewelry collection, which I had become familiar with over the years. No doubt, much of it had been purloined by her servant. I went to her storage facility to collect her furs, but no one in Sun Valley was wearing furs anymore, and I had no idea what to do with them. My mother was gone, and the world had moved on. I was entering a new era of possibility through the experience of spirituality.

When I returned to Sun Valley, Bill and I continued to hope for a good turn of fortune regarding finances for the resort. The Janss Investment Company, whose main business was to finance new commercial real estate developments, had been putting money into the resort for years. But now the Janss Company was no longer certain that Sun Valley was a winning proposition. Also, First Security Bank was beginning to doubt whether the resort was a good investment that would be able to pay back its increasing loan debt.

Wally recalls that Bill had for years been taking half-million-dollar losses in Sun Valley, then taking short-term loans to pay back the debt. Over the years, it had all built up, and there was concern as to whether the debt of $6 million to First Security Bank could be paid off. Company managers were wondering whether a bankruptcy was imminent and they would lose their jobs.

Housing development still held the prospect of improving the resort's fortunes. The proposed luxury Wildflower Condominiums might serve to draw high-end clientele. But it soon became apparent that despite all their promises, Chuck Dwight and Dick Fenton had no collateral. There was no funding at all behind their proposed development, no investors, and no loan financing for the condominiums or their overall Sun Valley development plan. They were forced to turn to Bill for start-up costs.

Bill was advised by his accountants and lawyers and the Janss Investment Company to cancel the contract and no longer pursue their development plan for the commercial area of Sun Valley. Dwight and Fenton apparently expected this. They were prepared and had figured this into their scheme, keeping complete records of all conversations. Knowing that Bill served on the board of First Security Bank, they applied for a loan from that bank and, when they were turned down, blamed the situation on a conflict of interest on Bill's part and sued him. It was then that I learned the term "lis pendens," which means "suit pending," a situation that resulted in an encumbrance on the property that would forestall the sale of the resort until the lawsuit was settled. All recorded conversations of Bill and his legal team with Dwight and Fenton over their contracts became part of the ongoing lawsuit.

Bill could see that the legal conflict plus the increasing debt ratio for Sun Valley Company were likely going to prevent him from realizing his dream for the resort. He had been heartbroken years before when his older brother Ed had sold the skiing rights to Aspen while developing Snowmass. He wanted to make up for this loss in Sun Valley. He wanted to turn things around and make Sun Valley a great success. But the greatness that he began implementing for Sun Valley would not be completed during his tenure as owner.

Bill received a final edict from Joe Leggett during the summer of 1977. As president of the Janss Corporation, Joe advised Bill that he should not invest any more of the company's funds in the resort; Bill would have to rely solely on continued loans from First Security Bank. Then, bank president George Eccles issued the same message that additional funding would not be forthcoming. Spence Eccles and Don Bren were so distressed—their hearts were in this resort—that they agreed to be partners in a purchase of the company. But Spence's father, Spencer S. Eccles, would not support investment in a ski resort that he considered a losing enterprise requiring untold amounts of capital improvements before ever becoming viable.

At the next Sun Valley Company board meeting, Joe Leggett stood up and said, "I have something to say." With that, he began taking off his suit jacket and slowly placed it on the back of his chair. He then removed his tie and placed it on top of the jacket, all very slowly and purposefully. When he had everyone's attention, he began to unbutton his shirt. He then drew aside the shirt to reveal a t-shirt with Bill's picture on it and underneath it the words: "Would you buy a used resort from this man?" We all laughed and were thankful for Joe's wry sense of humor.

Bill still had to deal with Dwight and Fenton. He relied on O'Melveny & Myers, a prestigious Los Angeles-based legal firm that had served the Janss Corporation for many years. Dwight and Fenton sought $200,000 as payment to settle the lawsuit. Bill refused to pay it. The lawsuit went to court in Boise, and the judgment ruled in Bill's favor.

Prior to the final verdict, a notice that Sun Valley Resort was for sale appeared in the newspapers, including the *Wall Street Journal* and the *Salt Lake Tribune*. The rest is history. Sun Valley Resort sold to Sinclair Oil and the Holding family in July 1977 once the lawsuit was over. The Holdings had been the sole prospective buyers. Chuck Dwight and the Ankas left the area.

John Truyens, about whom my parents so enjoyed teasing me when I was a girl, went on to marry Lilly Disney. Lilly bought a Lodge Condominium in Sun Valley and came for many years to visit, so I saw them both frequently. Lilly eventually bought a winery in Napa Valley called Silverado Vineyards, which produced very excellent wines. It happened to be across the Silverado Trail from my brother Peter's property. It's such a small world.

Following the sale of the resort, our lives began to change in ways I could not then imagine. The stress of those years had taken their toll on Bill, but we were not going to let this limit our joy of exploration and adventure. A new path emerged—one we would walk in a quieter way. We entered a tunnel, slow dancing and hanging on tight, not knowing what would be at the other end.

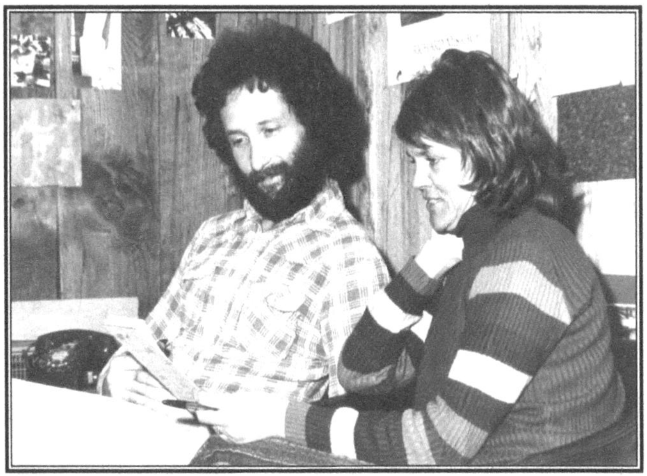

Jim Belson and I meeting in 1973 to discuss classes and the artists who would be invited to that summer's Sun Valley Creative Art Workshops, which would soon be renamed the Sun Valley Center for the Arts and Humanities.

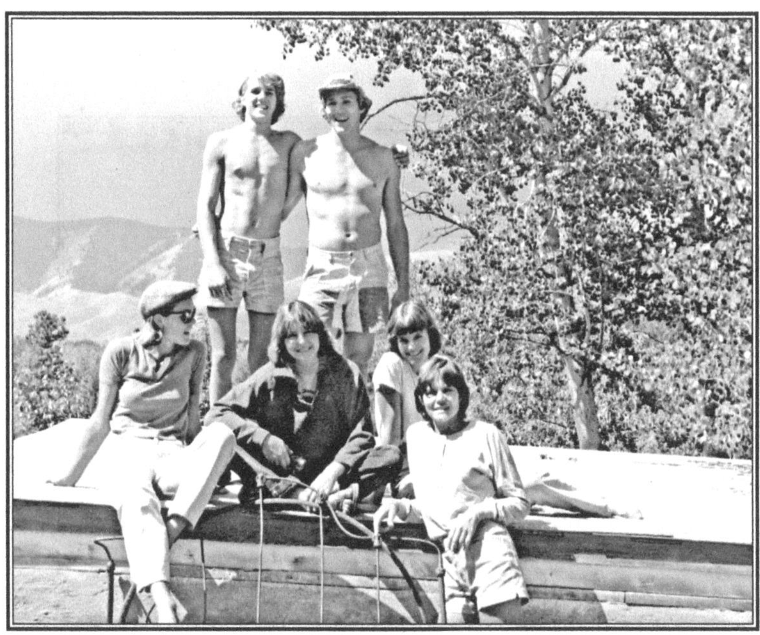

My family in 1970 at our Last Resort farm: Brant, Cameron, Kelley, Christin and Candy. I'm on the right. This was a time of retreat for us so there were no radios, telephones or TV's at this 20-acre working farm near Salmon, Idaho.

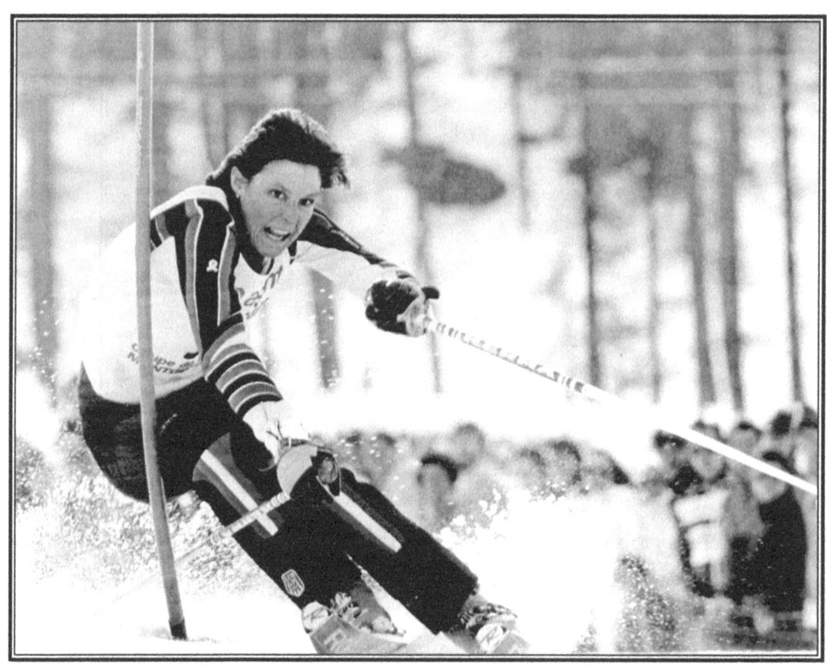

My daughter, Christin, skiing at Montgenevre, France,for a first place slalom at the World Cup finals in 1982.

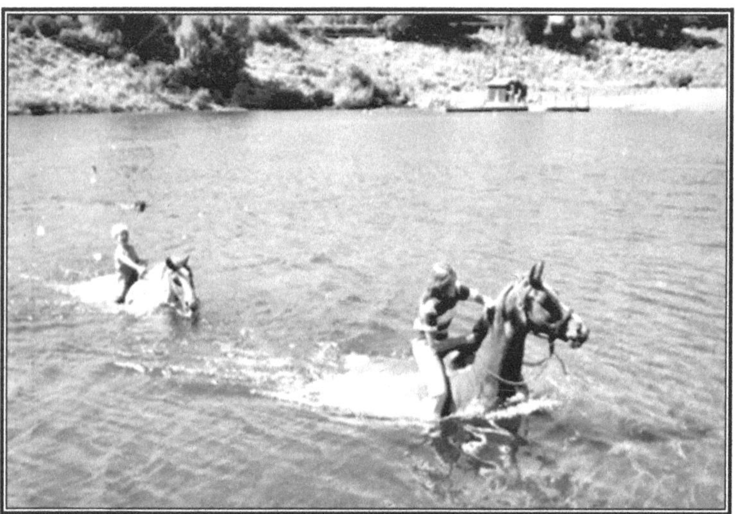

After moving to Sun Valley in 1969, my children Candy and Brant, the oldest and youngest, swam their horses in Sun Valley Lake. Police Chief Guy Coles drove by, shook his head, and just drove away. There were no regulations against such things in those days.

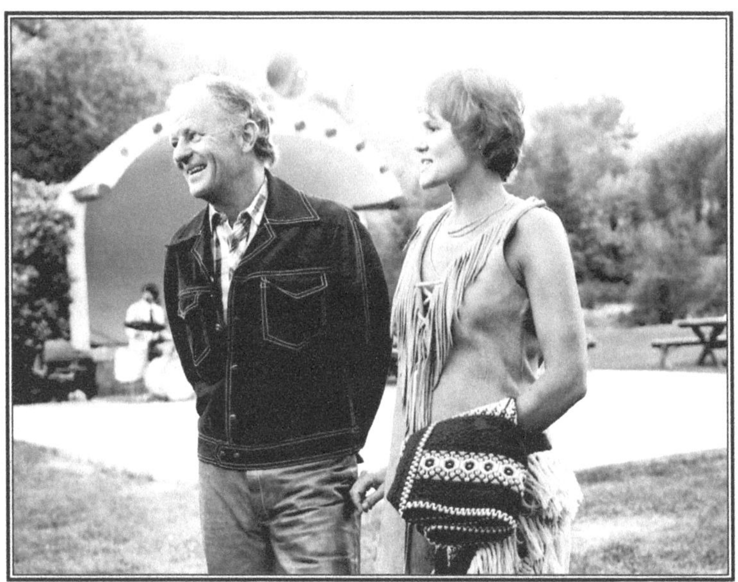

Bill and I spent time at an evening barbeque at Trail Creek in the mid-1970s.

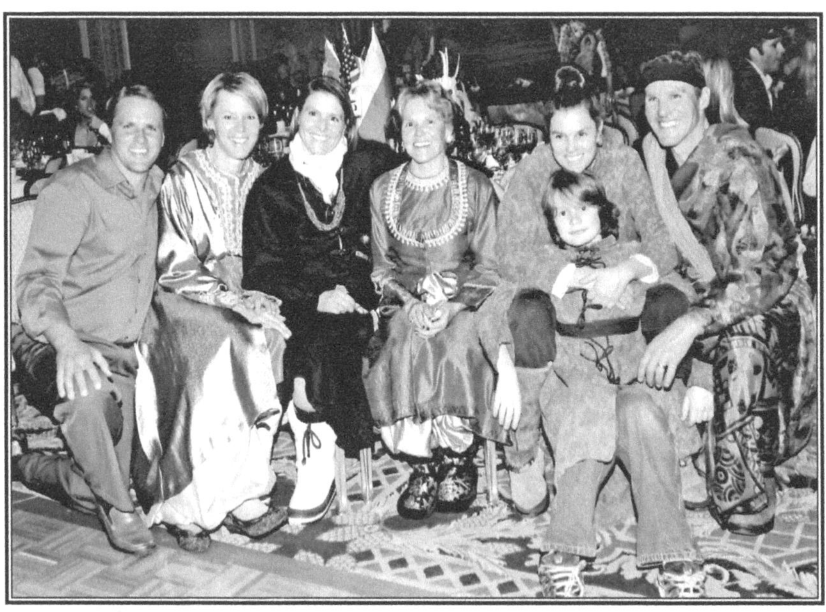

All my children gathered for a Sun Valley Ski Education Foundation fundraiser in 2004. The youngest is my grandson, Nicholas Popkey.

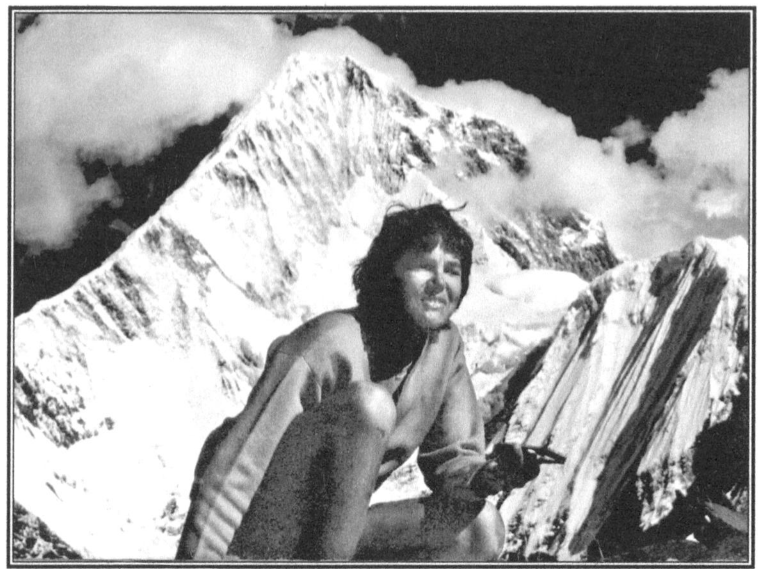

This picture of me was taken at nearly 20,000 feet of elevation in the Himalayas near Mount Everest in 1974. I was so grateful to have been able to climb that high.

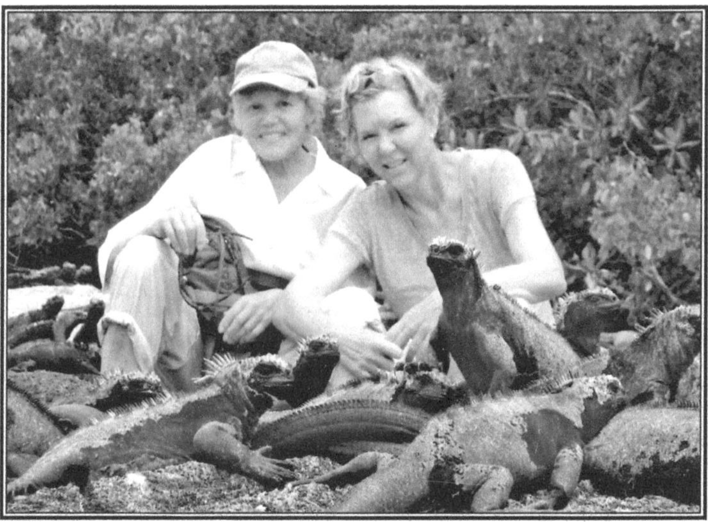

My daughter Kelley and I visited the Galapagos Islands in 2012, finding ourselves at one time in the midst of iguanas. The trip was a lesson in conservation due to the strict limitation of tourists at any one time.

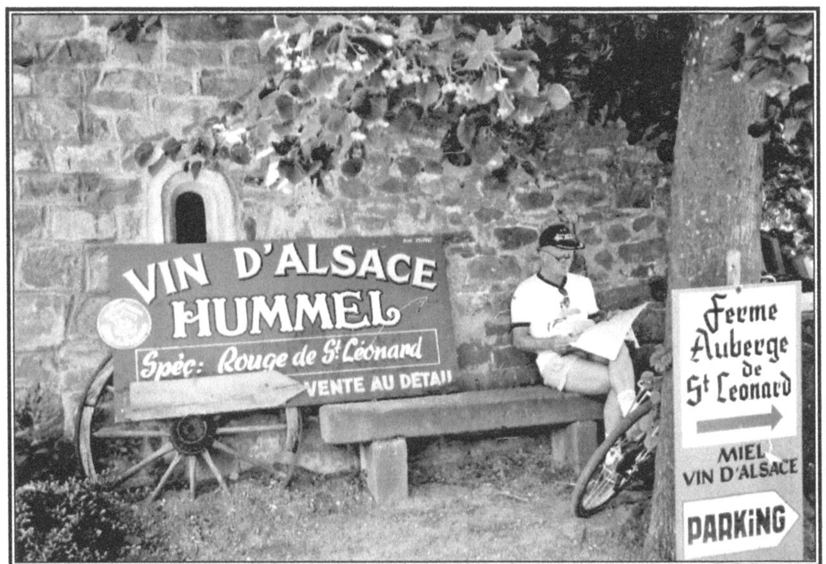

Bill always began his morning bike ride in France with a reading of the International Herald Tribune at the nearest coffee shop.

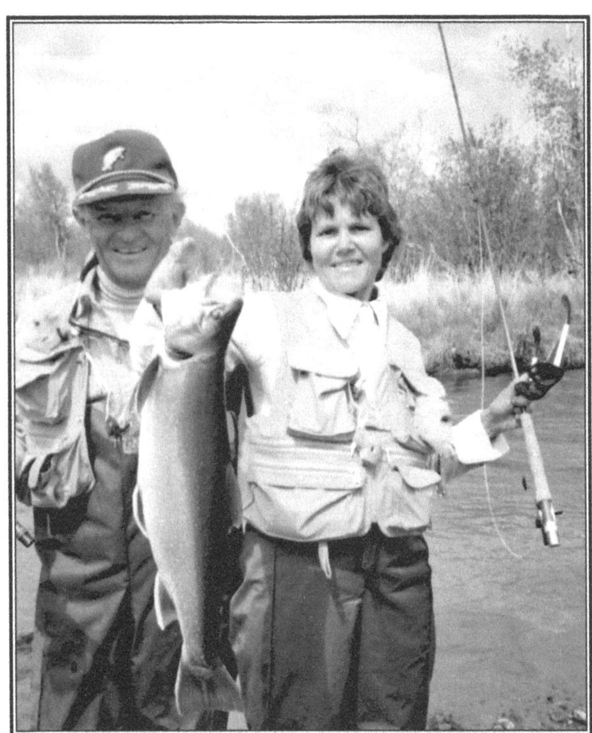

Bill and I fished in Alaska during the 1970s. It wasn't my favorite thing to do, so I would most often be happy to watch quietly from the shore.

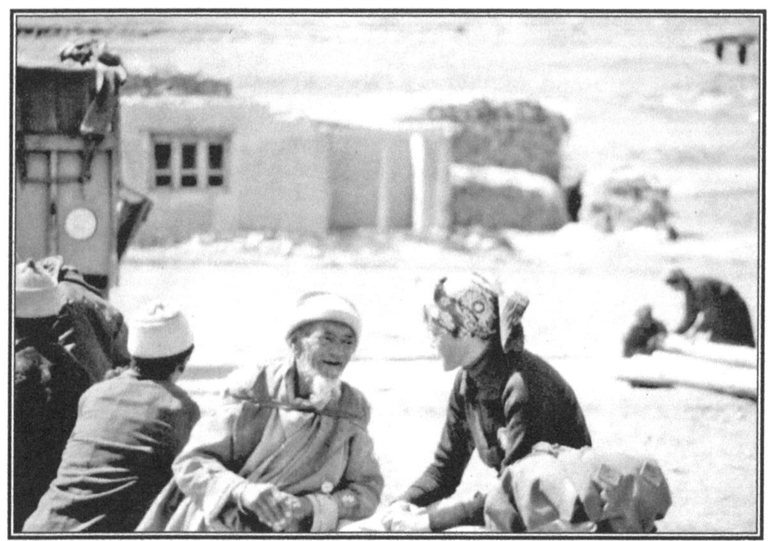

I chatted with the chieftain of a village in Southeast China near the Tibetan border during a trekking journey in 1975.

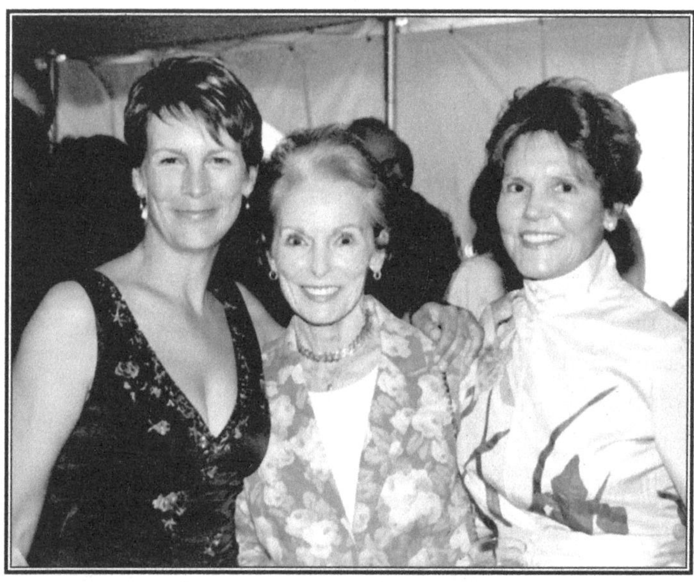

I celebrated with my friend Janet Leigh Brant and her daughter Jamie Lee Curtis, left, at a Sun Valley Center Wine Auction in the 1980s.

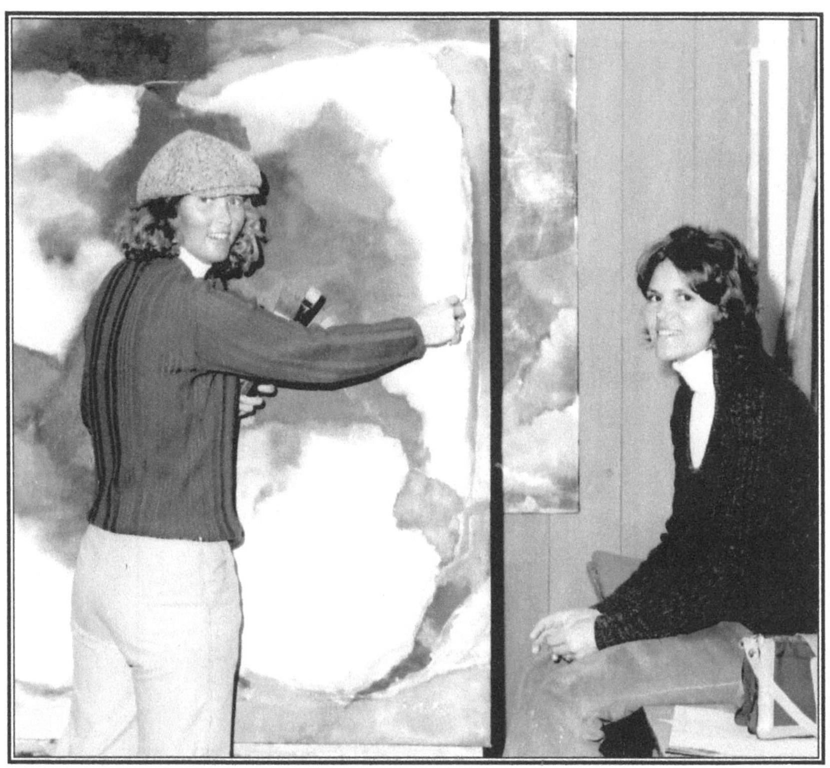

I watched as Mary Rolland demonstrated her painting talents during the early years of the Sun Valley Center for the Arts and Humanities.

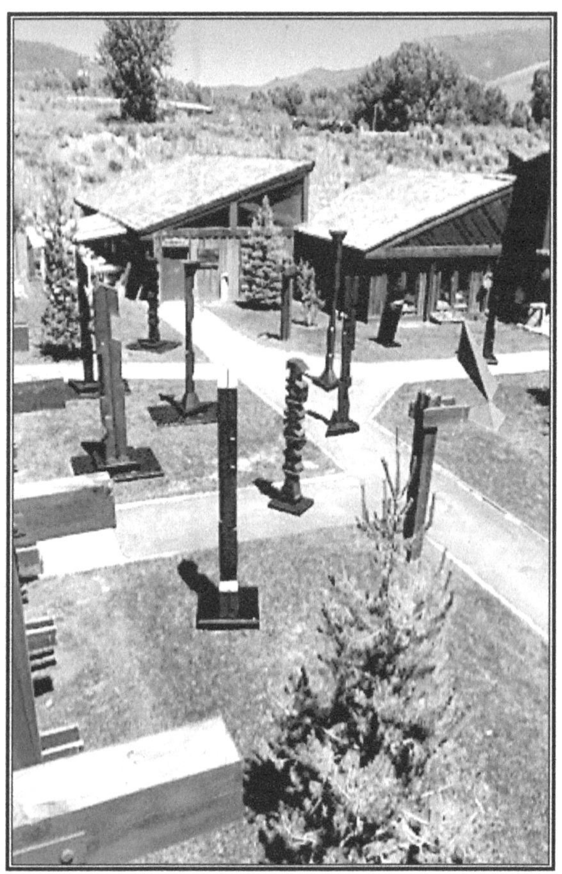

The Sun Valley Center campus in the 1970s was the perfect showplace for Rod Kagan's sculptures.

PART VI

Interim Paradise

CHAPTER THIRTY-EIGHT

Back Pay Way

The home where Bill and I lived together for twenty-three years was up the road he built into Back Pay Canyon above Fairway Road in Sun Valley. Bill could have chosen any available lot in Sun Valley at a time when he owned it all. This was his choice spot, high on the slope of a hill with a commanding view of Bald Mountain. The Sun Valley City Council had no real concern at the time for development planning, so it was left to Sun Valley Company. During a walk together on Fairway Drive, Bill once gestured toward the house of our old friends, the Zanucks, saying they had built just a little too far up the steep slope than was allowed by "company regulations."

At first, we didn't know how large a home we needed because several of the children were still young enough to live with us yet also old enough to want to be on their own. We could build one giant house with a separate entrance for the children and another full story, or a one-bedroom house just for us. As we deliberated, a fortuitous option presented itself. An older woman in Ketchum came forward with seven acres of vacant property to sell along the Big Wood River in town. It was an ideal location that we knew would provide a good investment for the children. The acreage, which became known as the Cooperville Subdivision, is still on the city plats under that name. There was ample room in Cooperville to build three cabins and still have another three lots with co-ownership split across the acreage. Bill purchased the acreage, and I financed and built three homes, one for Cameron, one for Brant, and one for the three girls together.

The Back Pay Way house was originally designed for the two of us but contained ample room for entertaining. The top of our road opened to one of Sun Valley's most popular hiking trails, which climbed gently up the canyon and across the hilltops to descend into the Trail Creek Cabin area. We were required to give access to hikers and bikers, but that was never an issue for us. We welcomed people onto our property; it was not considered trespassing in those days, just a good neighbor policy of giving access to a popular trail.

Our location was also popular with grazing sheep. Our good friend Senator John Peavey, now long married to Diane Josephy Peavey, was often missing a sheep that had strayed from his flock. One afternoon, my granddaughter Glenn, Kelley's daughter, found a sheep wandering around the Sagebrush Arena, where she trained with her horse in Hailey. She was so excited that she led it home and promised she would teach it to jump like a horse. This plan was foiled when John called to say he had lost one of his sheep and came the next day to pick it up.

Our friends often wanted to come to Sun Valley and stay with us; after a few years, Bill and I decided to build a guesthouse on the road below us. It had its own view of the valley and the pond below, which was fed by a stream that ran beside the new house using water that was recycled up from the pond. The guesthouse was its own private retreat.

Bill filled the pond with trout and took pride in these thriving schools of fish. Each week, he brought leftover bread loaves from the lodge, and everyone enjoyed the feverish feeding display after small pieces were thrown into the pond. Some of the workmen asked to fish the pond and caught a number of them, but they later said they would never return because our fish tasted like bread. We decided to feed them commercial fish pellets, which we stored in our garage until one night two striped raccoons entered through the doggie door and overturned the entire stash of fish food onto the floor. They only ate a few morsels. For them, it was all about finding something and making a mess of it. After the racoon incident, the fish soon went back on Sun Valley Resort bread rations.

One fall day I found a ewe that had apparently gotten lost while grazing by our guesthouse. I thought I had better close it in the garage for the night and called John Peavy, who said he would come in the morning. I found some leftover hay from a duck float we had made for the pond and left it with the ewe for the night. To my shock and dismay, when I entered the garage the next morning, there was blood everywhere. The hay had been used as a birthing bed. A tiny lamb had been born during the night, and both ewe and lamb were now dashing all over the garage.

When John arrived, he entered by the side door just as both animals bolted outside. They scooted under the back deck, where they felt safe, so John had to crawl through a narrow opening to pull out one after the other. He emerged covered in blood and carried the two scruffy animals to his truck. I considered it amazing that an Idaho senator would show up for such duty. It revealed his integrity. I never once teased him about it, but surely the memory would bring him a smile.

We loved entertaining, and Bill became famous for his wild duck dinners. He personally hunted and barbequed all the wild game at these parties. Invitations were coveted, and we were honored to have such wonderful guests. They included many artists associated with the Sun Valley Center for the Arts, as well as art dealers, developers, skiing friends, and family members. At the end of festivities and after a long, delicious dinner, Bill always stood to make his usual farewell. Clinking his wine glass, he would decisively declare: "I asked you for dinner, but not for the night." Everyone would stand, clap hands, and happily depart. They were usually tired and wanted to get up early to ski the next day.

I have come to think of those years as an interim paradise, a golden time in life that is spent with dear friends, the time passing so quickly that you only know in retrospect how lucky you have been. We held treasure hunts at the Busterback Ranch in the Sawtooth Valley, where our guests would look for hidden prizes on mountain bikes. Bill and I also enjoyed Middle Fork rafting and kayaking trips with our friends. He always insisted that we bring costumes. We took biking trips to Europe, and Bill and I once rented a house in Provence for a few weeks. There were other trips to places much farther away—to Nepal in the Himalayas and the ancient kingdom of Zanskar. But many of my favorite memories were made closer to home.

On several occasions, we were invited to the Silver Tip Ranch inside Yellowstone National Park, which had been homesteaded in 1913. Because no motorized vehicles were allowed there, we arrived at the ranch lodge after a long, dusty walk or a ride from Slough Creek in a buckboard pulled by the ranch's draft horses. It is still a mystery to us how this private ranch managed to coexist within a national park for over one hundred years. Slough Creek is grizzly bear country. The homesteader, Milton Ames, killed eight grizzlies the first spring he owned the ranch. Joseph B. "Frenchy" Duret, a French Canadian who took up residence in this secluded area, made his living as a hunter and trapper, supplying wild game to a number of buyers. He made nationwide headlines in 1922 when he was killed by a gigantic bear that, after he had trapped it, broke free and mauled him to death. This is what I would certainly call a "grizzly" death. Frenchy was buried at Frenchy's Meadow, adjacent to the lodge.

Before one of our trips to the Silver Tip, we stayed for a few days with Evelyn and Wally Haas at their ranch in Montana, which had some of the state's best fishing along the Boulder River. It was an honor to share their lodge and guest cabins with the Haas children and grandchildren and to be included in a Haas family event. Wally was an avid fisherman who traveled the world in search of perfect fishing spots. He was so knowledgeable that professional fishing guides invited him to accompany them on their trips. Wally had not only found but now owned the perfect spot he had been seeking for fishing and retirement.

At Silver Tip Lodge we were guests of one of the owner-members of the ranch, our friend Ralph Davidson. Bill and I always chose to walk the twelve miles to the ranch. It was flat and dusty, not like a hike in the Sawtooths. But it was exercise, something we prized in those days. We thought wishfully of mountain bikes, but they were not permitted in an area that was surrounded by a national park. Ralph was then executive director of the John F. Kennedy Center for the Performing Arts, so his guests were often Washington, DC, notables.

The conversations were always stimulating and thought-provoking, with everyone contributing. The day began with a hearty breakfast and talk of the coming day of fishing—who wanted what stretch of the river for their very own. One might never see another person all day, other than our assigned guides. Lunch was supplied to the fishers, or we could walk back to the lodge for a buffet meal. The afternoon offered fishing or a nap or both, with cocktails, a delicious ranch-style dinner and more invigorating conversation. Politics was never a topic, not in this fisherman's paradise.

One of Ralph's friends and guests whom I most enjoyed was Supreme Court Justice Sandra Day O'Connor, a great conversationalist who was always eager to discover unique details in the lives of others. Our first female high court justice, nominated by Ronald Reagan and confirmed unanimously, Sandra left her position on the Supreme Court to spend more time with her husband, who was suffering with Alzheimer's disease and unable to join her on fishing trips. It is rare that a justice retires from the US Supreme Court before a terminal illness or death, and I respected her for this compassionate decision.

On another trip to the Silver Tip, Ralph advised Bill and me after we arrived that he had invited President Jimmy Carter and his wife Rosalynn for several nights. Ralph seemed genuinely excited about it. Bill and I were not, as we had already experienced the consequences of a presidential visit, or the visit of any notable, during our years in Sun Valley. And we were right. The Carters flew in by helicopter from the Haas Ranch across the mountains. A separate helicopter carried six security personnel. The ranch was turned upside down for them. Ralph regretted the loss of peace and quiet that we usually enjoyed, but the Carters were a delightful couple, gracious and accommodating to all the other guests. I had the opportunity for a lengthy conversation with both Jimmy and Rosalynn around the barbeque fire one evening, where the three of us sat together on a log. One would never have suspected he had been president of the United States. He was just a regular guy on a fishing trip.

Back in Sun Valley, we hosted fund-raising dinners at Back Pay House. The nonprofit Conservation International held its board meeting in Sun Valley one year and expressed an interest in having its first evening reception in our home. Bill and I were eager to support them because we respected this organization for its global work in protecting the environment. I asked my two sons to bartend, and they set up a bar by the window overlooking the valley. The room was full of guests, and I was busy in a conversation when a gentleman came up to me and asked if we had a Charles Sheeler painting in our art collection. He obviously knew his twentieth-century American art. I said yes, it was over the transom of the door across the room. I immediately forgot the conversation and returned to talking with other guests.

A few minutes later, the gentleman came back to talk with me about the painting. I glanced over at Cam and Brant, aware that something was going on because they were laughing and indicating that it had to do with the man who was so interested in our paintings. I looked more carefully at him and suddenly recognized his voice. With the mustache he was wearing, I didn't recognize him at first, but then I realized that I was talking to Harrison Ford, so out of context from my movie memories of him—always on the run or in some wild adventure. I blushed, no doubt. Harrison eventually became the chairman of

Conservation International and has remained on that board for several decades. My sons never let me forget the shocked look on my face when I finally realized who was talking to me.

I am often clueless as to the identity of celebrities. Living in Sun Valley, we paid little attention to them as they lived amongst us. Only a year ago, I was in Napa Valley at the Chappellet Vineyard to attend the memorial service for my old dear friend Donn Chappellet. I was to give the opening eulogy the next morning; and during a dinner planned by Molly the night before, I was seated by a very handsome man. He pulled out my chair before I was able to see his seating card. I visited with him for quite a while, racking my brain to remember the voice and face I knew well. When he asked about my early ski resort memories, I finally realized it was Robert Redford, who of course had his own Sundance Mountain Resort in Utah.

For our family's Christmas dinners, Bill dressed like a "wise man," and the rest of us also wore costumes themed to the biblical Christmas story. Bill loved to dress in costume and insisted that everyone coming to dinner do the same. Our long table in the dining area and two smaller tables for the grandchildren allowed for a group ranging in age from two to sixty-five.

Bill's older children were comfortable with the idea of dressing up, but at first this was not well received by my teenagers, and I lived with their annual complaints. But as each year passed, they became increasingly enchanted with the idea and enjoyed competing with one another over who could come up with the best costume. They loved performing, so they competed over who played their role the best. They came dressed as Mary, Joseph, the wise men, shepherds, or anyone who might have played a role in the nativity scene.

Our long, steep driveway had several turns that made it a perfect racecourse for winter sledding competitions. The grandchildren had their own small sleds, and the adults brought their "tuned up" and latest speed sleds. There were couples' races—two to a sled—and the singles races. For this Sunday tradition, Bill directed the man who plowed snow for us to leave just the right amount of snow on the road surface for sledding. The uncontrollable speeds of a family competition would at times result in an accident or the launch of a sled off the track and down a hillside through powder.

We hadn't planned on renting our guesthouse, but a realtor friend called one Christmas season to ask if we would provide it to a developer named Donald Trump and his family. We were told they desired total privacy and that our place was ideal, so we agreed to the request. I knew the name Trump belonged to a New York City real estate developer, but I was asked not to divulge the name, nor would I have even considered doing so. I had no plans to meet our guests. I only knew that the man's wife, Ivana, was a skier and that they would be coming with two small children and a governess. I couldn't imagine how they were going to fit into our small guesthouse, but I didn't dwell on it. By then, my Christmas season was a busy family time at the homes of the Cooper children, who now had children of their own.

During the holidays, the realtor called to inform me that Mr. Trump would like to meet me and gave me a time when I should arrive at the guesthouse. I actually did not want to do this, but I agreed. He and I visited for an hour at the kitchen table. He told me all the things I could and should do to save costs in home construction. He advised me to follow the edicts of the planning and zoning commission or city codes initially and then just change everything after the inspection. I reflect now on this odd meeting with the man only because of what he became as our president and the glimpse I had into his character even then. We lived in a small community that prized accountability far from the urban world Donald Trump inhabited.

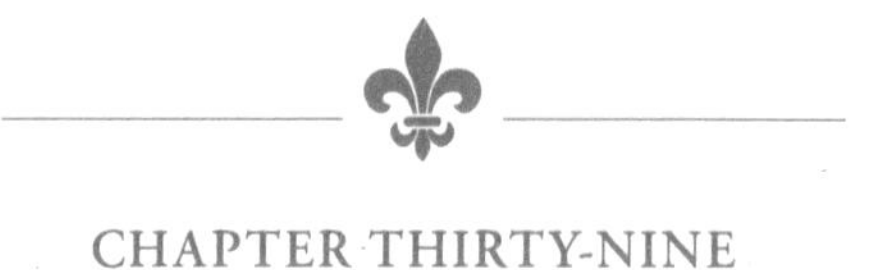

CHAPTER THIRTY-NINE

Mountainous Challenges in the Himalayas

In 1976, Bill and I flew to Kathmandu for what would be our first Himalayan adventure and my first trek in Nepal. We decided to journey through one of the more remote and less traveled areas in the Mount Everest region—the thirty-five-mile-long valley of Rolwaling, which extends from the Bhote Kosi, a river in the west, to the imposing 19,100-foot Tesi Lapcha Pass. My son Cameron came along, as did Bill's son, Bill Jr., and his girlfriend Jill.

This trek would take us from the subtropical lowlands surrounding the medieval-feeling city of Kathmandu to a high valley that parallels the Tibetan Plateau, an area that had seen few Westerners since being held off-limits following the Chinese invasion of Tibet in 1959. The area was home to the Khampa chieftains who had fought against the Chinese in support of the Dalai Lama.

The trip would be arduous. We were warned by the Mountain Travel Sobek facilitators that travel to such high altitudes could result in hemorrhages, brain damage, and the dreaded pulmonary edema, a filling of the lungs with fluid akin to slow drowning. We were instructed to get in shape and undergo a stress test for high output cardio-pulmonary exercise.

Only after we signed on did we realize that the trip would be the first Himalayan excursion for our guide, Jack Turner, although he had led numerous other trips in the Karakoram Range and elsewhere. There were fourteen "sahibs," or guests, in the group and a dozen Sherpas, both male and female, plus twenty to forty hardworking porters who, along with their yaks and other beasts of burden, carried everything from soup pots, vegetables, and live chickens to tents and rattan stools for the sahibs. We started out in t-shirts and shorts, but within two weeks we turned to winter mountain coats as we approached the Khumbu region of Everest.

Our group was diverse and athletic. We would all be humbled in one way or another by the experience. One man showed up with a wild grin, wearing a Fu Manchu-style mustache. My first thought was, "Oh, I hope he isn't going along with us." This turned out to be Bali Szabo, a Hungarian chef who fled his war-ravaged country to the United States when he was thirteen, arriving at the Austrian border with a machine gun hanging from one shoulder. Bali proved to be one of the most competent and engaging members of our group.

After two days of seeing the sights in Kathmandu, we climbed into a cramped Mercedes bus for a three-hour drive to the trailhead at Bharabise along the Sunkosi River. I say trailhead, but it really was the terminus of a major thoroughfare—not a roadway, but a major foot trail nexus that led to thousands of miles of foot trails that served as the primary routes of transportation throughout the region. Few Westerners had ventured past the Sunkosi since the opening of Nepal. The Tesi Lapcha Pass that lay ahead was one good reason to take a different route to the Everest region. We had been told by Mountain Travel to prepare for snow and ice climbing at the higher reaches of the pass.

On the first days of the journey, we passed through lowland villages surrounded by rice paddies and grazing water buffalo. This was the land of the Tamangs, who were descended from the Mongols and worked for the trekking companies but were not well-suited physiologically for the higher altitudes. The indigenous Sherpas were high-mountain people, as of course were the ethnic Tibetans, who stood out from the lowlanders with their wide Asian features and ruddy tan faces.

Making about ten to twelve miles each day, we often looked back to see our porters struggling with their heavy loads a mile or so back, looking as small as ants. We were spending at least $3,000 each for this adventure, including airfare. The porters and Sherpas were making fifty cents to a dollar per day. We all relied upon one another to survive in this rugged place, yet the vastness of the region surrounded by peaks higher than twenty thousand feet brought a sense of solitude and foreboding. These sacred hidden valleys, or beyul in Tibetan, were known for hundreds of years as secret places for worship and meditation, and they were said to be blessed by Padmasambhava, the Indian meditation master who first brought Buddhism to Tibet in the eighth century. The peaks were named after gods and goddesses.

With its cultural history, a spiritual energy permeated the area, inspiring in us a sense of respect and wonder. We passed by ancient Buddhist chortens at the highest points on passes, small ornately decorated stone shrines built to symbolize the path to enlightenment—a superconscious realm beyond duality, a place accessed only through wisdom and compassion and derived from an acceptance of impermanence.

Everywhere along the trails were flat rocks and stone slabs elegantly carved with *Om Mani Padme Hum* in the ornate Tibetan script. This mantra includes the ethical imperatives of Buddhism and is said to also transcend literal definitions to induce a mystical experience during its recitation. Occasionally, we passed a monastery where "reincarnated lamas" taught ancient lessons and meditation practices.

We trekked through a mossy rhododendron forest on one hillside and an alpine evergreen forest on another, until we reached the village of Beding, at twelve thousand feet, where many of the Sherpas went to town for Tibetan chang, or rice beer, returning to camp with samples for the rest of us. On our trip, one of the trekkers blew up small, colored rubber balloons for children whenever they appeared, yielding smiles of delight.

The more remote Nan Goan village, at fourteen thousand feet, was mostly dug into the hillsides, with slate roofs at ground level surrounded by potato fields, dark autumn heath, and grazing goats, sheep, and yaks. Grilled yak meat was often on the dinner menu for the sahibs. When we arrived at Nan Goan, it became clear that our arrival had been expected. The trail through the village was rimmed by entire families that put on their Sunday best to welcome us—men in wide-brimmed black hats, women wearing coral and garnet necklaces and silver bracelets. They carried the children on their shoulders so they could get a better view of these tired and rare Western trekkers. The locals made an effort to make eye contact with, the exotic travelers from another world. They wanted to be close to us, touch us, or just hang around the camp to see what we ate. Clearly, they had seen few Westerners.

Somewhere along the trail, Bali Szabo had recognized a large green plant that was growing wild on the side of the trail. He broke off branches from time to time and attached them to his backpack. He pointed out to us later that this was apparently a custom, as the plant has some herbal significance. I supposed that Bali had plans for cooking with it.

As we traveled, we all got to know one another. One member of the Himalayan support crew was called the Egg Man—he was so sure-footed that he was entrusted with a stack of cases containing raw eggs when we headed up the steepest hills. There was a Buddhist monk who also worked as a porter. He ventured only as far as Nan Goan. After delivering a sanctifying or purifying ritual and prayer and receiving one dollar for his efforts, he turned back for home.

The trail was in some places nothing more than stone and mud steps reaching upward, farther than I would ever have imagined. We climbed up and up, then had a brief respite on a plateau before descending once more into a canyon just as perilously long and steep, perhaps crossing a delicate bridge, before ascending up and up again once more.

To travel only a mile or two as the crow flies could take half a day on foot. It seemed as if that was our mission, to go up and down, never around—incessant climbing and descending day after day that became a meditation in itself. It rained most days, and then the sky cleared and the temperature became cold as we moved toward the higher elevations. In a single day, the temperature ranged from fifty-five degrees in the afternoon to ten below zero at night. As the support crew set up camp, we sometimes helped pitch our tents and then rested before dinner. One man in our group hiked the entire route in tennis shoes.

Bali, the wild Hungarian, reminded me of details of the trip as he was writing about it later. He made friends with the head Sherpa, Ang Lakpa, and the head cook, Nyima Tzering. He let them know that he decided to put his now-dried green branches to work in the form of dessert brownies. I had never experienced marijuana before, but out here in the middle of nowhere, I thought it would be a good idea, especially since I was at a time in my life of serious risk-taking and experimentation. The entire trip to Nepal was a novelty like no other. I felt transported to another world or parallel universe that was based on religion and spirituality as opposed to the materialistic tenets of the Western world.

Bali made what he called "magical" brownies, instructing the cooking staff to only eat one-half of one each, lest they become very stoned. He also made regular brownies, but they were not as popular. But the next day, Tzering was shouting at Bali, while the cooking crew lay about on big boulders staring at the sky, happy and useless.

The cooks had eaten far more brownies that they should have. "You cook dinner!" he shouted at Bali, who was happy to comply.

Cameron delivered a few magical brownies to us; and after eating them, Bill and I disappeared into our tent for a good long while. We were careful not to eat too much as we were already at high altitude and might be especially susceptible to their influence, but I do recall that many laughs were had by all as Cameron came barreling into our tent as if shot out of a gun to say, "High guys!"

Bali later tore two pages out of *War and Peace*, the book he had carried along, and rolled joints with them, climbing into his own small tent with Cameron, trip doctor Andy Leavitt, and four others for a smoke. He recently shared with me something he wrote about that day while high in the mountains, in more ways than one:

> "We started our drift among the clouds, letting our minds wander at will, savoring the rush of insight or illusion unique to the drug. The time passed uncharted until dinner. We sat huddled in the dinner tent, not too useful when it came to passing the sugar, the coffee, the meat, the soup. We were absorbed in the others, listening, watching, drawing the bead, slicing and dicing their personalities, lingering over little things, or life's great questions, as the case may be. As the grip of the pot weakened and we ran out of content to grasp, we calmly faded into our sleeping bags."

Within a few days, we stood at the base of the Rolwaling Glacier, where we heard the occasional rumbling of falling boulders and saw huge chunks of ice come crashing into a lake. We knew we were now to face the final climb up the Tesi Lapcha Pass, well beyond the altitude for which human beings had been designed. The air held less than half the amount of oxygen found at sea level.

Bali had some trouble and perhaps was suffering from early stages of pulmonary edema. Jack gave him plenty of time to rest, then put him at the front of the group and had him proceed at his own pace, which was brilliant. The rest of us followed. After some dreamy gazing at the surrounding mountains, the hardest part of the trek was over. We had survived the worst challenge to our bodies and were on our way back down on the other side of the pass. Although there had been several injuries on the journey thus far—sprained ankles, bruises, and various cases of dysentery or other stomach problems, we were now home free as we ambled down past the Drolum Bau Glacier to Thami, Namche Bazaar, and more towns and villages. After some of us trekked to the Everest base camp at eighteen thousand feet for its spectacular views, we all gathered again to trek out to Lukla and eventually make our way back to Kathmandu.

This first trip to the Far East was the most amazing journey I had yet taken. I had no idea what lay ahead for me, that there would be many more trips that brought even more dangerous and challenging circumstances, but I will never forget Nepal because it was the first trip that brought me into contact with people from cultures completely distinct from my own.

I was able to stay in contact with Bali over the years because he moved to the Wood River Valley and, while there, wrote about his travels, including our Nepal trip, in the local newspaper. In his later years, he lived in Hailey, where he built the Garden for Nonhumanity on reclaimed city property. It was filled with herbs and flowering plants for the animals near his apartment building.

Travel is an indispensable feature of life. We gain perspective from being out of our element and come home with new and creative ideas about life's possibilities—that is, if we are lucky enough to make it home at all. I learned that the man who trekked along with us in tennis shoes returned to Nepal the following year and, at some point in his journey, slipped off a ledge and fell to his death.

Some years later, in 1982, Bill and I took one of our most challenging trips—to the ancient hidden kingdom of Zanskar, an even more remote region in the Himalayas, bordering on Ladakh. A Tibetan book I had been reading described it as a land that was found by divine beings: "The gods opened up the earth, discovered the valley beneath it, and thus revealed it to existence. Because of this it is a very sacred place." There were no available Mountain Travel Sobek guides trained for trekking in this area, and the trained porters we expected never arrived. Instead, we relied on people booked out of Delhi, whom we could not trust at a time when the nearby region of Kashmir was in upheaval over the passing of Sheikh Mohammad Abdullah.

Deep down, we understood that these far-flung trips were for us meaningful tests of our competence and courage against the natural elements. Yet, political events can create unexpected hazards in a region like Kashmir, where war often erupted over border quarrels with Pakistan, as is still the case. Zanskar in 1982 was considered inaccessible and therefore tantalizing. It exists within one of the highest valleys on our planet at 13,150 feet and extends for two hundred miles. Access was possible either through the great Himalayan Range, its lowest pass being 17,300 feet, or over the barren, little-known, and difficult Zanskar Range to the north. The passes into the valley are closed for eight months of the year, leaving its people largely isolated.

Our small group was joined by my son Brant Cooper and Jack Davis, the man from New Jersey who sank with me in Gerry's motorboat at Lava Falls during our ill-fated attempt to make it up the Colorado River in a speedboat. Since that frightening failure, he had become a seasoned traveler who welcomed unique and dangerous challenges. We flew from New York to Istanbul for two days of touring the historic sites of the city. Bill relished the hours he spent in the expansive bazaar, where he could bargain undisturbed for his purchases.

Istanbul was a city full of history and wonder, a treasury of monuments from east and west, gathered through the ages by many of its ruling dominions. The history of the Roman and Turkish civilizations is voluminous and reaches back to an obelisk erected by Theodosius in 1471 BC. Of the 1,120 mosques in the city, Hagia Sophia is one of the world's architectural wonders. It was constructed under the rule of Justinian the Great, AD 532–537. Operated as a museum since 1935, Turkish president Recep Tayyip Erdoğan recently ordered Hagia Sophia to be reclassified as a mosque.

We flew to New Delhi and then to Srinagar, where there was no one to meet us. We searched for any transportation we could find to the city, remembering the warning that all transportation would be in lockdown. We found only one bus, already filled with Indian families and their babies, goats, and chickens. We squeezed in, as erect as statues in the aisle of the bus and giggled all the way to the center of town over the ridiculousness of our situation while the bus weaved among pedestrians, Brahma cattle, and bicycles.

Once in Srinagar, we toured the lagoons in a lavishly decorated Victorian-style houseboat, eventually finding an ad hoc group of guides who, over the next four weeks, managed to take us up thousands of meters in elevation to the Himalayan Plateau with severely limited supplies. I was reminded of Yvon Chouinard's comment: "When everything goes wrong, that is when the adventure begins." Some journeys are like that, and they often prove to be the most rewarding.

We drove fifteen hours toward our destination on poor roads, dodging donkey caravans, goats, and cows. Local families were working on roadside building efforts. We reached the town of Galhar, near the trailhead, and parked by what looked like a guesthouse, where we were directed up a ladder onto a rooftop where several gypsies had already spread out their bedding. We did the same. In the warm, starlit night, we were hoping for a good night's sleep, but the barking watchdogs of every family in the town prevented that. I was awakened as John rose to hasten down the ladder toward the growling dogs, urgently seeking the bathroom after unwisely drinking from the driver's water bottle early that day. As the sun rose amidst fleecy clouds, I arose to take a look from the rooftop where we had slept. The view left me breathless. The house was built on the edge of a cliff two thousand feet above a river. If John had been disoriented and walked in the wrong direction, he would have fallen to his death.

It turned out that our guides were unfamiliar with the region, but they were eager for work. Seven-hour days turned out to take twelve hours. Nothing went as planned, and Bill was often upset at having spent a fair sum for an organized trip, but the landscape was astonishing. We hiked by streams and waterfalls through pine and oak forests or through green fields to villages perched on hilltops full of happy, busy villagers who would surround us, filled with curiosity. The portals of the Hindu temples we passed were carefully carved with animistic themes.

After making it over a high pass, we entered the most beautiful valley I have ever seen, with rice fields spreading beneath towering mountains. The people appeared happy, healthy, cleanly dressed, and friendly. Perhaps this was the Shangri-la we had been expecting. The Tibetans, with their distinctive wide faces, wore colorful hats of burgundy wool and heavy wool garments of the same color. The women wore heavy beaded necklaces. We had gradually been climbing over the past five days and had now reached an altitude of 9,000 feet. The next campsite would be at 10,500 feet, with the final campsite at 12,500 feet, before we crossed the Zanskar Pass.

With only two days before the pass into Zanskar, we climbed out of the forests and took in the view of the glaciers and snow-covered peaks of the Himalayas. We were in the Valley of Pregnant Horses, where we were to be met by fresh porters, donkeys, and supplies. In this desolate valley, short on food, we waited until seven porters arrived—instead of the sixteen we had been expecting. There was much haggling over the prices to be paid, as the porters argued that it was harvest time. They said travel over the pass at this time of year was too dangerous due to possible heavy snows, and they claimed that it was the toughest pass they had ever crossed, straight up through snowy fields and crags. The porters declared that they would not carry over forty pounds, so we agreed to carry more weight. We had given away all items deemed nonessential in order to lighten our loads. As we quickly gathered what remained of our belongings and left the campsite, we saw every porter picking up a load to test it, setting it back down, then moving to test another. The next two days' trek to the high campsite at the base of the pass was daunting. We climbed along steep glacial terrain and over roughly pocketed ice to reach Umasi Glacier. Some of the porters were suffering from altitude headaches, and we learned that our head guide, Yacub, was freezing cold. He revealed to us that he had no proper clothing with him. That night, at our high-altitude glacier camp at 16,000 feet, we loaned him all the extra warm clothing we had.

We started our day of crossing the pass at five in the morning, opening the tent flap to an inch of new snow. With the wind blowing, it was extremely cold, but we climbed methodically up the steep snow slopes to reach the pass at 17,300 feet in two hours. We were in good shape after acclimatizing along the route. A porter gave me a prayer flag to plant with those already on the rocky mount, then we descended over snow-covered boulders to the bare ice of the Zanskar Glacier, a slow descent around giant boulders that had stood for eons, strewn across the trail. It was colder than it had been at 16,000 feet, with wind and snow still blowing across the trail when we at last reached a meadow. Another twelve-hour day lay ahead of us, and we wanted nothing more than to crawl into our sleeping bags.

We found ourselves in a broad, flat valley with barren mountains rising on each side—a quiet valley that was strangely pleasing after the noisy bantering of the porters. We encountered Tibetans again. A truck with supplies, fresh ponies, and Zanskari porters greeted us. It seemed a profusion of luxury. We were also met by a SITA World Tours travel company representative, who informed us of yet another change in schedule, which came as no surprise. We would not be able to go to Padum, the largest city and capital, as the bridge was out. Instead, we were happy to set out on foot for the town of Karcha in what had once been the kingdom of Zanskar. Like a monastery, the town was set on the side of a steep, rocky mountain. We climbed up steep stairs into the village and inquired of a man where we could find refuge. He kindly invited us into his house. More stairs to the third floor and an empty room—except for the children who stared at us and began to sing. So we sang back, knowing together only "Row, Row, Row Your Boat." We soon all joined in to dance together as well. It was a welcoming experience between our disparate cultures.

Yacub found us there and told us to follow him to the edge of the swollen, rapidly flowing river below the town. For some reason, we were relegated to setting up camp across the swollen river. Our camp could only be reached on the backs of our ponies after the supplies had been removed. I was terrified, and I giggled all the way across as the waters swirled around me and even over the saddle. Giggling was the only way to dull the fear.

What lay ahead was unknown, but it appeared that the trek could go no farther. Winter had blown in early, and crossing the next Zanskar Range was deemed impossible since no ponies or porters would be willing to make that journey. We took out our maps and agreed to turn back after seeing that three more passes remained ahead. We realized now that we could get stuck here for the winter and that if it continued to snow, even the lorries would no longer be able to drive the only way out of the valley on the road to the town of Kargil.

Travel is best when it is a pilgrimage of some sort, but oftentimes the destination is unreachable. I had so wanted to make it to the Thonde Monastery, an active monastic community just ten miles farther on. No one else seemed to care. One voice was not enough. After a year of planning and a lot of money spent for this unique experience, we had finally reached the hidden kingdom of Zanskar. And now it was decided that we would rush back to our hot baths and familiar luxuries. I was outnumbered and went into my tent to cry. There will perhaps always be a fantastic place just a bit farther on, just as we will sometimes be limited by time from reaching our ultimate goal. Ours had been a journey into the past. The "Zanskar Chronicles" I'd read described it as "a land where fairies congregate." I suppose we all need a magical place to believe in, to move toward, and to one day discover.

A philosopher at heart, I have a need to always plumb my thoughts about an experience in order to gain perceptions that can bring wisdom. In the sixteenth and seventeenth centuries, philosophers such as Descartes and Francis Bacon taught us that nature was only a mechanical process to be studied and researched. Any sense of its spiritual essence was removed as we sought to control and exploit the natural world for its resources. As a result, we tend to work only on human-to-human relationships, having deserted our original Earth-to-human relationship.

I considered this trip to Zanskar to be one of entering a true wilderness that offered many enriching gifts, despite its disappointments. A wilderness can be chaotic and disorganized, but behind that chaos dwells its wisdom, available to us if we listen. I felt a deep connection to another dimension of the universe—its spiritual dimension. In connecting with this dimension, I found myself living fully in the present moment and accepting any vagaries that the universe might impose upon us. The journey reconnected me to the totality of living beings and our earliest human relationship to the Earth.

We need to honor our leaders for their return to the wilderness—people like Henry David Thoreau, who gained his understanding and wisdom of the universe through directly experiencing the natural world. It is our responsibility to reject the belief that we need to control nature. We must commune with nature to gain its secrets. We need a worldwide change in consciousness. This will bring forth our true being as it relates to all living things. If we do this, nature and its wildness will whisper their secrets to us, and the wisdom gained from such an experience will change our lives forever.

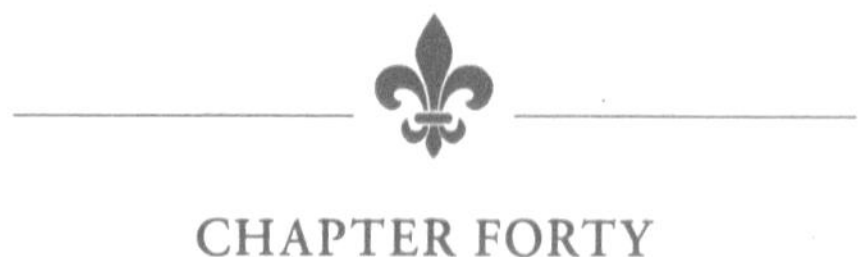

CHAPTER FORTY

My Spritual Path

Everyone has a life story, a path to follow. One person's path may be filled with more challenges than others. What matters is how we walk it. A path walked in truth and kindness, with perseverance, courage and acceptance, leads to the greatest happiness. I came to these realizations during the late 1970s when I began to see my life and the lives of those around me in new and different ways. I allowed intuition to flow into my soul, enabling my higher spirit to enter my life story.

Having finally found true love in my life with Bill Janss, and with fewer immediate parenting responsibilities, I was able to deeply explore my spirituality for the first time. Allowing this spiritual consciousness to emerge brought me a renewed sense of personal destiny. Many of the ideas and experiences from that time have carried me through many years of adventure and continued service and still resonate today.

These explorations coincided with a spiritual movement in Ketchum led primarily by Ed Moffat and Jenny Walton at their Paradise Natural Foods store and café. The store sold books and promoted ideas that changed my life. This couple seemed to know everyone in the new emerging spirituality movement—all the gurus, significant teachers, methods, and theories. Cheryl Welch of Chapter

One Bookstore was part of the wider New Age movement that inspired many of these ideas.

Ed and Jenny's early symposia were called "Dreaming the New Dream," and they created the feeling that anything was possible. Our small community responded with enthusiasm; many people were excited and eagerly took part in the numerous sessions the store hosted. Teachers came to the valley to provide astrological readings, past life regressions, rebirthing sessions, and individual psychic interviews. We learned how to meditate and what it meant to have one's aura read.

An entire new world was opening up for me, one to which I had never been exposed. My head was reeling, and the excitement I felt was overwhelming. It seemed as though ideas that I knew intuitively had become hidden, forgotten, and neglected behind my earlier, rational approach to life, an approach until then that had enabled me to meet the challenges of my life and move ahead. I began to believe that there was not only hope for me but also for the rest of humanity to evolve in love and truth.

I was not the only person in the family exploring new perspectives. During this time, my daughter Christin and I took a course in Transcendental Meditation taught by a local teacher at his Sun Valley condominium. We concentrated on a personal mantra—a word or phrase to focus the mind—which allowed us to transcend ordinary thinking to a realm of pure consciousness. This practice became its own guide over many years during the evolution of my "Being." I say Being because this period of my life was about spiritual evolution or "being" rather than "doing." As the years went by, I endeavored to bring meditative consciousness to all of my activities—not just while sitting in a meditative posture but also while vacuuming or washing dishes. Any activity can be done with added consciousness and care.

While we were waiting for our new home to be built on Back Pay Way and living in a three-bedroom Lodge condominium, only Brant and Christin were still at home with us. The other Cooper children were attending far-flung boarding schools—Candy in Italy, Kelley at Colorado Rocky Mountain School, and Cameron at Lawrenceville in New Jersey.

Oftentimes, the door to Brant's room was closed; I assumed he was watching TV. I found out later that he was instead sneaking out through an open window to join friends who gathered in the evenings at the ice rink to smoke pot, something I could not yet imagine happening in my family. When he later climbed back through the window, Brant always came in to say goodnight, gushing with atypical emotions. "Oh, Mom, I love you so much," he said, with red eyes and lengthy outpourings of affection that were a bit out of character. This was definitely something else speaking through him. I eventually realized that he was high and accepted that this was part of a new era.

One day, Bill and I took Brant hang gliding with us at Elkhorn. Bill and I loved this exciting new sport, but we only ever took off from Elkhorn Hill, which is much smaller than Bald Mountain. Before Brant took off, none of us had considered how light he was and what this could mean for the distance of his flight. Instead of landing nearby like the rest of us, he just continued on and on, gliding with no apparent plan to come down at all. He finally did land when it became apparent to him that the possibility of alighting on soft snow ended at the edge of a parking lot full of automobiles. Brant loved hang gliding, but in this instance, it did not provide a fond memory for his mother. I felt like I was watching my boy Icarus falling from the sky.

My own adventures during those years were more spiritual in nature. This involved exploring ideas that Bill may have thought were ridiculous. Regardless of where my interests led me, though, Bill supported me all the way. He even wryly suggested that I change my license plate to MME WU, meaning Madame Wu, as in "she's a little woo-woo." Rather than taking offense at his remark, I replaced my GRANYVAN license plates on the Volkswagen with MME WU plates. I installed them with a chuckle, embracing my new identity.

Bill was grounded, rooted in physical reality. Busy trying to make Sun Valley Resort work financially, he seemed not to need religion or spirituality in his life as a support system. Nevertheless, he let me pursue my own spiritual adventures, even when this meant traveling outside of Sun Valley for workshops. For me, this was an opportunity to explore my potential as a human being as well as my evolution as a soul during my brief time on this planet. It meant beginning to live a loving, fulfilling, and rewarding life in all of its potential. Bill understood and accepted unconditionally my commitment and need for travel during this time of searching, even though it must have seemed irrational to him.

The new ideas and practices I encountered were so vast and detailed that I would be hard-pressed to explain them all. It took commitment for me to incorporate them, and I could not begin to absorb them all at once. The guide or teacher who most fulfilled my quest for meaning and fulfillment was Jack Schwartz, a Dutchman who had fought against the Nazis as a young man. He did not have the education or flair for writing in English, but the content of his teachings and his belief system were clear in his books, which I still cherish in my library—books about "human energy systems" with such titles as *I Know from My Heart* and *The Path of Action*.

Jack's theory and practice of autogenics is a mental and physical therapy that can develop an inner awareness of our self-generating psychological processes. We learned how to control and monitor our own body-mind interactions, how to eat well, meditate, and sleep soundly. Jack taught us about our natural energy systems and how to control them for optimal health. He also provided a framework for spiritual living that extended beyond the physical body. Back then, the idea that we could use our minds to control blood pressure and even pain was not yet accepted, but now these practices have become part of mainstream complementary care at hospitals.

Jack and his wife maintained a retreat outside Ashland, Oregon. At least once a month, I would go there for a number of days. Jack would read a person's "aura" before beginning a session with them. He described my aura—the intangible, colored glow around my body—as lilac or light purple. This color represents the most spiritual and least physical of all possible aura readings, he said, indicating that this came with a large sense of responsibility to humanity. This knowledge fulfilled in me a belief that I had carried since childhood, that I was to bring love and guidance in any way that I could to all those in my life—not just my family but those who honored me with leadership roles in the communities where I had lived, was living, and would live in the future. Jack's observations confirmed for me the direction and path I had been following.

I began to read many volumes by other teachers, well-known to students and disciples of spirituality. Each confirmed what I had learned with Jack. These teachers included psychologist-turned-guru Ram Dass, Jean Huston of the "human potential movement," and David Bohm, a theoretical physicist who was deeply interested in human consciousness. I read books by Charlotte Beck, Wayne Dyer, and Larry Dossey, MD. Just recently, I received a new book in the mail from author Duane Elgin, a researcher at the Institute of Noetic Sciences, an organization I became increasingly involved in over the years.

As exciting as I found these first years of exploration, the next stage of my spiritual evolution was to take what I had learned through books and teachings and make it manifest in my life—in my Being. The spiritual path needs to be one of deeds, not just words and ideas. In years to come, I would move beyond the reading of books into assuring that my belief system became an actuality in my life.

Some of the practitioners I was exposed to in the 1970s were surely charlatans, including the Filipino "psychic surgeons," who came to town at this time. Bill had been diagnosed with a cancerous tumor and would do anything I suggested. He agreed to participate in the "surgery." These practitioners had already been reported as scammers, but why not give it a try? Some people seemed to completely believe in them as they pulled bloody objects from a patient's body, objects that were later found to be chicken entrails, which they cleverly placed onto the patient, seemingly having removed them from the body. It looked like a magician's performance.

These Filipino surgeons quickly disappeared from the United States after being thoroughly debunked. Yet, so much that I found during those years of spiritual exploration provided a foundation for further learning that has remained vital to my life. After our new Back Pay house was completed, astrologer David Pond stayed in our guesthouse each spring for many years. Beginning in 1980, he provided readings for people in the community. At first, I thought that having him do a reading of my birth chart would be merely interesting, but I was stunned by how accurate it was. I began to have readings done for all of my children and then their children, and now we all request annual chart readings for the upcoming year.

David has played an important role in my evolution and understanding about people through their astrological charts. A chart reveals their varied temperaments and the timing and meaning of events in their lives. David can also do a relationship chart, with positives and negatives for an individual in relation to someone else. When Bill and I planned to marry, I had David do a co-relationship chart for the two of us to see how we would synchronize and what conflictive personality traits might affect us. I learned that it would be better for me to make suggestions rather than tell Bill what to do. Bill learned that I too am a leader and want to be responsible for organizing my own life. We have both let each other have our freedom, and that is why ours became and remained such a beautiful relationship.

Perhaps the greatest luxury in life is to live deliberately enough to see the many miracles that can pass us by if we are not paying attention. Once my children had grown up enough to be beyond my control, I had time to reflect, invite intuition, and reconsider the myths that had informed my early studies in philosophy and art history. I also found my way to an intersection between science and spirituality, between the hyperrational person I was compelled to become in reaction to a chaotic childhood and the freedom of mind that entered my later life.

I believe that changes happen, messages reach us, when we are ready, and that life paths, although they feel new to us, have been trodden many times before by others. It seems timely that I just recently came to identify with the myth of Aletis, the Wanderer. She was the daughter of Icarius, who learned from Dionysus how to make wine. After Icarius's death, she wandered the world looking for him everywhere and has come to be seen as the archetypal figure in the heroine's journey, as distinct from the hero's journey popularized by Joseph Campbell.

While male heroes tend to move outward to prove their masculinity, passing tests and confronting various archetypal characters along the way to maturity, a female heroine can instead "travel deeper and deeper into her own psyche as she comes to value the uniqueness of her own being." I borrow these words and ideas from *Jane Eyre's Sisters: How Women Live and Write the Heroine's Story*, by Jody Gentian Bower, who writes that a woman's quest can extend far beyond the role of mother as her life becomes "the story of a woman who must travel from place to place searching for love, freedom, or answers."

Some writers propose that the entire hero's journey is about a man learning to integrate his feminine side. In a society where women are seen as inferior, a man's quest to honor his feminine aspects may be so challenging that it seems to take on its own heroic proportions. Joseph Campbell says that women in these myths represent "the totality of what can be known," whereas the hero is the "one who comes to know."

Only in retrospect have I come to view the perils and opportunities in life as invitations to a higher consciousness, responses that call that awareness into action. As a result, I have sought a path beyond the mundane in search of explanations for the miraculous, reflecting on the links, both good and bad, that seem to connect us as spiritual beings.

Take, for instance, a miracle of coincidence that occurred the night when two of my daughters nearly died on two different roads while driving many miles apart. I tell the story reluctantly, wary of the emotions it will awaken. It was early summer in 1976. Kelley and Christin decided to do what they had always dreamed of: bike the West Coast from the Oregon state line to San Francisco. They raved about the experience, sleeping in their sleeping bags along the route for ten days and enjoying the beauty of the beaches and craggy cliffs. However, by the time the trip was over, they were sick of each other and decided to drive home in their separate cars along different routes.

Kelley drove her Volkswagen convertible through Oregon's Klamath River Valley. At five in the morning, it was just getting light when she came over a rise to see a deer darting across the road in front of her. There was no time to stop; the deer struck the vehicle and was thrown to the top of the car, where its hooves ripped opened the canvas sunroof. Out of control, the car rolled over an embankment. Kelley and all of her possessions were scattered. Because she was not wearing her seat belt, she was thrown far from the car but survived. Had she been wearing the seat belt, the car would have come down on top of her and crushed her.

Kelley managed to crawl back up to the road, where she saw

that the deer had been pregnant and a fawn had died as well. She sobbed as she crumpled into a ball and waited for a passerby, bleeding profusely from the barbed wire that had arrested her flight from the car. Several cars passed her before she was rescued and eventually brought to Boise. She was able to use a phone along the way to call me before being dropped at a hotel. Bill and I rushed to his plane and flew to Boise as quickly as possible. We had her home by noon.

As Kelley slept, Candy and Christin joined me on the front steps of the girls' cabin in Ketchum to talk about their sister's miraculous survival. I happened to glance at the garage carport and see the light blue rooftop of Christin's car, somehow separated from the automobile. I mentioned it, wondering how it got there, and they decided that they had better confess what happened. Like Kelley, Christin had driven through the night, wanting to get home, but she fell asleep at the wheel just before reaching Fairfield.

"I drifted into the oncoming lane and then off the road on the other side," she told me, waking just as she went over the edge of the road. "I knew not to jerk the wheel too abruptly, but the lip of the asphalt still caused the car to flip. The wheels were turned slightly to the right, and over the course of rolling four times I found myself back across the road and in the field on the opposite side of the road, landing straight up and facing backward, from where I had just driven."

Christin crawled through the open sunroof, the glass of which she retrieved in the nearby field. Wearing her seat belt saved her from being crushed during the rollover. "It was like a movie," she said. "Total stillness and beauty and silence at dawn on the Camas Prairie. All alone, this thing had just happened, and I am standing in a field next to my wrecked car, completely unhurt, not a scratch, not a sound."

A passing motorcyclist had gone for help, and now my two daughters were home safe. Suddenly, the shock of it all hit me—two cars totaled on two separate routes at almost the same time. How is one to assimilate this apparent connection: two sisters having dual crashes at the same time in different places with seat belt survival options as the crucial part of the story line? By what strange forces could their destinies have been connected on that early morning?

For years, I have tried to resolve this coincidence, and I am still at a loss to explain it. I can only take it as a gift that we are on blessed journeys and connected in mysterious ways. I have always embraced the notion that if you are so blessed, it is your obligation to improve the lives of those less fortunate. I am still seeking to uncover the mystery of those forces that operate behind the scenes in our lives.

While the spiritual movement was under way in Ketchum and Sun Valley, my friend Toni Goodrich and several other spiritually adventurous friends started a metaphysical book club in town. We met once a month to explore topics that ranged from shamanism, yoga, and astrology to the Tarot and a study of mythological archetypes. Toni had worked as a dental hygienist in the Bay Area and in 1970 started taking a yoga class in Palo Alto. The Bay Area was a mecca for spiritual exploration, and Toni discovered Transcendental Meditation while studying at Stanford University. One member of the metaphysical book group, Ellen Fisher, who was a popular and active member of the community, had an aggressive form of breast cancer. Our goal was to explore alternative therapies for her and perhaps gain new perspectives on her illness.

Ellen confided many things to us during the months before she died, things that she may not have been able to talk about with others. "Ellen brought us into her experience," said Toni, who still lives in Sun Valley. As the disease progressed, we took turns visiting Ellen in her hospital room. It was a heartbreaking loss for our group when she passed away, and the metaphysical book club slowly disbanded. Perhaps everyone was too disheartened to carry on the monthly meetings.

At this time, Toni and I got to know Paul Neary, a clairvoyant whose essential idea was that we are cocreators with God in our own lives. There were other people who "channeled" disembodied spirit beings from other dimensions, such as "Ramtha" and "Gaia." Some of the books Toni remembers from that era changed her life, including *The Crack in the Cosmic Egg*, by Joseph Chilton Pearce, and *The Teachings of Don Juan*, by Carlos Castaneda. "It was as if an egg broke and all these ideas came pouring out," recalls Toni.

I was able to bring these spiritual interests to a new level and combine them with my passion for logic and scientific understanding after meeting Lynne Twist around 1980. She and her husband Bill came to visit Bill's daughter, Suzie Janss Ferguson, Lynne's schoolmate at Stanford. Lynne and I connected right away, and she later told me about a fascinating organization—the Institute for Noetic Sciences (IONS).

IONS was founded by astronaut Edgar Mitchell, who had an overpowering mystical experience while viewing Earth from a lunar module. He was overwhelmed by the realization that everything in human experience had taken place on this tiny globe within a limitless universe. "What I experienced during that three-day trip home was nothing short of an overwhelming universal connectedness," Mitchell wrote. "I perceived the universe as in some way conscious."

Lynne told me that when Edgar Mitchell saw the Earth from space, he had a "transcendental experience," that it opened up not only his heart but a whole new level of consciousness. "This was a huge breakthrough in the consciousness of our species probably," Lynne said. "He became aware that our individual consciousness is very, very narrow in comparison to what is available."

After Edgar returned to Earth, he founded IONS to explore the inner dimensions of our consciousness. As an astrophysicist and scientist, Edgar legitimatized some of the ideas IONS was researching on the perimeters of modern science: intuition, instinct, and the experience of prior lifetimes. His goal was to expand and explore consciousness in a way that gave credence to some of the things that we all know are real but which have never been scientifically proven. As Lynne professes, we all have out-of-body experiences, instincts, and intuitions that we respond to and trust.

My personal belief system parallels that of IONS in the joining together of the rational or scientific with the mind or spiritual consciousness. I'm reminded of my days of studying philosophy and the proposition introduced by seventeenth-century philosopher René Descartes that the rational and the spiritual are not one but two completely different entities. Descartes is remembered as a mathematician and scientific thinker. His work led to a cold, rationalistic, and calculated concept of the human being. He is remembered for saying, "Cogito ergo sum," translated as, "I think, therefore I am."

For Descartes, the truth was attained by method, evidence, and logical sequence. Chance must be set aside in order that truth may be found according to a set of rules or immediate knowledge. This was his rational approach, credited to him as the scientific method. Because it was innovative, Descartes was recognized as one of the founders of modern philosophy. Acceptance of this approach extended through the eighteenth-century Age of Enlightenment and beyond. There was no place for God or spirit in this philosophy. Science and religion were two disparate fields. Much of what I was learning during those years at IONS questioned this proposition.

I would often talk with Edgar about math and physics, quantum energy and black holes. The board respected and honored him for his astute sensitivity and broad perspective. He often sat alone, so I would go sit down with him to converse on many questions of physics and metaphysics. I could talk to him for hours. Before we parted, he would always remind me: "We are not just physical beings. We are spiritual beings, highly conscious."

Lynne joined the IONS board in 1988, after being involved in the 1970s in the early days of Erhard Seminars Training (EST), a workshop that grew out of the Human Potential Movement. Lynne was working with The Hunger Project, examining hunger as an integrity issue, a reflection of a breakdown in the consciousness of the human family. She invited me to join the board of IONS in 1993; I agreed, and became immersed in its world of innovative research.

Lynne had long known Willis Harman, the author, engineer, and futurist who cofounded IONS and served as its president. The executive director of IONS was Winston "Wink" Franklin, who later became IONS president after Willis's death. Others involved at that time were Marilyn Schlitz, IONS director of research for many years, who continues to lead programs bridging consciousness, science, healing, and transformation; Dean Radin, author of *Entangled Minds* and *The Conscious Universe*; and IONS chief scientist Brendan O'Regan, who conducted early research in spontaneous healing from fatal diseases, the use of imagery in healing, and additional significant work that led to now-accepted practices in the field of psychoneuroimmunology, which has to do with the effect of the mind on health and immune function.

Thanks in large part to IONS, these ideas were beginning to be accepted by the mainstream. Brendan wrote The *Heart of Healing*, a companion volume to the Turner Broadcasting System television series of the same name, which examines cross-cultural and historical perspectives on mind-body science that include acupuncture, creative and healing visualizations, homeopathy, and energy healing. It was also featured in Bill Moyers's documentary and book, Healing and the Mind.

IONS researchers also published studies on meditation and the placebo effect. They were at the cutting edge of what came to be known as alternative and then complementary medicine, practices now widely accepted in the medical community. Other research at IONS included "remote viewing" studies in a laboratory. A participant would focus on a certain image—say, a sailboat—and another participant outside the building would then draw an image of a sailboat. Or a person in Texas could somehow tell the government about things going on in the Soviet Union.

IONS scientists studied the power of meditation and the impact of a mother's mood on her baby's development, recalled Lynne. "These things are so obvious now; but at the time, they were outside the reality of science. Now people recognize there is an energy field around the mother that impacts the development of the brain and consciousness of the baby. IONS research proved unequivocally that these things are true way before anybody else."

When Lynne joined the IONS board, she was asked to chair an IONS fund-raising committee. From that position, she moved into being vice chair and then chairman of the board. She wrote *The Soul of Money* while serving on the IONS board. This groundbreaking book was a journey into the consciousness of our relationship with money. Lynne now travels widely speaking on this subject.

IONS board meetings lasted three or four days every two months, and I never wanted to miss one. The meetings began with an extraordinary experience such as swimming with dolphins in the Bahamas, fire walking, or holotropic breathing with Stanislov Grof. An experiential component always opened our meetings, facilitating the exploration of memories and visions for the future. We expanded our consciousness so that when we were in business meetings the next day, our own individual consciousness would have been broken open, more able to assess ongoing scientific research and results that were outside our realm of normality. Each board meeting was an amazing journey into some realm of consciousness that we were privileged to enter together as a group. The board grew close and intimately involved with one another because we shared these experiences together. I delved much deeper into my own self-awareness during those years because I believed in what we were doing and understood that it was a search for higher consciousness.

People on the IONS board were already familiar with many of these cutting-edge ideas and oriented toward this kind of innovative thinking. Often, they were invited to join the board because IONS already affirmed and validated their work. The board included Paul Temple and his wife, Diane Temple, who invited us for meetings at their home in Marin County. Sandra Hobson, a medicine woman, served on the IONS board for twenty years. Her IONS service validated her work as she gained further understanding and expertise from board experiences.

Many board members took the experience of deeper levels of consciousness into their business lives, including George Zimmer, the founder of Men's Warehouse. He was already oriented toward expanded consciousness; but as a member of the IONS board, he was inspired to manage his company in an extraordinary manner outside the usual businessman's way of seeing things. It affected his whole company. His experience caring for his mother, who died of cancer, led him to support research into the therapeutic use of MDMA, better known as ecstasy, as well as an effort to legalize cannabis. In 2004, George nominated spiritual guru Deepak Chopra for the Men's Warehouse corporate board.

Paul Temple, formerly the head of Standard Oil in Spain, was for many years chairman of the IONS board. Lynne told me that his experience of serving on the board expanded his idea of God and Christianity to include other dimensions of spirituality. Paul invested in experimental cancer treatments that were not only medical but spiritual and metaphysical in approach.

I aided Lynne in her fund-raising for IONS. She credits me with being one of the most competent and able board members. Because I respect and admire her, I take to heart her praise more than that of most people. "In terms of getting things done, when things got stuck in a conversation, you always brought us to closure—a conclusion and action," she told me. "People can get a little nutty when there is a lot of money and land involved, but you were really good with how much money we should we be putting into land development and how much into programs. You had a competency with finance and budgets that calmed some of the waters we were in."

When IONS was based in Sausalito, the board had a vision that they should be on a beautiful piece of land in Marin County. We settled on two hundred acres of rolling hills and oak trees—the former campus of World College West. The board had no idea how they would manage this purchase. The cost was estimated to be $9–10 million dollars. We used very "noetic" processes, like meditation and visualizations, to manifest it. Through our Native American liaison, Angeles Arrien, a Basque shaman from Idaho who was also trained as an anthropologist, we consulted with the indigenous people whose land it once had been. The result of our efforts came to be known as Earthrise, harkening back to Edgar Mitchell's revelation upon seeing our planet out of a spaceship window.

At one board meeting, I was called on to explore a myth that I felt resonated within my own life—a personal connection to Siddhartha, the Indian prince who defied his father's authority to escape the palace walls in order to experience the truth of existence. His spiritual search involved a series of adventures before he became the spiritually elevated Buddha at the end of his life. He faced the misery and frailty of human existence beyond his privileged circumstances and set upon a path to spiritual freedom through compassion. I felt that Siddhartha's path resonated with my own path and his revelations helped me make sense of my choices and commitments to an understanding of the nature of reality and humanity.

Lynne and I were two IONS board members who always spoke of an appreciation for the environment and the natural world. She said she looked up to me for the way I raised my five children and carried on the legacy of my husband Bill Janss. "As a woman, activist, philanthropist, mother, and female leader, you helped me understand who I am and the role I wanted to play in this world," Lynne said. "You set an example for women—to not be afraid to speak our minds and play a leadership role in this world."

Lynne became committed to work in the Amazon in 1997. Today she is working with indigenous tribes in the sacred headwater region of the Amazon River and has been taking three or four trips each year to the region. Her work is with the Pachamama Alliance, supporting land rights and native resilience in the face of encroaching development. She said her work is "primarily spiritual" in nature and takes place within wide-ranging practices in her efforts to ensure native sovereignty.

Looking back on those years, I can now appreciate how the early inquiring spirit of my youth yielded such amazing relationships. The search for truth through new experiences was so deeply embedded in my psyche that I never questioned its source, only wanting to probe its deepest secrets. I moved early on from a dependence on traditional religious values to an inner acceptance of what I now call our collective universal destiny within a conscious universe. This is different than the conventional notion of God as a man sitting on a cloud.

Thanks to IONS, I was exposed to thinkers like David Bohm, whose books I read for their expansive and provocative ideas about precognition and nonlocal consciousness. As a physicist, he had a great impact on my thinking and the development of holographic philosophy. Another innovative thinker who impacted my beliefs was Rupert Sheldrake, a Cambridge University biologist. His books propose that the scientific record is very much a work in progress and its laws are never static. The Big Bang theory of how the universe came into being all at once was only posited in the 1960s, he reminds us. We have been led to believe that the laws of the universe are static and universal, but Sheldrake proposes that these laws evolve. He also introduced the idea that every species has its own energy pattern, which evolves when necessary to meet adjustments to life on Earth. For Sheldrake, the evolution of these patterns for humans, animals, plants, or any living organism is a field of energy, which he terms a "morphic resonance," or changing energy pattern. Ideas and theories such as these can make sense of the extraordinary connections that underlie our relationships and sometimes defy rational thinking.

I believe there is something directing the evolution of the universe that we may never fully understand. Who knows what might be considered "scientific truth" in the generations to come? I do believe there is a life force that resides within us and the rest of the universe, ever present and evolving. Religions tend to put human beings first, but I have come to consider us merely a small part of the web of life. Think of the many miracles surrounding us; no one has yet fully explained the homing instincts of some animals, for example, or how butterflies migrate over several generations and through multiple life stages back to the same spot, why some people are drawn to one another's ideas as though they already understand one another, or how two sisters driving cars on the same night far from home would nearly simultaneously roll their cars and nearly lose their lives but for their seat belt choices.

Surely, more answers will come, but the universal energy of which I speak can only become known to those who seek and find the ability to give of themselves, quieting the ego and communicating with the collective consciousness, trusting ourselves to the energy of this greater power for guidance. The intuitions we so often feel could be related to all the souls that have gone before us and, thus, to the collective soul of the conscious universe. There is so much of value that comes from beyond us through the soul and psyche, and not through the rational mind.

There will always be mysteries. But when seeking answers, I have found that it is possible to communicate with something outside myself, through meditation or by walking in nature. We all will find our own ways of communicating. All of our education and rational thinking are important, but those spontaneous "aha!" moments bring answers as though from a mysterious source. Was this spiritual consciousness here from the beginning? Was it there when I was staring at the colorful airplanes while clinging to the airport's chain link fence when I was three years old? Yes. But my sense of wonder was then just beginning to lead me toward explanations that make rational sense of the world. We must guarantee as well that humanity carries forward our amazing human inventions through intuition and creativity. Science will only continue to create and succeed if it does not remove our basic sense of wonder at the miracle of existence and the vast universal consciousness of human minds.

While we are on planet Earth, we are part of this universal energy and can connect with it and participate with it. We can recognize it, feel it, enjoy its mystery and power, accept its guidance, and evolve with it. It is all around us, here before us, and here forever after us in its own evolution.

CHAPTER FORTY-ONE

AN OLYMPIC RETURN TO SUN VALLEY

WITH THE REST OF MY CHILDREN AWAY AT SCHOOL, Christin remained in Sun Valley to train and travel to compete on the World Cup ski racing circuit. She often stayed as a guest for weeks at a time at the home of physician Richard Steadman and his wife Gay in Lake Tahoe. While she was there with other injured racers, they named themselves the Tahoe Fracture Team because they were the early guinea pigs for Steadman's progressive surgical and rehabilitation methods. His revolutionary rehab protocols changed the understanding of ski injury recovery, including those injuries that at one time would have ended a racing career.

Richard Steadman, or "Steady," as he was known, founded the US Ski Team's medical pool in the 1970s. From that pool, a doctor would travel on his own finances to a ski training camp in Chile, New Zealand, or elsewhere and then be financed by the US Ski Team for his time and travel to major events like the Olympics or the World Championships. Physicians rotated throughout the season for this coveted position. Dr. Steadman was the attending physician when Christin broke her ankle in Portillo, Chile, in 1977. He accompanied her home for surgery and then welcomed her into his home for recuperation. Christin became part of the group of recovering ski racers who named themselves the Grateful Steadys and who came together in 2016 for an appreciation bash in Vail, Colorado. It was a massive tribute from athletes and the medical community to honor this orthopedic wizard and pioneer in his retirement.

Dr. Steadman was committed to the whole patient, not just the injury—a philosophy that left a lasting impact on sports medicine and particularly on the US Ski Team. He left Tahoe in 1990 following a generous offer from Vail Associates to provide him with support facilities, and so the original Steadman Clinic was founded. The clinic eventually added the Steadman Philippon Research Institute, both of which ultimately became part of the fifty-nine-thousand-square-foot Vail Medical Center.

Another man came from France to help make sports history in Sun Valley. In 1978, having made his home in Sun Valley, Michel Rudigoz was hired away to coach the US Men's Team. One of his charges was Sun Valley's Pete Patterson, who won a bronze medal in the 1978 World Championships under Michel's guidance.

Following the 1980 Lake Placid Olympics, Michel became head coach of the women's team, with a roster of talented athletes considered capable of winning at the highest levels of competition. My daughter Christin became an important member of that women's team, her rise coming after the badly broken ankle she suffered while training at her first US Ski Team camp in Chile at the age of seventeen. In 1980, at age twenty, she made her first Olympic Team, and Bill and I traveled to Lake Placid to cheer her on.

What a spectacular time that was for America. We were able to get tickets for the hockey finals between Russia and the United States, probably because no one expected it to be the game of the century. We feared for our lives when the crowd in attendance jumped up and down on the wooden platform bleachers that swayed with excitement for the US team about to win the match. US speed skater Eric Heiden won a record five gold medals on the downtown open-air rink; Phil Mahre won silver in the slalom behind the legendary Ingemar Stenmark of

Sweden; and Christin, taking seventh in the giant slalom and eighth in the slalom, was the top American finisher in both events.

By 1982, with Michel at the helm of a talented and determined US women's squad, Christin was in top form. That season, she won two World Cup races and three medals at the World Championships in Schladming, Austria, the first American skier in history, male or female, to accomplish the feat. She remains today the only female American skier to have done it. Under Michel's leadership, the team also won that year's Nation's Cup by amassing more World Cup points than any other country. Michel often remarked on what a feat that was, especially against the Austrians, Italians, Germans, and Swiss. No US team, male or female, has managed it since. "It was a very emotional moment for me," Michel told me recently. "They trained hard and were a powerful team."

In *The Story of Modern Skiing*, author John Fry described Rudigoz's coaching style as "a combination of athletic trainer, psychologist, Solomon, den mother, and happy time coordinator." That mix served to create what Fry described as "the greatest US Women's Ski Team of all time."

Michel and Christin's careers ascended in tandem and reached their pinnacle together at the 1984 Winter Olympic Games in Sarajevo. Bill and I had previously taken several trips to Europe for Christin's ski races and championships. Exactly twelve months before the 1984 Winter Games, we were in Les Diablerets, Switzerland, watching a World Cup downhill training run from our hotel balcony when we saw a racer fly off course and crash in spectacular fashion. It turned out to be Christin. Her season-ending crash resulted in a compression fracture to her left knee requiring a bone graft from her hip.

Recovering in time to be in form for the Olympics was far from guaranteed, but Christin was determined and focused, training harder than I had ever seen her train before. She never doubted that she would make the Olympic Team. A group of us traveled together to support her and the US team in Sarajevo. It was so different from the Lake Placid Games. Sarajevo's citizens were asked to ration their limited electricity, with the city turning off their electricity at nightfall for the benefit of visitors to the games, and residents contributed their food coupons for our use. The hotels were so poorly built that we could hear everything through the walls until two in the morning, when the dance music on the ground floor ended. But the Yugoslavian people were so gracious. They wanted their Olympics to be a success and gave everything they had to the world, including their milk and meat coupons, so that we could enjoy ourselves. It made us sad, but they were so insistent that we could not refuse.

For Christin's slalom event, the mountain was fogged in. She should have won it—the slalom was her stronger event at the time. Instead, she won silver in the giant slalom, just .40 seconds behind her teammate, Debbie Armstrong, who was a surprise winner of the gold. US teammate Tamara McKinney nearly made it a US medal sweep, missing bronze by only.43 seconds behind French skier Perrine Pelen. Christin won the first run, and Tamara the second, but Debbie was consistent enough over two runs to become the Olympic champion. It was an extraordinary showing for the team—especially with Bill Johnson winning gold in the downhill event and the twins, Phil and Steve Mahre, taking gold and silver in the men's slalom. It was a record medal haul for the United States.

Christin had competed in five Alpine World Cups, winning five World Cup races in three disciplines. She competed in the Olympic Winter Games of 1980 and 1984 and the World Championships of 1978 and 1982. She was the first American skier to win three medals in a single Worlds competition—a bronze and two silver medals in the 1982 World Championships. As of 2016, this feat was unmatched by any other female US skier.

The Wood River Valley turned out to welcome Michel and Christin back to town at the end of the World Cup season with a parade and celebration unlike any other ever planned in Sun Valley. The local coach-turned-hero and his local-junior-star-turned-Olympic-medalist rode in a convertible through the Sun Valley Mall to the Challenger Inn, where a boisterous crowd was waiting. It seemed the entire town was there. A man in a Ronald Reagan mask took to the stage, surely to remind everyone of Christin's infamous phone call with the president after her win. She had answered irreverently with, "Hi Ronnie," instead of, "Hello, Mr. President," which amused her fans to no end but angered more than a few American "patriots."

Mayor Ruthie Lieder was on stage to see Christin presented with a sign renaming a Bald Mountain run in her honor. Christin's Silver run would memorialize her achievements from then on. Nearby on Seattle Ridge is Gretchen's Gold run, celebrating the career of another Sun Valley legend, 1948 Olympic champion Gretchen Fraser, the first American skier to win an Olympic medal and my good friend. In 2019, two life-sized bronze sculptures were installed at Festival Meadows on Sun Valley Road, celebrating two of the community's legendary women skiers—Christin and Gretchen, who was always a mentor for Christin. During the unveiling ceremony, Christin said it was appropriate that Gretchen's statue stand quite a bit taller than hers since she "always looked up to her and is proud to be forever carving in her shadow."

After the 1984 Winter Olympics, Michel started Michel's Restaurant in Trail Creek Village, bringing all of his French culinary expertise from his home city of Lyon back to Ketchum. Some years later, he moved into the classic Christiana Bar and Restaurant. There, at Michel's Olympic Bar, the walls are covered with framed photos of Michel and his many famous charges, including Christin and her teammates. For more than thirty years, it has been a gathering place for the community and countless visiting champions and skiing families with connections to international competitions.

PART VII

Wisdom of the Wilderness

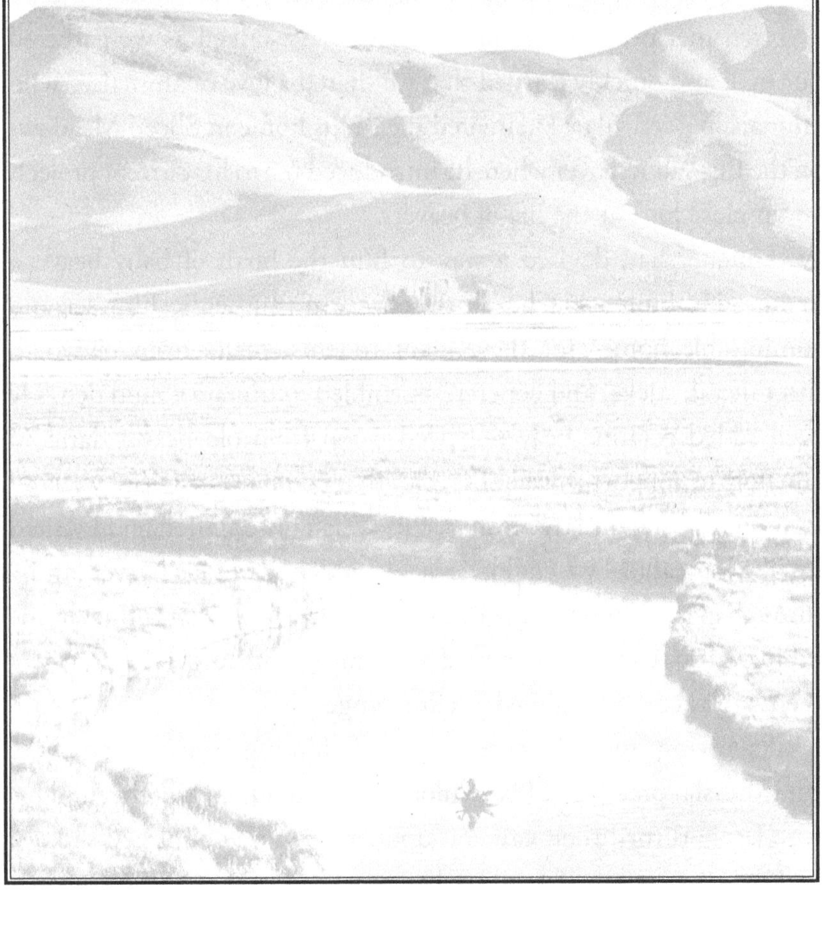

CHAPTER FORTY-TWO

Living Among Wolves

I first met Jim Dutcher at the Sun Valley Post Office, where I often met people from around town. We talked as we gathered our mail and quickly learned that we shared a love of animals—wild animals in particular. He invited me to his home in Sheep Meadows on the Big Wood River where he introduced me to his current project, an up-close look at the life of beavers.

Dutcher had devised a way to film the birth of baby beavers, or kits. He built what he described as an "authentic film set and comfortable home" for these giant rodents, made from plywood, sheet metal, sticks, and concrete assembled to imitate a mud den. He even added genuine beaver-chewed wood from old beaver dams in an effort to support this vital species that could create entire wetland ecosystems using its large front teeth. When my children and I visited his "beaver cabin," we could view the hidden life of his beaver family through glass windows. The beavers waddled through a tunnel in the cabin wall out into an enclosed swimming and feeding area where their habits could be filmed at close range.

Following several more years of filming cougars and the controversial practice of Idaho mountain lion hunts, Dutcher and his wife Jamie turned their cameras upon a far more politicized species. In 1972, the gray wolf was listed as protected under the Endangered

Species Act. By that time, the gray wolf, which had once inhabited much of North America from the Canadian Arctic to Central Mexico, had been almost eliminated. In the late 1860s, hunters known as "wolfers" laced carcasses of bison with strychnine, killing a thousand wolves each winter. Livestock owners lobbied state governments to continue killing wolves to protect livestock. Bounties were paid for dead wolves. In 1995, the US Fish and Wildlife Service produced a recovery plan for wolves that would introduce sixty-six wolves to Central Idaho and Yellowstone National Park. Dutcher served as a consultant to the gray wolf reintroduction project for the design of holding enclosures for the fourteen wolves brought to Yellowstone from Canada. The enclosures were necessary to ensure that the reintroduced wolves would not immediately return to Alberta. "At that time, there were only fifteen wolves in all of the western states," Jim said.

Jamie was the perfect partner for Jim Dutcher. She began her career as an assistant in the hospital of the National Zoo in Washington, DC. She and Jim later led three National Geographic expeditions to Alaska, joining revered wolf biologist Gordon Haber to study the social lives of wolves. In 1990, five years before the first reintroduction of wolves into Idaho, the Dutchers obtained a special use permit from the US Forest Service to set up a tented camp within a twenty-five-acre enclosure to study and film a pack of wolves. The Dutchers adopted a family of wolf pups, bottle feeding them from the moment they opened their eyes so that they could establish a relationship of trust. The pups had been born to captive parents that were part of a research study in Montana.

It was a true privilege to bring my grandchildren to the Dutcher home and for them to be able to hold and cuddle the pups. It was a unique experience that increased my grandchildren's understanding and appreciation of wildlife and the value it brings to the Wood River Valley and the Sawtooth Mountains. During those years, I joined the board of Living with Wolves, a nonprofit formed by the Dutchers, meeting at their home late into the evening for long discussions about maintaining and funding wolf reintroduction strategies.

I was already familiar with Jim's early reputation as an underwater filmmaker who produced educational films about coral reefs, sea turtles, and other sea creatures in the Caribbean. When he came to take on the wolf project, he confessed to me that he was nervous about speaking to an audience, which was part of his job as an advocate. Jim recalled for me those years of my support, especially after I introduced him to Governor Cecil Andrus, who took an interest in the environmental documentaries the Dutchers were producing. "I appreciated your belief in me," Jim said. "You financially supported us, but even more importantly, you supported us with encouragement and connections to the community."

When the wolf pups grew too large for the enclosure at the house, the Dutchers moved them to a secret, hidden enclosure in the Sawtooth Mountains. There, they had erected a sturdy, winterized yurt on stilts above the wolves' living area. When Cameron and I were invited to visit, we jumped at the invitation. One subzero winter day in 1995, we drove to the specified parking area on Highway 75 and waited for the Dutchers to arrive on their snowmobiles and take us to the hidden enclosure.

When I say that the Dutchers were living with the wolves, I mean exactly that. They were truly camping within the enclosure, with the wolves all around them, howling day and night to one another with no fear or mistrust of the humans living with them. We enjoyed lunch and then were instructed how to meet the wolf pack in order to be accepted. We crouched low to appear deferential in the presence of Kamots, the alpha male, who approached us warily. In our crouched positions, they were as tall as we were. We quickly learned that a wolf greets a person by licking every inch of their face, just as they greet each other. Jamie Dutcher described this greeting as "a warm, fluffy tornado of tongues."

Cam and I adjusted by keeping our mouths closed, which was difficult because we were having so much fun that we were giggling aloud. After this energetic greeting, Kamots climbed onto Cam's shoulders. Only Cam was strong enough to sustain such weight. After we passed muster with mighty Kamots, the rest of the wolves also wanted to meet us. I retreated so as not to end up flattened on the snow with licking wolves all over me. During the six years of their unprecedented experience of living with the wolves, the Dutchers produced three prime time documentaries for the American Broadcasting Company (ABC) and the Discovery Channel. The films won three Emmy Awards, and their story was covered by more than two hundred media outlets around the world, including the *Today Show, Good Morning America, Dateline*, and the British Broadcasting Company. Their mission has been to spread information about the wolf's social and caring family behavior and its importance as a keystone predator species in the environment. The Dutchers went on to write eight books about wolves, and their films continue to circle the Earth. They give presentations and tell their story worldwide.

"We would have preferred that the wolves that were reintroduced to Idaho could have come back naturally instead of being captured in Canada," Jim told me recently. "That way, the recovery of wolves would have kept their protection as an endangered species, and they would not be hunted as they are now. The current wolf population in Idaho has yet to become a sustainable population."

In 1994, I nominated Jim Dutcher for the Take Pride in Idaho award, which he won. He went on to serve on the wolf introduction oversight committee for five years. When it came time to end the Sawtooth wolf project, I aided in the creation and funding of a new educational foundation to continue the Dutchers' work by creating a permanent home for the pack on Nez Perce tribal land to the north. The Nez Perce had supported wolf reintroduction at a time when the state of Idaho refused to adhere to the federal mandate. Jim and Jamie tell of a visit they paid to the pack a few years later on tribal land and their amazement that the wolves responded to their calls. The pack came running out of the forestlands and jumped on them, happily licking them with their memories. "At the end of the project, we couldn't set the wolves free," Jamie said. "It would have been illegal and unethical. By giving us their trust, the pack had lost the one thing crucial to their survival: a fear of humans."

In 2005, the Dutchers set aside their filmmaking gear and created the nonprofit Living with Wolves, which now demands all of their time. The organization was groundbreaking in its study of wolves and wolf habitat as well as its mission—finding solutions for wolves' coexistence with humans. I was invited to become an advisor to that organization, and I readily accepted. My friendship with the Dutchers has been a highlight of my life. It brought me a reward I never felt possible, an opportunity to return to the wild a top predator that is essential to a balanced ecosystem.

I entered into this amazing experience believing in the mission from the beginning but never envisioning the extent to which it would become accepted and the impact this educational opportunity would end up having on our country. Young people, especially, understand that the social family behavior of a wolf pack is no different from the caring and interdependence of the human family. I believe there are many more connections between us and the nonhuman world that are not yet accepted by humanity or science.

My own family's bonds have remained strong through the years, despite many challenges and surprises. In 1980, Bill suffered another heart attack and was told that he would need to undergo bypass surgery, so we started making plans for it and the weeks of recovery to follow in Los Angeles. We could not leave before the coming weekend, as Candy was to be married.

The Western-themed ceremony and party were planned at Trail

Creek Cabin, and the entire family had rented costumes from a costume shop in Boise. Sun Valley Resort and the Holding family supported us in every way. We entered the Trail Creek picnic grounds in a restored Sun Valley carriage drawn by draft horses. Stepping down from the carriage in our flowing Western dresses, we made a perfect entrance. The French chef hired by the Holdings had prepared a Western barbeque feast. The contemporary band had everyone hotfooting it, except for Bill and me. The doctor had given Bill strict instructions not to dance, not to do anything that might raise his heart rate. We were advised to live more carefully now and acknowledge how precious our days together had become. If only we could carry this perspective every day of our lives.

CHAPTER FORTY-THREE

The Nature Conservancy

I WAS DEEPLY INVOLVED with the creation of the Sun Valley Center for the Arts and Humanities during the early 1970s when Bill first asked me to join an organization that was dedicated to preserving local wetlands, streams, and ranches for future generations. The Nature Conservancy provided an opportunity for me to pursue my passion for environmental conservation and led to a new chapter in my life filled with organized team building and studies of the natural sciences.

The years that followed were filled with adventures to wild places around Idaho, across the United States, and around the world—extraordinary places that deserve our attention and care. Bill and I had always loved wilderness travel, but our plans for these adventures seemed to come to a halt in the mid 1980s, when our lives took an abrupt spiral out of control. This was when Bill was diagnosed with nodular lymphoma, a slowly advancing disease that could only be contained with chemotherapy and surgeries. The disease would periodically scatter through his neck, abdomen and groin, where lymph glands work to fight infections. I might never have known the severity of his prognosis had Marian French, Bill's secretary, not told me of it following a surgery to remove a growth from Bill's groin.

For Bill, the malignancy discovered by his doctors simply did not exist. He seemed not to believe it was a threat and decided to lead his life as he always had, with bravado, intensity, and enthusiasm. After all, we had already hiked some of the highest mountain passes in the Himalayas. We had many more plans for such adventures, and Bill was committed to continued travel in his remaining years. It made no difference to him whether he was feeling weak or unable to hike or bike as fast as he once had. He always pushed on.

In 1993, I took up the offer to join the Idaho Nature Conservancy board. By then, I knew that if you really want to make sense of this world, you have to see it in all its natural glory. I was blessed to have lived in proximity to vast open spaces all my life, whether it was on the edge of an ocean or beside a mountain wilderness. I am grateful for the peace provided by this universal legacy to mankind and remain committed to the path of honoring and preserving untrammeled regions of the natural world so that others can experience them well into the future.

The wisdom of the wilderness can be elusive, but how can someone not be moved by a forest, standing proudly through ages that predate the human race? The trees, animals, and other creatures in this forest have endured through many evolutions and devastations on this ever-transforming planet. They can convey secrets if we listen. Wilderness provides a safe place for wisdom to emerge. When we enter a forest and follow a trail deep into the woods, perhaps it is the silence that brings answers. Thoughts emerge from one's inner being in proportion to the vast unfolding universe. I always exit the forest with renewed understanding and perspective.

My entry into the world of environmental conservation began with an awe of nature and led to a dedication to service. I told Bill that I was ready for this new commitment, not knowing how long it would last. It turned out to be a deeply rewarding part of my life for the next twenty years. I chaired the Idaho TNC for eight years before serving on its National Board of Governors for eight years, until 2005. After five years away, I so missed working on TNC's conservation mission that I rejoined the Idaho state board from 2010 until 2016.

The Nature Conservancy was the first land trust in the United States, founded in 1951 by a group of individuals to protect environmental assets they shared in common. For years, a group of scholars and private individuals had been seeking a way to preserve ecologically sensitive areas. The very first conservation project was organized in 1954 to protect a forty-acre wooded ravine in New York from development. The neighbors pitched in to buy it to keep it safe from development in perpetuity.

The Idaho Chapter of The Nature Conservancy was founded in 1965 by a group of students, professors, and community volunteers in Moscow, Idaho. For its first twelve years, they had no paid staff but succeeded in preserving small but ecologically significant areas from development—like Idler's Rest, a growth of old cedar trees on Moscow Mountain, which was a popular recreation area for University of Idaho students and faculty. What began as a local concern for many state TNC chapters such as ours eventually led to a broader mission to "work locally but think globally." This remains one of the mantras for Idaho TNC, which has expanded from preserving local sites that were too often over-loved and overused to a wider conservation perspective on entire ecoregions.

Starting in the mid 1980s, Terry Ring, owner of Silver Creek Outfitters in Ketchum, served on Idaho's TNC board for eighteen years, including six years as chairman. After attending Boise State University, he had come to the valley in the 1970s, when Ketchum was still a very small town. "At that time, you dialed just four numbers to call anyone in town," Terry remembered. "If you got the wrong number, whoever answered would likely know the number of the person you were trying to reach. And those four numbers you used for your phone number were the same four numbers you used for your credit account at Atkinsons' Market."

Terry was the youngest member of the board when he joined and was still the youngest when he left the board. Other members included Bob Hansberger of Boise Cascade; Bob Lane of West One Bank; Jack Hemingway, who was then on the Idaho Fish and Game Commission; Jim Bruce of Idaho Power; and Boise businessman and planner Pete O'Neil. "There was no owners' manual about how to do this," Terry recalled. "We started out like cowboys, shooting from the hip, and then scaled up. I was a young guy with a fly shop and felt so lucky to meet so many people and learn so much—people like Don and Gretchen Fraser and Clara Spiegel, who came to the valley in 1939 with two young children, and, of course, Bill Janss."

Terry bought Silver Creek Outfitters with a partner from Dick Alfs Fly Shop in 1980 and has been the managing partner ever since. He met Bill soon after the Janss Corporation purchased Sun Valley Resort. "Bill came into the shop to buy some flies. I was only twenty-three years old, but he was very interested in what I was doing," Terry said. "He asked where I was from and what my plans were. He wrote details on his arm with a ballpoint pen to remember things. He was eager to give advice."

In the early days, the TNC's goals could have been as simple as protecting a creek that ran though everyone's backyards, said Terry. He said he knew the Idaho TNC would resonate in a generous community like the Wood River Valley, where nonprofits played a huge role. One of the many things the Janss Corporation provided to the community was a donation of land for Our Lady of the Snows Catholic Church on Sun Valley Road, in memory of John F. Kennedy.

TNC provided a pragmatic approach and the legal tools necessary to pursue environmental conservation projects. Over the years, Terry became involved in creative ideas and visited places like Ritter Island near Hagerman, where TNC would one day preserve some of the last undeveloped areas of Thousand Springs. This is where an ancient underground aquifer pours out of a cliff in waterfalls into the Snake River.

Lou Lunte recently stepped down from his position as Idaho TNC deputy director; he has been with the Idaho chapter for thirty-four years, our longest-serving staff member. He provided invaluable details to back up my vague memories of the organization's early years. He and his wife Cindy became Silver Creek Preserve comanagers in July 1988. Lou has served Idaho TNC in a variety of positions, including five times as interim executive director. The Luntes have returned happily to their original job managing Silver Creek Preserve. Cindy is Lou's "full-time volunteer," and they now take winters off.

Lou recalled, it was in 1975 that Bill Janss was approached by Jack Hemingway, who had become concerned about the deteriorating condition of Silver Creek, a world-renowned trout fishery that flowed from a perennial spring about twenty-five miles south of Sun Valley. Jack's father, Ernest Hemingway, had fished there, along with Gary Cooper and other celebrities who fished and hunted waterfowl with the Purdy family of Picabo during the earliest days of the Sun Valley Resort.

In the 1960s, Silver Creek existed within a cattle ranch that partly belonged to Sun Valley Resort under its ownership by Union Pacific. The railroad company had purchased 480 acres many years earlier, when it had a train station at the nearby Hayspur Fish Hatchery. During the summer, anglers on their way to Ketchum and Sun Valley could disembark at Hayspur to fish. Trains were discontinued in 1964, the same year the Janss Investment Company purchased the resort along with Stalker Creek, otherwise known as Stocker Creek. This area eventually became part of the Silver Creek Preserve.

Due to competing ranching interests in the area, Silver Creek was in a deteriorated condition by 1975; grazing cattle churned the creek banks to mud where they entered the stream to drink. Jack had grown up fishing Silver Creek. His first thought was to designate it as an Idaho Fish and Game Wildlife management area. But he knew from experience that this would not be the best option since the Fish and Game Department's plan to build campsites and open more access routes into the area would jeopardize Silver Creek's fragile ecology. Jack also knew that the partisan nature of state agencies could make the area vulnerable to unanticipated changes in state politics.

The fragile ecology I describe reflects the unique spring-fed stream of Silver Creek, a treasure of wandering crystal-clear waters that originate from an aquifer somewhere under the desert around Picabo. Its abundance of wildlife includes eagles, hawks, songbirds, waterfowl, coyotes, bobcats, mountain lions, deer, moose, and elk. The aquatic system at Silver Creek boasts one of the highest densities of stream insects in North America, and over 150 species of birds have been identified there. Brown trout in the stream grow to enormous size and attract anglers from afar.

Jack Hemingway asked the Idaho TNC for help in approaching Bill Janss, who by 1968 had purchased the Sun Valley Resort and its holdings near Silver Creek from his family's development company. Bill agreed to sell the property for conservation purposes at a bargain price of $500,000. The few lots that had already sold on the land reflected its potential for real estate development. A great deal more money could have been made by developing the ranch, and although this had been the mission and policy of the Janss Company for three generations, Bill was committed to conservation at Silver Creek and did not hesitate in his decision. Jack later asked Bill who should be invited to join the Idaho TNC board, and he responded, "Why don't you ask my wife, Glenn?"

From his contacts, Jack was able to raise $300,000 of the purchase price in just a few weeks. The rest came from Idaho TNC donors, including devoted fishermen who wanted to preserve this prized fishing venue. The largest gift came from a surprising donor:

the Boise Cascade lumber company, which contributed $100,000 toward the purchase thanks to the company's CEO, John Fery, and his passion for the area. Fery later built a home on Fairway Drive, near our house, and spent his retirement years in the valley. These days, his son Bruce Fery is the overall manager of the Sinclair resorts, including the Sun Valley Resort.

In its early years, the Idaho TNC had to depend on expertise from the San Francisco and Portland TNC offices, which had more experience with conservation easements, the legal and financial tools used for compensating landowners in exchange for suspending development rights on all or portions of a property in perpetuity. The TNC mission is a simple and far-reaching one—"to conserve the lands and waters on which all life depends."

I recall the visits of Spencer Beebe from Portland and Henry Little, TNC's western field representative from San Francisco. Little moved to Ketchum to guide our local chapter until we had our own staff. Over his two years in residence in the Wood River Valley, he became a close and admired friend. As with so many loyal staff members, he remained with the organization until retirement, including his years at the national office, or what would later be referred to as Global TNC.

Spencer Beebe was a Peace Corps veteran and Yale Forestry School graduate who played an important role in events that followed at Silver Creek and beyond. After fourteen years with TNC, Beebe went on to found Conservation International in 1987. Author Ernest Schwiebert has written about the day at Silver Creek in 1980 when Spencer and Bill shook hands, sealing the agreement that Sun Valley would sell its Silver Creek holdings to the TNC. "Few who knew us well would believe that we did not fish Silver Creek that day, although [Jack] Hemingway's tan Peugeot was stuffed with our fishing gear," wrote Schwiebert.

In later years, the Idaho TNC gave the local Wood River

Land Trust its first conservation easement at Lake Creek, north of Ketchum. In this way, TNC delegated conservation successes to other organizations with similar local goals so that it could move on to use its financial resources for other important projects around the state.

In 1979, the Idaho TNC hired Guy Bonnivier, a true outdoorsman and conservationist who remained on staff for twenty years. He was originally hired as a carpenter to build a two-room dual-purpose visitors' center and caretaker's cabin at Silver Creek, but he proved to be effective in many other ways.

Despite what we considered to be broad community support for the Silver Creek project, the local ranchers, our neighbors, did not yet want to work with TNC; they did not trust the goals of a conservation organization and feared the recommendations for change that our presence portended. Guy built trust with these neighbors and also became a confidant of John Fell Stevenson, a son of American diplomat and politician Adlai Stevenson. John owned a large cattle ranch to the west of Silver Creek, and he helped Guy fence the cattle out of the riparian areas that fed into the Silver Creek Preserve. This process of patiently working with farmers and ranchers over time and gaining their trust in our ecologically beneficial methods has proved to be an invaluable approach.

Guy also became friends with the owners of the nearby 840-acre Stocker Creek Rod and Gun Club. There were eight partners in the club, Bill Janss being one, along with Gretchen and Don Fraser, Jim and Harriet Barnett, and the Wynn Gray family. Together, we enjoyed a small, rustic clubhouse where we could sign up for a weekend stay. Guy struck a deal to buy this clubhouse from the partners. To fund the project, 440 acres of Silver Creek were sold to adjacent ranchers and some of the gun club owners contributed part of their interest toward the organization's conservation goals. Bill, the Barnetts, and the Frasers retained a membership, providing us continued use of the cabin.

Guy was the first Silver Creek Preserve manager. His success was noted by the TNC board when he was later appointed its first state director. He introduced changes to the board and the eventual relocation of the state office from Boise to the Ketchum area. This move was not supported by all trustees. Some resigned. One board member stopped supporting TNC for the twenty years that Guy served as director. The year that he left in 1988, this member gave $1 million toward the protection of Box Canyon near Wendell, Idaho. This is an indication of the significance of personal relationships in nonprofits. The Idaho TNC has now protected more than ten thousand acres in the state through conservation easements.

The new board eventually settled in. Guy's friendship with Mary Hemingway resulted in the eventual gift of the Hemingway House north of Ketchum to the Idaho TNC, with stipulations that the surrounding acreage become a preserve and the house never be sold. The house that Ernest and Mary once called home became the TNC staff offices and Guy's residence. It was there that Lou Lunte first came to apply for a job, dressed in a suit and tie and looking very professional. He found that the job would be somewhat more casual. "I knocked on the door, and down the stairs came Guy wearing shorts and no shirt, surrounded by his dogs," Lou recalled.

The restoration and resource management work on Silver Creek continues to this day. We had to have patience, but within twenty years we slowly influenced many landowners to provide conservation easements on their land and fence out cattle. Silver Creek is a key example of how land donations and the purchase of conservation easements along stream banks can be effective. Silver Creek Preserve is considered to be one of the most successful private stream restoration efforts ever undertaken for public benefit and reflects the importance of TNC being an owner with a voice that can speak with experience. It remains the largest project ever undertaken by Idaho

TNC and now covers 874 acres along Silver Creek. The Fish and Game Department has been an important resource for the funding of the continuing restoration work at Silver Creek Preserve. Ranchers like John Fell Stevenson became loyal supporters for research on innovative farming methods in the area. In 2003, Idaho TNC hosted the Silver Creek Symposium, which gathered experts in water and fishery habitat to share what they knew about the creek and how to plan for the future.

The Idaho TNC is now a fully staffed and effective organization, but when I became chair in 1994, I found the organization crying out for just that—some organization. The chapter had yet to adopt formal bylaws and set the terms for board service. After fulfilling these requirements, it was important to establish the essential committees to support the staff: an executive committee, finance committee, nominating committee, and development committee. These were skills I learned from founding other nonprofit organizations.

The chapter was soon growing rapidly, with projects all over the state, including Thousand Springs near Hagerman, the South Fork of the Snake River, the Flat Ranch on Henry's Fork, the Forty-five Ranch in the Owyhee Canyonlands, Garden Creek in Hell's Canyon, and Cougar Bay on Lake Coeur d'Alene. During my tenure as chair, we acquired or preserved all of these. With my former fund-raising experience, I was able to work closely with Guy Bonnivier to seek out donors. Traveling all over the state to raise funds, we rapidly learned that the ideal scenario was to find a willing donor close to a designated TNC project.

I learned a great deal about our state beyond the Wood River Valley and was delighted to work with staff to plan board meetings and bring our trustees to project sites. We had many key and influential board members during that time. One in particular was Laird Noh. His family had created the Noh Sheep Company in the Magic Valley area in 1912, and Laird ran it for thirty-five years, in between serving as an Idaho state senator and chairing the Idaho Senate's Resources and Environmental Committee. Laird was a respected member of the Idaho Legislature and a respected sheep rancher in Southeast Idaho. There were few such legislators who had any background or interest in environmental issues at the time. He introduced rotational grazing on his ranch, which highlighted the benefits TNC had found in allowing grazing areas to rebound periodically. Laird also provided invaluable experience with government and conservation policies, moving the political base toward a recognition of the value of forests, open spaces, farmlands, and wildlife habitat for their recreational potential.

Under my board tenure, the Flat Ranch was our last acquisition, and the staff and I wanted to schedule a trustee meeting there so the board could have a firsthand experience of its beauty, importance, and conservation significance. This acquisition would reflect our policy of owning a property that we could restore, thereby setting an example for new methods of farming that provided a simultaneous renewal of habitat in and near spring-fed streams. We wanted to demonstrate how our proven techniques, like rotational grazing, would benefit the land's production and cattle health and weight, and therefore be profitable to the rancher. The 1,600-acre Flat Ranch was also strategic because of its nearness to other ranchers we hoped to impress with our grazing practices. A working cattle ranch, it was close to habitat that the TNC wanted to preserve near Yellowstone National Park.

At that time, there were no buildings on the Idaho TNC's Flat Ranch land for a board and staff meeting. We had acquired a cabin on an adjacent property in a beautiful location, with pines surrounding a large spring where moose would come to water. The cabin barely kept out the elements, and pack rats lived there, but we did some cleaning—everyone pitching in—and set up tables to welcome the twenty-five trustees and staff members for a meeting and a tour of the ranch. We never quite knew what creatures might join us during those early meetings in sometimes desolate landscapes.

Our board meetings were also scheduled in places where we needed more exposure to donors, including Boise, where Bob Lane, a former Idaho TNC chairman, invited us to use West One Bank's executive office suite, overlooking the capital city of Idaho. Receptions and events were planned there to introduce carefully selected people to our mission and plans for the state. In 1996, I was invited to take my efforts to a new level and join the TNC National Board of Governors. At this time, Bill was very sick with cancer and I knew I could not travel. Nevertheless, I accepted the invitation and said I would begin my service as soon as I could.

During those years, Bill and I were living through many challenges related to his illness. I have come to consider them as "blessed years" because we never knew how long they would last. We lived them in the realization that every moment we had together was precious. We joined a trip to Italy with the International Council of the Museum of Modern Art, a remarkable and extraordinary opportunity. We were to be granted access to art treasures not available to tourists, including a viewing of Leonard Da Vinci's *Last Supper,* which was then under restoration and closed to visitors. The plane ride overnight from New York to Milan seemed ordinary. I fell asleep and assumed that Bill was sleeping also. We taxied to the hotel and checked into our room, and only then did Bill admit to me that he had not been able to urinate during the entire journey. I called the hotel doctor, who examined Bill and admitted him to the hospital at once, telling me that I should follow later.

When I inquired of the front desk where the hospital was located, I was directed to take an elevator to the basement floor and walk in a tunnel under the street to a hospital across from the hotel. This strange passage led to a shock when I found the basement entrance hallway lined with stretchers and patients awaiting admission. I found Bill on a stretcher in this hallway, waiting for attention. After he was finally admitted to a room, I was allowed to join him. There were two doctors by his side, speaking in rapid Italian. There was no one I could ask for details. They implied with a diagram that they would release the urine, place a catheter for the trip home, but not perform surgery to remove the growth causing the pressure and painful blockage. They gave him a sedative for the night and said we should depart for home the next morning. Back at the Mollie Scott Clinic in Sun Valley, surgery removed the growth, and I hoped that would be the end of it.

We planned another trip to Italy, this time biking through Umbria, known for its tough rides through the hilly countryside. We had taken similar trips with Sun Valley biking buddies through the Veneto region and the Tuscan countryside. Bill and I decided to rent a country guesthouse for two weeks beforehand to just enjoy touring the quiet Italian countryside on our own. History repeated itself upon our arrival, with Bill suffering suddenly from severe abdominal pains. The owner of the property suggested I take him to the hospital immediately and gave me directions.

If only an ambulance had been an option. Finding my way in the dark of night through a deluge of heavy rain in the craze of Italian traffic left me close to tears. I stopped several times and in my limited Italian asked, "*Dove l'hospitale*?" Once in the emergency room, Bill was discovered to have another tumorous growth. They kept him for the night, and I returned for him the next day. They gave him strong medications, and we decided to cancel the biking tour but remain for the rest of our trip at the country house.

After returning home, we searched for unique but less physically demanding trips, ones that offered access to air flights and hospital care. Bill continued to approach trips with courage and determination. On the climb up a steep hill in the Canadian Rockies, he hiked slowly behind us. He did not want anyone to wait for him, saying he would meet us at the top and make it in his own time. On a bike ride in the hills of Burgundy or Tuscany, he would dismount his bike and push it up the hill amidst cheers from our companions.

These years were the final ten with Bill, a jumble of increasingly terrible periods countered by the best of hopeful outdoor adventures. Through our commitment to one another, I felt closest to him in those years. He blessed me every day with his presence in my life. Bill needed me and expressed his appreciation with each passing day. And I so needed him. He never indicated his needs, maintaining his courage in the face of this debilitating disease. We were able to hang on to one another and dwell in our love, which now seemed to reach back in our lives to the friendships between our families many years before.

The tragedies we had shared with one another also brought us closer together. Bill had lost his sister Patricia to an automobile accident. During our early years of marriage, he woke from nightmares during which he relived the tragedy of the house fire in which he lost of his daughter Kathy and his wife Anne suffered terrible burns and miscarried their unborn child.

Bill and I understood one another's emotional scars. We shared our losses with one another and supported each other through our pain. This man who had survived so much had earned my deep and constant love. He had proved himself a strong and dependable life companion. Despite whatever traumas might confront us, we overcame them together and became even more devoted companions. We enjoyed all of life's gifts together as one—our children, the arts, music, wine, good food, and a path of adventure. And now the reality was that our days together were coming to an end.

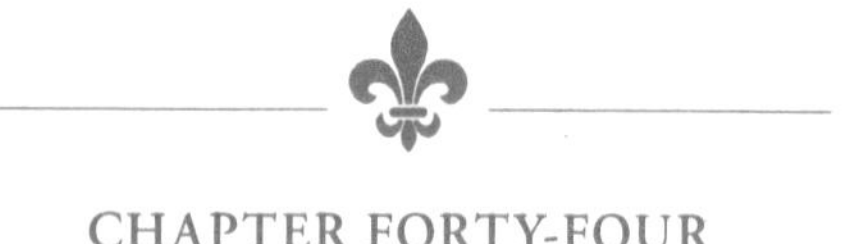

CHAPTER FORTY-FOUR

A Passage into Memory

Memories dissipate and evolve over time. They diverge in a multitude of ways, depending on who carries them. We want to be comfortable with our memories, yet even as we dare to covet them, they can carry such pain. Living through the last months with Bill as his cancer advanced was the most painful time in my life. I wrote in a journal to capture and interpret the feelings that I could not face immediately. Sometimes our souls must play catch-up with the more heartrending experiences in our lives.

Again, I would watch as this disease took my husband from me, staying by his side as his companion and nurse. There were no other choices for either of us. I had to participate deeply in whatever was to come. As I reread the journal I kept of the daily routines during that time, I am now reminded of the sense of unreality that accompanied me on my journey of farewell to someone I had been with for twenty-three years. It was a chaotic yet strangely ordinary period of time; heartbreaking, yet—like so many excruciating experiences—it held the potential for bringing out the deepest devotion.

As Bill fought against the disease that slowly took away his coordination, his determined rationality, and then his life, I wondered if his last memories flowed together, as mine do now, back through our extraordinary adventures: trekking to the Mustang District on the Tibetan Plateau, cycling through Provence with our Busterback Ranch treasure-hunting buddies, or sailing to distant ports with Harry and Diane Rinker on their yacht. Did his concerns revolve around his children and grandchildren, or the business legacy he would leave behind?

"I don't care if I ever see another Greek temple," Bill said one afternoon in southern Italy after I dragged him on yet another art adventure. He was living then on patience during the day and fine Sicilian wines at night. Did his mind flash on that close call with roadside bandits in Salerno who were after my Louis Vuitton luggage, or the sword-carrying horsemen in the Himalayas? At those times, life was suddenly more real and precious than it had been before the danger. Simple urgency has a way of turning life into a pure and unhindered blessing.

Our tastes for experiences didn't always match. But they did that day when Harry Rinker dropped anchor near a surf break in Costa Rica so that we could paddle over to ride the waves together, just Bill and me; and they did during any number of dinners when, in good company, we were laughing, dressing up, or telling stories. Bill and I were perfect partners. But after driving, rather than trekking, a fair portion of the Way of St. James in Spain and stopping routinely at my request to explore yet another sturdy architectural church masterpiece, Bill would sigh and say, "I will be just fine if I never see another Romanesque church." I wondered if Bill might have flashed on the day when we woke up in the Seychelles. I talked him into walking out nude onto the beach. He must have thought I was crazy. We got sunburned in places where one's body doesn't usually get sunburned and, as a result, were unable to celebrate our romantic holiday in the ways we had planned.

Our traveling companions always remembered Bill as having his head buried in the latest edition of the *International Herald Tribune* while sitting at a piazza café, preferring to study world news and business reports instead of murals and frescoes. At the castle of Chateau Židlochovice in the Czech Republic, we joined the seven-hundred-year hunting tradition at a pheasantry with the Rinkers and their carefully selected hunting guests. Driven by men and dogs, thousands of birds took flight above us. As the shots rang out, they fell in bunches all around me and at my feet, trembling in their last throes of life. I closed my eyes to shut out the picture of death. Soon there were endless rows of dead pheasant arranged carefully on blankets. I chose to leave this devastation and, with Maggie Wetzel, hired a guide to tour the region over the next few days. We had always enjoyed the luxury of choice.

Now, in this experience with Bill, there was no way to avoid the inevitable, even as I was bombarded by a slideshow of intimate experiences that assaulted me at will as my beloved's presence diminished before my eyes. To be in reality and unreality simultaneously took me back to the early Malibu years with my family when life was both real and surreal in its organized chaos; only some higher power or principle could ever make sense of it. The counsel of Wood River hospice director Carolyn Nystrom helped me accept the presence of both realms. Without this incredible lady and her gracious volunteers, I would have been denied the soulful experience of being there for Bill as he passed into memories. Thanks to her, I was able to accept the roiling emotions that persisted while remaining present for the man I loved.

Bill, in his gallant way, skied every day during that winter in 1996. He followed his usual routine of banging the boots on the fireplace, quickly downing breakfast, and then running through the usual checkout: "gloves, goggles, money clip, and ski pass," before he roared out the door to meet Pete Smith at the Warm Springs lift. The years had long since passed when the lift operators recognized him and called him by name. There was no longer any need to be first in line up the lift. And yet, a blast of wind seemed to carry him out the door, and then all would be silent. The two men would ski hard until noon. After that, Bill went to the office, then home for lunch and a nap. He loved that routine but complained of being very tired.

"But Bill, you are almost eighty—you should feel tired," I responded, which did not make him feel any better. We had been living those blessed years in which our children had grown and our grandchildren's lives were taking shape. The years of stress from business challenges had passed. We had been granted time to travel, enjoy our families, and reflect. Bill had lived in near-complete denial of his illness and yet often spoke of "putting his ducks in a row" and of the need to "do it right" at the end. He had required no surgeries or follow-up chemotherapy for two years, so we were hopeful that we might be seeing the end of this disease forever. It was magical thinking to ignore the earlier prognosis. That summer would be the most difficult season of my life because I had never accepted the possibility that Bill could actually succumb to cancer. I had drifted into denial because, after each surgical ordeal, he had always sprung back, regaining his energy and his ability to enter back into sports through sheer will and joie de vivre.

One night before going out, he complained about not being able to button his top shirt button. I shrugged it off with my usual positive outlook, suggesting the cleaners must not have replaced it in its correct spot. During a trip to Santa Fe and then New York, we visited Jane and Bill Pitcher, companions from the Snowmass development days. A swelling on Bill's neck had enlarged and seemed to resemble a spider bite. There were lots of bugs in the house, and so we both embraced that possibility—another case of wishful thinking.

During a dinner party given in our honor by my cousin Leslie Barclay and her husband Rutgers, I noticed that Bill was uncharacteristically quiet and avoided participating in the conversation and laughter. Perhaps he was bored, fatigued, or maybe just preoccupied. We flew on to New York from Santa Fe in late May to organize an art exhibit scheduled by John Berggruen in his San Francisco gallery to honor Bill's modernist expertise and reflect the insight and sensitivity represented in his art collection. We needed to inform art dealers in New York, such as Richard York, who had Bill's works on consignment. Richard had wanted the exhibition to premier in his gallery on the East Coast, but James Corcoran and John Berggruen had masterminded the arrangement for the show to open in California. Such were our concerns, which seem trivial now. I had begun to notice how much Bill's walking had slowed. He always walked faster than me, wondering why I had to wear high heels on Madison Avenue while visiting art galleries. "Shades of my mother" was always my retort. Now, no matter how slowly I walked, he fell behind.

On Memorial Day weekend, Bill decided to cut his New York trip short and fly to Los Angeles to see his doctor at St. John's Hospital in Santa Monica. Had I realized how disoriented he truly was, I would have gone with him and simply delayed organizing the exhibition. Bill followed my suggestion and stayed at the UCLA Guest House for his first night in Los Angeles, calling Dr. Sheldon Herman on Monday for an appointment on Tuesday.

I flew to Los Angeles on Wednesday and went directly to St. Johns with a premonition that this time things would be different. The staff informed me that a tumor had been removed already that morning. Dr. Herman was nowhere to be found, so I set up residence in Loews Santa Monica Beach Hotel. It was not until the following Monday, after a concerted effort, that I was able to intercept the doctor for a brief moment. The news was the very thing we had dreaded for the last decade. The severity of his cancer had progressed from its original detection at a grade of four to a grade of seven out of ten. At that number, it would progress rapidly with little to no hope for Bill's survival. After he received heavy doses of chemotherapy, we returned to Idaho and began the search for a local oncologist.

The new prognosis brought about a dramatic change in Bill's behavior. The bravado that had been such a part of his personality was suddenly and mysteriously gone, replaced by a lack of interest in life and a general dullness in his demeanor. The first weeks at home passed without change, and our hopes resurfaced. But the true beginning of the end arrived in the middle of one night when Bill stumbled to the bathroom, shaking in a cold sweat, and then passed out in bed. I called for an ambulance, which arrived at once. My real Bill was gone. He was disoriented and unable to speak. I felt bereft and adrift, out of control without a plan, no assurances, and no vision into the future as this shocking new reality surrounded me.

Carolyn Nystrom introduced me to a book, *Final Gifts*, that she said might shed some light on our circumstances and provide an enlightening perspective on Bill's final passage. In reading it, I began to take notice of special happenings, such as how one lone female duck at our pond never came to feed with the rest. Bill so loved the ritual of feeding the flock of dozens of ducks that circled and landed on the pond in summer before swimming to the bank beside us. I felt sad for this lone duck and wondered how she would fare in the coming winter months. Messages, dreams, and symbols continued to emerge during these final months and well into the years that followed, messages that only my intuition could decipher. I have come to believe that death is a passage from our singular consciousness into the soul of the many through this reconnection with our deepest being.

The next weeks passed with Bill in St. Luke's Hospital in Boise. The care was excellent, but Bill was difficult: disoriented, hyperactive, nervous, and agitated. He had to be chased by nurses in his many escape attempts. He did not sleep at night and distressed the nurses and patients with his disoriented wanderings. Further complications and diagnoses followed, along with the relentless medical fight against cancer that included radiation to his brain daily.

I suggested some weekends at home, and this did restore a semblance of his old self. We enjoyed swimming the dogs and feeding the ducks and fish—quiet, familiar, and valued time together. Friends and family came to visit. A return to Boise and more radiation brought further mental confusion. Chemotherapy led to carsickness, and it became clear that the disease was winning. We accepted the blessing and clarity of a simple daily routine rather than the relentless battle for recovery. Hospice care began, and even a walk to the pond was soon out of reach.

I wanted so badly to have someone else be responsible for his well-being and survival, fearing that I would not be able to handle his erratic behavior. Memories of not being able to care for my mother when I was a child haunted me. I accepted Carolyn's assurance that I would be able to handle Bill's passing at home, where he preferred to be, but I was surprised to find myself angry about this plan. I was angry at my father for leaving me to care for my mother when I—a child—was totally unprepared for the consequences of looking after her. My mother then had me to blame. Her anger fell upon me for anything I did that stood in the way of her drinking. I was also to blame for her rescues and her deliveries to the hospital rehab. I was angry, too, with Gerry for dying and leaving me alone with five children to raise. I did not want a third such awesome responsibility, for which I felt so unprepared.

All of my angst was in the past, and yet I had to remain present. I soon learned that by remaining at Bill's side I was able to share his feelings and worries and, most importantly, the inspirations of his last days, which to the uninitiated would seem to be mere delusions. Bill loved to fly and travel more than anything. At times, he appeared to drift in dreams of many destinations: where he was going in his Aerostar airplane, who was going with him, who was to be there when he arrived, and whether he had packed everything he needed. He wanted everything to be right on this last journey. I might have missed all these messages had I not been present for him. I wouldn't have been able to comfort him during those worrisome hours if I had not learned to listen for the symbolic messages that he was sharing with me, that this last trip had to be done just right, in a way only he could organize.

I dreamed one night that Bill and I were taking a trip. We were going to meet Gerry, my first husband. They were both still alive, though Gerry was sick, and it seemed important to me that they meet. In the dream, all was perfectly normal, with me busily packing. I remember thinking in the dream that they would like one another. Upon waking, I thought the dream had been a harbinger of Bill's approaching death, when he and Gerry could meet in the afterlife. Several nights later, I dreamed that Bill was trying to escape an upper bunk because he insisted that he needed to arrange something. This indicated to me that he was not ready to die—not until everything was just right. At some point, while drifting between consciousness and unconsciousness, reality and unreality, Bill seemed to regain his senses; and he informed me that he was ready for his trip anytime.

"Who will be traveling with you, Billy?" I asked.

"Kelley will fly me," he said.

"Kelley does not know how to fly an airplane," I responded. I asked more questions, and Bill said we would all be going, but he would not be coming back, and Kelley needed to bring me back. Bill knew that I talked frequently to Kelley and that we were close, so she must have come into his mind as the person who could be most trusted to get me home. I agreed with the plan, and he was calmed.

This was the first time that Bill had said he would not be coming home. There had always been a "we" in his trip taking, never an "I" or "you." Earlier, I had asked Carolyn if there would ever be an end to the "we." She said to just wait and it would come clear in time. I came to realize that the dying are in another world of their own, very clear to them and not at all confused or irrational. It is essential that we support them in this world, not question it, but accept it and query them so we can learn more about their experience, share in it, and make them feel comfortable in it.

One night, he abruptly sat up in bed and reached out for something. I asked, "Who is out there? Flossie? Your sister Patsy? Your daughter Kathy?" He responded with certainty, "No, they are not there yet," and laid back down in peace, as if he knew they would be there soon, and he was no longer anxious.

Carolyn ordered a hospital bed for the library. With a day bed for me, Bill and I could stay upstairs. Friends and family came daily. Marian French delivered the mail. Neither Bill nor I left the house. Close friends came to sit with Bill at the table that fronted the fireplace—Michael and Leslie Engl, Pete and Becky Smith, Tim Ryan. Hospice staff would spell me occasionally to go to the market. Carolyn came by in the evening, when we were seated by the fire listening to classical music. She remarked on how peaceful it all was.

My children had found that the best way to pass the time with Bill was to give him paper and his familiar felt pens and encourage him to draw. He would just rearrange the pens and paper to his satisfaction and then rearrange them again. He had returned to that childhood wonder that so many people have described. The day after Thanksgiving, Bill passed into the unconscious realm of the dying. Old friends from across the country called in with condolences: Jane and Bill Pitcher, Justice Byron White, Nancy and Bill Maynard, Joe and Carmen Leggett, Ralph Davidson, and Spence Eccles. Don Bren flew in to say farewell. Bill's children did the same. I left all these visitors alone with him for as long as they desired.

Bill died December 4, 1996, the very day I had prayed he would not—Brant's birthday and the date on which Gerry had also died. Why, out of 365 days, would he have chosen this day? I told Brant that he had been honored by the passing of his two fathers on this particular date because he had been given the legacy of responsibility for the family, a legacy he has taken seriously all these years.

There was a remarkable event that night after Bill passed away. It had been snowing for ten straight days, and together we all shared the thought that this was to honor Bill's love of winter. It was still snowing when I went to the window at dusk. I had long before stopped feeding the ducks, and the pond was now frozen and covered with snow. I noticed that the lone female duck from earlier in the summer had flown in and was resting on the duck dock, now locked in ice. Why had she returned all alone now? I pondered that she might have come back for Bill. It darkened and snowed another two feet. In the morning, she was gone. For me, it seemed she had come to say farewell and carry his spirit away.

We are all free to believe as we wish, and I suppose the heart and mind work to make sense of the incomprehensible. Love leads sometimes to grief and loss but also to faith, and faith can transform memory into healing. It takes time. For me, Bill will always be a spirit in flight, always in space—in fact, a space cadet of sorts. He loved flying amidst the clouds and in the sky with the birds. That is how he was to all who knew him—a visionary, always looking to the future for the betterment of his community and the larger world.

I wanted a true celebration of his spirit with a memorial service that would itself never be forgotten, one that would include the entire community he so loved. I took on the obsession that Bill always had about everything needing to be done exactly right. I needed the printed program, with its picture of Bill's face after crashing though powder snow, to be correct. I drove to the print shop in Hailey for a few proofreading and correction sessions regarding the biblical passages and who would read them, the people to be thanked, the speakers, and the hospice and other nonprofits to be mentioned. After the program was printed, Candy caught one mistake—the "e" was missing from Anne Janss's name. She handed out a stack to each family member, and they carefully wrote in the missing "e." By then,

I did not know who I was or where I was. I just kept busy.

Pete and Becky Smith, who agreed to plan the memorial, organized a send-off in the Sun Valley Inn Limelight Room with a celebratory reception afterward for the community at the River Run Lodge. It was grand and expensive; but Joe Leggett had said that Janss Corporation would pay all expenses, and Sun Valley Resort offered the support of all its services, including a torchlight parade of ski instructors and ski patrollers down Bald Mountain. Other skiers were allowed to join in. All of my children skied in it, and Christin was allowed to lead the parade, despite ski school director Rainer Kolb's worries.

The lodge emptied out to cheer the skiers on and meet them at the base with an orchestra playing fanfares. The night of the service, I met everyone at the door and thanked them for honoring Bill by attending. Frederic Boloix had asked to handle the music, and Paul Kenny oversaw the ski instructors, who all came in their uniforms. Julie Gallagher handled arrangements with Sun Valley and the sequence of events. The entire conference room was filled to overflowing with those who came to honor of Bill. The lights on the Christmas trees decorated for the annual Christmas Ball gave a festive brightness to the room. Pete Smith was master of ceremonies and Reverend Berger led the prayers. Bob Maynard and then Bob Craig spoke. Frederic spoke of Bill's unique love of so many worlds—music, art, and skiing. His words were followed by the perfect choice of music by the Boise Symphony Brass Quintet.

Wally Huffman, with his wonderful sense of humor, captured Bill's personality, telling stories about the many years they worked together. "Huffman, this is Janss," he would hear on the phone, as if it was a surprise call from someone unknown. Wally always knew who it was. He likened Bill to a Hans Hoffman painting that hung in our home—it had splattered balls of color, as if thrown upon the canvas. This painting had lost a few gobs of expensive paint over the years at the hands of my mischievous children. A collector somewhere might be interested to know.

All of my eight grandchildren, dressed in their festive Sunday best, crossed the speaker's platform, each of them carrying their favorite toy to leave there for Bill before descending the stairs to their chairs. Most of the toys were beloved stuffed animals, and the array was impressive. We promised them that they would be getting the toys back, but there was honest fear on some tiny faces, despite our assurances.

Guy Bonnivier was the last to speak, sharing numerous tales of his and Bill's duck hunting ventures and Bill's lifetime commitment to conservation and the restoration of Silver Creek. The reception was open to the entire community. My dearest friends Molly Chappellet and Bunny Fleming flew in for the occasion. I circulated to greet as many guests as possible. A lavish buffet was served, and dancing was still going on at midnight when I left. It was an event that will never be duplicated or forgotten. The gratitude of the community was evident for this man who labored so hard to provide a world-renowned resort for them. Together, Bill and I had worked to build a community that honored the total human being in mind, body, and spirit.

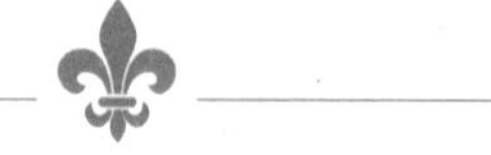

CHAPTER FORTY-FIVE

Working for Global Conservation

"Wilderness is not a luxury, but a necessity of the human spirit."—Edward Abbey

Despite the pain of loss that I felt upon Bill's passing, or perhaps because of it, I had to stay busy and connected. The mission of The Nature Conservancy continued to beckon to me. In 1997, I joined TNC's National Board of Governors, which had just committed to a global perspective. The following year, TNC introduced Conservation by Design, based on analyses of ecological regions in the United States and abroad.

This exciting new initiative gave TNC a more realistic approach to prioritizing where the most crucial work was needed. We would now be focused on threats to biodiversity within "ecoregions" across multiple states, areas that were deemed by wildlife biologists and other specialists to be linked in ecological significance. While a biological perspective made sense, it didn't always square with the conservation aims of current state boards. Nevertheless, it was apparent to me that the goals of the former would ultimately transcend the latter.

States were asked to work cooperatively with adjacent states, thereby jointly reducing the greatest threats to biodiversity within an ecoregion. Biologists had revealed that Idaho shared five ecoregions with other states, yet the priorities from state to state didn't always match up. An Idaho forest might not be as high a priority as one in

Washington, for example, when considered within a broader ecological context.

Lou Lunte tells me that my appointment to the national board was due to my hard work at the Idaho chapter. Although this may be true in part, it was also due to the recommendation of Ward Woods, an Idaho TNC board member who also served on the national board. A resident of Blaine County, Woodie was a highly respected CEO of a major New York-based investment company and chairman of TNC's finance committee.

The CEO of TNC's national board at that time was a brilliant academic by the name of John Sawhill. I had met John in Sun Valley several summers earlier when he was there on a family vacation. He had been told to look up the Janss family, perhaps as a way of also looking me over for a national board position. John was wonderful to work with, highly organized, and effective. A professor of economics, his appointment as president of New York University was followed by a stint as deputy secretary of the Department of Energy under the Carter administration. By 1997, he was a member of the Harvard Business School faculty as part of the school's Social Enterprise Initiative.

Henry "Hank" Paulson was chair of TNC's national board at that time. He and my friend Julie Wrigley had previously served together on the board of The Peregrine Fund. Hank's wife Wendy and Julie were friends. Julie grew up in Newport Beach, California, studied anthropology at Stanford University, and earned a law degree from the University of Denver. In 1981, she married Bill Wrigley, heir to the vast Wrigley chewing gum fortune. Although Julie credits me with being an important mentor for her, she joined TNC because she cared about the environment. As a child, she searched for abalone on the beach and enjoyed a clear view of Catalina Island, twenty miles away, which was owned by the Wrigley family. She and her husband Bill treasured the island for its pristine natural beauty, and they worked together to place 90 percent of it into a conservancy that would protect it from development.

"At that time, there were some people who wanted to develop Catalina like Coney Island," Julie recalled. Her husband Bill had passed away and, as she says, "bequeathed" to her a number of philanthropic duties. She joined TNC's national board in 2000.

Hank Paulson was CEO of Goldman Sachs when he became TNC's national board chair. He later served as secretary of the treasury under President George W. Bush. His timing with us was providential. Goldman Sachs had just finished a battle with the IRS, and so Paulson had experience working with the agency, which had grown suspicious of any property purchase by a TNC board trustee. The IRS was concerned about the supposed practice of placing a conservation easement on a property for a particular owner and then reselling it for a profit. In fact, temporary trustee ownership provided TNC with a source of income to opportunely buy and preserve important threatened land. TNC had already placed restrictions on itself that would not permit a trustee to profit from the resale of a property after the three years required to retain it.

For instance, I stepped up when Idaho TNC needed to acquire Summit Creek Ranch near the divide between the Pahsimeroi Valley and the Little Lost Valley. Summit Creek is a tributary of the Little Lost River. This ranch was important for the preservation of wildlife, including deer, elk, and pronghorn. It also provided important aquatic habitat for bull trout, a listed endangered species.

At the time, there was concern that ranchers would divert water out of the stream for other uses. By changing management of the property, TNC was able to enhance habitats for both the stream and upland wildlife game. Placing a conservation easement on the ranch protected it from any future development. Three years later, TNC sold it to a "conservation buyer," someone who accepted the development restrictions imposed by a TNC conservation easement placed on the land. It was a win-win for all involved and an example of the benefit of trustee involvement in the temporary purchase of ecologically sensitive areas.

John Sawhill appointed me chair of the nominating committee for TNC's national board, a committee he directed since he knew better than I did the background and conservation experience of the potential trustees under consideration. TNC was now recognized internationally as the largest conservation organization in the world. I had the opportunity while on the board to visit countries where our involvement would lead to conservation successes: Brazil, Peru, Argentina, Chile, and China. I joined hiking groups for trips to Patagonia. TNC opened an office in Bariloche, Argentina, and that became a destination for board participation, with the added fun of fishing and birdwatching. I embraced this global perspective of networking beyond US borders because it was obvious to biologists and conservationists that vital, interconnected ecosystems were threatened and being lost forever. The need to identify these corridors for preservation often crossed state and national boundaries.

In 1998, I was fortunate to join a delegation of TNC officials that visited the Yunnan Province of China. Thanks to Henry Paulson, TNC was allowed to work in China after receiving an official introduction to the Chinese government. Bill and I had traveled to the country in 1978, when there were still food carts on the streets of Beijing and everyone was dressed like Chairman Mao. I was eager to see how China had changed.

Paulson persuaded President George W. Bush to allow him to spearhead US-China relations, and he later led the US-China Strategic Economic Dialogue, a forum under which the two countries could address their joint global areas of current and future strategic economic concerns. Paulson touted TNC's capability to bring attention to rising conservation needs in China. After launching TNC's China program, he created its Asia Pacific Council, a group of top leaders from Asia and the United States who focused on the regional issues of conservation and sustainable economic development.

TNC staff member Carol Fox had been serving as director of program development for TNC's Asia Pacific region in 1998. She had an exceptional record of building new programs and developing sources of funding. It was no wonder that Paulson selected Carol to lead a trip into China to test the role of TNC "on the ground" and verify the value of practical, concrete ideas for conservation on a local level. I was invited to come along and represent the global board of directors in hope of influencing policy in China to head off what was considered to be a looming environmental crisis for the country. Carol had been working to start a conservation program in China for several years, but no one at TNC understood just what Carol was doing. She needed to convince the board of directors in order to gain support. One of her goals was the creation of a national park in Yunnan Province, around the quaint town of Lijiang. Conservation leader Ed Norton, who was familiar with national parks processes, was interested in her efforts, and Carol invited him to join our trip.

Lijiang lies close to one of the treasures of Yunnan Province, Jade Dragon Snow Mountain, which boasts a glacier and thirteen dramatic mountain peaks within a highly biodiverse area—likened to a huge dragon flying over the clouds. The local Naxi people call the central mountain Oulu, which means "silver mountain rock." Nearby is Tiger Leaping Gorge, considered the Grand Canyon of China. The gorge is located where the river passes between the mountains of Jade Dragon Snow Mountain and Haba Snow Mountain at a series of rapids below two-thousand-meter cliffs. Local legend has it that a tiger leaped across the gorge at the narrowest point to escape a hunter. Tiger Leaping Gorge had just been opened to foreigners in 1993.

Ten of us made the journey in 1998, and we met in Lijiang, which borders Sichuan Province. This was the home of the Naxi and several other minority ethnic groups. Jiang means "river"; the Naxi people, who had settled there from Tibet, spoke a unique Tibetan-Burmese language. The old town of Lijiang is a historic and culturally significant city built in the late thirteenth century. It is the most well-preserved Naxi-style ancient town in China, and in 1997 it had been included in the World Heritage List of the United Nations Educational, Scientific, and Cultural Organization (UNESCO).

A commercial center in the 1300s and the center of silk embroidery for all of southwestern China, Lijiang still has its old town of cobblestone streets and a central market square. At one time the most important stop on the ancient Southern Silk Road, it is revered for its views of Jade Dragon Snow Mountain. Traffic was very manageable in Lijiang. Wide berth was given for bicycles and pedestrians, but it was clear that if traffic in the city grew, there was no infrastructure capable of handling it. I mention this because of the shock I felt upon returning to visit this area with TNC just six years later. Traffic was at a standstill, and bicycles and pedestrians were relegated to a narrow strip of road beside the congested travel lane. Never had I seen such rapid development.

In 1998, I was not prepared for the numerous official dinners we were expected to attend. These were important events in the lives of Chinese officials. Anything out of the ordinary provided an excuse for an official dinner. To my surprise and chagrin, as the only representative of The Nature Conservancy Board of Directors, I was the appointed "speaker" at all of these functions. Speeches, given amidst the many courses of food and wines, were taken very seriously.

English was still little spoken or understood in China, so my conversation with my host at the end of the table was minimal, managed only with the help of an interpreter. It was important that we come across as officials, so I fashioned my presentations to stress environmental concerns and programs, which included the need for forest management with an eye toward safeguarding biodiversity. I was not confrontational, instead touting the success of TNC programs in the United States. I also stressed the need to preserve Chinese heritage, including the extraordinary architecture of Lijiang.

I am not certain that I was understood, and perhaps I was too idealistic. It seemed that conservation and the environment were not yet issues on official agendas. However, Carol encouraged me by saying that they were impressed with a woman leader and liked the idea of a woman making presentations to them. At that time, it was certainly a unique experience for these local officials. We traveled by van into more remote areas, north along a rugged road to Zhongdian, a Tibetan town. Our mission was to stress to them the importance of preserving their cultural heritage.

I found the Chinese to be industrious people; they worked as a family. Sons still remained with their working families, living in the simplest of stone huts, which we visited to gain understanding of how our proposed fuel program would work. Trees were being cut down indiscriminately. As an wood alternative, we were introducing the idea of drying the dung of their farm animals and using that for biogas fuel in stone-built stoves. TNC had planned the installation of these stoves for local families across vast areas.

We visited the forest habitat of the golden monkey, high in the lower mountains, but we never managed to glimpse one. This is not unusual as they are very secretive. This area is now an official wildlife reserve. The golden monkey is a revered animal throughout the country.

As we traveled in China, we slept in everything from dirty, cold dormitories with outhouses on a hillside to nice guesthouses and hotels. It was a year of heavy rains, and the flooding of the Yangtze River aided our goal of helping officials and the Chinese public understand what would happen if they continued to denude the hillsides along the river. We were appalled to see the muddy waters and flood devastation. Mud was thick and deep along the riverbanks, and agricultural fields were ruined. After this flood, the cutting of wood in the area was outlawed.

We toured monasteries, schools, and city government facilities to educate ourselves about the needs of the local Chinese residents and officials in Yunnan Province, but I came to wonder what was behind our visits to some of these facilities. When I queried Carol Fox, she told me quietly and confidentially that Ed was being considered to head TNC's first conservation program in China and it was crucial for him to experience all that he could before making a decision about such a major life change. Ed did accept this post and went on to create a comprehensive program for all of Yunnan Province. A lawyer from Washington, DC, Ed was already a leading environmental advocate. The program he set forth was so successful that, in 2002, Jiang Zemin, the president of China, said he wanted to have Ed's Yunnan Great Rivers project serve as a model for all of China.

I was honored to have been on this trip, which created a "bulkhead" for TNC in China with its first office in Lijiang, from which many conservation ideas were originally implemented. My work for the Idaho TNC chapter helped me realize that we needed to be part of such global conservation efforts. After attending a national board meeting, I would return to open an Idaho board meeting with a review of what I had learned about the work we were accomplishing internationally.

Responses were mixed. Some trustees were not happy with this new and expanded mission, fearing it would limit our impact in Idaho and dilute our power to make informed local decisions. I simply reminded trustees that we all share this planet and that many species across the globe depend on habitats similar to Idaho's. The creatures in a riparian area, fragile desert ecosystem, or mountain forest don't know what country they are in and which borders they cross. It was our job as stewards of the land to rise above the human differences that often block conservation efforts. "No conservation organization can save everything," I told them. "But we must consider one of the most important forests in the world, the Amazon, when considering the preservation of forests elsewhere."

By the early 2000s, TNC had a million members and was involved in multiple conservation programs overseas. Julie Wrigley and I were two directors on the national board representing Idaho and its importance in conservation projects like the Silver Creek Preserve. When we traveled to what was now the global headquarters of TNC in Arlington, Virginia, Julie described it as "galactic headquarters" because there was so much going on there. The nonprofit organization had been growing in significance in recent years under the leadership of John Sawhill, but he died unexpectedly in 2000. A national search for his replacement was launched under the leadership of highly respected California TNC executive director Steve McCormick, who was ultimately chosen to fill the job himself. He quickly shifted the goals of state TNC chapters toward global projects, perhaps too quickly from the perspective of many state chapters.

In McCormick's first speech to the TNC national assembly, he told the state directors that what they were doing in their home areas would no longer be as important as the overseas initiatives the global board was rolling out. He wanted each local TNC chapter to now select an international project to support and to commit an additional monetary amount to it each year. Some people saw this as taking away from the responsibilities of the state organizations and their local projects, since the real strength and support for TNC came from these local chapters. McCormick's mission to merge state chapters into regional departments was met with resistance by many state boards and many corporations that were represented on those boards.

McCormick left after five years, and Hank Paulson took over to keep the organization on track with its new goals until a new executive director could be hired. By 2003, my local conservation companion, Julie Wrigley, had left the global board to serve the World Wildlife Fund and Conservation International. A few years ago, she made a $50 million donation to Arizona State University's Global Institute of Sustainability, which was recently renamed in her honor.

McCormick sent TNC Western Division director Rebecca Patton to Idaho to make a presentation before the Idaho chapter to request that we become more financially supportive of TNC's global work. Idaho was her first presentation to a state board. Her prepared remarks were not well received by a state board, which still had only local priorities in mind. Her perceived lack of appreciation for state priorities drew tirades from trustees who as of yet had no global vision. She subsequently softened the context of talks she delivered to other state chapters.

During the McCormick years, TNC went through many different attempts to raise funds for global programs through the local chapters. Mandatory payments from chapters were short-lived. Another accounting approach was to require each chapter to commit to a global fund-raising goal that was negotiated between state and division directors. The general expectation was that the chapter would commit 10 percent of its operations revenue to support global programs. Lou Lunte said this was done by stewarding specific donors to support global efforts. He recalled,

> It did vary by state. Some had smaller goals, some larger, depending on their fund-raising capability. While these goals were certainly taken very seriously and part of the state director's performance review, they were officially considered "voluntary" goals; and if a chapter was unable to hit the goal through specific donor requests, no funds were taken from the chapter to fill the gap. The fund-raising approach has become far more collaborative over time, but during McCormick's early years it was a huge fight between state chapters and TNC global.

Despite initial challenges, TNC now has a strong foundation for this global, scientific approach to species conservation. Over time, it became clear that larger and more effective conservation projects could be undertaken jointly with other states. Formerly reluctant trustees then joined the fervor. By the time Guy Bonnivier retired in 1998, it was clear that the new global and ecoregional policies had superseded his initial conservation commitment. Guy resented them being imposed, as he saw it, on his chapter.

Although it has evolved over the decades, Conservation by Design is still used today as a foundation for analysis of the most significant global threats, including what is now the greatest transcendent issue of our time: climate change. Although worldwide collaboration is increasingly important to fight the causes of extinctions at our doorstep, including possibly our own, environmental conservation always begins at a local level.

I had an opportunity to experience other state priorities during the first capital campaign, which I initiated as Idaho TNC chair in 1999. Until that time, the chapter had raised funds only for specific projects. It was now apparent that the organization needed funding to buy conservation easements, move staff to other parts of the state to establish offices, and fund our increasing number of projects statewide. I agreed to chair the campaign, and we set a goal of $20 million. The goal seemed formidable, but staff and trustees spread out across the state to contact new donors. We relied on development staff to formulate a list of major potential donors, a list that incorporated business contacts, former donors, and conservation enthusiasts. A board member from somewhere in the north—Coeur d'Alene, for example—would help create a list from that area and then organize a fund-raising event there.

We achieved our goal within three years and created a base of new donors that have remained strong supporters to this day. It was due to this fund-raising experience that I was appointed to cochair with Ian Cumming the Western Region of the Campaign for Conservation, the first national fund-raising campaign in many years. The United States was divided into geographic ecoregions rather than states. Key trustees in these ecoregions were appointed to chairmanships.

Ian Cumming was an amazing individual. Some noted philanthropists strive for notice in the public eye while others stay so busy behind the scenes that they simply have no time for it. Cumming was an unsung hero of the philanthropic world. I nicknamed him the "iron marshmallow" because he was shy of the media and yet extraordinarily effective in his business life. In the press, his personality was contrasted with that of fellow Utah billionaire-philanthropist Jon Huntsman Sr. While both men were immensely successful, they supported different political parties. I knew in my heart that conservation had to remain a bipartisan issue—to be successful, TNC needed to work with people of all political persuasions.

Cumming was born in Canada and received his MBA at Harvard Business School in 1970. Working largely behind the scenes, he was involved in an array of business ventures. He started Terracor, a real estate development company, created a successful holding company, owned ski resorts, and supported the Democratic Party. With his business colleague Joe Steinberg, he founded Leucadia National Corporation, one of America's most successful banking firms. When Cumming retired in 2013 after a thirty-four-year career, an article about the company in *Crain's New York* noted, "While Cumming's track record compares very nicely with Mr. (Warren) Buffet's, he is as unknown as the Oracle of Omaha is famous."

Cumming and his sometime opponent Jon Huntsman Sr. died on the same day. *The Deseret News* reported, "Ian Cumming Lived Life with Little Fanfare and Died the Same Way." There was little notice made of his death, which seemed only fitting given his reclusive nature. Both men grew up in humble circumstances, but much was known about Huntsman, who welcomed the press. A friend of Ian Cumming said of him, "He was more of a self-actualized person who did not see any value in what it meant to be known by the media."

I understand this sentiment now more than ever. Public acknowledgments are no guarantee of a person's sense of fulfillment. Ian quietly gave large contributions to the University of Utah, was a member of it board of regents, and was instrumental in hiring two successive presidents. In this sense, he was not reclusive at all but busy working his wonders, leaving large gifts to the David Eccles School of Business, the John A. Moran Eye Center, and other worthy causes.

I decided that the best way to inform a state chapter about our Campaign for Conservation would be to personally attend one of their board meetings, make a presentation, and invite follow-up questions. After Bill's death, I welcomed travel opportunities. My presentation was based on the reasons for global outreach. I took on the role that Rebecca Patton had bravely undertaken in Idaho, but for me the presentation needed to be made in twelve additional states.

I was accompanied by a key TNC staff member, Olivia Millard, who traveled with me, carrying a laptop and a PowerPoint presentation for me to use as I introduced the capital campaign. Millard set up all the flights, hotel reservations, rental cars, and dates of our presentations with each of the chapters. Thanks to her organizational skills, we were able to complete the state presentations for the capital campaign within one year, sharing fun memories along the way. I met the trustees of all thirteen western state TNC boards, including Hawaii and Alaska.

These western states had a diversity of conservation plans and priorities. In the deserts of New Mexico, water conservation was a priority. The coastlines of California had a different focus entirely, where sea mammals needed protection. Washington state TNC trustees were focused on forest and wetlands protections. In Hawaii, the TNC wanted to help eradicate the wild boar and so took to trapping and removing them instead of shooting them as hunters preferred. Some local Hawaiians were not in favor of removal, so TNC regretfully abandoned the preferred trapping plan.

Understanding local conditions and priorities is essential to making good decisions. It is why TNC seeks the advice of local people. I experienced a good example of this when I ventured to Alaska without a staff member. After my presentation at the board meeting in Juno, I flew north by seaplane with my son Brant and his two young sons to Lake Minchumina, or Menchuh Mene' in the local indigenous language. We stayed at a remote fishing retreat. The children did not understand why they had to go to bed while it was still light, and they fought through exhaustion to stay awake. They were not at all taken with dry fly-fishing, especially after their deep-sea fishing excursion out of Juno. At this lake retreat, I was hiking down the road from the cabins and noticed several igloos with dogs chained to them. Back home, I would have charged off with a complaint to People for the Ethical Treatment of Animals (PETA). Why were they so cruelly chained? I learned that they were sled dogs and, if left to run free, they would run off into the woods and be killed by wolves.

My visit to this remote fishing retreat confirmed for me the need for conservation that is in accord with local indigenous traditions. The tradition of dogsledding fascinated me, and I programmed it quietly into future family plans for a seventieth birthday winter visit and a sled trip to Mount McKinley. Doubtless, there was still some competitive fervor in me that was activated to prove I could still participate in such adventures and survive. I had no idea how tough such a trip was going to be for dogsled novices such as ourselves, but I survived through pure will and commitment to our family legacy of competition.

Visiting other state preserves and learning about their methods and successes was beneficial information to take home to Idaho. An unexpected reward from these statewide visits was getting to know the executive directors of each state, many of whom remained in these positions for their entire careers with TNC, and the board chairs, many of whom later became trustees at the national level. While on these travels, I often found that it was simple pleasures that brought the most valued memories. Some hotels had freshly baked chocolate chip cookies at the reception desk. Olivia and I giggled over our good fortune when we discovered these and filled our mouths and pockets.

Following its research into our trustee purchases and resales of land, the IRS strongly suggested that TNC reduce its national board from thirty to twenty members. For a temporary period, this left us unable to fill our committees to a productive number, which is essential for the effectiveness of a nonprofit organization. A committee with only three people is incapable of fulfilling its goals. When Hank Paulson called to see if I would be among those willing to leave the board, I did so. I had already served eight years of my nine-year term. I understood that it was more important to reserve the now limited board positions for those with more scientific expertise or corporate contacts.

With my travels over and nonprofit work at an end, I was ready to turn my attention to matters of personal reflection. As I made my plans to quietly leave town for Tetonia, I realized that the Wood River Valley was no longer the same place where I had raised my children. In many ways, the dreams Bill and I once had for developing a multifaceted community had been fulfilled. The proliferation of nonprofit organizations, and the social and economic benefits they bring, had transformed the valley. There were now lectures, concerts, and arts and education programs galore to serve the burgeoning population. Sun Valley had become a year-round destination resort, and it was no longer a quiet place.

Yet, a large part of the local population, including a substantial immigrant population, still worked hard to make a living in the valley, and I was drawn into an effort to build a YMCA complex that would serve their health and wellness needs. Beginning in 2005, I participated in what I now think of as my "swan song" of fund-raising. It brought me back to honoring the friendships that Bill and I enjoyed during the earliest days of his Sun Valley Resort ownership.

Plans for an eighty-four-thousand-square-foot YMCA facility gained widespread public support. The city of Ketchum came through with a one dollar per year, ninety-nine-year lease for land near the Big Wood River on Warm Springs Road across from Rotary Park. I went to work raising money for a planned aquatic center that would feature a lap pool for swim lessons, aqua aerobics, water polo, scuba diving, and kayaking; and an expansive recreation pool for parents and kids that included a waterslide. There would be nothing like it for many miles around.

Cynthia Murphy chaired the Wood River Community YMCA board for ten years while the facility was planned and developed. A natural leader, she also sits on several other nonprofit boards in the valley. She reminded me recently that one of the most important swimming programs at the YMCA, in the Bill Janss Aquatic Center, is the Learn to Swim Program, a free program that teaches every second grader in Blaine County how to swim. She explained to me that drowning is one of the leading causes of death among young children in Idaho. "The Blaine County School District loves this program as it teaches the children to swim but it also builds self-esteem, confidence, and friendships," Cynthia said. In the years to come, thanks to continuing generous donations, no person will be turned away due to a lack of money, and no child growing up in the Wood River Valley will lack the opportunity to learn to swim.

When I took on this fund-raising project, I reached out right away to Spence Eccles, a man whose family has been involved with the valley's economic and social development for generations. Back in the 1880s, Spence's grandfather, David Eccles, had a sawmill in Gray's Gulch near Hailey. Bill Janss and his brother Ed had received financing from First Security to purchase Sun Valley Resort from Union Pacific when Spence Eccles was the bank's senior vice president. The only problem for Spence with regard to supporting the YMCA project was that Spence's family foundation was only supposed to make grants in the family's home state of Utah. He told us that it would require obtaining an exception to the rule. Nevertheless, Spence and his wife Cleone came to town for a meeting to consider a donation.

During the meeting, Spence shared stories about how important Bill had been to the community and how it wouldn't be the same place today if not for him. He spoke of his deep friendship with Bill, and in the end he decided to make an exception and fund the pool. He said he felt good about it because he and Bill had been such great friends. Spence wrote me a long personal letter memorializing the good times gone by, his family's history in the valley, and the faith it had taken to support the Sun Valley Resort.

It meant a lot to me that Spence and the YMCA board would honor Bill's legacy in this way. The $1 million I was able to raise from Spence (along with an additional $1 million I raised from a group of private donors) meant that Spence's foundation would have the naming rights for the facility. Thanks to support by the George S. and Dolores Doré Eccles Foundation, the YMCA's extraordinary swimming facility is known as the Bill Janss Aquatic Center, with funding by the George S. and Dolores Doré Eccles Foundation.

When news broke in 2007 about the donation, Spence shared his feelings with the *Idaho Mountain Express*:

> Bill and my uncle, George Eccles, were close friends from the earliest days of Sun Valley. I have had the distinct privilege in my life of sharing, and working toward, a common vision with Bill Janss of the evolution of Sun Valley into the "grand dame" of year-round family resorts. . . . Our foundation appreciates the opportunity to help create this new aquatic facility bearing Bill Janss' name. We know it will be a great asset for the whole Wood River Valley, helping to carry on Bill's legacy of sharing in this community and area, benefiting both children and adults for many years to come.

People don't always understand the importance of personal relationships and teamwork in pulling together such lasting institutions. When you pass through the YMCA, you can see the names of the donors honored on the wall—hundreds of people who came together and continue to give to fulfill a vision. On one hallway, I found a picture that brings me all the way back to Malibu, a photograph of me standing with Janet Leigh Brandt and her daughter Jamie Lee Curtis, who emceed for us during a "YMCA Classic" fundraiser. These events, fun as they are, are also foundational to the success of the community. At some point during one of the YMCA Classics, Johnny Mathis was singing in a tent. My kids secretly convinced him to sing "Wonderful, Wonderful" to me, and it was just so memorable. These fundraisers, organized by Bud Yorkin, featured a celebrity golf tournament. Clint Eastwood and Tom Hanks graciously showed up for the good cause, but there is nothing like having Johnny Mathis sing you a song.

I was soon ready to depart from the Wood River Valley, having fulfilled so many of the dreams I once shared with Bill. A new generation of residents were now here to usher in a new era. Would they ever know how much effort had gone into supporting the community's needs and expanding its opportunities? I closed out this final effort and began my move to the Teton Valley. Few people knew my plans. I took such pleasure in knowing that this new swimming complex at the YMCA would be one last sign of Bill's legacy. This complex would honor the man who over four decades worked to provide his community with all that was needed to benefit the life of the total human being—spirit, mind, and body. In ending my own life story, I dedicate a similar path taken in the hope that I have accomplished something of significance for the benefit of my beloved community.

EPILOGUE

My Final Tidal Pool

"I would rather sit on a pumpkin and have it all to myself than to be crowded on a velvet cushion."—Henry David Thoreau

I've been blessed with the luxury of reflection to look into my past and to accept it in all honesty, including my regrets, transgressions, and mistakes. The poet Rumi wrote, "Out beyond ideas of wrongdoing and right doing there is a field. I'll meet you there. When the soul lies down in that grass, the world is too full to talk about it." I strive to meet myself "there" and am grateful that I could live to tell my story. I awake every morning in deep gratitude for my good fortune in life, for my mind and body that have so loyally supported me into the last year of my eighties. I take a cup of coffee onto my deck and listen to the birds, watch the mother robin search for worms in the lawn below and then fly to her two waiting babies in a nest over the lantern behind me on the deck. I look out over green fields as far as I can see to the low forest pines and aspens and on to the rising Grand Teton Range. I listen to the horses whinnying on the adjacent property and to the creek as it bubbles past below me.

I am in one of those liminal spaces where we sometimes find ourselves, either by chance or by choice. I have had three of these periods in my lifetime, each resulting from the need for change or a desire to follow new inspiration. My first tidal pool of reflection came after my college graduation when I moved into married life.

Having five children came to encompass every moment of my time. The second time of reflection came after the tidal wave of divorce in Malibu left me bereft and searching to recover my own truth and inner soul's needs. This led to our fortuitous move to rural Sun Valley and all that would take place there. I continued the responsibilities there that I had learned as a girl while representing my family in place of my mother at social events. This led me into the deep involvement in Sun Valley social life and nonprofit event attendance for nearly half of my life. I followed this path with eagerness, grateful to be of service. But my soul's needs changed. I left Sun Valley after forty years rather than continue giving excuses to avoid the ongoing social demands. I found myself saying I would not be in town for an event or party and then take the chance that someone would catch me in my white lie at the market. I had to be truthful to myself and to others and seek more suitable circumstances for a final respite.

The third tidal pool of my life is my current and final journey. It began when I chose to leave the social responsibilities and expectations behind and begin again. I found an entirely new life where I knew no one, in Teton Valley, which is reminiscent of the Wood River Valley when I arrived there to live in 1969. It is rural and peaceful with generations rooted in a legacy of connection to the land. The town of Driggs eight miles from me has only one traffic signal on its main corner. After a period serving here on the Teton Regional Land Trust and then for a second time on Idaho's Nature Conservancy board, I realized that, at age eighty-five, it was time for me to retire from public service and give myself up to a quiet time of assessment and evaluation.

It has been a rewarding challenge to assess whether I have followed my destiny and lived to the fullest the life path I chose to follow. With this work accomplished, I live now in a place of peace and acceptance, alone, with no responsibilities beyond the welfare of myself and my rescued feral black cat. I cherish this final independence and peace as the greatest final joy of my life. I never knew that I could in these last fifteen years be so happy with what I have come to call my "aloneness." It is not loneliness that I feel, but a comfort in my Being-ness, with few obligations. I can go to Tai Chi class at the Senior Center, or not. I can work in the yard with the weeding and pruning, perfecting it, or not. I welcome visits from some of my few surviving friends, my children and grandchildren, and the birds and animals that come to my house to share in my peace and remoteness.

I am surrounded by nature—not the nature that I have known in its wildness, but the nature of the early settlers who brought production to the land and still bring it from their fields annually by their toil. I watch the storms come from the west and pass over me and through me as they are wind-driven east over the Tetons and beyond. I can rest in observation of the passing clouds and the shapes they take as they change every moment. I live in constant wonderment. I have been inspired by love and compassion in this life and now I rest in my space, my final tidal pool of deep reflection before entering a universe of energy and light where each of us will have our lighted spark of energy all our own that will drift with the energy of all before us. In the end, it's not what you gather but what you scatter that tells what kind of life you have lived.

ACKNOWLEDGMENTS

The inspiration I followed to examine my past was aided by many helpers who made this book possible. Thank you to the many people interviewed for this book and to those who helped fill in the gaps in my memory. The list is too long to mention here, but I hope I have mentioned them all in these pages.

I would like to thank Tony Tekaroniake Evans, my coauthor, for his professionalism and patience with an unskilled writer who beleaguered him with questions about how to improve my writing skills. He interviewed numerous people, provided essential research, and worked to refine and present my memories in an orderly fashion. Saul Turtletaub read early chapters and provided helpful feedback and good humor. Julie Weston saw the project through as a reader, supplying crucial advice and catching many errors. Thanks to Christina Dubois for her excellent copyediting of the final draft.

I am grateful to my teachers at Wellesley College in the late 1940s, who inspired me to search for answers to life's mysteries; and to David Pond, who advised me to tell my story when the time was right. I want to thank the many wonderful people I have known and worked with at the Los Angeles County Museum of Art, The Institute for Noetic Sciences, the Idaho Centennial Commission and Idaho Heritage Trust, the Sun Valley Center for the Arts and Humanities, The Nature Conservancy, Boise Art Museum, and other organizations mentioned in this book, and the many donors who ensure their ongoing success.

I also want to thank the communities of Malibu, Sun Valley, and the Wood River Valley for providing the network of friends where my children grew up. Thank you to Anne and Bill Janss for their initial encouragement to establish an arts center in Sun Valley. Lastly, I want to express gratitude to my family for their encouragement during the five years it took to tell this story. They, more than anyone, have made my life worth living and my story worth telling.

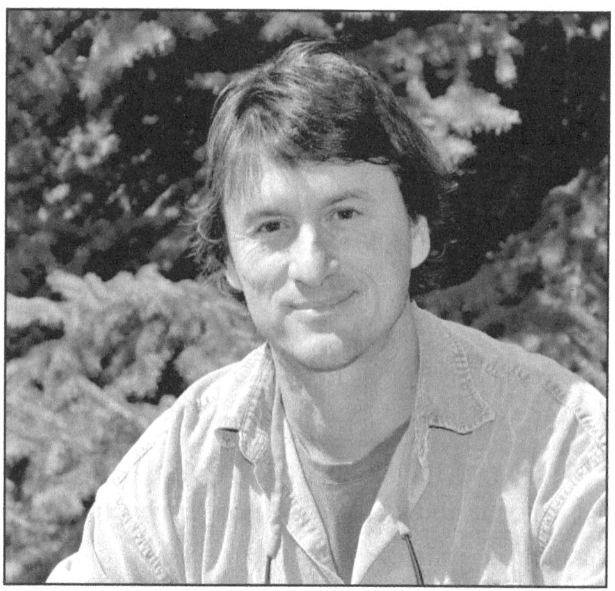

ABOUT THE COAUTHOR

Author of *Teaching Native Pride* (2020) and *A History of Indians in the Sun Valley Area* (2017), Tony Tekaroniake Evans is an award-winning writer and columnist at the *Idaho Mountain Express* in Ketchum/Sun Valley, Idaho, which won the National Newspaper Association's General Excellence Award in 2018 and 2020. He studied cultural anthropology and biology at the University of Colorado at Boulder and won the Expatriate Scholarship to the Prague Summer Writing Workshop at Charles University in 1996. Since then, he has written for the *Mountain Gazette, History.com, High Country News, Taos News, Santa Fe New Mexican,* Multihulls International, *Idaho Arts Quarterly, Boise Weekly,* and *Environmental News Network;* contributed reporting to the BBC live Sunday Edition and Boise State Public Radio; and offered creative writing workshops in Ketchum. He is a citizen of the Mohawk Nation, Kahnawake Band, and a member of the Bear Clan. Tony can be reached at twoskies@ hotmail.com.

INDEX

D

E

K

L

N

Q

R

S

Y

Z

www.ingramcontent.com/pod-product-compliance
Ingram Content Group UK Ltd.
Pitfield, Milton Keynes, MK11 3LW, UK
UKHW012253290726
14090UKWH00016B/628

9 780578 985459